Education, Social Background and Cognitive Ability

Are socioeconomic inequalities in education declining? Is socioeconomic background becoming less important for people's occupational class or status? How important is cognitive ability for education and later occupational outcomes? How do countries differ in the importance of socioeconomic background for education and work?

Gary N. Marks argues that in Western industrialized countries, pervasive views that socioeconomic background (or class background) has strong and unchanging relationships with education, and later socioeconomic outcomes, resistant to policy and social change, are unfounded. Marks provides a large amount of evidence from many countries showing that the influence of socioeconomic background on education is moderate and most often declining, and that socioeconomic background has only very weak impacts on adults' occupation and earnings after taking into account education and cognitive ability.

Furthermore, Marks shows that cognitive ability is a more powerful influence than socioeconomic background for educational outcomes and that, in addition to its indirect effects through education, cognitive ability has direct effects on occupation and earnings. Its effects cannot be dismissed as simply another aspect of socioeconomic background, nor do the usual criticisms of cognitive ability apply. The declining effects of socioeconomic background and the importance of cognitive ability support many of the contentions of modernization theory.

This book contributes to a variety of debates within sociology: quantitative and qualitative approaches, explanatory and non-explanatory theory, the relationship between theory and empirical research, the role of political ideology in research, sociology as a social science, and sociology's contribution to our knowledge about contemporary societies. It will appeal to professionals and students in economics, education, psychology and sociology, policymakers and anybody interested in social stratification and its reproduction.

Gary N. Marks is a Principal Research Fellow at the Melbourne Institute of Applied Economic and Social Research, the University of Melbourne, Australia.

Routledge Research in Education

For a complete list of titles in the series, please visit www.routledge.com.

84. **Virtual Literacies**
    Interactive Spaces for Children and Young People
    Edited by Guy Merchant, Julia Gillen, Jackie Marsh and Julia Davies

85. **Geography and Social Justice in the Classroom**
    Edited by Todd W. Kenreich

86. **Diversity, Intercultural Encounters, and Education**
    Edited by Susana Gonçalves and Markus A. Carpenter

87. **The Role of Participants in Education Research**
    Ethics, Epistemologies, and Methods
    Edited by Warren Midgley, Patrick Alan Danaher and Margaret Baguley

88. **Care in Education**
    Teaching with Understanding and Compassion
    Sandra Wilde

89. **Family, Community, and Higher Education**
    Edited by Toby S. Jenkins

90. **Rethinking School Bullying**
    Dominance, Identity and School Culture
    Ronald B. Jacobson

91. **Language, Literacy, and Pedagogy in Postindustrial Societies**
    The Case of Black Academic Underachievement
    Paul C. Mocombe and Carol Tomlin

92. **Education for Civic and Political Participation**
A Critical Approach
Edited by Reinhold Hedtke and Tatjana Zimenkova

93. **Language Teaching Through the Ages**
Garon Wheeler

94. **Refugees, Immigrants, and Education in the Global South**
Lives in Motion
Edited by Lesley Bartlett and Ameena Ghaffar-Kucher

95. **The Resegregation of Schools**
Education and Race in the Twenty-First Century
Edited by Jamel K. Donnor and Adrienne D. Dixson

96. **Autobiographical Writing and Identity in EFL Education**
Shizhou Yang

97. **Online Learning and Community Cohesion**
Linking Schools
Roger Austin and William Hunter

98. **Language Teachers and Teaching**
Global Perspectives, Local Initiatives
Edited by Selim Ben Said and Lawrence Jun Zhang

99. **Towards Methodologically Inclusive Research Syntheses**
Expanding Possibilities
Harsh Suri

100. **Raising Literacy Achievement in High-Poverty Schools**
An Evidence-Based Approach
Eithne Kennedy

101. **Learning and Collective Creativity**
Activity-Theoretical and Sociocultural Studies
Annalisa Sannino and Viv Ellis

102. **Educational Inequalities**
Difference and Diversity in Schools and Higher Education
Edited by Kalwant Bhopal and Uvanney Maylor

103. **Education, Social Background and Cognitive Ability**
The decline of the social
Gary N. Marks

Education, Social Background and Cognitive Ability

The decline of the social

Gary N. Marks

LONDON AND NEW YORK

First published 2014
by Routledge
2 Park Square, Milton Park, Abingdon, Oxfordshire OX14 4RN

and by Routledge
711 Third Avenue, New York, NY 10017

First issued in paperback 2015

Routledge is an imprint of the Taylor & Francis Group, an informa business

British Library Cataloguing in Publication Data
A catalogue record for this book is available from the British Library

Library of Congress Cataloging in Publication Data
Marks, Gary N.
Education, social background and cognitive ability : the decline of the social / Gary N. Marks.
pages cm
Includes bibliographical references.
1. Education–Social aspects. 2. Children with social disabilities–Education.
3. Educational equalization. 4. Cognitive learning. I. Title.
LC191.M2665 2014
306.43–dc23
2013012887

ISBN 13: 978-1-138-92322-5 (pbk)
ISBN 13: 978-0-415-84246-4 (hbk)

Typeset in Galliard
by FiSH Books Ltd, Enfield

Dedicated to Kerry, our children, my parents and those who have helped me on the way.

Contents

Tables

Abbreviations

ACT	American College Testing assessment
AFQT	Armed Forces Qualification Test (US)
ALLS	Adult Literacy and Life Skills Survey
BCS	British Cohort Study
BHPS	British Household Panel Survey
CASMIN	Comparative Analysis of Social Mobility in Industrial Nations
EEI	Effectively Expanding Inequality
EGP	Erikson, Goldthorpe and Portocarero occupational class schema
EMI	Effectively Maintained Inequality
ESCS	Economic, Social and Cultural Status (PISA)
g	general ability factor
GCSE	General Certificate of Secondary Education
GPA	Grade Point Average
GSEOP	German Socio-Economic Panel
GSS	General Social Survey (US)
HS&B	High School and Beyond (US)
IALS	International Adult Literacy Study
IEA	International Association for the Evaluation of Educational Achievement
ISEI	International Socioeconomic Index
IQ	Intelligence Quotient
ISCED	International Standard Classification of Education
LSAY	Longitudinal Surveys of Australian Youth
MMI	Maximally Maintained Inequality
NAEP	National Assessment of Educational Progress (US)
NCDS	National Child Development Study (UK)
NCES	National Centre for Educational Statistics (US)
NELS	National Education Longitudinal Study (US)
NLS	National Longitudinal Study (US)
NLS72	National Longitudinal Study of the Class of 1972 (US)
NLSY	National Longitudinal Survey of Youth (US)

OCG	Occupational Changes in a Generation Study (US)
OECD	Organisation for Economic Co-operation and Development
OLS	Ordinary Least Squares (regression)
PIRLS	Progress in International Reading Literacy Study
PISA	Programme for International Student Assessment
PPVT	Peabody Picture Vocabulary Test
PSID	Panel Survey of Income Dynamics (US)
RRA	Relative Risk Aversion
SAT	Scholastic Aptitude Test
SES	Socioeconomic Status
TIMSS	Trends in International Mathematics and Science Studies
WAIS	Wechsler Adult Intelligence Scale test
WLS	Wisconsin Longitudinal Study (US)
YITS	Youth in Transition Survey (Canada)

Chapter 1

Introduction

There is a widely held set of inter-related views – among professional social scientists, journalists, policymakers, bureaucrats, social commentators and other educated publics – that socioeconomic background largely determines educational and subsequent occupational and economic outcomes in contemporary Western societies. Differences between students or schools in test scores, overall student performance, early school leaving, entry to university or college and overall educational attainment are mainly due to socioeconomic background. This explains why there is so little intergenerational mobility in Western countries. Relatedly, the status or socioeconomic level of people's occupations has a close association with that of their father or family of origin. Similarly, inequalities in earnings, income and wealth mainly reflect economic and social inequalities in the parental generation. These understandings feed into political debates about what policies should be implemented to create a fairer society.

There is also a pervasive misunderstanding that cognitive ability is irrelevant to education and subsequent socioeconomic inequalities. There is a variety of arguments: the concept is somehow invalid; there is no such thing as cognitive ability; there are multiple intelligences; IQ tests measure nothing of any more consequence than performance in IQ tests; cognitive ability is simply not important for educational and adult labor market outcomes; or that its apparent importance is simply a reflection of socioeconomic background. Furthermore, the very concept of ability, it is argued, perpetuates socioeconomic inequalities through the propagation of false meritocratic ideologies. In contrast, non-cognitive attributes – for example, "leadership", "motivation", personality factors, "being in control" and especially "culture" – are understood as more important for education and the labor market than cognitive ability.

Finally, there is the widespread belief that nothing has changed – the reproduction of socioeconomic inequalities in contemporary societies remains as strong as ever – despite massive changes in educational participation, specific policies implemented to reduce inequality of opportunity, and dramatic improvements in health, welfare and economic wellbeing. Despite meritocratic ideals, education does not reduce the reproduction of socioeconomic inequalities across generations but instead perpetuates them. This pessimistic view implies that policymakers are wasting their time and gives credence to the surprisingly enduring, but often unsaid, argument that the reproduction of socioeconomic inequalities in contemporary Western societies can only be alleviated by the radical transformation of societies' economic and social institutions.

There is far less consensus on explanations for the supposedly strong and enduring reproduction of socioeconomic inequalities across generations. Theoretical explanations may emphasize: financial factors, such as the capacity to buy "success" for one's children; rational decision making, in that pursuing further education is not rational for working-class students; "culture" which either advantages those from high socioeconomic backgrounds or creates barriers for those from low socioeconomic backgrounds; or schools and the overall organization of education systems, especially the differentiation of students into different types of schools or curricular clusters within schools.

The purpose of this book is to show that, in Western industrialized countries, arguments that the reproduction of socioeconomic inequalities across generations is strong and enduring and that cognitive ability is irrelevant, are simply not true. Therefore, many of the theories surrounding the reproduction of socioeconomic inequalities are incorrect since they assume strong and enduring socioeconomic inequalities. In addition, many of the explicit and implicit contentions and claims made by such theories are not consistent with the bulk of the evidence from scientifically orientated empirical studies.

The sociological perspective

The sociological perspective emphasizes the importance of ascribed social characteristics – for example, class or socioeconomic background, religion, gender, race and ethnicity – for people's lives. "People's lives" encompasses their education, occupation, income, social interactions (including marriage), political orientations and other attitudes and behaviors. To some, the sociological perspective entails a science of society: the careful development of theory, models and measures, and the objective application of statistical and other methods, in order to uncover important social processes and produce a cumulative body of knowledge. Ideally, this facilitates the implementation of policies that would successfully reduce social inequalities and improve society for all (Cole 1994a: 130; Lipset 1994). The sociological perspective is clearly superior to notions that social outcomes are the result of the actions of deities or other supernatural forces, or simply part of the natural order. Arguably, it is more valuable than purely historical, psychological or economic approaches.

The overwhelming importance of social background and social group membership on what people did and thought was the generally accepted wisdom within sociology before the 1970s. The central sociological relationships were those involved in the intergenerational reproduction of socioeconomic inequalities: in education, occupation and income. It was taken for granted that socioeconomic background and a few other sociological variables (gender, religion, race, ethnicity and possibly region) closely predicted children's development during infancy and early childhood, their performance at both primary and secondary school, the type of courses they took in high school, the age at which they left school, their final level of educational attainment, and their occupational standing and income at mid-life. Thus, the cycle of socioeconomic inequality is perpetuated across generations. The task of sociological theory was to account for these supposedly enduring and strong relationships.

Divisions and challenges

The sociological perspective was never a paradigm in the Kuhnian sense: a set of practices, beliefs and body of knowledge common to the discipline's practitioners. The strongest division was between scientific and humanistic perspectives. The "scientific" school assumes that scientific principles could be applied to the study of society, albeit with modifications, in much the same way as psychology and economics do and are considered social sciences. In contrast, others understood sociology as a humanity, much more like history, philosophy or even literary criticism. This division was reflected in the type of sociology practised: quantitative sociology involving surveys and the statistical analysis of data were firmly in the scientific camp; historical sociology, social philosophy and much of what passes as theory fell in the humanities camp; and qualitative studies of small groups and organizations could fall into either.

From about 1970, the discipline became more openly hostile to the scientific study of society. Increasingly, critiques of "positivism" – defined generally as the application of scientific methods – almost invariably concluded that the scientific study of society was impossible (for a prominent example see Gouldner 1970). Furthermore, the goal of objectivity was ridiculed and sociologists proudly announced their political leanings (Berger 1992: 12). Although most prominent sociologists in the United States (US) of the pre- and early post-war years were clearly on the progressive, often socialist, side of politics (see Lipset 1994), a consequence of the anti-war and civil-rights movements of the late 1960s was pressure for sociology to become openly radical and politically active (Lipset 1994: 207).

From the mid-1960s, there were also empirical challenges. A variety of studies undermined some of the most cherished assumptions of sociology. In the US, the Coleman report, *Equality of Educational Opportunity* (Coleman *et al.* 1966: 301), found that only very small proportions of the variance in students' verbal test scores could be uniquely accounted for by their economic or educational backgrounds. Furthermore, after taking into account measures of home background, schools and variations in their resources and curricula made little difference to student outcomes (1966: 22–3, 301). Based on the first large-scale national study of social stratification, Blau and Duncan's (1967) *The American Occupational Structure* found a large amount of upward occupational mobility which was increasing (1967: 77, 106). Furthermore, a surprisingly low amount of the variation in educational attainment was accounted for by father's occupation and father's education (1967: 174). In the analysis of occupational attainment, years spent in formal education was a very much stronger influence than father's occupation (1967: 170). Blau and Duncan's groundbreaking study analyzed a theoretical model that linked socioeconomic background with education, occupation and earnings by path analysis, a sophisticated technique then only recently introduced into sociology (Duncan 1966).

At much the same time, a number of studies concluded that cognitive ability has consequences for socioeconomic outcomes, especially educational attainment (Eckland 1967; Sewell and Shah 1968; Taubman and Wales 1972). Intelligence along with other social-psychological variables was incorporated in the Wisconsin model of status attainment, which was an extension of the Blau–Duncan model (Sewell *et al.* 1969). A few years later, Duncan *et al.* (1972: 104) concluded that intelligence "has a substantial influence on occupational attainment, apart from its correlation with family background factors" and "bears an important relationship to income (net of social origins) for men of equal schooling and occupational statuses". At much the same time, the publication of Jensen's (1969) paper, "How Much Can We Boost IQ and Scholastic Achievement?", initiated the first of a series of acrimonious debates on the nature of intelligence and its role in education and social stratification.

The challenges to sociological orthodoxies were consolidated in Jencks *et al.*'s (1972) book, *Inequality*. The book concluded that: economic variation between families explains only a fraction of the variation in children's cognitive scores (1972: 81); high schools and their resources make little difference to test scores or educational attainment (1972: 93, 159); the most important determinant of educational attainment (after family background broadly defined) is probably cognitive skill (1972: 159); the role of a father's socioeconomic status "in determining his son's status is surprising small"; family background is not the primary determinant of occupational status (1972: 179); and there is almost as much income inequality among adult men from the same socioeconomic background as among men in general (1972: 215). Jencks *et al.*'s (1972: 8) conclusion that socioeconomic success depends on on-the-job-competence and "luck" provided little scope for conventional sociological explanations.

Empirical studies from other countries also found considerably weaker sociological relationships than usually presumed. A comprehensive cross-national study of occupational mobility in Western countries found that "all countries studied are characterized by a high degree of mobility" leading to the conclusion of "widespread social mobility" (Lipset and Zetterberg 1959: 72, 25). Much later, Goldthorpe and Llewellyn (1977) demonstrated that conventional views that there was little social mobility in Britain and that the limited amount that existed was mostly only short range were incorrect. In a later cross-national study, Erikson and Goldthorpe (1992: 190) found an even greater amount of absolute mobility than Lipset and Zetterberg. Analyses of the Blau–Duncan status attainment model conducted in other countries also found that educational attainment was only moderately accounted for by socioeconomic background and that educational attainment had a much stronger influence on men's occupational destinations than socioeconomic background (Boyd *et al.* 1985; Broom and Jones 1976; Halsey 1977).

These findings tended to confirm many of the claims of theories of industrialization and post-industrialization, or more generally "modernization" theory. In contrast to "pre-modern" societies, modern societies, that is industrialized Western societies, are comparatively open, exhibiting substantial amounts of social mobility. The process of socioeconomic attainment is governed much more by (educational) achievement than by social ascription, and the demands of industrial society mean that ability and competence are more important for occupational attainment than class or socioeconomic background. Western societies are to a considerable extent meritocratic, given the importance of cognitive ability for educational attainment and the strong effects of education for subsequent labor market outcomes. The more "modern" the society, the more meritocratic it is, and the weaker the impact of ascribed characteristics, such as socioeconomic background, but also gender, race, ethnicity, and other attributes from one's birth.

These challenges to conventional sociological understandings were soon met with strong resistance. Blau and Duncan's work was critiqued for an apparent preoccupation of method over substance, for not including the ways in which classes and interests groups shape the stratification system (assuming that they can and do), and for focusing almost exclusively on men (Acker 1973; Coser 1975). The statistical analysis of survey data was increasingly critiqued for being positivistic and empiricist, although it was not clear what this meant, only that such research and its findings could easily be dismissed (see Marsh 1982: 3, 48–51). Critical theory, neo-Marxist accounts of contemporary societies, anti-scientific critiques of quantitative sociology and activist "social action" research were gaining prominence. Empirically, Bowles (1972) argued that the Blau–Duncan and Wisconsin models of status attainment did not adequately measure socioeconomic background because they did not include income and wealth, and did not take into account measurement error. In a well-cited article, Collins (1971) posited two general explanations for the expansion of education: functionalist and conflict. Functionalist theories understand the expansion of education as a response to increased technical requirements of the labor market, whereas conflict theories focus on privileged social groups imposing their cultural values on the selection process for higher-status jobs. A consensus emerged that conflict theories much better accounted for social phenomena than functionalist explanations which were increasingly derided. This was followed by Bowles and Gintis's (1976) book, which argued that, instead of transmitting knowledge and skills, the education system primarily prepared students for their appropriate roles in a class-stratified society. The root of the problem was the capitalist economy. Ignoring much of the US attainment literature, Bourdieu's (1977) theory of cultural capital received widespread acclaim as an explanation for the supposedly strong and enduring socioeconomic inequalities in education and thus society more generally. Jencks *et al.*'s (1979: 10) second book, *Who Gets Ahead*, states that "background characteristics seem to exert appreciable effects on both occupational status and earnings even among men with the same test scores and education", which was widely misinterpreted as reestablishing the primacy of socioeconomic background.[1] In contrast to the liberal-functionalist expectation of increased openness in occupational mobility due to industrialization, Erikson and Goldthorpe (1992) characterized social mobility in modern societies as in "constant flux" by focusing on the relative odds of social mobility.[2] Cross-national research on educational transitions from one level to the next concluded that, generally, socioeconomic inequalities in education have not declined (Blossfeld and Shavit 1993; Shavit *et al.* 2007b). Similarly, cross-national studies employing log-linear analysis on the cross-tabulation of educational attainment by class or educational background also concluded there has been no change over time (Goldthorpe 1996a; Pfeffer 2008).

There are therefore two general perspectives on the reproduction of socioeconomic inequalities in Western countries. The first "modernization" perspective argues that socioeconomic background, social class and other ascribed attributes have become, or are becoming, less important for a range of social outcomes. The opposing perspective, often referred to as reproduction theory, contends that the reproduction of socioeconomic inequalities has remained strong and/or enduring, characterized as "persistent inequality", "persisting class differentials", "maximally maintained inequality", "constant flux", and "trendless fluctuation".

The fundamental question is: In modern societies, do socioeconomic origins have only a weak or declining influence on educational and subsequent socioeconomic outcomes, or has the intergenerational reproduction of socioeconomic inequalities remained strong despite societal changes and policies aimed to reduce inequality of opportunity?

The question is central to sociology as a discipline and is important beyond the discipline relevant to a number of fields in economics, education and psychology. It is also of great interest to policymakers and politicians.

The response to this question should involve a series of inter-related theoretical generalizations that can account for the findings from the large number of relevant scientifically orientated studies.

Chapter outline

The next chapter is about theory. The first part discusses the state of sociological theory and the paucity of appropriate explanatory theories that logically account for a range of related empirical phenomena. Much sociological theory bears little resemblance to scientifically oriented explanatory theory: hermeneutic-type analyses of the texts of prominent sociological theorists, critiques of almost every aspect of Western societies from Marxist and other radical perspectives, epistemological discourses on science usually concluding on the impossibility of a science of society, and of course, "postmodernism" which explicitly rejects Western and scientific ways of acquiring knowledge. The second part of Chapter 2 discusses modernization theory. Much of sociological theory has been about contrasting industrial society with preindustrial society, industrial society with post-industrial society and the consequences for individuals from further modernization or modernity. Modernization and reproduction theories provide the theoretical background for this book.

Chapter 3 discusses the measurement of the major concepts used in this book: occupational class, occupational status, educational attainment, socioeconomic background, cognitive ability, ability-type measures, and non-cognitive attributes. The last section of Chapter 3 briefly summarizes the statistical techniques referred to throughout this book.

Chapter 4 deals with many of the issues surrounding "cognitive ability": whether there is such a thing as human intelligence, its measurement and dimensionality, its stability over time, the extent to which cognitive ability can be attributed to socioeconomic background and education, and the relative importance of genetics and the environment. It also discusses non-cognitive attributes, their stability, associations with cognitive ability and if they too have any genetic basis.

Chapter 5 demonstrates that ability has sizable associations with a range of educational outcomes: student achievement or test scores; student performance (e.g. grades at school); educational differentiation, which is the allocation of students to different types of schools (tracking) and within-school curricular differentiation (streaming); school completion and non-completion; university entry and completion; and overall educational attainment. The effects of non-cognitive attributes for education are also discussed.

Chapter 6 shows that cognitive ability is also associated with labor market outcomes: participation in the labor market, unemployment, occupational attainment and earnings. Its effects are substantially reduced when taking into educational attainment, but it has non-trivial effects, net of education, throughout the occupational career. The chapter also discusses the importance of non-cognitive attributes for occupational attainment and earnings.

Chapter 7 provides evidence that socioeconomic background, no matter how it is measured, is only moderately associated with educational outcomes. Chapter 8 evaluates various theoretical approaches that attempt to explain socioeconomic inequalities in education: economic, social, school-based and cultural approaches. Chapter 9 evaluates the evidence for declining socio-economic inequalities in education and the extent that aspects of modernization theory can account for over time and between country differences.

Chapter 10 focuses on occupational attainment, the magnitude of the association between parents and their adult child's occupations (including a section on occupational mobility in Western countries), the relative importance of socioeconomic background and education across countries and changes over time, and the relevance of modernization theory.

Chapter 11 discusses the intergenerational reproduction of economic inequalities. Since about 1990, a major subfield in economics concludes that the intergenerational transmission of inequalities in earnings and income is much higher than earlier studies claimed, at least in Britain and the US. The chapter reviews work on the magnitudes of the intergenerational earnings "elasticities" and correlations, changes over time, cross-national differences and the extent to which economic inequalities among adults can be attributed to economic resources in the parental generation or to other factors.

The final chapter discusses how reproduction and modernization theory has fared under intense empirical scrutiny and the implications of this study for policy and stratification theory. The chapter also outlines an inchoate theory that incorporates socioeconomic background, ability, education and occupational outcomes which is consistent with the bulk of the empirical findings cited in this book.

Notes

1 Socioeconomic background usually refers to father's and mother's education and occupation, family income and wealth, as single indicators of socioeconomic background or in some combination (see page 39). Social background usually includes race, ethnicity, family size, region, possibly religion and other sociodemographic factors as well as (some) indicators of socioeconomic background. Family background is usually measured in sibling studies of brothers and/or sisters. Siblings have much more similar educational and socioeconomic outcomes than do non-related individuals of the same age. The similarity between siblings' outcomes compared to individuals from different families provides a measure of the total impact of family (as opposed to socioeconomic or social) background. See page 129 for a definition of family background and use the index for references to sibling studies referred to in this book.

2 The focus was not on gross movement upwards or downwards but on the relative odds which produces seemingly larger class-of-origin differences in class-of-destination and most often invariance in relative mobility chances over time and cross-nationally.

Chapter 2

Theoretical matters

Sociological theory

Sociological theory,[1] as generally understood within the discipline, is not theory in the scientific sense but something quite different. Hedström and Swedberg (1996) point out that much contemporary sociological theory is not about explanation but about the interpretation of social phenomena, which they describe as non-explanatory discourse. Prominent contemporary theorists, such as Giddens and Alexander, see theory's purpose not as explanatory but as discourse or conceptualizations of a more philosophical nature (see Goldthorpe 2000: 2). A sizable component of sociological theorizing is critical theory, which seeks human emancipation from oppression by analyzing the forms of oppression, mainly capitalism and other Western institutions (corporations, marriage, the health and education systems, the labor market, etc.). Another type of non-explanatory theory is normative theory, which is about what societies should be rather than what they are. These so-called theories do not allow the development of testable propositions and so are immune from falsification (Goldthorpe 1990: 405; Lenski 1988).[2] "Theory" immune from falsification is essentially a system of beliefs. For these theorists and their disciples, much empirical work is simply not relevant, since it is based on contestable and unacceptable "positivist" assumptions. If quantitative empirical work is referred to at all, it is in a very cursory, dismissive or uninformed way.

Sociology is a unique discipline in that the theoretical and empirical strands of the discipline are generally quite separate enterprises. Goldthorpe (2000: 2) views the "manifest lack of integration of research and theory" as the great scandal of sociology. Hedström and Swedberg (1996: 127) see contemporary theory as having "less and less bearing on empirical research". Theories are not so much connected to a particular field of research but to prominent individuals; beginning with the "founding fathers" Marx, Weber, and, less often, Durkheim; the Frankfurt School theorists; since the 1970s later critical theorists, such as Althusser, Poulantzas, Habermas, and Bourdieu; and, more recently, Foucault, Giddens, and Beck. Focusing on prominent theorists rather than theories about empirical phenomena is not a sound basis on which to develop explanatory theories. Lenski (1988: 165) points out that "By teaching theory for its own sake, rather than in conjunction with a distinctive research tradition, we tend to raise up new generations of theorists who too often emulate the old masters in ways that hinder, rather than advance, the cause of macrosociology".

Very often, sociological theory has the hallmarks of a religion; theorists have an almost godlike status and their writings are treated with the utmost reverence.[3] A major enterprise within some parts of the discipline is to analyze theoretical texts to try and understand the author's insights which apparently, although this is never demonstrated, allow a better understanding of contemporary societies. The interpretation of theoretical texts is a difficult task even for the most educated reader because they are often written in an obscure and difficult way, and the concepts and ideas tend to be vague, slippery and, on some readings, contradictory.[4] Also, there is often the issue of the quality of the translation since a true understanding is not really possible for non-native speakers of the original language. Understanding these texts is supposedly facilitated by self-appointed experts who, like priests, are best able to interpret the text. Among these experts, there is little consensus about what is the true or intended meaning, so debate ensues spawning more text, as Goldthorpe (2000: 7) notes, "books being written out of books . . . that extends indefinitely" and with almost no reference to empirical evidence. This is all very disempowering for students and disappointing for anyone interested in comprehensible, non-ideological, explanatory theories about modern societies.

Sociological theory and the sociopolitical context

Although "theory" has a high status in sociology, theories (apart from the writings of classical theorists) are almost invariably short lived. They are discarded not because they are found to be inadequate explanations of the social world but because they simply become unfashionable. Their popularity is sensitive to prevailing political orthodoxies which can alter in response to political events. The Vietnam War and the events of May 1968 changed sociological theory. Parsons' overly voluminous theorizing, so prominent until this time, was dismissed because he was viewed as too conservative, although there is no doubt he was politically to the left.[5] Similarly, Merton and the formal theory movement of the 1960s and early 1970s were judged as positivist and therefore not worth considering. Taking their place were neo-Marxist critical theories, which were largely critiques of the existing capitalist social order, often heralding (and welcoming) its demise. Marcuse's (1964) *One-Dimensional Man* argued that increased wealth and consumerism meant that workers were being duped into supporting an economic system detrimental to their "true" interests, which was supposedly state socialism. According to Habermas (1975) in *Legitimation Crisis*, the ideological support bases of capitalism were being eroded, evidenced by the growth of the counter-culture and the anti-war movement, which meant that, in the future, capitalist societies would not be able to maintain their legitimacy among their citizenry. Over 40 years later there is no sign that capitalism is facing a crisis of "legitimacy".

The economic problems of the 1970s, high inflation and high unemployment, were further confirmation that capitalism was failing and Marx's predictions of proletarianization, emiseration and polarization were at last being realized.[6] Marxist critiques on the nature of work in capitalist societies by Braverman (1974) and Burawoy (1979) concluded with arguments that "workers" – which ranged in definition from piece-rate workers to all employees – would be much better off under a socialist economic system akin to, but not the same as, the Soviet Union. The recession of the early 1980s, together with Thatcherism and Reaganism, were further evidence that the system was collapsing, or at the very least required careful analysis from a Marxist or critical perspective. In the 1980s, prominent theorists from the Marxist perspective were concerned about the nature of class, given changes in the occupational structure and the growth of the welfare state, and whether these developments could account for the really pressing issue of the time: the absence of mass revolutionary movements in Western countries. By the mid- to late-1980s, the absence of mobilizing issues like the Vietnam War and improvements in Western economies made these theories largely redundant. Post-structuralism emerged, in part, because of disillusionment with the Soviet Union and other socialist states – which were far from emancipatory – and the declining strength of socialist and communist organizations in Western countries. Post-structuralists were concerned with critically analyzing culture and discourse in order to better understand their oppressive effects, hopefully leading to liberation. In post-structuralism, there was no point in discussing social structures since classes were fluid and only crystallized at pre-revolutionary moments. This view was for the faithful. It explained why social class was less relevant politically and socially but, at the same time, the ultimate basis of contemporary societies, and at some apocalyptic time in the future (judgment day) the true power of class would be revealed.

A series of unforeseen events – the 1989 collapse of communism in Eastern Europe and two years later in the Soviet Union,[7] the decline of the once-popular communist parties of Western Europe, the adoption by China of many aspects of market economies, the absence of an exemplary existing (or for that matter past) socialist society – all contributed to the virtual disappearance of Marxist theory in academia. The ideology that had lasted for over a century and permeated almost all countries, that capitalism would inevitably be replaced by a much-superior socialist economic system, was largely abandoned in the West, and with it the attendant sociological theorizing on the reasons why this was, was not or should be happening. The vacuum created by the demise of Marxism was quickly filled by postmodernism.[8]

Postmodernism

In the early 1990s Turner summarized the then state of sociological theory as being concerned with:

> 1) the faults of positivism and scientific sociology;
> 2) the ontological and epistemological problems of theorizing about human interaction and organization;
> 3) the offering of alternatives which (pick your favourite combination) take into account human agency, indeterminacy, history, context, or contingency;
> 4) the advocacy of critique of technology, capitalism, and assorted evils or the offering of a program and plan for when all the philosophical issues are worked out;
> 5) the worship of the masters through the history of ideas, name dropping and quoting, or scholarship on particular theorists;
> 6) the fine-tuning of the lost art of discourse (on just about anything non-empirical).
>
> (Turner 1992: 54)

The major difference between 1992 and now is the growth of postmodernism, which shares many of these features, but is primarily concerned with "deconstructing" language and communication because, apparently, it is the source of social power. The postmodernist position is well summarized by Goldthorpe:

> There is no world "out there" existing independently of our representations of it or, that is, the ways in which we socially construct it through our language; thus the criterion of the truth of statements cannot be correspondence with such an independent world; truth is not discovered but is rather *made*, and is made, moreover in many different ways always with a moral and political intent; thus, all truth is "local" and "contextual"; there is no knowledge that can claim a privileged, objective, and universal status by virtue of the methods through which it is secured, only "knowledges" that are specific to particular communities, cultures and so on, and that serve their purposes.
>
> (Goldthorpe 2000: 8)

In common with other parts of sociology, including quantitative sociology, postmodernist sociology focuses on social inequalities. However, postmodernism assumes that these inequalities are extreme and unchanging, and it is the task of postmodernism to expose how these inequities are maintained by deconstructing language and text.

Postmodernism takes an uncompromising social relativist position. It argues that the conclusions reached by scientifically orientated sociology, or indeed any science, are a product of the sociopolitical context, so invariably support that context, and are no better than commonsense or non-scientific explanations. Of course, this argument can be directed at postmodernism itself; its ostensible mission in exposing the linguistic basis for society's supposed rampant inequities and evils is simply a political strategy to reinforce the political and economic position of its practitioners and has no more authenticity than any other approach.

There is nothing particularly new about postmodernism; it has commonalities with sociological and philosophical critiques of science and knowledge, hermeneutics, critical theory, post-structuralism, and the "social construction of reality" school in sociology. Postmodernism also shares similarities with aspects of Marxism, in that ideology, science, culture and other aspects of the "superstructure" are understood as reinforcing and maintaining the existing social order. The major difference is instead of objective reality or "truth" being established through careful Marxist scientific methods or by the revolutionary proletariat, an objective understanding is not possible. Other aspects of Marxist theory, "discourses" on the malevolent role of social institutions (the education system, the division and organization of production, the press, the political system, marriage etc.) and culture in maintaining the inequitable social order are left largely intact. There is a particular emphasis on class, gender and race: a holy trinity.[9] As was characteristic of Marxism, postmodernism is highly critical of existing Western societies[10] and calls for an emancipatory research methodology and agenda that eschews "scientism". The similarities between postmodernism and Marxism are exemplified by the publication of Sokal's (1996) hoax article; a postmodernist critique of the natural sciences in the avowedly Marxist journal, *Social Text.*

Despite dismissing the very possibility of a scholarly discipline, postmodernism has spread throughout sociology and with surprisingly little criticism (Smith 1995).[11] Inglehart (1997: 23–5) takes a benign view of postmodernism compatible with his thesis of post-materialism as logically following from Weberian and Marxist accounts of modernization. However, its influence is not at all benign. Sociology is particularly vulnerable to postmodernism because it does not have a strong shared body of research findings and has a history of accommodating (even welcoming) epistemological and ontological critiques of itself, unlike economics or psychology. Smith (1995: 58), citing Turner and others, notes that if postmodernists had their way sociology would be little more than critiques about Western societies, science and technology, accompanied by unbridled but poor philosophizing. Unfortunately, this is truer today than when it was written.

The policy implications from postmodernism are disturbing. It takes as a given that modern Western societies are characterized by severe, enduring and irrepressible injustices largely and ultimately perpetuated by language. So, if these injustices were to be eliminated and stopped from reasserting themselves, it would be necessary to control language, as well as radically reforming society's institutions. Contrary to its apparent relativist façade, postmodernism does not accept views contrary to its own often extreme political and ideological positions; opposing ideas are viewed as pernicious and vehicles of oppression. As in the case of Marxism and other radical ideologies, its agenda is ultimately totalitarian, requiring control of all aspects of society, and the "removal" of reactionary elements, in the name of some ill-defined greater good.

Consequences of non-explanatory theory

Although it is often recognized that there is a chasm between theory and empirical research in sociology, the detrimental consequences are much less often acknowledged. Since it is not possible to derive testable hypotheses from these types of theories, they serve only as a backdrop. It is not uncommon for "research" studies to be peppered with references to prominent theorists, no matter how unrelated to the topic, and for them not to engage with the actual theory itself or even its implications. Instead, it signals to the reader their familiarity with "theory", so not to be accused of "mindless empiricism" and to show where the researchers' ideological and political allegiances lie.

Non-explanatory theory facilitates politicization. The political position of much of sociology is from a radical-left perspective, which sees social problems in individual societies and the world as the result of capitalism, patriarchy, racism, and the economic and cultural imperialism of the US and other Western countries (see Berger 2002; Klein and Stern 2006). Horowitz (1994) argues that sociology has changed from having a central place in the social sciences to an ideological outpost of political extremism. Klein and Stern (2006) argue that sociology is compatible with classic liberalism but such a political position is virtually absent (they suggest "forbidden") from the discipline. The discipline was more politically left in the early 2000s than even in the late 1960s (Burawoy 2005). There is the pervasive view that if only capitalism could be replaced by something else – something like a centralized, possibly supranational, bureaucracy that controls the production, distribution and exchange of goods and services, and importantly ideology, run by like-minded people – the world would be a much better place. This is extraordinary, given the dismal failure of the radical-left regimes to generate reasonable standards of living for their citizens, and their contempt and abuse of human rights over the past century. It is not contemplated that market economies, wealth production, the Western traditions of human rights, law, parliamentary democracy, pluralism, and the values of the Enlightenment could and have substantially improved people's lives.[12]

A high-profile manifestation of sociology's political position is Burawoy's (2005) speech promoting "public sociology", given while he was president of the American Sociological Association. After providing an allegory to contemporary societies with the Nazi army about to overtake Paris, he speaks of "unfettered capitalism" fuelling market tyrannies and untold inequities on a global scale, and describes democracy as a "a thin veil for powerful interests, disenfranchisement, mendacity, and even violence" (2005: 260). Nielsen (2004) expresses serious concerns about "public sociology" and notes that its advocacy of certain political beliefs emanating from a particular moral-political agenda is incompatible with a scientifically orientated profession.

"Theory" is often explicitly or implicitly defined by political position; there is Marxist, feminist, postcolonial, critical, queer and postmodernist theories, in various combinations and hues, which awkwardly mesh scholarly research with activist politics or political ideology. Weak evidence and poor arguments are used to strongly promote a particular political position. Findings incompatible with the dominant ideologies and political positions are either ignored or vehemently attacked. The politicization and ideological nature of the discipline was one of the reasons Berger (1992) wrote "Sociology: A Disinvitation?", lamenting the politicization of the discipline and its inability to predict societal changes. Later, Berger (2002) notes that the "core scientific principle of objectivity has been ignored in practice and denied validity in theory".

"Critical theory" has hijacked critical thinking. Critical thinking should mean critically evaluating an argument for its logic, the appropriateness of the supporting evidence and the fair treatment of contrary arguments and evidence. Critical thinking also means being conscious of the various strategies that proponents (on either side of a debate) can make to support their case, such as: dubious or irrelevant analogies, metaphors and similes; slippery concepts that change their meaning to suit the argument; appeals to a higher authority (e.g. prominent theorists, noble prize winners); the use of emotive language; and *ad hominem* attacks. Instead, "thinking critically" has become the ability to parrot standard polemics on positivism, capitalism, patriarchy, imperialism, and take an extreme left-wing position on a range of social and political issues.

In addition, the critiques of science and the production of knowledge so characteristic of contemporary "theory" substantially contribute to the absence of a generally agreed upon cumulative body of knowledge in sociology, which is understood by the field's professionals and practitioners and transmitted to its students. This would be the discipline's contribution to the corpus of human knowledge.[13] It is very difficult to find a single conclusion from sociological research conducted over the past half century or so, on which a general consensus would be reached among professional sociologists. Almost all the conclusions are contestable in some way or other.

The prominence of non-explanatory discourse is important to the popularity of qualitative research. Although there are examples of qualitative research in sociology that adhere to scientific procedures, such studies are becoming less common. Qualitative research is popular because it is more compatible with non-explanatory discursive theory. Increasingly, qualitative research strongly avoids any aspect of the research process that could be viewed as positivist. It often sees itself as emancipatory: highlighting the plight of the disadvantaged or social minorities, or the wickedness of the privileged. Furthermore, it does not require the technical and statistical skills necessary for quantitative research, arguing that it is inclusive and can supposedly benefit the subjects being studied. As a result, "anything goes", because there is no need to follow established procedures; endeavor to be objective; or worry about technical issues such as sampling, validity, reliability, hypothesis testing; or guard against spurious interpretations. The disregard for scientific protocols creates serious problems for the usefulness of much of qualitative research in sociology. Ideally, qualitative research should dovetail with quantitative work by addressing research questions about social processes from *the same general body of theory and accepted body of knowledge* that are difficult to examine through quantitative approaches. However, it is characteristic for qualitative research to ignore the findings of relevant quantitative work, but cite other qualitative studies with similar ideological orientations. Often the research is based on "grounded theory", which is no theory at all, but theory as you go.[14] If quantitative researchers set out to develop theory as they learn more about their data, they would be accused of "data dredging", "mindless empiricism", and of being atheoretical.

Qualitative research is typically based on a small number of subjects selected on an *ad hoc* basis but often quite illegitimately makes general conclusions about much larger populations. Scientific sampling techniques are rarely used and, even if they were, the number of subjects examined would be too small to make valid inferences about the sampled population. Furthermore, there is a lack of an appreciation of variability. There is an implicit assumption that all subjects with the same characteristics have the same outcomes, and the aim is to identify the social processes involved. However, this is hardly ever the case: the variation in outcomes among individuals with the same social characteristics is most often considerable.[15] A couple of carefully selected quotes may support the study's original contentions, but it is rarely made clear whether these quotes are typical (modal) or only expressed by a small minority. Furthermore, qualitative studies do not routinely make appropriate comparisons since they usually focus on a single group. There is no consideration that the null hypothesis may be true, that the variation in outcomes for the studied social group is no different from that of a comparable group. If the variations in outcomes for comparable groups are much the same, then conclusions arguing that particular social processes explain the difference cannot be made since there was no difference to begin with. One of the most disturbing aspects of many qualitative studies is that they almost invariably support the original contentions. This should sound alarm bells since it is rare in quantitative work to strongly and unambiguously confirm original hypotheses.

The long shadow of non-explanatory discursive theory also falls on quantitative research. Because so much of what passes as theory are simply attacks on just about every aspect of quantitative research – its epistemology, ontology, assumptions, measurement, analytical techniques, and inferences – quantitative researchers are very wary of "theory". Unfortunately, they do little to defend it against these largely ill-informed and misguided attacks.[16] Since the social space for social theory has already been filled, quantitative researchers seldom claim to be theorists, as well as researchers or analysts. Since quantitative sociologists shy away from taking the high ground on theory, this is taken as further evidence that their work is atheoretical. It is almost *de rigueur* for text books in quantitative sociology to strongly emphasize the importance of theory when doing quantitative research, so as not to be advocating "mindless empiricism". However, if a keen student followed this advice and went to prominent theoretical books or journals at any time over the last 50 years, they would find little guidance from theory with ill-defined concepts and few testable propositions.

Explanatory theory remains undeveloped. Only when prominent theorists make causal claims that can be examined do quantitative sociologists engage in that type of theory. Bourdieu's theory of cultural capital endeavoring to account for socioeconomic inequalities in education is a good example. Needless to say, the proponents of cultural capital theory take little notice of quantitative research on cultural capital theory. If pressed, they would argue that the said quantitative research has not, and cannot, fully appreciate the scope, complexity and subtly of the theory; in effect, arguing that it cannot generate unambiguous falsifiable propositions. In the effort to be "theoretical", quantitative researchers can also misuse theory. It is perfectly acceptable for a book or academic article to present a chapter or section on theory; again, for example, Bourdieu's cultural capital theory, followed by the presentation of statistical findings that have little connection with the theory discussed. It is enough to present analyses showing that there are socioeconomic inequalities in education (which there are) and conclude that the foregoing research work strongly supports the said theory and, of course, there should be further research in the area.

Rejecting the principle that academic research should strive for objectivity, there is no attempt to try to minimize the influence of the researcher's political views and ideological orientations. Against the advice of Sherlock Holmes, it is quite legitimate in much of sociology to theorize with few facts.[17] Of course, the response is that "facts" are cultural products contaminated by political and ideological content. However, it is not tenable to argue that "facts" are so riddled with ideology and political content that none can be considered relevant to theory building. Data and facts do have cultural content but are usually not tied to a particular political ideology. A good theory is one that is consistent with a large number of observations often from disparate sources. A bad theory is one that rejects inconvenient facts for ideological or political reasons. It is one thing to say that the research process involves human agency but quite another to reject objectivity entirely and, with it, rigorous standards of evidence, deductive and inductive reasoning and thus the very possibility of developing modest theories that adequately account for empirical phenomena.

This disjuncture between theory and empirical research, the highly politicalized nature of what passes as theory, postmodernism, and the rejection of scientific methods are disastrous for institutional sociology.[18] Because of various critiques of positivism, whole swathes of high-quality research are irrelevant to almost all non-quantitative sociologists and thus their students. It is sometimes claimed that a unique strength of sociology is its pluralism in that there are many different types of sociologies. However, as Goldthorpe (2000: 7–8) argues, it is not a genuine (nor fruitful) pluralism because there is no shared paradigm to work on. There are also implications for the refereeing process in academic journals and the appointment of editors.[19] The system of reviewing theses, manuscripts and research proposals breaks down if referees are highly politicized, and intolerant of normal science and its assumptions. Funding agencies with limited resources are less likely to fund research in a highly fragmented discipline with significant segments questioning the very idea of acquiring knowledge. Many departments are characterized by warring factions that, at best, ignore each other and, at worst, are openly hostile in full view of students and university administrators.[20] The recruitment of new staff is often fraught given ideological and methodological divisions. Attracting high-ability students is problematic for many departments and this is not helped by the obsession with impenetrable theory and critiques of quantitative approaches (see Cappell 1995). Another casualty in several countries is the lack of higher-level research skills among graduate and postgraduate students and, in many instances, staff. Over the last 40 years, there have been major methodological advances in the analysis of non-experimental data (structural equation modeling, generalized linear models, event history, fixed and random effects models to name a few), but these developments do not permeate into the discipline much beyond specialist groups. Owing to the reasons outlined above, much of the discipline is irrelevant to policymakers and policy development. They do not want to be confronted with (or pay for) epistemological pieces about the impossibility of knowing about the social world or thinly veiled ideological treatises.

Critiques of quantitative sociology

One of the most unfair criticisms of quantitative sociology is that it makes causal claims that cannot be justified. Debates on causality range from the epistemological to high-level statistics. The three most commonly proposed conditions for establishing causality are correlation, temporal sequencing and the absence of other plausible causal factors (spuriousness). The adage "correlation is not causality" is true, but correlation does serve as a strong basis to further examine causality. Without some kind of correlation, there can be no causality. Statistics and the quantitative social sciences, from their beginnings, have been concerned with the issue of "spuriousness" or the "omitted variable problem".[21] If *x* is correlated with *y*, and assuming that *x* precedes *y*, *x* may not necessarily cause *y*, because there may be a third factor (or factors) *z*, that causes both *x* and *y*, and so is responsible for the observed association between *x* and *y*. Isolating the independent (non-spurious) effects of factors is the main reason for the extensive use of multivariate techniques in quantitative social science. These have become increasingly complex, with particular methods developed for binary, ordinal and polytomous outcomes, and to take into account measurement error and unobserved influences.

Sociological studies almost invariably make causal claims; since without such claims the studies would have little or no point. Oddly, critiques centered on causality are mainly directed at quantitative sociology. Qualitative sociology, critical theory and even postmodernism characteristically make causal claims from much weaker (or no) evidence, often without data or considering technical issues such as representativeness or spuriousness. Qualitative research also invariably makes causal claims that a particular factor or process is important for the social outcomes of a particular group. However, only quantitative approaches allow the issue of causality to be addressed in a systematic, sophisticated and rigorous way.

This is not the place to discuss the philosophical issues surrounding the acquisition of knowledge. A couple of points need to be made about positivism. In the critiques of quantitative sociology, positivism is characterized as rampant empiricism rejecting all speculation that is not empirically based. Marsh (1982: 49) points out that, within the discipline, it is never clear what positivism really means, although it should be avoided at all costs. Often the critique is extended to science in general: the critique of scientism. Generally quantitative sociologists do not take the view that knowledge can only be gained by sense experience – the extreme position of the logical positivists. If pushed, they would most likely take the position of the critical realists who acknowledge an objective world out there, but humans are involved in knowing about it. What the anti-positivists do not seem to realize is that, although it is acknowledged that humans are involved in every part of the research process, from the choice of a research question to the conclusions made, this does not mean that the conclusions reached are wrong or utterly subjective. Humans are also involved in the physical sciences, which have produced very plausible theoretical explanations for a wide range of phenomena. If the argument is to reject science and scientific methods then logically one must also reject the theories and ideas of important people who have shaped contemporary society and modern thinking.

The structure–agency issue is often promoted as something so important that it must be resolved before sociological research can begin. It is often used as further grist to the mill in critiques of scientifically orientated social science, which is apparently ignorant of the issue. Yes, societies do consist of structures and institutions. These can be formal legal institutions created or supported by legislation (such as the education system, religions, employing organizations, marriage) or more informal structures (such as the occupational structure, the patterning of income and wealth, non-institutionalized religions and other belief systems, social norms and values). And, yes, people "negotiate" their lives within and across these structures, and these social structures are populated, managed and changed by people. This is hardly revelatory; it would be difficult to find an individual who disagrees that both structure and agency are involved, when put in reasonably comprehensible terms. Furthermore, it is not necessary to include these concepts in every piece of social science research; in much the same way as other aspects of the human condition – that they have needs and desires; are cognizant; use language; are sexual; are aware of their own morality; make choices; are both rational and emotional; are social beings; have bodies etc. – are true but irrelevant to most social science research questions.

It is often argued that the lack of core knowledge in sociology and relevant explanatory theories is because of special problems with the subject matter. People are not atoms; they have feelings, desires and motivations, so the methodologies appropriate to the natural sciences cannot be applied to sociology. By the natural sciences, what is usually meant is "physics", ignoring the diversity of procedures used in other natural sciences, or indeed within physics. It is supposedly difficult for sociologists to objectively study society because they themselves are part of it (Cole 1994b). There is a range of other arguments: societies are far more complex than the natural world; sociology is limited to non-experimental methods whereas causality can be more convincingly demonstrated by experimental methods (which is true, but equally applicable to all largely observational disciplines); and there is a multitude of influences and unpredictable events. So the argument is that the main reason that sociology does not have a knowledge base and lacks explanatory theories is because of the difficult nature of its subject matter: human beings living in contemporary societies.

These arguments are simply rationalizations for the poor state of sociological knowledge and theories. As a discipline, sociology should be in a much stronger position. There is no absence of information about present-day societies with high-quality administrative, survey and other data. Not only is there abundant data but also a range of sophisticated and appropriate statistical methods that importantly can evaluate the effects of several influences on an outcome in non-experimental contexts. The abundance of information about contemporary society contrasts with other disciplines. In history, there are few primary sources and those that remain could be viewed as biased, a product of educated elites from wealthier, conquering or literate societies. The further one goes back in history, the more limited, biased and unreliable the information. For archaeology, there are rarely written records and the evidence is based mainly on surviving artifacts; there is no way of knowing how representative these artifacts are. Anthropologists often have to rely on their own observations and informants, who may or may not have their own agendas.

Other disciplines have succeeded in developing a body of knowledge despite difficult subject matters and/or limited data. The whole study of human evolution, another largely non-experimental discipline, is based on a small number of fossils, which, if put together, may fill up a large room. Evolutionary biologists and paleontologists are able to say sensible things about animals, plants and microorganisms that lived tens and hundreds of millions of years ago based only on the surviving fragmentary records. Astronomy deals with phenomena which are light years away, incomprehensively large phenomena (e.g. galaxies), objects that cannot be seen or that only theoretically exist and events that occurred billions of years ago. The subject matter of nuclear physics, molecular biology and cosmology, to take several of many examples, is not easy; there is great complexity in what goes on within atoms, molecules, cells, and in this and distant galaxies. Progress has been made by the process of normal science, through logic and using instruments intelligently. It is not credible to argue that quasars, the Earth's geological history, atoms or the biochemical reactions within a cell are so much easier to study than people living in existing societies.

A common argument is that sociology cannot be scientific because it is impossible to make accurate predictions. This is not unique to sociology. It is also not easy to predict revolutions or other political events, financial crises (or, for that matter, stock market prices), earthquakes, hurricanes, the position of electrons, the next supernova visible from Earth, the flight path of a bubble bee, plane crashes or next Tuesday's weather. The inability to predict a particular phenomenon does not mean that the corresponding disciplines are not scientific. Furthermore, reasonably accurate predictions can be made about many aspects of the social world. Reasonable predictions for, say, the year 2030, could be made about the level of religiosity in various Western societies, the levels of support for the Labour party in the United Kingdom (UK), or the level of income inequality in the US or Sweden, or the strongest influences on educational attainment and earnings in industrialized societies.

At this point, the postmodernists and others would reiterate their critique of science and argue that scientific explanations are no better than any other "way of knowing". The logical consequence of this view is that they put themselves in the same camp as creationists, alchemists, astrologists, religious fundamentalists, and the like. A less radical response is that progress can occur in the physical sciences, but not in the social sciences because of special problems; citing any one of the issues discussed above. Psychology, economics, criminology, anthropology, and other social sciences have not reached such a paralyzing and embarrassing impasse on the relationship between theory and empirical research, nor is it commonly asserted that an objective, even partial, scientific understanding of their subject matter is impossible. The reason that sociology has not progressed theoretically and has not created a generally agreed-upon body of knowledge is because of much of what passes for "theory" is non-explanatory, the predominance of anti-scientific ideologies and anti-quantitative critiques, its highly politicized nature and other aspects of its institutions. It is not because of "special" problems with the subject matter being studied.

What should sociological theory be? To reiterate the obvious, sociological theory should comprise a logical set of interrelated statements that account for a range of related empirical phenomena. Theories should allow the generation of unambiguous research hypotheses that can be falsified (Lenski 1988). Theories should not be normative, concerned about how things ought to be, but how they are. Theories should be able to accommodate and deal with ideologically unpalatable findings. Explanatory theories should strive as much as possible to be objective and not be conflated with political advocacy. The assessment of theories should rest solely on their ability to account for a range of empirical findings. Theories should not be judged by the popularity, politics or ideology of their originators, or by their possible implications for policy or political ideologies.

Modernization theory

For social stratification, modernization theory contends that, as societies modernize, the influence of socioeconomic background and other ascribed attributes for education and subsequent socioeconomic outcomes decline. Societies become more meritocratic, with educational attainment more strongly associated with cognitive ability than socioeconomic background, and achievement in the education system becoming a much stronger determinant of occupation and earnings than ascribed attributes. The twin questions of modernization – changes over time and cross-national differences – have driven many studies on the reproduction of educational and socioeconomic inequalities.

Modernization is the process exemplified by contemporary industrialized societies characterized by a complex economy and division of labor, mass communications, both economic and cultural globalization, a decline in the role of community in self-identification, increased individualism, and a decline in the power of traditional social institutions such as social class, the church and the family.

Before industrialization, the circumstances of a person's birth – class, gender, ethnicity, religion and region – largely determined their lives. The Industrial Revolution changed all this. The demand for factory labor undermined the traditional roles in rural and village life and the socializing influence of the church, the family and the local community. There was massive migration from the countryside to urban centers. New occupational groups emerged: enterprises required supervisors and managers, and the use of technology in production and the need for infrastructure created demand for skilled engineers, technicians and scientists. The rise of larger businesses meant that the family firm was less viable. Education expanded, industrial growth produced more occupations (e.g. clerical workers, accountants) that required skills in literacy and numeracy. Furthermore, social reformers advocated that children should be learning at school rather than working on farms or in factories. As electricity replaced steam, production was on a much larger scale, further increasing the division of labor and the demand for specific skills and credentials. A credential signals that an individual has the appropriate knowledge and skills for a particular occupation.

The competition between companies, at first in regional markets (facilitated by better transport and communication), and later in larger domestic and global markets, meant that it was not economically viable to retain employees who do not perform, no matter their social background or social connections. The increased social surplus (from profits) and the demand for welfare, health and other social services expanded professional and paraprofessional occupations whose entry is governed by educational credentials. The surplus also facilitated the expansion of the government sector, which employs bureaucratic selection procedures (such as examinations for entry).[22]

Post-industrialization produced further changes. The bulk of the workforce worked in non-manual occupations, with further increases in professional, paraprofessional, technical and service occupations. Education continued to expand and university education changed from an elite to a mass system. Entry to institutions and courses offering the most sought-after credentials became increasingly based on performance. With post-industrialization, large working-class communities surrounding heavy industries declined. Manual workers became more affluent, moving away from traditional working-class districts. The welfare state has taken over the role of the family in many aspects of children's socialization. Movies, television, and more recently the internet further undermine the socialization effects of family, friends and local communities.

Modernization is not a theory in the sense of comprising a series of logically interconnected statements generating specific unambiguous hypotheses. It is better understood as an organizing rubric, a collection of diverse and varied but related hypotheses which generally contend that, as societies develop, they become richer, more equal, more democratic, more open and more achievement orientated; and what people do and think becomes less tied to their socioeconomic background, other ascribed characteristics, and their current social position.

Modernization and sociological theory

Modernization theory has occupied a central position in sociology and related social sciences. Modernization theory has its origins in the social evolutionary theories of the eighteenth and nineteenth centuries, in which all societies were viewed as progressing towards contemporary European societies. The origin of sociology as a discipline can be attributed to the profound and widespread social changes that were taking place in the wake of industrialization (Berger 2002). Similarly, Giddens (1978: xii) argues that the political climate from the French Revolution and the economic changes from the Industrial Revolution provided the context for the emergence of the discipline of sociology.

Early sociologists contrasted the change from traditional, rural and religious societies with little division of labor to larger, urban and more secular industrial societies. Nineteenth-century social scientists developed a number of dualities and typologies summarizing the change from preindustrial to industrial society. Comte (1798–1857) argued that industrialized societies were entering the "positive" phase of development, with science becoming the dominant mode of inquiry and humanity the basic social unit, rather than the family or the state. There is a universal order and a prevailing sentiment of "benevolence". This contrasted with the earlier metaphysical stage characterized by organized religion, royalty, tradition, and explanations of both natural and social phenomena based on divine will. Spencer (1820–1903) contrasted "industrial" society with its contractual obligations and complexity from "militant" societies which were simple and ordered, and where relationships were based on social norms and tradition. Toennies (1858–1936) distinguished *Gemeinschaft* and *Gesellschaft*. *Gemeinschaft* was the general term for preindustrial communities where social ties were intimate and informal, and work was limited to a small number of general occupations: farming, soldiering, religious work and some specialized trade and commercial occupations. In contrast, *Gesellschaft* (modern) communities were characterized by formalized ties, impersonal relationships and a large number of occupations. Similarly, Durkheim (1858–1917) contrasted mechanical and organic solidarity. In small preindustrial communities, social cohesion was brought about by shared beliefs and practices: mechanical solidarity. In large-scale industrial societies, social cohesion is maintained by a shared acceptance of the interdependence of social units involved in a complex and specialized division of labor: organic solidarity. Redfield (1897–1958) proposed a folk–urban continuum, where folk societies were small, homogenous and based on religion, and the division of labor was only defined by age and sex. At the other extreme, urban industrial societies were secular and individualistic. Marx differentiated societies by their mode of production and saw European societies as progressing from feudalism to capitalism. This change undermined the social relationships (e.g. loyalty, honor, fealty) that characterized feudal society. Weber saw growing rationalization and bureaucratization as characteristic of modern society, reducing the role of social ties and tradition.

Taking some of the ideas of Weber, Parsons and functionalist theory, Levy (1966: 240) associated modernization with "rationality, universalism, and functional specificity". Blau and Duncan also emphasized "universalism and science":

> ...a fundamental trend toward expanding universalism characterizes industrial society. Objective criteria of evaluation that are universally accepted increasingly pervade all spheres of life and displace particularistic standards of diverse ingroups, intuitive judgments, and humanistic values not susceptible to empirical verification. The growing emphasis on rationality and efficiency inherent in the spread of universalism finds expression in rapid technological progress and increasing division of labor and differentiation generally, as standards of efficiency are applied to the performance of tasks and the allocation of manpower for them.
>
> (Blau and Duncan 1967: 429)

Not only were these changes limited to Western countries, Kerr and others (Kerr 1983; Kerr *et al.* 1964) argued that industrialization generates convergence between societies with different political and cultural systems: then, specifically, communist and capitalist societies. According to Dunlop *et al.* (1975: 37) "the logic of industrialization results in advanced industrial societies becoming more alike, despite cultural and political differences, and certainly more alike than any one of them is like a less developed country".

Bell (1973: 9) argued that the emergence of post-industrial society further reduces the importance of social ascription. Post-industrial society would be a meritocracy in which status and income are based on education and skill. Universities would become the arbitrator of class position (1973: 410). Bell (1973: 426) contrasted modern society to "estate society", in which only the birthright of inheritance allowed access to land and honorable positions in the army and the church. He also argued that post-industrial society heralds a shift in power relations:

> In industry, family capitalism is replaced by managerial capitalism; in government, patronage is replaced by civil service and bureaucratization; in the universities, the exclusiveness of the old social elites, particularly WASP domination of the Ivy League colleges...The post-industrial society, in this dimension of status and power, is the logical extension of the meritocracy; it is the codification of a new social order based, in principle, on the priority of educated talent.
>
> (Bell 1973: 426)

More recently, Inglehart (1997: 10–11) reformulates modernization theory, emphasizing four points: change is not linear; modernization theory is not deterministic; modernization theory is not interchangeable with Westernization; and "democracy" is not an inherent aspect of modernization. His main contention is that "technological and economic changes tend to be linked with specific types of cultural, political and social change" and these changes move in theoretically coherent and predictable ways (1997: 11).

Aspects of critical theory and postmodernism resonate with modernization theory. Following from Weber, Habermas (1984, 1987) focused on the undesirable consequences of increasing rationalism, Giddens (1990) on "modernity" and Beck (1992) on the risk society because of the hazards and uncertainties created by modernization. "Reflexive-modernity" argues that the foundations of the traditional social order are dissolving undermining social identities and societal expectations and destabilizing contemporary societies (Beck and Beck-Gernsheim 2002). They are also concerned with rise of "individualism" and whether modern citizens are in the process of being "released from the forms of industrial society (class, social layer, occupation, family and marriage)" (2002: 30). Among sociological theorists there are debates about "modernity", "modernism", "postmodernism", "post-industrialization" and, of course, "globalization" (Kumar 1995). As Kumar (1995: 67) points out there is no consensus of what these terms mean but they all imply disintegration of the major sources of stratification predominant in industrial society.

Similarly, strands of postmodernism are similar to modernization theory in that postmodernists see world-wide processes dismantling older social structures. Postmodernists argue that modernism has run its course and industrial societies are entering a postmodernist phase characterized by "relativism" and a decline in the power of dominant social discourses. Postmodernism has a seemingly contradictory position regarding modernization. On the one hand, it celebrates the withering away of what it sees as capitalist, colonial, patriarchal and racial hegemonies but opposes privileging science and Western ways of knowing.

Critique

From about 1970, modernization theory was critiqued for being evolutionary, unilinear, and Eurocentric for assuming that Western society (or, worse still, US society) represents the pinnacle of human achievement, for being overly optimistic, for assuming that progress is inevitable and desirable, and for not considering the well-documented negative aspects of industrialization, colonialism and imperialism. Modernization does not necessarily mean social progress. These are all reasonable criticisms. Modernization theory was largely discarded from the early 1970s, because of such criticisms but other factors were also at work further undermining its appeal. The economic downturns of the 1970s demonstrated that continuing economic progress was not inevitable and added credibility to existing critiques of capitalism. Similarly, many "developing" countries were clearly not on the pathway of increasing prosperity and democratic rights.

A large proportion were (and still are) ruled by despotic and authoritarian regimes and, apart from the political elite, remain impoverished. In the area of societal development, modernization theory was replaced by dependency and world systems theories, where Western countries were understood as the problem, not the solution. These Marxist-inspired approaches focused on cultural and economic neocolonialism: Western countries exploiting the resources, cheap labor and markets of developing countries, keeping them perpetually undeveloped. Modernization theory did not sit well with the more radical and sometimes activist perspectives in sociology such as neo-Marxism and feminism, which became prominent from the late 1960s and early 1970s. It could easily (but unfairly) be characterized as pro-capitalist, politically conservative, patriarchal and imperialist.[23]

Reproduction theory

The counter to modernization theory, reproduction theory – which also has many diverse strands – assumes that the intergenerational reproduction of socioeconomic and other inequalities is strong and unchanging and attempts to explain these strong and enduring inequalities.

An important difference between modernization and reproduction theory is their respective conceptualizations of the role of education in modern society. In modernization theory, education provides a means whereby those from disadvantaged social origins are able to achieve higher levels of social status, whereas reproduction theory holds a very different view of education. For reproduction theorists, education maintains the status quo, acting in the interests of the privileged.

A variety of social processes has been proposed, explaining what is assumed as strong and unchanging social reproduction. There are both deficit theories that focus on the disadvantages associated with being working class while others focus on the advantages of the middle class or social elites. Bernstein (1971) argues that education discriminates against working-class students, since they do not have the linguistic grammars to cope with the language of the curriculum. Another approach focuses on working-class culture that places less value on education or academic pursuits so their youth leaves school early and obtains (gender appropriate) paid work (Hyman 1966). According to Boudon (1974: 29–31), class differences in aspirations will mean that working-class students will have lower educational and thus occupational attainments than comparable middle-class students. Since they have lower aspirations, working-class students choose lower status educational and career paths than middle-class students, even with the same level of academic achievement. The related rational risk aversion thesis focuses on the different economic costs and benefits for middle- and working-class students continuing with their education (Breen and Goldthorpe 1997). Bourdieu's (1977) cultural capital theory argues that education systems reward students from privileged backgrounds since their cultural understandings are much the same as that which underpins schooling, the curriculum, textbooks and the criteria which teachers and examiners use to assess students. The Maximally Maintained Inequality thesis, which focuses on the transition from one educational level to the next, maintains that class differences in education only decline when the transition for higher-class students has reached saturation (Raftery and Hout 1993). Lucas's (2001) related Effectively Maintained Inequality argues that educational differentiation within schools, where higher-class students are more likely to enroll in the more academic courses, contributes to the maintenance of inequality. Alon's (2009) Effectively Expanding Inequality argues that cognitive tests are the key mechanism by which privileged classes reproduce their positions, since cognitive testing is increasingly used for college admissions.

The meritocracy argument focuses on the increasing importance of cognitive skills for education and the labor market. Correspondingly, some reproduction theorists argue that non-cognitive skills contribute to the intergenerational reproduction of social inequalities. According to Bowles (1972: S225–6), working-class jobs require obedience, predictability and willingness to accept external controls, whereas higher-class jobs require independence and internal discipline. He goes on to argue that parents tend to have similar personality traits and, in children, the same personality traits are developed from a young age and continually reinforced through social processes. Therefore, children acquire the personality characteristics appropriate to their parents' occupations. The socialization to appropriate personality attributes is reinforced by schools. Working- and middle-class students attend different schools and experience different socialization patterns that facilitate the reproduction of the class structure (Bowles and Gintis 1976: 132–3). Their "correspondence principle" contends that the social relationships of education replicate the hierarchical division of labor or the social relations of production (Bowles and Gintis 1976: 131). These complementary relationships serve to reproduce social class differences in personality from one generation to the next. Farkas (2003: 556) contends that non-cognitive skills, for example conscientiousness and good work habits, in conjunction with cognitive skills, contribute to school success, schooling and occupational attainment. He notes that arguments about the importance of non-cognitive attributes for social reproduction can be linked to cultural capital arguments in that (non-cognitive) skills, habits and styles are important for socioeconomic success rather than cognitive ability (2003: 545).

Debates, contentions and hypotheses

Modernization has been and is a central issue in sociology, and is the source of a large number of theses, hypotheses, propositions and contentions.

Modernization theory implies that cognitive ability is becoming increasingly important in contemporary industrialized societies: the meritocracy thesis. Levy (1966: 218) argues that modern societies increasingly require "experts" and cognitive ability is involved in the selection of these experts. Because of the demands by employers and universities for easily comparable, transparent and reliable information on student performance, assessment has become increasingly based on generic skills about comprehending, manipulating and making logical inferences from text and mathematical expressions. Such skills are very similar to the operational definitions of intelligence. With the dismantling of social barriers, success in the education system and society more generally comes to depend more and more on meritocratic criteria, which is generally understood as ability plus effort.[24] Bell (1973: 44) argued that the meritocracy principle is central to the allocation of position in the (post-industrial) knowledge society. In the UK, the meritocracy debate began with Saunders's (1995) provocatively titled paper "Might Britain be a Meritocracy?". He showed that the observed patterns of intergenerational occupational mobility were not incompatible with a meritocratic model, given that ability is to some extent inherited and is important to educational and labor market outcomes. Rindermann (2008: 137) concluded that cognitive ability is involved in the causal nexus of cultural, political and economic "modernization". Subsequently, Rindermann and Thompson (2011) argued that the cognitive ability of a nation's intellectual class is associated with accomplishments in science, technology, engineering and mathematics, and predicts the quality of the nation's economic and political institutions which in turn influences the generation of wealth.

A central contention of modernization theory is that modern societies are becoming more open. In other words, socioeconomic or social class origins are less important as social selection is based on more rational criteria. Cross-national studies on mobility were motivated by the American exceptionalism thesis, that more modern societies – with the US as the archetypical modern society – show higher levels of social mobility (Lipset and Zetterberg 1959). After the American exceptionalism thesis could not be supported empirically, the Lipset–Zetterberg thesis became prominent, contending that the patterning of social mobility is much the same in industrialized countries that have reached a certain level of industrialization, although the extent of mobility in different countries is likely to be related to the rates of industrialization and urbanization (Lipset and Zetterberg 1959: 13, 49). Part of the theoretical background to Erikson and Goldthorpe's (1992: 3–9) *The Constant Flux* is the "liberal thesis of industrialism" – which makes much the same arguments as modernization theories.

In the context of occupational attainment, modernization theory holds that, as societies develop, they become more open, socioeconomic achievements become less tied to social background and other ascribed characteristics, and education becomes more crucial to subsequent socioeconomic outcomes (Blau and Duncan 1967; DiPrete and Grusky 1990). Put simply, social background becomes less important and social attainment becomes more based on universalistic criteria (Goldthorpe 1997).

Blau and Duncan view the increasing importance of achieved characteristics (which they call heightened universalism) as having important implications for modern societies:

> Heightened universalism has profound implications for the stratification system. The achieved status of a man, what he has accomplished in terms of some objective criteria, becomes more important than his ascribed status, who he is in the sense of what family he comes from. This does not mean that family background no longer influences careers. What it does imply is that superior status cannot any more be directly inherited but must be legitimized by actual achievements that are socially acknowledged. Education assumes increasing significance for social status in general and for the transmission of fathers to sons in particular.
>
> (Blau and Duncan 1967: 430)

Treiman formally derived several propositions on the intergenerational reproduction of socioeconomic inequalities:

> 1) The more industrialized a society, the smaller the influence of parental status on educational attainment.
> 2) The more industrialized a society, the smaller the direct influence of father's occupational status on son's occupational status.
> 3) The more industrialized a society, the greater the direct influence of educational attainment on occupational status.
> 4) The more industrialized a society, the smaller the direct influence of education on income.
>
> (Treiman 1970)

The final proposition is surprising. Treiman argued that the impact of education on earnings (rather than income) should decline, because the expansion of education should lower the market value of educated workers. However, in the context of modernization theory, higher educational qualifications should mean greater skills and hence productivity, so employers will reward higher levels of education. The relationship should become stronger over time.

Ganzeboom and Treiman (2007) add the "political intervention" thesis, which hypothesizes that the importance of achievement vis-à-vis ascription will change according to the political context. The most prominent political context, during the twentieth century at least, is communism or state socialism, in which there was an explicit ideology regarding removing the influence of ascriptive criteria on occupational outcomes. In addition, left-leaning governments in almost all Western nations have implemented policies aimed at reducing the effects of socioeconomic background and other ascriptive criteria on educational and occupational outcomes.

The following hypotheses summarize the major claims of modernization theory for socioeconomic stratification:

- Cognitive ability is a strong predictor of educational and subsequent labor market outcomes.
- The effects of cognitive ability are increasing over time for educational and labor market outcomes.
- The effects of cognitive ability are stronger in economically more developed countries.
- Socioeconomic background has a relatively weak influence on educational and labor market outcomes.
- For educational and labor market outcomes, the effects of socioeconomic background are declining.
- For occupational and economic outcomes, the effect on educational attainment is larger than that for socioeconomic background.
- For occupational and economic outcomes, the impact of educational attainment is increasing.
- For education, occupational status, and earnings, the contribution of the environment is smaller than that for genetics (which includes inherited cognitive ability and non-cognitive attributes).
- For education, occupational status, and earnings, the contribution of the environment is declining and the genetic component is increasing.
- Many of these changes can be attributed to modernization.

It is important to distinguish between the overall association of socioeconomic background with educational and socioeconomic outcomes, and the effects of socioeconomic background. The bivariate correlation may remain constant over time, but the sociological processes that produce the correlation may have changed substantially. For example, the correlation between socioeconomic background and student achievement could be entirely due to the economic and cultural resources of the family. However, it may also be due, at least in part, to the effect of cognitive ability on student achievement, the correlation between parents' and their children's cognitive ability, and the correlation between parents' cognitive ability and the family's socioeconomic status. The causal pathways linking socioeconomic background and later educational and socioeconomic outcomes are more complex because they involve the inter-correlations and relationships between a larger number of variables: parents' and child's cognitive abilities, student achievement and, for occupational and economic outcomes, education. Substantial changes in these intercorrelations and relationships could occur without reducing the overall correlation between socioeconomic background and the socioeconomic outcome (occupation or earnings). For example, the intergenerational correlation for earnings (between parents' and their adult children's earnings) could even increase with several changes consistent with modernization theory: a stronger association between parents' and their children's cognitive abilities, an increased importance of cognitive ability for educational attainment, and an increase in the impact of education on earnings.

Notes

1 A version of the first half of this chapter was submitted to two highly ranked theoretical journals. After about 6 weeks, the editor of *Sociological Theory* said he "declined" to send it out for review. After 7 months with *Theory and Society* it was rejected:

> The theoretical discussion and indeed the meta-theoretical discussion you develop are well done. However our articles need to combine the theory with an empirical case for which the research has been carried out or extended examples and data, that apply or illustrate the theory or are used to construct the theory. As the journal's title suggests, its articles need to weave connections between theory and society.

Referee reports were apparently sought and received but not forwarded.

2 Rather than falsification, it is more accurate to portray Popper as focusing on a constant dynamic between "criticism" and reformulation of solutions or theory (Popper 1976a: 89–90). Falsification is, of course, an important component of criticism. It is interesting to note that Popper strongly objected to being labeled as a positivist by the critical theorists and found the title of the book, *The Positivist Dispute in German Sociology*, quite objectionable (Popper 1976b).

3 Lenski (1988: 165) observes that "the teaching of sociological theory has more in common with seminary instruction in theology and biblical studies".

4 Aron (1967: 150) makes this point in relation to Marx: "there remain a number of obscurities or ambiguities which account for the many interpretations his thought has provoked". A similar criticism is made of Parsons (see Lenski 1988: 165). Lamont and Lareau (1988: 55) make a similar point in relation to Bourdieu, noting the diversity of meanings and "radically different roles" of the concept of cultural capital by Bourdieu himself. Kingston (2001: 89) makes the point more strongly "Bourdieu's explanations are often vague, even contradictory. Because his conceptual arguments are weakly linked to specific, concrete referents, researchers have an uncertain guide about how to proceed with empirical tests".

5 In fact, this common caricature is not correct; Parsons saw sociology as a vehicle for social reform. See Lipset (1994) for an interesting essay on the politics and personalities of post-war US sociologists.

6 Proletarianization is the process where employers, the self-employed and independent farmers become wage laborers; emiseration is the steady decline of the living conditions of the proletariat; and polarization is increasing inequality between the increasing mass of workers and the declining numbers of capitalists.

7 Nielsen (2004) parallels the response of Marxist theorists to the collapse of communism to that of a religious sect after their predictions of cataclysm were not realized. The events were quickly reinterpreted and new predictions made.

8 A good example of the importance of political events and perceived political position on the popularity of sociological theorists is Giddens who, during the 1990s, belonged to the pantheon of contemporary sociological theorists. His subsequent close relationship with UK Prime Minister Blair and thus the Iraq war put an end to his widespread acclaim.
9 Berger (2002) refers to a "class, race, and gender" mantra prevalent in some strands of sociology.
10 Postmodernists are strangely silent about truly oppressive regimes, especially if they are anti-capitalist or anti-American. The oppressiveness of such regimes is glibly attributed to a history of colonialism, present-day economic imperialism and various nefarious activities by the US and other Western countries.
11 Fukuyama (2006) saw postmodernism and critiques of modernity as potentially destructive to liberal democracies.
12 Mead (2005/06) argues that it is the Anglo-Saxon democracies with their rule of law, good governance and free trade that created the wealth for Britain and the US to lead the world militarily and politically, "the peerless capacity of capitalism, law, and consent to generate wealth and power" (2005/06: 7). Furthermore, they have "an unusually long history of governing in accord with individual rights".
13 Cole (1994b), Goldthorpe (2000: 9–10) and Huber (1995) also note that sociology lacks core knowledge.
14 Grounded theory is generating theory from data, inductive as opposed to deductive reasoning. There is nothing wrong with this in principle, but after more than 40 years since the publication of Glaser and Strauss's 1967 book, it is expected that grounded theory would have served its preparatory purpose.
15 This is reflected by the small to moderate correlations between social group membership and many outcomes.
16 Goldthorpe (1990, 2000) is a notable exception, but also Marsh (1982), who exposes the sophistry of the critiques of surveys and quantitative analysis. It was very unfortunate for British sociology that she died at a young age.
17 From *A Scandal in Bohemia*. "It is a capital mistake to theorize before one has data. Insensibly one begins to twist facts to suit theories, instead of theories to suit facts".
18 There is no shortage of despairing commentaries on the state of sociology, not all from a "scientific" perspective (e.g. Cole 1994a; Lenski 1988; Berger 2002; Goldthorpe 2000; Lipset 1994).
19 For an insight into ignorant reviewers at a high level, see Stolzenberg (2008), who provides several examples of what he described as "methodological shamanism".
20 Lipset (1994) and Goldthorpe (2000: 9) also make this point.
21 In econometrics, this is known as "unobserved heterogeneity": the existence of unobserved variables which are correlated with the observed variables, meaning that the estimates for the observed variables are biased (usually upwards).
22 The introduction of examinations for the British civil service in the 1870s was in Young's (1994) book, the beginning of the meritocracy.
23 Berger (1992: 14) notes that modernization theory was understood as a vehicle of Western imperialism.
24 Young's cautionary tale of a future meritocracy begins with the proposition that ability + effort = merit (Young 1994: xiii).

Chapter 3

Concepts, measures and statistics

This chapter looks at the conceptualization and measurement of the major concepts discussed throughout this book: social class, occupational status, education, socioeconomic background, cognitive ability and ability-type measures, and non-cognitive attributes. The last section provides a basic understanding of the statistics cited throughout this book.

Concepts and measures

Occupation

"Occupation" is unarguably a major aspect of the stratification system of modern (and past) societies and is among the strongest aspects of social identity. The answer to the question "What kind of work do you do?" provides the best single clue to a person's standing in society (Treiman 1977: 1). A person's occupational role is their most important social role outside their immediate family; occupations indicate the technical and social skills that people bring to the labor market and thus their likely present and future economic situation (Hauser and Warren 1997: 184). Across societies and over time, occupation is associated with social standing, political influence and income (Featherman and Hauser 1978: 19).

Occupation-based measures have several advantages over other measures of socioeconomic standing. Asking respondents about their present or past occupation generates far less missing data than family income or personal earnings. Information about occupations is less problematic in terms of refusal, recall, reliability, and stability that plague the measurement of income or wealth (Hauser and Warren 1997: 179). Furthermore, the reliability of occupational data is high; respondents can reliably report their own occupations several months apart or several decades earlier and that of their parents (see Hauser and Warren 1997: 184–8; Looker 1989; West *et al.* 2001).[1] Among adolescents, parental occupation is more accurately measured than parental education (Lien *et al.* 2001).

There are two general types of stratification concepts based on occupation:

categorical measures of occupational class or occupational group, and continuous measures of occupational attainment.

Social class

Occupation is the basis of most, if not all, theoretical approaches to social class in sociology. Traditional Marxist theories defined classes by their relationship to the means of the production. The bourgeoisie own and control the means of production while the proletariat are non-owners who are paid less than their value to production. The third class is the petty bourgeoisie comprising shopkeepers, farmers and other self-employed workers who may employ a small number of employees. They differ from the bourgeoisie since they work alongside their employees and do not generate enough profit for capital expansion. Weberian approaches define classes in terms of market and work situations. Market situation refers to the possession of skills which are able to be sold on the marketplace for a given economic return (Giddens 1980: 78). Work situation is defined by Lockwood (1958: 15) as the set of social relationships workers experience by virtue of their position in the division of labor. This fundamental role played by the labor market in both approaches leads to occupation becoming the primary indicator of social class, since individuals in the same or similar occupations tend to be in similar market and work situations or have similar relationships to the means of production.

During the 1970s and 1980s, Neo-Marxist and Weberian writers proposed a variety of theoretical approaches to the class structure in contemporary Western societies (Giddens and MacKenzie 1982; Wright 1980). These approaches stem from the increasing proportions of middle-stratum employees such as managers, administrators, professionals and clerical workers, who cannot be unambiguously assigned to the classes of the classical class schemas: the proletariat, the bourgeoisie and petty bourgeoisie. Empirically, both the middle and working classes are too heterogeneous economically, politically and socially to be considered as social class. Within the Marxist perspective, the middle stratum presents problems as to the relevance of Marxist notions such as the exploitation of surplus labor and ownership and control of the means of production. To a Weberian theorist, the issue is whether particular occupational groups differ in their market and work situations to such a degree as to justify their allocation to different classes. The criteria by which social classes are distinguished – ownership and self-employment, qualifications and credentials, authority, managerial role, number of subordinates, size of enterprise, private or public sector, etc. – was a particularly vexed issue (the so-called boundary problem) in stratification research during the 1970s (Parkin 1979: 11–28, 119–23). As Kingston (2000: 37–59) points out, to be of any analytical importance, classes should be theoretically and empirically meaningful homogeneous groups. There are always plausible arguments that particular occupational groups are so distinct economically, socially or politically that they constitute a separate social class. However, there is little consensus on how best to conceptualize and thus measure social class.

Giddens (1980) coined the concepts "class structuration" and "social closure" to argue that modern capitalist societies consist of three classes: an upper class, a middle class and a working class. He focuses on the three major forms of market capacities extant in modern society (the ownership of property, possession of education qualifications and possession of labor power) which are more or less translated into these three classes (1980: 105–7).

Another approach focuses on the political and ideological orientations of occupational groups. The main focus is on intellectuals or, more broadly, relatively high-income professionals working in non-market organizations. As long ago as 1972, Kristol (1972) suggested that the "new class" comprised college-educated engineers, scientists, teachers, social scientists, psychologists, etc. Gouldner's (1979) "New Class" comprised radical left-wing intellectuals challenging many aspects of modern societies. More recently, sociocultural specialists are distinguished as a separate social class because of their distinct political leanings (Güveli *et al.* 2007; Jansen 2011; Oesch 2008). As Pakulski and Waters (1996: 59) observe, such new classes turn class analysis on its head, with classes defined by their political and ideological orientations rather than their economic situation.

The first international study of occupational mobility by Lipset and Zetterberg (1959) used the simple manual and non-manual dichotomous measure of social class (the study excluded agricultural workers). For studies of occupational mobility in the US, Featherman and Hauser (1978: 89) used a five-class schema comprising upper non-manual (professionals and managers), lower non-manual (proprietors, clerical and sales workers), upper manual (trades, foremen), lower manual (service workers, operatives and laborers) and farm (farmers, managers and workers). The Erikson *et al.* (1979) or EGP class schema has become the standard measure of social class for mobility research and is commonly used in education. The disaggregated measure comprises 11 social classes, collapsible to seven-, five- and three-class schemas (Erikson and Goldthorpe 1992: 35–8; Erikson *et al.* 1979). Its popularity is mainly due to its use in the Comparative Analysis of Social Mobility in Industrial Nations (CASMIN) project – an international project comparing mobility patterns in several countries. One typical aggregation comprises six classes: an upper and lower service class (classes I and II), other non-manual employees (IIIa and b), technical and supervisory manual workers (V), small employers and the self-employed (IV), skilled and unskilled manual workers (VI and VIIa) and manual agricultural workers (VIIb). The commonly used five-class measure may combine semi-skilled and unskilled agricultural workers with other semi-skilled and unskilled manual workers

(VI, VIIa and VIIb). The most privileged group is the service class (Goldthorpe 1982), which comprises higher-level professional, administrative and managerial employees as well as owners of large corporations. Members of this class enjoy superior market and work situations to other workers.

Occupational status

The idea behind occupational status is that occupations form a status hierarchy. The concept of occupational status originated from community studies of social prestige conducted in American towns from the 1920s. Social prestige governed the social interaction between families. Families tended to socialize with other families of similar social prestige. Prestige scores index commonly held understandings of the relative rankings of occupations. They are an indication of the "desirability" of occupations. According to Ganzeboom and Treiman (1996: 203), prestige measures "reflect the classical sociological hypothesis that occupational status constitutes the single most important dimension in social interaction". Occupational prestige is measured by assigning scores to occupational groups obtained from surveys on the prestige associated with each occupation (see Bergman and Joye 2005: 18–23; Mueller and Parcel 1981).

There are high levels of consistency in the ratings given to occupations by different groups within a given society, and cross-nationally (Hodge *et al.* 1966; Kraus *et al.* 1978). Measures of occupational prestige show very high correlations (0.99) over time (Gilbert and Kahl 1992: 41; Hodge *et al.* 1966). There are examples of occupations with cross-national variations in social standing, but these cases are rare and the cross-national variation is small compared to differences within countries in the social standing of occupations (Treiman 1970). In the US and Australia, the correlations between different measures of occupational prestige scales are high (over 0.90) (Featherman *et al.* 1975: 342–3). Davis (1994: 180) claims that the robustness of occupational prestige is the only important discovery of empirical sociology.

The problem with prestige measures, based on survey respondents' evaluations of the prestige of occupations, is that it is not possible to assign a prestige score to all occupations. Although most occupations can be assigned a prestige score – Jones and McMillan (2001: 541) provide an example where three in four occupations can be assigned prestige scores – not all occupations are covered. Research in the area took a major step forward when Duncan (1961) developed a procedure to assign prestige scores to all occupations by regressing the proportion of high-income earners and the proportion with a high-school diploma in each occupational group on their prestige score. The resultant regression weights, together with the education and income levels of each census occupation category, were used to assign status scores to all occupational groups. Therefore, measures of occupational status can be calculated from census and other administrative data. Socio-economic indices of occupation have also been constructed for Australia (Jones 1989; Jones and McMillan 2001; McMillan *et al.* 2009), Britain (Goldthorpe and Hope 1972), Canada (Blishen and McRoberts 1976; Boyd 2008) and New Zealand (Davis *et al.* 1999). Since measures of occupational status are based on the classification of occupations, they need to be changed with each substantial revision to the coding scheme employed by the respective national statistical agency. Education and income are the dominant characteristics, with education being slightly more powerful than income (Ganzeboom and Treiman 1996).[2] The International Socioeconomic Index (ISEI) is the most well-known cross-national measure (Ganzeboom and Treiman 1996; Ganzeboom *et al.* 1992). The index is based on estimating the scores for occupational categories, which maximizes the impact of the continuous measure of occupation on earnings (ISEI), net of education.

The socioeconomic indices of occupational status (derived from the education and incomes of the incumbents of occupational groups) are only imperfectly correlated with prestige measures (measured by respondents' evaluations of the status of occupations).[3] In addition, because they show stronger relationships in analyzing intergenerational relationships, they are preferred to prestige measures (Featherman and Hauser 1976; Featherman *et al.* 1975; Hauser and Warren 1997: 190; Kelley 1990; Treas and Tyree 1979).

Education

Educational attainment is usually measured in one of three ways. The first is to measure the number of years of formal education. Therefore, high-school graduates in the US are assigned a score of 12, since they have spent 12 years at school, and college graduates have a score of 16 (12 years of school plus four years of college). At the other end of the scale, no school education is assigned a score of zero and completion of primary or elementary school only is assigned a score of six. Although crude, this linear measure is very convenient to analyze and is appropriate for studies of single-path education systems in which individuals' educational attainment is simply how far they progressed in the system. The "years of education" measure may be inappropriate for multiple branching educational systems, which branch at various points into academic, vocational, or generalist tracks. An alternative measure is an ordinal measure of the highest qualification obtained. For example, for the UK, measures of educational attainment often comprise: no qualification, "O" (Ordinary) levels (GSCE or General Certificate of Secondary Education), "A" (Advanced) levels, bachelor degrees and postgraduate degrees. Such measures avoid problems with the years of education measure in tracked school systems, though a difficulty with ordinal measures of educational attainment is where to place school and post-school vocational qualifications. A third approach is to conceptualize education as a categorical variable and to analyze it as one would analyze any nominal variable, which is more complex statistically and more difficult to report than analyses of years of education or an ordinal measure of qualifications.

Socioeconomic background

Although there is a general, shared, understanding that occupational socio-economic background relates to privilege and disadvantage in the family of origin, there is little agreement on the conceptualization of socioeconomic background and thus its measurement. A high socioeconomic background may mean coming from a wealthy family, or from a family where one or both parents have high-prestige occupations (such as medical specialists or lawyers), or a family in which one or both parents are highly educated. A quite distinct approach focuses on more recognizable forms of disadvantage, such as parental receipt of social security benefits or free school lunches, but this approach is not appropriate for over-time or cross-national comparisons.

Single indicators

In research on educational outcomes, father's occupation (either class or status), and father's or mother's education are the most commonly used single-indicator measures of socioeconomic background. Household income and wealth are less commonly used indicators mainly due to the lack of appropriate data. Mother's occupation is rarely used as a single indicator, because of the lower levels of women's participation in the labor market. Other aspects of the home environment used as indictors of socioeconomic background include educational resources, books in the home, parents' participation in "high" cultural activities, and social networks.

For studies of school students, measures of occupational class are sometimes based on simply assigning their parents' occupation (usually their fathers') to one of several occupational class groupings. Criterion-scaled measures of occupational status assign scores to occupational titles so that the final scores maximize the bivariate correlation of occupation with the criterion variable, usually student achievement or educational attainment (Comber and Keeves 1973: 258; Marks 2011).

Parental education is arguably of greater relevance to educational outcomes than parental occupation. High-income parents who are not highly educated may not emphasize their children's education as much as do highly educated parents. On the other hand, highly educated parents without other resources (such as a business, farm, or large amounts of capital) are more likely to view education as the key to their children's futures. The practical advantage of parental education as an indicator of socioeconomic background is that every parent has an education, whereas not everyone has an occupation (Looker 1989). In addition, a parent's educational level is generally stable over the lifetime whereas occupation, income and wealth are not. On the other hand, school students, and respondents in general, are less likely to provide accurate information about their father's or mother's education than about their occupations.

In the cross-national context, the conceptualization and measurement of parental education is more problematic than for occupation. Educational arrangements differ markedly between countries. While the relative standing of doctors, teachers, unskilled workers, and other occupational groups are much the same across the developed world, it is more difficult to maintain that educational levels (so many years of education, school completion and particular qualifications) are equivalent across countries. Vocational qualifications are particularly difficult to compare cross-nationally. Because of problems in constructing comparative measures of education, the education schemas designed for cross-national work, such as UNESCO's International Standard Classification of Education (ISCED), and CASMIN developed by occupational mobility researchers, comprise quite broad categories (Brauns and Steinmann 1997; Müller *et al.* 1989; OECD 1999).

Multiple and composite measures

Several indicators of socioeconomic background in the same analysis (e.g. a regression analysis) constitute a multiple measure of socioeconomic background, whereas composite measures are single variable measures constructed by combining several indicators of socioeconomic background (Buchmann 2002). Analyses using either composite or multiple measures explain more of the variation in the outcome variable than do comparable analyses with a single measure. This implies that single-indicator measures do not capture all aspects of socioeconomic background.

The intercorrelations among indicators of socioeconomic background are not particularly strong. Of the socioeconomic background variables, mother's and father's education are the most highly correlated (at around 0.5), indicating substantial educational homogamy. Across industrialized countries, father's and mother's education and occupational status, books in the home, and cultural aspects have only moderate intercorrelations at around 0.4, often lower (see Marks 2011: 227). Mueller and Parcel (1981: 16) dismiss using parental education as a proxy for occupational status since the correlation is only around 0.5 to 0.6, and there is considerable heterogeneity in income and occupation within educational categories. Intercorrelations involving family income and wealth are also not strong: 0.31 for wealth and income, around 0.38 for both education and occupational status with income, and 0.18 for both wealth and education, and wealth and occupational status (Bowles 1972: S225). Since the indicators of socioeconomic background are only moderately intercorrelated, composite measures do not constitute a highly reliable scalar measure. Furthermore, the weak or only moderate intercorrelations undermine the commonly held assumption that socioeconomic background is a one-dimensional concept measured interchangeably by a range of educational, occupational and economic indicators.

Multiple indicator approaches make comparisons difficult for cross-national analysis and analysis over time, since their effects are to some extent dependent on the intercorrelations of the indicators and these intercorrelations are likely to differ between samples. The more indicators included, the less clear cut is the comparison. One solution is to construct a sheaf coefficient, which a summarizes the effects of multiple indicators for a given outcome (Heise 1972; Whitt 1986).

Cognitive ability

Cognitive ability or intelligence is defined as "a very general mental capability that, among other things, involves ability to reason, plan, solve problems, think abstractly, comprehend complex ideas, learn quickly and learn from experience" (Gottfredson 1997a: 13). Similarly, Neisser *et al.* (1996: 77) define intelligence as the "ability to understand complex ideas, to adapt effectively to the environment, to learn from experience, to engage in various forms of reasoning, to overcome obstacles by taking thought". The terms "general ability", "general cognitive ability", "general mental ability", and "ability" are synonyms for the psychological concept "intelligence" (Adey *et al.* 2007: 76).

The measurement of cognitive ability began over 100 years ago as a way of identifying children who were likely to be academically successful. Intelligence is measured by specifically designed tests, such as Stanford-Binet, the Wechsler Adult Intelligence Scale (WAIS) or the non-verbal Raven's progressive matrices. The tests usually comprise multiple choice items testing verbal and mathematical reasoning, pattern recognition, spatial and other abilities. Different IQ measures are usually highly intercorrelated, suggesting they are measuring the same underlying concept. The median correlation of IQ tests with other IQ tests range from 0.64 to 0.81, averaging about 0.77 (Jensen 1980: 314–15; Jensen 1998: 91).

Studies with ability-type measures

Besides conventional IQ tests, there is a variety of ability-type measures found in studies or data collections where the primary focus is not the measurement of intelligence. These include national and international studies of student achievement and adult literacy, national and regional birth cohort studies, longitudinal surveys of young persons, cross-sectional surveys and household panel studies. The ability-type measures are denoted by a variety of concepts, such as "army qualification tests", "academic aptitude", "student achievement", "adult literacy", "scholastic achievement", "quantitative reasoning" or, more simply, "test scores".

General tests of literacy, numeracy and problem solving, and tests of cognitive ability are conceptually similar. Rindermann (2008: 128) maintains that there is no important theoretical difference between student achievement and ability tests, since they both assess "thinking and knowledge". In the OECD's Programme for International Student Assessment (PISA), literacy is defined generally as "concerned with the capacity of students to apply knowledge and skills in key subject areas and to analyze, reason and communicate effectively as they pose, solve and interpret problems in a variety of situations" (OECD 2007b: 16). "Adult literacy" closely relates to general cognitive ability since "both assess skills that appear to represent verbal comprehension and reasoning, or the ability to understand, analyze, interpret, and evaluate written information and apply fundamental principles and concepts" (Baldwin cited by Gottfredson 1997b: 109). These definitions closely resemble operative definitions of intelligence. Baumert *et al.* (2009) point out that like intelligence tests, reading and mathematical assessments involve reasoning and making logical inferences. Jencks *et al.* (1972, 1979) have no hesitation in focusing on test scores in chapters entitled "Inequality in Cognitive Skills" and "The Effects of Academic Ability". Scores in a US adult literacy test are referred to as "cognitive skill" by Kerckhoff *et al.* (2001). According to the OECD, the 2012 adult literacy study collects an unprecedented amount of information on "basic cognitive skills" (Thorn 2009: 19).

Studies of student achievement

Large-scale national or international studies of student achievement monitor performance over time and cross-nationally. One example of a national study is the National Assessment of Educational Progress (NAEP) in the US, which is able to monitor changes in test scores over time (NCES 2008). There are similar national and regional studies in other countries.

Since the early 1960s, cross-national studies of student achievement have been used to compare student performance across educational systems. The aim of these studies is to draw conclusions on the influence of policy and institutional arrangements for both performance and social inequality. Data are collected on student performance in mathematics (numeracy), reading (literacy), science, and, in some instances, problem solving.

The International Association for the Evaluation of Educational Achievement (IEA) has a long history of international studies in student achievement. The very first international study of student achievement, conducted between 1959 and 1961, was a feasibility study for the first group of IEA studies, with 12 countries participating (Thorndike 1962, 1973).[5] This study was followed by the first reading literacy study and the first and second international mathematics and science studies, conducted during the 1970s and 1980s. The mathematics and science studies were combined to form TIMSS and the reading literacy studies evolved into PIRLS.

The OECD's (2001, 2004, 2007b) PISA program has a three-year cycle and uses age-based (15-year-olds) samples rather than the grade-based samples in the more recent IEA studies. PISA tests students in reading literacy, mathematical literacy, scientific literacy, and, in some years, a fourth domain: problem solving. Each year of testing has a major domain and two (or three) minor domains. All students are tested in the major domain. In 2000, the major domain was reading, in 2003 it was mathematics, in 2006 science and in 2009 reading again. The sample sizes for each country are at least 4,500 students and an increasing number of partner and non-OECD countries participate in PISA.

Since the early 1990s, students' scores in each cross-national study are scaled to a (pooled country) mean of 500 score points and a standard deviation of 100 score points. For PISA, the mean and standard deviation are based on OECD countries only. The tests are based on item response theory, which assumes that the probability of a student correctly answering a test item is a function of student ability and item difficultly. This allows very flexible test designs, since test items are considered as a sample from the population of test items, each with difficulties that can be estimated.

Adult literacy studies

Since the early 1990s, the OECD and Statistics Canada have run cross-national studies in adult literacy: the 1994–1998 International Adult Literacy Survey (IALS), the 2002–2006 Adult Literacy and Life Skills Survey (ALLS) and the current OECD Programme for the International Assessment of Adult Competencies. The purpose of adult literacy studies is to assess the "skills of their adult populations in order to monitor how well prepared they are for the challenges of the knowledge based society" (Thorn 2009: 4). The domains covered by adult literacy tests include numeracy, problem solving, practical cognition, prose literacy, and document literacy. They consist of test items not too dissimilar to student achievement tests.

Birth cohort studies

Since a major focus of birth cohort studies is on cognitive development, they typically include several measures of ability (sometimes conventional IQ tests). The ability debate in sociology in the UK focused largely on data from the 1958 National Child Development Study (NCDS), which is one of several British birth cohort studies that included ability measures going back to a Scottish birth cohort study in 1921 and forward to the 1970 British Cohort (BCS) and Millennium Birth Cohort Studies. Similarly, there are regional birth cohort studies in New Zealand: the Dunedin and Christchurch birth cohort studies.

Longitudinal studies of youth

Longitudinal studies of young people often incorporate ability-type measures. A prominent example is the 1979 National Longitudinal Survey of Youth (NLSY) in the US – the data source for *The Bell Curve* – which included the Armed Forces Qualification Test (AFQT). The 1979 NLSY is one of a number of longitudinal surveys of youths and adults, beginning in the 1960s and continuing with a second NLSY cohort initially surveyed in 1997. A satellite study surveys the children of 1979 NLSY mothers. A similar study was conducted of children of the NCDS respondents in the UK. In addition, there is a series of US education-focused longitudinal studies, such as the 1972 study of high school seniors (NLS72), High School and Beyond (HS&B) and the 1988 National Education Longitudinal Study (NELS). The Wisconsin Longitudinal Study (WLS) of high school seniors, which commenced in 1957, generated an extensive sociological literature. There are also longitudinal surveys of the school-to-work transition conducted in other countries, which include test scores in literacy and numeracy, taken in middle secondary school, for example, the multi-cohort Longitudinal Surveys of Australian Youth (LSAY) study. Australia, Canada, Denmark, Switzerland and several other countries conduct longitudinal studies based on the initial PISA samples of 15-year-olds (OECD 2010b: 120).

Cross-sectional and household panel studies

Several repeated cross-sectional and household panel surveys include shorter and thus weaker measures of ability. The US General Social Survey (GSS) and the Panel Survey of Income Dynamics (PSID) included vocabulary and sentence completion tests. In one year, the German Socio-Economic Panel (GSOEP) included symbol correspondence and word fluency tests administered to a sample of parents and their children.

Correlations of ability-type measures with cognitive ability

Test scores are closely associated with general intelligence. The correlations are about the same magnitude as the intercorrelations among IQ tests. According to Gottfredson (1997b: 109), literacy as measured in the 1992 US National Literacy Study correlates about 0.8 with the "academic *g*" factor. In a more recent review article, she (2008: 554) concludes that cognitive ability correlates also at around 0.8 with performance in standardized academic achievement tests. Herrnstein and Murray (1994: 584) show sizable correlations of over 0.7 and up to 0.9 between the AFQT measure and standard ability tests with a median correlation of 0.8. The correlations between measures of *g* derived from the Armed Services Vocational Aptitude Battery by factor analyses and the Scholastic Aptitude Test (SAT) and the American College Testing (ACT) are around 0.8, leading the authors to conclude that these tests for college admission are mainly a test of *g* (Frey and Detterman 2004; Koenig *et al.* 2008).

Performance in cross-national achievement tests is also strongly correlated with ability. In the PISA study, the high intercorrelations of student performance across the domains of reading, mathematics and science are strongly suggestive of a single underlying ability dimension.[6] At the country level, there are strong correlations between performance in cross-national achievement tests (TIMSS and PISA) and general ability (Lynn *et al.* 2007; Lynn and Mikk 2009; Rindermann 2007). Rindermann (2006, 2007: 687) concludes there is a strong *g* factor of cognitive abilities for international student assessments, such as PIRLS, TIMSS and PISA. There is evidence at the individual student level from the 2000 German PISA study in which students undertaking PISA also sat German cognitive abilities tests. The correlations between general cognitive ability and test scores, corrected for measurement error, are around 0.8.[7] Analyzing these data, Brunner (2008) estimate correlations of around 0.8 for fluid intelligence with verbal and mathematical ability. Baumert *et al.* (2009) demonstrate that student achievement (in TIMSS or PISA) is not identical to general cognitive ability because large-scale student assessments measure, to varying extents, knowledge acquisition.

Hauser and Huang (1997) report a correlation of 0.8 between the GSS vocabulary tests and general intelligence and a correlation of 0.7 between the short sentence completion test they used in their study and a general ability test for the army. Weakliem *et al.* (1995) cite several sources arguing that the simple vocabulary test they use is highly correlated with standard measures of intelligence. The sentence completion test used in the PSID was developed from the Lorge-Thorndike intelligence test and shows reasonable correlations (around 0.5) with several components of intelligence tests (Veroff *et al.* 1971: 35).

Non-cognitive attributes

The conceptualization and measurement of non-cognitive attributes is much less developed than that for cognitive ability. Non-cognitive attributes encompass a very broad variety of attributes such as locus of control (the extent that individuals feel they are in control of their lives), self-esteem, the "big five" personality traits (openness, conscientiousness, extraversion, agreeableness, and neuroticism), industriousness, perseverance, leadership, self-confidence, emotional stability, persistence, willingness to assume responsibility and ability to take initiative (Anger 2012; Farkas 2003: 544;

Grönqvistb *et al.* 2010). In longitudinal studies, non-cognitive attributes (like cognitive ability) are typically measured during late childhood or adolescence. Jencks *et al.*'s (1979: 122) non-cognitive traits included personality self-assessments of sociability, social sensitivity, impulsiveness, vigor, calmness, tidiness, culture, leadership, self-confidence, mature personality, and several indirect measures of personality. "Locus of control" is often included in analyses of education and labor market outcomes. Jencks *et al.* (1979: 132–45) further broadened non-cognitive attributes with behaviors during high school, including group activities, dating, hobbies, sport, student employment, intellectual and science fiction reading, attendance at cultural events, and attitude to the importance of insurance. These were understood as indirect measures of personality. Covay and Carbonaro's (2010) measure of non-cognitive skills incorporated students' attentiveness, organization, flexibility, task persistence, learning independence, and eagerness to learn.

There is a tendency in the literature to treat non-cognitive attributes as desirable and sometimes to advocate their development through schooling. However, it should be noted that labor market success may also involve undesirable non-cognitive attributes such as aggression, egocentrism and ruthlessness. This was the point of Olneck and Bills's (1980) reference to the novel *What Makes Sammy Run?* in which the central character is particularly Machiavellian.

Statistics

The statistical analyses used in the studies cited in this book range from very simple percentages and correlations to quite sophisticated structural equation and fixed-effect modeling. This is not the place to explain these methods and all can be found in textbooks and on the internet. The following outline should be useful to non-expert readers in understanding the statistics referred to throughout this book.

- The correlation coefficient provides a convenient summary of the strength of the relationship between two variables. A correlation of zero means there is no relationship and correlations close to one (or minus one) indicate an almost perfect linear (or inverse) correspondence. A strong correlation is above 0.5 or 0.6, a moderate correlation around 0.3 and a weak correlation is 0.2 or lower.
- A regression coefficient is the predicted change in the outcome variable for a one-unit change in the predictor variable. In the bivariate case, the coefficient is the slope of the line of best fit when the y variable is plotted against the x variable on Cartesian axes.
- In multiple regression, the regression coefficient is the predicted change in the outcome variable for a one-unit change in the predictor variable, net of the other predictor variables. In other words, it is the effect of

the predictor variable on the outcome variable "purged" of its associations with the other predictor variables. The "purged" variables are not correlated with each other. This is why the coefficients obtained in multiple regression are referred to as independent of, net of, or controlling for other predictor variables, or *ceteris paribus* or other things equal.

- The standardized regression coefficient (beta or β) is the predicted change in the outcome variable in standard deviation units for a one standard deviation change in the predictor variable. It is used to compare the size of the effects of predictor variables. It can be understood as the correlation, net of or controlling for, other predictors, although it can theoretically fall outside the –1 to +1 range for correlations. In the bivariate case, the standardized regression coefficient is equal to the correlation coefficient.
- The value of R square provides a summary of the explanatory power of the model or the proportion of the variance in the outcome variable explained. It ranges from zero to one, and in the bivariate case, the R square value is the square of the correlation coefficient. In multiple regression, the multiple correlation is the square root of R square.
- Earnings or income are usually logged (to base e) when analyzed as outcome variables, since their distribution is highly skewed. The regression coefficient is then the percentage change in earnings (or income) for a one-unit change in the predictor variable.
- The hypothetical relationships or causal sequence among a number of related variables can be analyzed by path analysis. For example, the relationships between socioeconomic background, test scores, and educational attainment can be represented by a path diagram, with paths from socioeconomic background to both test scores and education, and a path between test scores and education. Path coefficients are typically standardized regression coefficients. With path analysis, the correlation between two variables can be decomposed into direct and indirect effects.
- Factor analysis refers to a variety of statistical techniques which aims to represent the correlations of a set of variables in terms of a much smaller set of underlying (or latent) dimensions. Factor analysis was developed about 100 years ago by Spearman (1904) to account for the correlations observed in student performance in a range of subjects – classics, French, mathematics, music etc. – with a single underlying (latent) dimension denoted as "general intelligence". The method is related to path analysis, in that the observed scores of students in a number of tests (the manifest variables) are hypothesized as a function of the underlying latent variable(s) and a unique component (including error). The loadings of manifest variables on latent variables can be understood as correlations or path coefficients.

- Structural equation modeling is a combination of confirmatory factor analysis and path analysis. It allows researchers to specify and test a theoretical model. The model involves concepts (latent variables) and measures of concepts (manifest variables). The structural equation model is a very powerful statistical tool that provides estimates of the pathways between concepts, it allows tests of competing models indicated by the extent that the model can reproduce the observed correlations or covariances between the observed variables, and allows the calculation of direct and indirect effects.
- For categorical outcomes – such as school completion, participation at college or university and some labor market outcomes – logistic regression is commonly used. The published research literature for categorical outcomes usually expresses the relationships in terms of odds ratios (the exponent of the logistic regression coefficient), which is a ratio of two odds; for example, the odds of attending university rather than not attending for the middle class, relative to the comparable odds for the working class. Although the scale is not linear, a larger odds ratio is indicative of a stronger relationship. An odds ratio of one means no relationship.
- Fixed-effect models allow for controlling the effects of a higher level cluster variable that includes two or more observations. Examples are families where there are separate observations for siblings, so the fixed effect for families controls for everything siblings have in common, such as family income and socioeconomic status, but also typically unmeasured factors like family attitudes and values. Similarly, in longitudinal studies where there are multiple observations for students' test scores or individual earnings, fixed-effect models control all unobserved (time invariant) differences between individuals, such as ability, personality and appearance.
- Log-linear modeling focuses on the counts in a cross-tabulation of the two variables. The two variables could be educational background and educational attainment, or class-of-origin and class-of-destination. The rationale for using log-linear modeling is that the association between the two variables is independent of their marginal distributions. The association parameters can be converted to odds ratios; for example, the ratio of the odds of a university degree rather than no university degree for those from upper-class origins to the comparable odds for those with lower class origins. For over-time analyses, changes in the marginal distributions between cohorts or time points are also modeled as independent of the association. In the context of the relationship between educational attainment and socioeconomic status or class, the marginal distribution for education changes substantially because of educational expansion and there also changes in the distribution of class or educational background. These changes are sometimes referred to as structural changes.

Notes

1 Hauser and Warren (1997: 188) report a study with correlations of over 0.9 for father's occupational status from fathers' occupations reported by ninth and twelfth graders and their fathers.
2 New Zealand is an exception with a greater weight to income than earnings (Jones and McMillan 2001).
3 The correlation between Treiman's standard international occupational prestige scale (based on averaging national prestige ratings for jobs) and Ganzeboom and Treiman's international socioeconomic index is only around 0.8 (Ganzeboom and Treiman 1996: note 13).
4 This study compared student achievement in mathematics, reading, geography, science and non-verbal intelligence across 12 countries (Belgium, England, Finland, France, the Federal Republic of Germany, Israel, Poland, Scotland, Sweden, Switzerland, the US and Yugoslavia) (see Foshay *et al.* 1962: 7–20).
5 According to Bond and Fox (2001: 259) the intercorrelations (for PISA 2000) are 0.82 between mathematics and reading, 0.89 between science and reading and 0.85 between mathematics and science. These correlations are after "conditioning", a regression based technique which reduces measurement error. The intercorrelations are smaller but remain substantial with the unconditioned or raw estimates: 0.70 between mathematics and reading, 0.64 between mathematics and science, and 0.72 between reading and science (author's own analysis).
6 Author's own analysis. The correlations between cognitive ability and student performance in reading, mathematics and science were 0.79, 0.80 and 0.78, respectively. Note that the PISA test scores have been "conditioned" to reduce measurement error.
7 The counts in an individual cell (f_{ij}) in a cross-tabulation of class origins (I categories) by educational attainment (J categories) is a function of the geometric mean of all the expected cell frequencies (η) multiplied by the marginal distribution of class origins (F_o^O), the marginal distribution for the levels of educational attainment (F_e^E) and the association between class origins and educational attainment (A_{oe}^{OE}). For over-time analyses, there is also a parameter for cohorts (or time points). These terms are logged to estimate an additive model, λ_o^O, λ_e^E and λ_c^C for origins, destinations and cohorts. Changes over time are indicated by changes in the association by cohort or time point.

Chapter 4

Cognitive ability I

Conceptual issues, stability and origins

Cognitive ability is an important concept in the social sciences, not only in psychology, but also in education, sociology and economics. In psychology, cognitive ability is a key concept involved in a range of mental processes, including problem solving, adaptation, comprehension, reasoning, knowledge acquisition, abstract thought, and the ability to make connections. The concept is important to education because of cognitive ability's strong relationship with learning. During the 1970s, cognitive ability featured prominently in landmark publications in sociological studies on educational and subsequent socioeconomic attainments (Duncan *et al.* 1972; Jencks *et al.* 1972, 1979; Sewell and Hauser 1975: 91–100). In economics, the concept of ability is important to the central human capital relationship between education and earnings. In the wage equation, ability is the most prominent of the "unobservables" (or omitted variables).[1] The return on human capital (i.e. the increase in earnings attributable to education) is understood to be overestimated in the absence of controls for ability, since ability influences earnings and is correlated with education.

In some quarters, cognitive ability is a taboo concept and publications that conclude that ability is important to educational and occupational outcomes often generate considerable controversy. The most recent dispute occurred in the mid-1990s soon after the publication of Herrnstein and Murray's (1994) *The Bell Curve*, which was one of a series of acrimonious debates stretching back to the late 1960s. In response to *The Bell Curve*, there was no shortage of edited collections of critiques (Arrow *et al.* 2000; Devlin *et al.* 1997; Fisher *et al.* 1996); and numerous highly critical book reviews (for a summary of the reviews, see Nielsen 1995b).[2] The more prominent criticisms about its conceptualization and measurement are that:

- the concept of intelligence is nebulous and may even not exist;[3]
- there is no such thing as general cognitive ability, instead there are several (or multiple) largely independent human intelligences;
- IQ tests are culturally biased, and are not valid measures of intelligence;
- intelligence is not an enduring human trait;

- intelligence is simply a reflection of socioeconomic background, social class and other social factors;[4]
- ability is a consequence of, rather than an influence on, schooling;
- there is little or no biological basis to cognitive ability: environmental factors explain its intercorrelations between parents and their biological children, and among siblings, twins and other genetically related people.

There is also the more radical view that the study of human intelligence is inherently racist and/or contributes to the legitimation of socioeconomic and other social inequalities through propagating meritocratic ideologies (Bowles and Gintis 1977: 229–31; Gould 1996: 28–36, 376–91, 400). According to Bowles and Gintis (1976: 108), "the predatory, competitive and personally destructive way in which intellectual achievement is rewarded in US schools and colleges is monument not to creative rationality, but the need of a privileged class to justify an irrational, exploitative, and undemocratic system". Gould (1996) and Fienberg and Resnick (1997) unfairly link the study of intelligence to the eugenics movements of the late nineteenth and early twentieth centuries.[5]

It is unfortunate the critiques are so pervasive that it is quite acceptable to ignore the concept of cognitive ability in research and policy discussions on educational and labor market outcomes. This omission is easily justified, given the abundance of critiques on just about any aspect of the concept, its measurement and its use. Nielsen (1995a: 704) notes that, despite the evidence from published research, these critiques confirm existing ideological preferences and reinforce "a comfortable state of denial". Although largely mistaken, these criticisms appear to enjoy much greater support among educated publics, policymakers and many social science communities than the largely consensual body of knowledge established by academic research in the field.[6]

In response to the large number of, often outlandish, critiques of *The Bell Curve*, Gottfredson's (1997a) "Mainstream Science on Intelligence" response outlining "conclusions regarded as mainstream among researchers on intelligence" was co-signed with 52 prominent signatories from academia. Similarly, Neisser *et al.*'s (1996: 79) "Intelligence: Knowns and Unknowns", published in the *American Psychologist*, had 11 co-authors. Subsequent research generally reiterates the conclusions and summary statements contained in these two publications (see Deary 2012; Gottfredson 2008; Jensen 1998: 105–36). In addition, there are calls for cognitive ability to lose its taboo status and be incorporated into research and policy discussions. Nash (2001) argues that IQ and its intellectual pedigree should at least be considered, if not incorporated, albeit in some revised form, into educational sociology. Similarly, several educational psychologists advocate that ability should be part of the deliberations about educational policy rather than pretending that it does not exist or is irrelevant (Adey *et al.* 2007; Brunner 2008; Rowe 1997).

Before discussing the role of cognitive ability for educational and labor market outcomes, which is the focus of the next two chapters, three issues deserve particular attention: the conceptualization and measurement of cognitive ability, its stability and origins. There are critiques on the existence of such a thing as "human intelligence", its measurement by intelligence tests, whether it is best understood as a single general dimension or multiple largely independent "intelligences", and whether the measures of cognitive ability are culturally biased. Instability over the life course in ability measures undermines the implicit claim that intelligence is an enduring human trait. The origins of cognitive ability are important because of arguments that intelligence is simply a function of social factors and has little or no biological component. This chapter also discusses the conceptualization, stability and origins of non-cognitive attributes.

Conceptualization and dimensionality

In the English language, there are many words relating to the idea that there is variation in human intelligence: canny, clever, brainy, bright, brilliant, dull, dumb, foolish, gifted, ingenious, quick-witted, sharp, simple, smart, and stupid. English is not alone in this respect (Neisser *et al.* 1996: 79). These words reflect something real about people and are not equated with social class, socioeconomic standing or social background.

In response to the many criticisms about the conceptualization and measurement of cognitive ability, Gottfredson (2008: 554) points out that no other concept in the social and behavioral sciences is as well established in terms of construct and predictive validity. This is in stark contrast to prominent concepts in sociology, such as social class, socioeconomic background, cultural capital, and social capital. Few concepts in sociology have generally agreed operational definitions. Education is also characterized by concepts that are conceptualized and measured in a variety of ways. Even in economics, there is no consensus on the conceptualization and measurement of the central concept of "human capital".

The general consensus is that there is a single overarching dimension of "general cognitive ability", rather than a large number of specific largely independent "intelligences". The development of factor analysis was closely associated with the measurement of intelligence. From data derived from responses to test items, factor analysis summarizes the correlations between test items to a smaller number of (unobserved) underlying factors. These underlying factors may distinguish between verbal, mathematical and other abilities, or fluid and crystallized intelligence.[7] Individual items load on (or are more highly correlated with) one rather than another underlying factor. Hierarchical factor analysis further summarizes the isolated factors into a smaller number of higher level factors or a single factor. In factor analysis, there is considerable indeterminacy: the number of factors isolated, their intercorrelations, the extent of unique and error variance for the individual test items, and the existence and form of a hierarchical structure. This indeterminacy was the basis for much of Gould's (1996) critique of the concept of intelligence and IQ tests, and contributes to debates about the nature of human intelligence.

According to Sternberg (1996: 11) the most widely accepted view is that intelligence is hierarchical in structure with general ability (*g*) at the top of the hierarchy and more specific abilities at lower levels. Sub-dimensions such as fluid and crystallized intelligence can be isolated but do not replace *g*. This is the view shared by almost all researchers in psychometrics (Jensen 1998: 74–5, 106). Carroll's (1993) widely cited three-strata model comprises a lower-order stratum of 50–60 narrowly defined abilities, a second stratum of 8–10 broad abilities and a higher single dimension of general intellectual ability (*g*). Different factor analytical models produce almost identical estimates of the underlying or generalized *g* (Jensen 1998: 81–3).

Factors independent of each other or only weakly correlated would be strong evidence for multiple intelligences. However, the factors isolated in multifactor solutions tend to be highly correlated. Thurston's three-factor model could not fit the data if the factors were defined as independent (Jensen 1998: 75–8). Epstein and Winship (2005) attempted to discredit the notion that ability is a uni-dimensional concept with confirmatory factor analysis, but their isolated factors were highly intercorrelated. Fluent ability (defined as numerical operations and coding speed) had correlations of 0.75 and 0.81 with verbal and quantitative ability, and the correlation between quantitative and verbal ability was 0.86 (2005: 272). These highly correlated factors are in fact evidence of a general underlying factor. Jensen (1998: 106) points out that Gardener's theory of multiple intelligences is contradicted by high correlations between at least four of the intelligences (verbal, logical-mathematical, spatial and musical). The high intercorrelations across dimensions of intelligence are much higher than the intercorrelations among socioeconomic status indicators, which are often used to construct composite indices. Carroll (2003) concludes that the notion that there is no such thing as *g* cannot be accepted, even if separate crystalline and fluid intelligences are isolated. One point that is often overlooked in the debates about dimensionality of intelligence is that highly correlated multiple dimensions are not useful for analyses of the influence of ability, vis-à-vis other factors, on educational and socioeconomic outcomes. In regression-type analyses, high multi-collinearity – a direct consequence of the highly correlated dimensions – will produce erroneous and useless estimates.

Cultural bias

Measures of cognitive ability are not culturally biased. After several decades of research on various forms of cultural biases and threats to validity, the consensus among professional psychologists is that tests of cognitive ability are not culturally biased (Gottfredson 1997a: 14; Jensen 1980; Neisser *et al.* 1996: 97). According to Brown *et al.* (1999: 208), claims of test bias found in academic journals and the popular media, and some textbooks, are not empirically justified.

Middle-class children typically exhibit higher average IQ scores than working-class children, but this is not necessarily evidence that IQ tests are biased. This is the so-called egalitarian fallacy that all social groups should score equally well on intelligence tests and any difference is *ipso facto* evidence of cultural bias. Bias occurs if the test is measuring something different in one social group compared with another. Jewish and many Asian groups also show higher test scores (see Lynn 1996; Lynn and Kanazawa 2008), but such findings are never presented as evidence of cultural bias. It is important to keep in mind that, although there are IQ differences between class, race and ethnic groups, the within-group variation is always very much greater than the between-group variation. Thus, there are substantial proportions of high-scoring individuals from low socioeconomic status or minority groups and low-scoring individuals from mainstream and privileged groups.

One argument revolves around the nature of the test items themselves; the test items are easier for white middle-class subjects, since many items are based on the same cultural norms and values. However, there is little difference in the relative percentages of correct answers across social groups between items with low or high cultural contents. In fact, black–white differences tend to be greater on the non-cultural items (Jensen and McGurk 1987). A second argument, that white middle-class students perform better because they are more familiar with tests and the test environment, is refuted by studies in which students already familiar with testing show similar class differences in IQ scores (see Guterman 1979). If the test items were measuring different things for different social groups then there would be substantial social-group differences in the ranking of test items in terms of item difficulty (the percentage of correct answers), the ranking of the correlations between individual items and total test score, and the underlying factor structure. Such statistical characteristics of the test data are almost identical for different social groups (Jensen 1998: 362–5; also see Gordon and Rudert 1979: 177–82).

Ability tests exhibit predictive validity across different social groups. If ability tests simply reflected white, middle-class, cultural understandings then they should be of little value in predicting educational outcomes for other students. However, Guterman (1979) shows that IQ predicted vocabulary, verbal comprehension, mathematical reasoning, and school grades equally well for middle- and working-class students. Gordon and Rudert (1979) found no substantial differences between black and white groups in the extent that IQ predicts a range of educational outcomes. Although IQ is a stronger influence on educational outcomes than socioeconomic status, for both blacks and whites, IQ tends to be relatively more important than socioeconomic status for black groups. Similarly, *g* tends to be a better predictor of occupational status and earnings among blacks than whites (Nyborg and Jensen 2001).

Stability

Cognitive ability is very stable over the life course. In the US, the correlation in test scores of the same students measured at ages eight to ten and 18 is between 0.7 and 0.8 (Jencks *et al.* 1972: 59–60). Jencks *et al.* (1972: 60) report correlations among adults in test scores averaging between 0.8 and 0.9 over 15 to 20-year periods. McCall (1977) estimates the correlation between childhood and adulthood IQ to be between 0.70 and 0.85. Jencks *et al.* (1979: 97), citing a book written by Bloom in 1964, comment that the correlations "between adolescent and adult test scores are typically at least 0.8".[8] In the 1958 NCDS, the over time correlations for test scores at ages 11 and 16 were 0.76 for mathematics and 0.78 for reading (McNiece *et al.* 2004). Bond and Saunders (1999: 230), using structural equation modeling, comment that "academic ability is remarkably stable", given that the first tests were administered at seven years of age, and settle on a stability coefficient of 0.84 (which can be understood as the correlation across tests adjusted for measurement error).[9] For New Zealand, the correlation between IQ at ages eight and nine with academic ability at age 13 was 0.83 (Fergusson *et al.* 2008: 285). A study of Norwegian children found lower intercorrelations (about 0.7) between ages five and nine and higher correlations of 0.8 between the ages of ten and 12 (Bartels *et al.* 2002a). For Israel, the correlation between test scores in the eighth grade and military screening tests at age 17 was 0.75, 0.87 after adjusting for measurement error. Analyzing intelligence at age 17, the reported standardized effects for intelligence measured at the eighth grade was 0.67 compared with standardized effects of 0.10 and 0.07 for mother's and father's education (Shavit and Featherman 1988: 45, 47). For Sweden, the correlation between ability measured at age ten and at military service entrance was 0.75 (Fagerlind 1975: 58). One of the most striking findings was a correlation of 0.7 in general intelligence measured at age 11 and old age (about age 80) based on the 1921 and 1936 Scottish birth cohort studies (Deary *et al.* 2004; Johnson *et al.* 2010b: 60).

However, intelligence is to some degree malleable and does change in response to environmental stimuli. In a review article, Ceci (1991) concluded that intelligence increased with schooling with an effect of about two IQ score points per additional year of schooling. Other US studies estimated a gain of two and four IQ points per year of education (Hansen *et al.* 2004; Herrnstein and Murray 1994: 591; Winship and Korenman 1997). Similarly, the allocation of students to higher academic tracks is associated with small but significant increases in ability of two or three IQ points (Gustafsson 2001; Shavit and Featherman 1988; Sternberg *et al.* 2001).

There is a reciprocal relationship between ability and education; higher ability increases educational achievements, and higher educational achievement increases test scores (Sternberg *et al.* 2001). Although IQ changes in response to schooling, the influence of prior IQ is much larger. In a chapter in an edited collection attacking *The Bell Curve*, Winship and Korenman (1997: 231–2) explicitly disagree with the contention that "the effects of education on IQ are considerably more important than the effect of early IQ on later IQ". They conservatively conclude that the impact of early IQ on later IQ is more than twice that of education.

Flynn effect

Evidence that intelligence is not fixed is provided by the "Flynn" effect: widespread gains in intelligence across cohorts during the course of the twentieth century (Flynn 1984, 1987, 1999). The Flynn effect is about differences between birth cohorts, not changes within individuals. In the US, average IQ scores increased by 13 points (nearly one standard deviation) over 46 years (Flynn 1984). Flynn (1987) documents "massive gains" for various measures of IQ in the Netherlands, Belgium, France, Norway, New Zealand, Canada and the US, and with weaker data for East Germany, Australia, Japan, West Germany, Switzerland and Austria. A later Swedish study estimates the gain to be as much as one standard deviation across cohorts born between 1909 and 1969 (Rönnlund and Nilsson 2008). In Britain, there were recent strong gains in IQ for both young children (three points per decade) and teenagers (six points per decade) between 1982 and 2008 (Lynn 2009a).[10] Much of the gain in mean intelligence was at the low ability end of the spectrum (Weiss 2010: 487; Teasdale and Owen 1989).

The two initial explanations for the massive gains across cohorts in IQ are increased "test sophistication", that is more practice doing tests, and educational expansion. Although repeated practice at doing tests does increase IQ score, a ceiling is soon reached, which is far below the observed increases between cohorts (Flynn 1984: 47). In a later article, Flynn (1987) concludes that the massive gains could not be explained by increased test sophistication, educational expansion or increasing socioeconomic status. The gains are strongest for culturally reduced tests, tests that minimize the need for specific skills or familiarity with the test-language and mathematics. Flynn (1987: 185) summarizes, "IQ gains since 1950 reflect a massive increase in problem-solving ability and not merely an increasing body of learned content". Jensen (1998: 319–20) also concludes that ability tests that emphasize scholastic content show the least gain and in several instances are declining. The explanation increasingly favored is improvements in infant nutrition (Lynn 2009b; Flynn 1984). Other explanations include changes in students' attitudes to test taking, an increase in the relative fertility of highly educated women, advances in obstetrics and public health reducing prenatal and perinatal incidents that impair cognitive functioning, breastfeeding and earlier maturation due to, among other things, the electric light and television (Jensen 1998: 318–33). In a cross-national analysis, Barber (2005) suggests that the increasing demand for cognitive skills in developed countries has promoted an adaptive increase in cognitive ability. Flynn himself hypothesized that the societal impact of technology has emphasized abstract rather than concrete approaches to problem solving, evidenced by the over-time increase in scores in abstract reasoning (see Weiss 2010; Kaufman 2010). These suggestions are, in effect, saying that modernization is involved in inter-cohort increases in cognitive ability.

Origins

Parental ability

There is a reasonably strong association between the cognitive abilities of parents and those of their biological children. A simple measure of ability in the PSID produced a correlation coefficient of around 0.50 between father's and son's IQ scores (Kiker and Condon 1981).[11] Bouchard and McGue's (1981: 1057–8) meta-analysis estimated an average correlation of 0.42 between parent's and child's abilities. Later estimates are very similar, around 0.4 to 0.5 for one parent (Daniels *et al.* 1997: 56; Deary *et al.* 2005a; Neiss and Rowe 2000; Scarr and Weinberg 1978). The correlations between mothers (original respondents in the 1979 NLSY) and their sons and daughters (aged around 14) were around 0.4 for both mathematics and reading test scores (Duncan *et al.* 2005: 34, 43). Based on a large number of studies, some with only small sample sizes, Bowles and Gintis (2002a: 10) conclude that the intergenerational correlations for cognitive ability range between 0.4 and a very large 0.7. The higher correlations are for studies with test scores available for both parents.

The correlations between children's and their parent's measured abilities increase with the children's age. Plomin *et al.* (1997) found that parent–child correlations in ability increased from around 0.2 in middle childhood to 0.4 at age 16. The correlation between mothers' IQ and their children in the 1979 NLSY was 0.38 for five-year-olds and 0.44 for nine- and ten-year-olds (Rodgers and Wänström 2007: 192).

Unsurprisingly, there is a strong correspondence between the cognitive ability of parents and their children in other countries. A Norwegian study estimated a correlation of 0.38 between father's and son's IQ (Black *et al.* 2009: 139). A similar Swedish study concluded that the correlation between father's and son's IQ was 0.36 (Björklund *et al.* 2009a). A later study again reported a raw correlation of around 0.35, increasing to almost 0.5 when correcting for measurement error (Grönqvistb *et al.* 2010: 13). A recent German study of GOESP data found the intergenerational correlation for cognitive skills (for adult children and both parents) was between 0.52 and 0.56 (Anger 2012: 401).

Socioeconomic background

The correlation between parent's and child's abilities cannot be dismissed as simply attributable to social factors, with socioeconomic background the most obvious explanation. The association between socioeconomic background and ability is much weaker than that between parent's and child's abilities. Citing a 1936 study, Duncan *et al.* (1972: 89) report correlations of only 0.20 and 0.25 between respondent's intelligence and father's occupational status and father's education. Sewell and Hauser (1975: 78) found that father's and mother's educational attainment, father's occupational status and family income averaged over four years could account for less than ten percent of the variation in students' test scores in mental ability. Among twelfth graders in 1972, Thomas *et al.* (1979: 143) could account for only 22 percent of the variation in scholastic aptitude with socioeconomic background, race and gender. The standardized coefficient for a composite measure of socioeconomic background – comprising father's and mother's education, father's occupational status and home possessions – was 0.33. Wolfe (1982: 219) found statistically significant but weak effects for family income on child's IQ at ages four and seven years. Family income and both mother's and father's education could only account for two to three percent of the variation in children's IQ. Stronger evidence is from White's (1982: 469) meta-analysis, where the average correlation between socioeconomic background and IQ at the student level across 74 studies was 0.33, indicating that about ten percent of the variation in IQ is accounted for by socioeconomic background.

In other countries, the correlations between cognitive ability and socioeconomic background are of a similar magnitude. For the UK, Saunders (1997: 267) reports a raw correlation of 0.24 between child's IQ and father's occupational status. In the Scottish birth cohort studies, the correlations were around 0.3 (Johnson *et al.* 2010b: 60; von Stumm *et al.* 2010: 207).[12] For the 1936 Lothian Birth Cohort, Johnson *et al.* (2010a: 275) report a correlation of only 0.2 between father's social class and the test score at age 11.[13] Connelly's (2012: 111) path analysis of the NCDS and BCS suggests that less than ten percent of the variation in child's test scores is accounted by father's EGP class and father's education. In a very large Swedish study, Sorjonen *et al.* (2011: 279) report a correlation of 0.30 between intelligence and class of origin. For the Netherlands, a reported correlation is 0.33 (cited by Flynn 1987: 188). For Israel, Resh (1998: 425–6) reports that socioeconomic status, gender and ethnicity could only account for ten percent of the variance in ability and notes that "the amount of explained variance is not very high".

In regression analyses of child's test scores with both parent's ability and socioeconomic background, parent's ability has substantially stronger effects than socioeconomic or class background. Often the impact of socioeconomic background is trivial or not statistically significant, net of parent's cognitive ability. Scarr and Weinberg (1978: 681) found that, among biological families, only 11 percent of the variation in adolescent IQ was accounted for by four socioeconomic background measures: father's education and occupation, mother's education and family income. The addition of two background factors – family size and birth rank – increased the explained variance to 15 percent. However, adding parents' IQ increased the explained variance to over 30 percent and the effects of the four socioeconomic background variables were no longer statistically significant. A multivariate analysis of intelligence – weakly measured by sentence completion – from the PSID showed strong effects for father's IQ score (with a standardized regression coefficient of 0.55), whereas the effects of father's education, father's occupational status and parental income (averaged over five years) were not statistically significant (Kiker and Condon 1981: 101–2). Analyzing data from children of mothers in the 1979 NLSY, Carlson and Corcoran (2001: 789) noted that mother's ability score (measured by the AFQT score) was the only maternal characteristic that significantly predicted reading scores in children aged seven to ten. The standardized effect was around 0.36.[14] Its addition to a model comprising measures of family structure, the child's demographic and mother's sociodemographic characteristics almost doubled the explained variance from 12 to 22 percent (2001: 787).[15] Mother's AFQT score had similarly strong effects for child's mathematics score (2001: 787–8). Duncan *et al.* (2005: 54) compared the impact of mother's adolescent mathematics test score on daughter's mathematics test score (at about age 14) with and without a suite of socioeconomic status controls (including mother's education and family income averaged over a three-year period). With the addition of the socioeconomic status variables, the standardized coefficient for maternal mathematics score declined very marginally from 0.23 to 0.22.

A study of families in Korea and Hawaii found that the impact of parental socioeconomic status on child's ability was small relative to parent's ability (Johnson and Nagoshi 1985). A more recent study on the Hawaiian sample concluded that parental occupational status and education had no impact on child's ability, net of parent's ability (Nagoshi and Johnson 2005). In an article attempting to critique *The Bell Curve*, Currie and Thomas (1999: 302) found standardized effects between 0.6 and 0.7 for maternal test score on offspring's score on the Peabody Picture Vocabulary Test (PPVT) compared with around 0.2 for socioeconomic status among children aged six and older. In younger children – where the measurement of ability is much less reliable – the effects of maternal ability and socioeconomic status were more similar, although the impact of maternal ability was more than twice that of socioeconomic status. Although Currie and Thomas (1999: 302) were very critical of *The Bell Curve*'s findings on a number of grounds, they conceded that "a central result has emerged that maternal AFQT is a powerful predictor of child PPVT scores, even after controlling for a host of background characteristics" (1999: 324). However, they then change tack completely and conclude that the AFQT is a very good marker of human capital, socio-economic status and other background characteristics, anything but what it is supposed to measure.

For other countries, the patterns are very similar. Analysis of the test scores of original respondents in the UK's NCDS and their children, found that the intergenerational transmission of test scores was reduced only marginally, when controlling for parental education and income which were "unrelated to their children's age 7 test scores" (Brown *et al.* 2011: 49). Analyzing the German GSOEP, Anger and Heineck (2010) found that the addition of parental IQ to the analysis of child's IQ reduced the effect of parental education to statistical insignificance. An exception is a Swedish study which claimed that 50 percent of the intergenerational association in IQ was due to family factors, since the correlation among brothers approached 0.5 (Björklund *et al.* 2009a). Their logic here is unclear, since the sibling correlation is considered a "broader measure of the importance of family background" with the admission that brothers share 50 percent of their genome. A simpler explanation for the discrepancy (a father–son correlation for IQ of 0.35 and a brother correlation of 0.5) is that the measure of father's ability is poor. The father–son correlation should be close to 0.5. The correlation in ability between brothers is to a large extent because of their shared genetic heritage (see below).

Biology and genetics

Evidence of a sizable biological component for ability comes from the comparison of children from biological and adopted families. The effects of parents' socioeconomic characteristics are much weaker for adopted children than for biological children. An early study found that among adopted children, the correlation of IQ with father's (and mother's) education was 0.15 (0.05) compared with 0.39 among biological children (Scarr and Weinberg 1978: 678). Only two percent of the variation in IQ in adopted children could be accounted for by socioeconomic background variables – father's education and occupation, mother's education and family income – compared to 11 percent in biological families (Scarr and Weinberg 1978: 681). A later study found much the same pattern. The correlations between parental education and child's verbal intelligence are substantially higher in biological (0.41 and 0.36 for mother's and father's, respectively) than adoptive (0.16 and 0.18) families. This study concluded that the environmental component of parental education accounts for only three to four percent of the variation in verbal intelligence (Neiss and Rowe 2000: 492–3). Plomin *et al.* (1997) found negligible correlations between parents and their adopted children's general and specific cognitive abilities (with the same tests). In biological families, the correlations were moderate (around 0.3 to 0.4).

The correlation in IQ among siblings is around 0.5 (Paul 1980). This is the expectation if IQ was purely genetic. Nielsen (2006: 202) reports a correlation of 0.4 for full siblings, 0.3 for half siblings and 0.08 for non-related siblings, strongly suggesting that genes are involved. Mazumder (2008: 697) reported a sibling correlation for AFQT test scores of 0.62, slightly higher than that for education (0.60), and higher than that for height (0.45–0.50).

Twin studies confirm there is a sizable genetic basis to cognitive ability. Monozygotic twins are genetically identical whereas dizygotic (or fraternal) twins share only 50 percent of their genome. In an early study, Goldberger (1978) reported very large correlations in IQ of 0.89 among monozygotic twins reared together and 0.68 among those reared apart. In Bouchard and McGue's (1981) meta-analysis, the average correlation in intelligence for identical twins reared together was 0.86, compared with 0.60 for dizygotic twins and 0.47 for siblings. For monozygotic twins reared apart, the correlation was still very high (0.72), but for siblings and dizygotic twins reared apart the correlations were much lower at 0.24.[16] A later study found that among monozygotic twins reared together the correlations on several measures of ability ranged from 0.76 to 0.88; and for monozygotic twins reared apart the correlations were surprisingly high, between 0.64 and 0.78 (Bouchard *et al.* 1990: 226). Jensen (1998: 177) reports correlations in IQ of 0.86 for monozygotic twins reared together, 0.60 for dizygotic twins reared together, 0.75 for monozygotic twins reared apart and 0.50 for siblings reared together. Even among siblings reared apart, during adulthood, the correlation in ability was around 0.5 (1998: 178). Solon's (1999: 1,775) review of several studies posits a correlation of 0.85 for identical twins reared together and 0.70 for identical twins reared apart. He notes that the latter correlation is much higher than that for siblings reared together and these correlations imply a genetic component to IQ. The observed familial correlations are similar to the theoretical correlations that assume ability is a continuous human trait governed by a number of genes: a polygenic mode of inheritance (similar to that for height). Under this model, the correlations would be 1.0 for identical twins; 0.5 for non-identical twins, siblings, parents and their children; 0.25 for stepsiblings and 0.125 for cousins (Teasdale and Owen 1984). This model assumes no assortative mating (the tendency to marry like).[17] Although genes for mental retardation have been located, no specific genes have been identified for general cognitive ability. It is likely that a large number of small genetic variations are responsible (Deary *et al.* 2010: 205–6).

Adoption, sibling and twin studies allow estimates of heritability (H^2); that is, the variation in IQ (or any other outcome) attributable to genetic factors as a proportion of the total variation.[18] The classic measure of heritability is twice the difference in the correlations between identical twins and non-identical twins or siblings (Jensen 1998: 200; Nielsen 2006: 201). A variety of studies generate heritabilities of 50–80 percent, with a much smaller proportion of the variance, typically less than 20 percent, being attributed to the shared environment (Deary *et al.* 2009; Nielsen 2006; Plug and Vijverberg 2003; Plomin *et al.* 1997; Rowe *et al.* 1999b; van Leeuwen *et al.* 2008). Even critics of *The Bell Curve* estimate heritabilities for IQ of around 50 percent and a much smaller effect for the (non-womb) environment at around 17 percent (Daniels *et al.* 1997: 54–8).[19] Plomin *et al.* (1997: 445) conclude that environmental transmission of cognitive ability from parent to child is negligible. Similarly, Nielsen (2006) concludes that the impact of shared environmental factors is relatively small, although there is a sizable unshared environmental component (i.e. unique to the individual).

Interestingly, the heritability of IQ is quite low among very young children and rises with age (Davis *et al.* 2009; Deary *et al.* 2009). Jensen (1998: 169, 179) documents heritabilities of 40–50 percent in young children, 60–70 percent in adolescents and young adults, rising to 80 percent among older adults. The environmental component tends to decline with children's age. It declines to zero in adulthood (Jensen 1998: 179–81; Neisser *et al.* 1996: 85). The increase with age in the heritability of IQ and decrease in the importance of the environment is contrary to what an environmental model would predict (Jensen 1998: 367). Heritability tends to be lower, and the shared environment more important, in low socioeconomic status and economically disadvantaged families (Harden *et al.* 2007; Rowe *et al.* 1999a; Turkheimer *et al.* 2003). These findings suggest that, as countries become wealthier, the heritability of intelligence increases and the influence of the family environment decreases. This conclusion is consistent with modernization theories.

Neisser *et al.* (1996: 86) point out that heritability does not mean immutability. Height and weight are inheritable but quite sensitive to the environment. Furthermore, heritability does not mean nothing can be done to reduce the chance of undesirable outcomes. There are hosts of genetically related conditions, ranging from minor disorders (e.g. prone to sunburn, short-sightedness, fallen arches) to very serious conditions (phenylketonuria, cancers and autoimmune diseases), all of which, to varying extents, are treatable.

Ultimately, there is a physiological basis to intelligence. Luo *et al.* (2003) conclude that mental speed is a major causal factor underlying the observed correlation between general intelligence and scholastic performance. Jensen (1998: 201–69) hypothesizes that *g* is explainable by the speed and efficiency of information processing. Reaction time from a single test item has only a moderate correlation of between −0.3 and −0.5 with *g*, but the reaction times combined for a range of tasks have correlations with *g* approaching −0.7 (1998: 229). He concludes that reaction time accounts for 70 percent of the inheritable variance in IQ (1998: 265). To take reductionism a little further, reaction time can be attributed to nerve conduction velocity, the degree of myelination of nerve fibers (which increases velocity) and the metabolism of glucose by the brain (Jensen 1998: 159–62, 204–5). In contrast, Deary *et al.* (2010) tend to favor brain network connectivity and efficiency.

Non-cognitive attributes

Unlike cognitive ability, it is not possible to isolate a single dimension of non-cognitive ability. There is much variation in the intercorrelations for non-cognitive attributes. Jencks *et al.* (1979: 126) reported the intercorrelations for nine composite measures of non-cognitive traits ranging from 0.28 to 0.62. Olneck and Bills (1980: 35) presented high correlations for some pairs of attributes: "industriousness" and "perseverance" (0.81), "perseverance" and "cooperativeness" (0.71), "integrity" and "cooperativeness" (0.71), and "initiative" and "executive ability" (0.59). For other pairs of attributes the intercorrelations were around 0.4 and 0.5.

Bowles and Gintis's (2002b: 12) "non-cognitive component of the returns to schooling" is the ratio of the regression coefficient for education on earnings controlling for cognitive ability, to the comparable coefficient not controlling for cognitive ability. They estimate a ratio of 0.82, suggesting that approximately 80 percent of the impact of education on earnings is due to non-cognitive attributes. With this definition, non-cognitive attributes include anything correlated with education and earnings, but uncorrelated with cognitive ability. This very broad definition may include factors normally not regarded as "skills" such as, time of year born, area of residency, gender, physical stature, personality, appearance and of course "error".

Non-cognitive traits tend to be stable over time but not as stable as cognitive ability. Judge *et al.* (1999: 635–6) report high correlations for adjacent time periods (0.6–0.8) and lower, but still substantial correlations for measures collected 40 or so years apart (0.3–0.4). Osborne Groves (2005b: 213–14) cites 9 to 19-year stabilities between 0.5 and 0.8. Correcting for measurement error would increase these correlations.

Non-cognitive attributes are often not independent of cognitive skills. Bowles and Gintis (1976: 320–1) calculate a correlation of 0.25 between an aggregate measure of non-cognitive skills and cognitive factors (IQ, verbal and numerical SAT test scores). Jencks *et al.* (1979: 146) report a correlation of 0.27 between composite measures of cognitive and non-cognitive skills. Farkas *et al.* (1990: 131) present sizable correlatives between basic cognitive skills and work habits (0.40), and appearance and dress (0.25). Using the 1979 NLSY, Heckman *et al.* (2006: web appendix, Table S3) report correlations of between 0.20 and 0.30 for components of the AFQT with measures of locus of control (the Rotter scale) and self-esteem (Rosenberg).

The intergenerational correlation for non-cognitive attributes tends to be considerably weaker than that for cognitive ability. Intergenerational correlations for the "big five" personality traits range from between 0.10 and 0.29 (Osborne Groves 2005b: 213). Duncan *et al.* (2005) found generally small mother–daughter correlations for personality traits: 0.13 for the Pearlin mastery (a locus of control measure), 0.16 for self-esteem, 0.08 for depression and 0.10 for shyness at age six. These compare with intergenerational correlations of around 0.40 for mathematics and reading test scores (2005: 34–5). For Germany, Anger (2012: 401) reported intergenerational correlations for non-cognitive skills ranging from 0.19 to 0.31. This contrasted with an intergenerational correlations up to 0.56 for cognitive skills. A study of Swedish conscripts found that the intergenerational correlation for a composite measure of non-cognitive ability – encompassing emotional stability, persistence, social outgoingness and willing to take initiatives – was correlated at 0.21, rising to a questionable 0.43 using instrumental variables (Grönqvistb *et al.* 2010: 13). Mazumder (2008: 697) reports correlations less than 0.3 for self-esteem among full-brothers and around 0.10 for the Rotter scale measure of "locus of control". These compare with a brother correlation of 0.62 for test scores, suggesting the family, broadly defined, is only a weak influence on non-cognitive attributes.

Like cognitive ability the intergenerational transmission of non-cognitive traits cannot be attributed to socioeconomic background. As well as analyzing the (minimal) impact of socioeconomic status on the intergenerational correlation of test scores, Duncan *et al.* (2005: 54) performed the same exercise for locus of control and shyness. For daughters, the coefficient for mother's locus of control on daughter's locus of control declined very marginally from 0.12 to 0.11 controlling for socioeconomic status from 0.14 to 0.13 controlling for shyness. Summarizing the impact of socioeconomic status on a large number of intergenerational correlations for cognitive, personality and behavioral variables (e.g. drug taking, sex at a young age, ever convicted) the authors conclude their analyses "provide little support for the idea that parental SES is the key cause of similarities in parents and children" (Duncan *et al.* 2005: 69). This confirms earlier work by Jencks *et al.* (1979: 132, 138) that found weak relationships between social background and self-assessed non-cognitive traits and indirect measures of personality. The explained variance was less than ten percent and, in some instances, less than five percent. Similarly, Lynn *et al.* (1983: 476) reported very weak correlations between personality factors and measures of socioeconomic background. The weak association between non-cognitive factors and socioeconomic variables is not consistent with Bowles and Gintis's (1976) correspondence principle.

There is also a biological component to non-cognitive attributes. The intergenerational correlations for non-cognitive traits among adopted families was estimated at 0.07 compared with correlations of 0.20 between parents and their biological but living away children (Loehlin 2005: 193). Loehlin (2005: 198, 205) concludes that the limited amount of parent–child resemblance in non-cognitive attributes is mostly, but not entirely, genetic. For a range of personality factors, the correlations among monozygotic twins reared apart are higher than those for dizygotic twins reared together: 0.48 (monozygotic) and 0.23 (dizygotic) for wellbeing, 0.56 and 0.13 for social potency, 0.36 and 0.13 for achievement orientation, 0.61 and 0.24 for stress reaction, 0.48 and 0.38 for alienation, and 0.46 and 0.14 for aggression. The heritabilities – the proportion of the observed variation due to genetic factors – ranges from 0.39 to 0.58. The shared family environment was statistically significant for only two of the 14 traits examined. The authors conclude "the common environment generally plays a very modest role in the determination of many personality traits" (Tellegen *et al.* 1988: 1035–7).

Among monozygotic twins reared apart, the correlations on personality inventories were surprisingly high around 0.50, much the same as the correlations among monozygotic twins reared together (Bouchard *et al.* 1990: 226). Another twin study concluded that "entrepreneurship" has a high heritability and the environment and upbringing had little effect (Nicolaou *et al.* 2008). On the Eysenck personality scales, monozygotic twins show higher correlations than dizygotic twins or other related individuals. The correlations for monozygotic and dizygotic twins are 0.29 and 0.11 for psychoticism, 0.51 and 0.12 for extraversion, 0.39 and 0.16 for neuroticism, and 0.47 and 0.22 for the lie scale (Eaves *et al.* 1999: 70). They conclude that "the shared environment plays a small and insignificant role in the creation of personality differences in adults" (1999: 76).

Conclusions

The arguments commonly used to discredit the concept of cognitive ability are simply not valid. Human intelligence is a well-recognized human trait existing long before its formal measurement. The various IQ tests that measure ability are highly intercorrelated. A single underlying dimension, generalized intelligence (*g*), accounts for much of the variation in the responses to test items. Alternatively, the responses can be accounted for by a small number of highly intercorrelated dimensions. Intelligence is an enduring trait. Studies of children, adolescents and adults in a variety of countries have demonstrated the remarkable stability of measures of cognitive ability over the life course with high correlations between childhood and adulthood.

Cognitive ability has a sizable genetic component. Typically, socioeconomic influences on children's IQ or test scores largely disappear when controlling for parental cognitive ability. There are only very weak effects of parental socioeconomic factors on adoptive children's cognitive abilities. The sizable correlations of cognitive ability among identical twins reared apart – higher than that for siblings reared together – cannot be accounted for by social factors. Heritability studies consistently find that environmental factors play a much lesser role than biological factors. However, this does not mean that human intelligence is *determined* by biology, is unresponsive to environmental stimuli or that policies aiming to improve the socioeconomic and other outcomes of disadvantaged groups are of no value.

Bowles and Gintis (1976, 2002b) argue that non-cognitive factors socialized by families and schools are important to the reproduction of socioeconomic inequalities. If non-cognitive factors are important to the inheritance of socioeconomic inequalities, then the intergenerational correlations for non-cognitive factors would be appreciable. However, the intergenerational associations are often substantially weaker than that for cognitive ability. If non-cognitive factors are important to the reproduction of socioeconomic inequalities then controlling for socioeconomic background would remove or substantially reduce the intergenerational correlations of non-cognitive factors. It does not. Furthermore, like cognitive ability the bulk of the intergenerational correlation for non-cognitive factors are due to genetic, not environmental, factors. The impact of the overall shared environment is very weak and often not statistically different from zero. These findings are all contrary to the Bowles and Ginitis argument that non-cognitive attributes maintain the intergenerational reproduction of socioeconomic inequalities.

Notes

1 What sociologists understand as "specification error" is, to economists, "ability bias" or more generally "unobserved heterogeneity".
2 For a critique of the critiques, see Nielsen (1995a).
3 Gould's (1996) *Mismeasure of Man* argues that the concept is nebulous given the ambiguity involved in factor analytical techniques.
4 The idea that IQ is largely a reflection of socioeconomic status is common in edited critiques following publication of *The Bell Curve*. This extraordinary argument that IQ is another measure of socioeconomic status has been made, among others, by Currie and Thomas (1999: 317–18), "One might argue that AFQT scores are a better indicator of the socioeconomic status of the mother and her family when she was an adolescent"; a statement that is followed by citations to Heckman. Similarly, Richardson (2002) claims that IQ tests are simply a test of class background.
5 Equally, and again unfairly, it could be argued that the insistence on environmental factors could be traced to the ideology of Soviet Marxism, which insisted that everything was environmental. This ideology promoted Lamarckian genetics, prohibited the study of Mendelian genetics, and the sacking and imprisonment of geneticists who disagreed (Bell 1973: 407).
6 Carroll (1995) makes this point in regard to the generally positive responses to Gould's (1996) *The Mismeasure of Man*.
7 Fluid intelligence is ability independent of acquired knowledge, whereas crystallized intelligences involves acquired knowledge.
8 Based on the same source, Duncan *et al.* (1972: 100) settle on a stability coefficient of 0.9 between ability measured at age twelve and maturity.
9 Structural equation modeling will invariably produce larger structural coefficients, if it includes a measurement model.

10 However, there is some recent evidence that the Flynn effect is slowing down, or of actual declines across cohorts in IQ scores. Declines have been found for Denmark, Norway and Britain (Shayer and Ginsburg 2009; Sundet *et al.* 2004; Teasdale and Owen 2008).
11 The author converted the unstandardized coefficient (b) to standardized coefficient β by the ratio of the standard deviations:

$$\beta = b\left(\frac{s_x}{s_y}\right)$$

12 For the 1936 Lothian Birth Cohort, Johnson *et al.* (2010a: 275) report a correlation of only 0.2 between father's social class and the test score at age 11.
13 Father's class tends to exhibit weaker correlations than continuous measures of socioeconomic background.
14 Calculated from the coefficient in Table 3 (0.478) multiplied by the ratio of the independent to the dependent variable (21.1/27.6) in Table 1. AFQT score was divided by 10 (Carlson and Corcoran 2001: 783).
15 Family income also had an impact but it was relatively weak. A doubling of family income increased child's reading score by about 3.2 percent. Percentage effect = coefficient*ln(2) (i.e. 4.573*0.69).
16 Goldberger (1978), from other sources, presents a similar pattern of correlations. For example, the correlation for IQ among monozygotic twins reared together is 0.89, and among twins reared apart is 0.68. Among siblings, parents and their children, the intercorrelations are also around 0.5. For adoptive children, the correlations with their adoptive parents and siblings are around 0.23.
17 Assortative mating describes the tendency for male–female pairs to have similar characteristics. The intercorrelations for IQ among spouses are around 0.4 to 0.6 (Goldberger 1978; Jensen 1998: 176; Scarr and Weinberg 1978: 678). The high intercorrelations for IQ among spouses are probably due to selection on education rather than on intelligence (Watkins and Meredith 1981). Assortative mating tends to produce over estimates of the environmental component in heritability studies (Bartels *et al.* 2002b: 551).
18 Estimates from these studies are typically based on the following logic:

> IQ is a combination of genetic, environment and unique factors. The variances can be equated as follows: Var(IQ) = Var(G) + Var (E) + Var(U).
>
> For monozygotic twins (reared apart or together), the correlation of the genetic component is 1.0. For dizygotic twins or siblings (reared apart or together), the correlation of the genetic component is 0.5. For step-brothers, the correlation of the genetic component is 0.25. For biologically unrelated siblings, the genetic component is zero.
>
> For twins or siblings reared together, the correlation of the environmental component is 1.0. For twins or siblings reared apart, the correlation of the environmental component is zero.
>
> These assumptions can be changed to accommodate various possibilities; for example, twins have identical environments but siblings do not, or the extent of assortative mating.

19 The Daniels *et al.* (1997: 54–8) model does not include a term for unique (or neither genetic nor environmental) influences. Also their model underestimates the IQ correlation among monozygotic twins reared apart, suggesting that the genetic component is underestimated.

Chapter 5

Cognitive ability II

Educational outcomes

Definitions of intelligence offered in Chapter 3 include references to learning quickly, solving problems, the ability to make connections, thinking abstractly, comprehending complex ideas, and reasoning. Similarly, cognitive ability is important to knowledge acquisition, more quickly understanding new ideas and using more effective problem-solving strategies (Baumert *et al.* 2009: 172). All these skills are involved in some form or other in educational settings, so it is expected that cognitive ability has a strong relationship with a range of educational outcomes.

The purpose of this chapter is to show that cognitive ability has strong relationships with a variety of educational outcomes: scores in standardized tests, grades and class rank, and other measures of student performance; educational plans, aspirations and expectations; tracking and streaming; early school leaving (and its converse school completion); participation at university or college, overall educational attainment and the transition from one educational level to the next. Typically, its influence is substantially stronger than that for class or socioeconomic background. The argument is not that ability "determines" educational outcomes and that socioeconomic background and other ascribed characteristics are of no consequence. The argument is that the influence of cognitive ability is important enough to be incorporated into theoretical explanations of educational outcomes and policy deliberations about education.[1] The final section of this chapter discusses the importance of non-cognitive attributes – personality traits, motivation, locus of control, height, etc. – on educational outcomes, because of arguments that non-cognitive attributes are, just as or, more important than cognitive ability for educational outcomes.

Theoretical issues

Modernization theory would contend that cognitive ability is becoming increasingly important in contemporary industrialized societies.

Many of the post-war educational reforms in industrialized countries were based on a meritocratic ideology: that success in the education system should be based on ability and effort, not social background and other socially ascribed characteristics. The implicit assumption was that, once the social impediments to educational success had been removed, ability and effort would largely determine educational outcomes. Various policies – scholarships, 11-plus exams, school tracking,[2] raising the school leaving age – were implemented, so that high-ability students from disadvantaged backgrounds would further their education. Similarly, low-ability students from high socioeconomic backgrounds would be weeded out by their weak performance, identified primarily by standardized tests. The 1944 Education Act in the UK was designed so that bright working-class students could attend academically orientated grammar schools (Saunders 2010: 52). The goal was to make education systems more meritocratic.[3]

There are other reasons why ability may have become more important. Increases in the influence of ability for educational and related outcomes may also come about passively, for example by changing parental attitudes and aspirations for their high-ability children's education which in previous generations would have encouraged their children to earn a living as soon as they could leave school, no matter their academic potential. Furthermore, colleges and universities have become more selective, with admission based almost solely on academic criteria (Alon and Tienda 2007; Thomas *et al.* 1979). This contrasts with earlier times, when "open admissions" policies meant that only those who could afford the fees and the time spent not earning a wage could attend.

The meritocratic goal that educational outcomes should, to a considerable extent, reflect ability and motivation can be critiqued as unfair for those unfortunate enough to be born with low levels of ability (Marshall and Swift 1996: 383; Rawls 1971: 104). Rawls (1971: 73–4, 107) argues that the distribution of wealth and income arbitrarily determined by the natural distributions of ability and talents is no fairer than the distribution by historical and social fortune. Similarly, "'equality of opportunity' means an equal chance to leave the less fortunate behind in the personal quest for influence and social position" (1971: 106–7). Therefore, social justice is only possible with equality of outcomes, which as Saunders (1996: 87) argues is unworkable, since there would be no incentive to perform. If an educational system based on ability and motivation is contrary to social justice, then it is very difficult to envisage what criteria would govern student assessment and access to different educational pathways. For example, rewarding students through lotteries or mandating quotas for those with particular social characteristics may satisfy some advocates of social justice, but they are simply not practicable or politically acceptable alternatives or for that matter particularly fair.

The hypotheses generated from modernization theory are that:

- ability has a strong effect for the range of educational outcomes;
- these effects cannot be dismissed as being due to socioeconomic background;

- the effects of ability are consistently stronger than the effects of socio-economic background;
- cognitive ability is becoming more important for education.

The expectations for increasing effects of ability need to be nuanced for some particular outcomes. For categorical outcomes, such as school completion and university entrance, the impact of ability is likely to increase and then decline with educational expansion. As school completion increases beyond the point where all high-ability students complete school, the effect of ability will decline, since increasing proportions of middle- and lower-ability students complete school. Similarly, the impact of ability for participation at college or university is likely to increase with the change from elite to mass systems as more high-ability students from less-privileged backgrounds participate. However, with further increases in participation from mass to universal systems, the overall effect of ability is likely to decline as increasing proportions of lower-ability students attend.[4] Similarly, it is very difficult to conclude if the impact of ability on tracking and streaming has increased. Since the 1960s, reforms to the education systems of most countries have usually included reducing educational differentiation. Furthermore, with the increases in university participation, the proportion of students in higher status academic tracks has tended to increase.

A methodological note

The standard criticism of comparing the effects of cognitive ability to that of socioeconomic background is that social science is not a "horse race", and there are statistical issues in assessing the relative importance of variables. King (1986: 673–4) argues that it is "theoretically 'good enough' to say that even after controlling for a set of variables (i.e. plausible rival hypotheses, possible confounding influences), the variable in which we are interested still seems to have an important influence on the dependent variable". A few points need to be made. In other contexts, social researchers commonly conclude that a particular factor is more important for a particular social outcome. The "horse race" criticism is particularly mounted in comparisons involving cognitive ability, especially when it is shown to be the stronger influence. Second, the size of the effect of a variable is crucial to theory building. Many factors have small effects on social outcomes and, in large enough samples, these effects will often be statistically significant. In order for theories to account for observed patterns, they need to focus on the most important influences. It is not "theoretically good enough" to conclude that a variable has a statistically significant impact and not to consider the magnitude of that impact. There is little point in a theory which contends that, for a particular outcome, a multitude of factors are somewhat important. A similar point can be made about policy. Policymakers wish to focus on the factors that make the most difference: the so-called "bang for the buck".[5]

It is true that there are statistical issues surrounding assessing the importance of variables (see Bring 1994; Hunter and Hamilton 2002; King 1986; Kim and Ferree 1981). The interpretation of a standardized coefficient is the expected change in the dependent variable in standard deviation units for a one standard deviation change in the independent variable. This does not make much sense for dichotomous variables such as gender, and is not at all appropriate for multinomial variables. Standardized effects cannot be compared across samples, if the variance of the independent variable differs. Standardized coefficients apply best to continuous variables with normal distributions. Furthermore, standardized coefficients can be misleading for variables that have comparable impacts. Often, the criticisms confuse comparing the same variable across different samples with comparing two variables within the same sample (Menard 2011: 1411). Although there are statistical issues in assessing the importance of predictors, some influences *are* more important than others. If the difference is large enough, a variety of statistical procedures – partial correlations, semi-partial correlations, standardized coefficients, standardized independent variables, effect sizes, t values, changes in variance explained – will all lead to the same conclusion.

Empirical evidence

The rough order for these discussions of the empirical results is the presentation of the overall (zero-order) correlations, focusing first on the US, then the UK and other countries. This is followed by a discussion on the effects of ability, net of other influences, with studies from a variety of developed countries.

Student performance

Chapter 3 documented the very strong associations between cognitive ability and performance in standardized testing programs mainly because both types of tests are measuring much the same generic skills. The correlations, unadjusted for measurement error, are between 0.65 and 0.85 and larger, adjusting for measurement error (see pages 44–5). These are very high correlations and cannot be accounted for by socioeconomic background, which has much lower correlations (up to 0.5 for multiple indicators but more commonly around 0.3) with student performance in standardized tests (see pages 114–16).

In the US, the correlations between student performance (usually grades) and IQ scores are considerable. In the WLS, Sewell *et al.* (1969: 88) reported a strong correlation (0.62) between ability and grades at school. Jencks *et al.* (1979: 96) reported intercorrelations between tests of ability, student aptitude or performance in specific subject areas of between 0.65 and 0.75. Analyzing data from the 1988 NELS study, Dumais (2002: 65) reported a correlation of 0.57 between ability and grades at school compared to a correlation of 0.33 between grades and a composite measure of socioeconomic status.[6] Other studies present slightly lower estimates; Ceci (1991) reports an average correlation of 0.55, Neisser *et al.* (1996: 81) 0.5 and Sternberg *et al.* (2001: 4) between 0.4 and 0.5. Jensen (1998: 278) concludes that the correlations between ability and grades are between 0.6 and 0.7 among primary school students, with smaller correlations in high school (0.5 to 0.6) and college (0.4 to 0.5) as students at the lower end of the ability continuum drop out, attenuating the correlation. He claims that the correlation between *g* and grades at school is close to 0.75 when correcting for attenuation.

For class rank, the association with ability is possibly stronger, since class rank has finer distinctions. Jensen (1998: 280) reports a correlation of 0.62 between the WAIS IQ test and class rank at graduation.

The correlations between performance at school and ability are also substantial in other developed countries. In the UK, as long ago as 1955, correlations as high as 0.7 were reported between intelligence and student performance in primary school; this compares to the then substantial correlation of 0.56 between socioeconomic status and performance (cited by Colom and Flores-Mendoza 2007: 244). In upper secondary school, Thienpont and Verleye (2004) estimate the correlation between a measure of IQ measured at age 11 and performance at the British O and A level examinations at 0.57 and 0.47, respectively; the comparable correlations are 0.37 and 0.27 for social class, and 0.34 and 0.26 for father's education. The correlation between *g* and overall performance in the English General Certificate of Secondary Education (GCSE) was around 0.7, and mostly between 0.5 and 0.7 between *g* and performance in specific subjects. Of those with average IQ scores at age 11, 58 percent obtained five or more satisfactory grades in the general certificate. For students scoring one standard deviation above the mean, the percentage was much higher at 91 percent; and for one standard deviation below the mean, it was only 16 percent (Deary *et al.* 2007). The authors estimate a correlation of 0.81 between the latent intelligence trait (*g*) from an ability test administered at age 11 and a latent trait of educational achievement (from GCSE scores). Micklewright and Schnepf (2006: 68) report a correlation of 0.76 between PISA test scores and performance in Key Stage 4 subjects.

For Australia, Marks (2010b: 31) reports a correlation of 0.59 between test scores at age 15 (from PISA) and tertiary entrance performance in the final year of school. This compares with a correlation of 0.25 for father's occupational status and 0.29 for the broad PISA measure of Economic, Social and Cultural Status (ESCS). All these correlations are attenuated because academically weaker and, to a lesser extent, lower socioeconomic background students have already left school or are not competing for university places. In Sweden, the correlation between cognitive ability measured at age 13 and grades is around 0.6 among cohorts born between 1967 and 1982 (Erikson and Rudolphi 2010: 295). For the Netherlands, Bartels *et al.* (2002b: 544) reported a correlation of 0.63 between IQ and performance in the national test of educational achievement (CITO) tests (which influences track placement) at 12 years of age. For IQ measured at ages 7 and 10 the correlations were still substantial: 0.5 and 0.6. For Slovenia, the correlation between intelligence and grades in the last four years of the nine years of primary school was 0.48 and the standardized beta was 0.39, net of a combined measure of parental education and cultural capital (Flerea *et al.* 2010). For Israel, Resh (1998: 425) reported correlations of 0.67, 0.57 and 0.45 for ability with reading and mathematics achievement, and mean grades. For Iceland, the correlations for verbal IQ and nonverbal IQ with GPA were 0.61 and 0.54 (Thorlindsson 1987: 705).

The large correlations between ability and student performance cannot be attributed to socioeconomic background or social background. A study of 1955 US high-school sophomores found that ability had a much stronger standardized effect ($\beta = 0.46$) for sophomore and senior class standing than a composite measure of socioeconomic status ($\beta = 0.08$) (Alexander and Eckland 1974; see also Sewell and Hauser 1975: 95). An analysis of the WLS data estimated a standardized effect of 0.59 for ability on high school grades with no significant effects for family income (obtained from tax records), father's occupation or father's or mother's education (Sewell *et al.* 1980: 566). Similarly, in an analysis of the NLS72, Thomas *et al.* (1979) found very strong effects of test scores for class rank with a standardized regression coefficient of 0.6. In that analysis, the effect of socioeconomic status was negative (–0.05), indicating that students with similar levels of ability from lower socioeconomic status households had higher class ranks than students from higher-status households. DiMaggio (1982: 195) reported standardized effects of around 0.3 of ability on grades in English, mathematics, history, and in all subjects, net of father's education, and several indicators of cultural capital. In the 1998 NELS study, the standardized effects for ability and socioeconomic status on grades at school (GPA) were 0.38 and 0.12 among eighth-grade boys, and 0.42 and 0.07 among eighth-grade girls (Dumais 2002: 56).

In New Zealand, IQ measured at age eight had strong effects for grades in the tenth grade, net of family income, parents' education and other background factors (Maani and Kalb 2007). The effect was equivalent to a partial correlation of 0.52. For Australia, the impact of test scores for university entrance performance was three times stronger than that for socioeconomic background (Marks 2010c). In Brazil, the correlation between intelligence and scholastic achievement was between 0.6 and 0.7, with no effects for parental income and education when controlling for intelligence (Colom and Flores-Mendoza 2007). In Israel, ability had much stronger effects on performance in reading and science than a composite measure of socioeconomic status

(Resh 1998: 426).[7] For GPA in Iceland, Thorlindsson (1987: 707) reports standardized effects (betas) of 0.54 and 0.26 for verbal ability and social class.

Nor can the impact of ability be attributed to unobserved aspects of family background. Reviewing previous studies, Teachman (1996: 36) concludes that intellectual ability "is by far the most important predictor of grades". His own structural equation analysis of sibling data concluded that ability explains between 59 and 67 percent of the between-family variance in students' academic grades. He concludes that the search for additional family background variables to explain the relationship between ability would be fruitless and the focus should be on within-family factors that differ between siblings (1996: 44–5).

There is some but only limited evidence that the impact of ability on school performance is increasing. In the US, Hearn (1991: 165) reported a correlation of 0.48 between tested ability and grades in the 1980–2 HS&B study. In a later comparative study based on the 1988 NELS study, Karen (2002: 208) reported a correlation of 0.59. Calculations from Barron *et al.*'s (2000) paper indicate that the standardized effect of ability on high-school rank, net of parental education, was of the order of 0.15 for students graduating in 1972 but around 0.30 for the class graduating in 1979.[8] For Australia, the effect of test scores on university entrance rank was higher in 2005–6 than in 1999 or 2002 (Marks 2009a: 33).[9]

Aspirations and expectations

Ability is also important in the formation of educational aspirations and expectations.[10] In 1953, Kahl (1953) concluded that ability and occupational class background were practically equal predictors of educational aspirations among US students. Alexander and Eckland (1974), analyzing data collected in 1955, found notably stronger effects for socioeconomic status than ability for educational expectations. However, other studies have found stronger relationships for cognitive ability. The correlations of mental ability with college plans and occupational aspirations among WLS high-school graduates (in the late 1950s) were both at 0.43. These correlations compare with correlations below 0.3 for father's and mother's education, father's occupational status and an accurate measure (from tax records) of family income (Sewell and Hauser 1975: 93). These correlations are attenuated because they are restricted to high-school graduates. From the 1979 NLSY, the correlations between cognitive ability and educational aspirations and expectations were 0.6 and 0.5, respectively. These compare with correlations between 0.35 and 0.40 for parental education and less than 0.2 for family income (Ganzach 2000).

The strong association between aspirations and tests scores is not confined to the US. Using cross-national data from 12 countries in the First International Science Study, Husen (1967: 39) reports sizable correlations among 13-year-olds between mathematics test score and years of education planned (0.42) and years of education desired (0.38). Analyzing data from over 40 countries from the PISA 2000 and 2003 studies, Sikora and Saha (2007: 71) conclude that higher academic achievement, measured by reading scores, is strongly related to expecting to complete a university education.

Multivariate studies indicate that ability has stronger net effects for educational aspirations than socioeconomic background when both are included in the same analysis. Sewell and Shah's (1968: 204) analysis of college plans in the WLS report stronger effects for ability (β=0.37) among males than father's education (β=0.14) or mother's education (β=0.13). Alwin and Otto (1977: 267) also reported stronger effects of ability (β=0.41) on college plans than a composite measure of socioeconomic background (β=0.20). In the Christchurch birth cohort study, cognitive ability had stronger effects on educational aspirations than family's socioeconomic status. The respective standardized coefficients were 0.47 and 0.27. Family's economic resources had no impact (Fergusson *et al.* 2008). Analyzing sibling data to gauge the importance of family background, Teachman and Paasch (1998: 704) conclude that three-quarters of the variation in students' educational expectations is attributable to differences between families but "only a fraction of this variation can be explained by standard indicators of socioeconomic status".

Tracking and streaming

Ability plays a much greater role than socioeconomic background in the allocation of students to particular educational locations within and between schools. Jencks *et al.* (1972: 34–5) found that, in the US, the correlation between curriculum assignment and test scores was around 0.50. The authors note that, to their surprise, "social class did not seem to play an important role in high school curriculum placement, except insofar as it influenced test scores". In an analysis of the NLS72, the relative standardized effects of test scores and socioeconomic background for curriculum track placement (college preparatory versus other) were 0.52 and 0.16 (Thomas *et al.* 1979: 43). Alexander and Cook (1982: 631) found that the coefficient for ability measured in the fifth grade had "by far the largest impact" for senior high school curriculum placement. Ability had stronger effects for academic track placement than a composite measure of socioeconomic status, net of grades and educational expectations, both of which are at least moderately correlated with ability (Jones *et al.* 1995).[11] Even at kindergarten and first grade, prior test score was the strongest determinant of the allocation of children to different ability groups (Tach and Farkas 2006).

Similarly, ability is strongly correlated with school track and curriculum placement in other countries. When students were allocated to different school tracks in the UK, the correlation between secondary schooling type and ability for the cohort born between 1933 and 1952 was estimated at around 0.6 (Halsey *et al.* 1980: 160–1). This compares with a correlation of 0.44 between school type and family's material circumstances. After school tracks were abolished, ability became a strong determinant of within-school subject differentiation. Davies *et al.* (2008: 241) concluded that general ability had the strongest effect for subject choice in English secondary schools.

For Australia, Fullarton *et al.* (2003: 34–5) found that enrolments in advanced mathematics, physics and chemistry were much higher among students with test scores (measured three years earlier) in the top quartile. For Israel, the correlation between ability and track placement was 0.59 compared to 0.38 for socioeconomic status. This study concluded that "ability and academic performance are strong predictors of track placement" (Resh 1998: 416, 425). For the Netherlands, the correlation between test scores and advice on which secondary school tract is most appropriate was also large: 0.59 and 0.66 for cohorts born in 1940 and 1965 (Vrooman and Dronkers 1986: 76). For Denmark, Jæger (2009: 1960) reported a multinomial regression coefficient of 0.82 (the predictor variable was standardized) for reading ability (from the 2000 PISA study) on participation in an academic rather than a vocational secondary school, net of parental occupational status (which was barely significant), father's education and mother's education. In Slovenia, the correlation between high-school track and intelligence was 0.50, with a beta of 0.37, net of background factors (Flerea *et al.* 2010).

In the Netherlands, the impact of ability on school type appears to have increased. The impact of test scores in relation to advice on which secondary school to attend was larger in the cohort born in 1965 compared with the cohort born in 1940 (Vrooman and Dronkers 1986: 77). For both cohorts, the effects of ability were quite large, with standardized effects of 0.44 and 0.58, net of social class. A second study of type of school attended using the same data found increases in the effects of ability: the standardized effect increased from 0.33 to 0.48 (Faasse *et al.* 1987). In contrast, in the US, the correlation between test scores and track placement appears to have declined substantially from 0.40 for the 1980–1982 HS&B study to 0.27 in the 1988 NELS study (Hearn 1991: 165; Karen 2002: 208). This decline may be due to the expansion of the academic track.

School completion and non-completion

Dropping out of school is strongly associated with ability. According to the US's 1979 and 1997 NLSY studies, nearly everyone in the highest ability quartile finished school, no matter their family's income level: about 80 percent in the 1979 NLSY and 90 percent in the 1997 NLSY (Belley and Lochner 2007: 46–7). A one standard deviation increase in ability reduces the odds of dropping out of high school by 5.6 times compared with 1.9

times for the same difference in a composite measure of socioeconomic status.[12] Korenman and Winship (2000) also found strong negative effects of ability for dropping out of school, net of socioeconomic background; a one standard deviation increase in ability decreased the odds of dropping out by about six times compared to 1.6 times for the same difference on a composite measure of socioeconomic status.[13]

For the UK, Halsey *et al.* (1980: 161) settled on a correlation of 0.49 between school leaving age and respondent's IQ. Bratti (2007) found that a one standard deviation increase in quantitative ability measured at age ten reduced the probability of not continuing with education at age 16 by five percentage points, and for verbal ability eight percentage points, net of social class, parental education, family income and other factors.[14] By comparison, the impact of a one standard deviation difference in family income was (maximally) about two percentage points (2007: 33). Analyzing not having obtained any O levels in the 1958 NCDS, Hobcraft (2001) reports very strong effects for a categorical measure of tests scores.[15] The effects for father's occupation and parental income were small and mostly not statistically significant. Bynner and Joshi (2002: 417) found that, according to the 1958 NCDS, children with low scores in either reading or mathematics were about five times more likely to leave school early than those with top scores.

According to the Canadian Youth in Transition Survey (YITS), based on the PISA 2000 cohort, the average reading score (measured at age 15) of high school "dropouts" was 457 compared with 547 for high-school graduates: a difference of about 0.9 of a standard deviation. The odds of students at the highest proficiency level (level 5) completing school were 17 times that for students at level 1, net of parental education, household income and other factors. This compares with an odds ratio of 2.1 for students from the highest income quartile compared with those in the lowest (Knighton and Bussière 2006: 8, 17). According to 2001 LSAY data, over 90 percent of Australian students in the top ability quartile completed school compared with 62 percent of students in the lowest ability quartile (Fullarton *et al.* 2003: 18). For the youth cohort aged 15-years-old in 2003, 97 percent of students in the top mathematics test score quartile completed school compared with 66 percent of the bottom quartile (Curtis and McMillan 2008: 9). Marks (2007) found that ability measured by PISA 2000 test scores had a strong effect on school leaving: a one standard deviation difference in the PISA test score decreased the odds of leaving school by 2.9 times. Its magnitude was two to three times greater than that for socioeconomic background. In New Zealand, a ten point difference in IQ scores measured at ages seven and eight increased the odds of finishing school 2.3 times, net of background and behavioral factors (Fergusson *et al.* 2005).[16] Another New Zealand study reported that the raw correlation between gaining a school certificate (that is completing school at a minimal satisfactory standard) and IQ measured at ages seven to nine was 0.40 compared with correlations of 0.30 for parental occupational status (Caspi *et al.* 1998: 446). In Israel in the 1980s, the average IQ of secondary school dropouts was 84, slightly more than one standard deviation below the mean (Shavit and Featherman 1988: 45).

Changes over time

In the US between 1916 and 1942, there was little difference in the average ability of high-school graduates and non-graduates. By about 1960, there was a gap of about 16 points in the average IQs of high-school graduates and non-graduates (Herrnstein and Murray 1994: 145–6). This suggests that the impact of ability must have increased between 1940 and 1960. In 1979, ability differences were large, with almost no one in the two top quintiles not completing school but 55 percent of the bottom ability quintile dropping out. Comparing 1979 and 1997 NLSY data, Belley and Lochner (2007: 51) conclude that ability has become less important for high-school completion. This is because the proportion completing high school increased (in these data from 79 to 90 percent) and almost everyone in the top ability quartile completed school as did over 80 percent in the second quartile. The increase in participation mostly came from the lower-ability groups. So the pattern is one of ability becoming more important as school completion increases but of decreasing importance as school completion approaches saturation.

For the UK, the available evidence suggests a similar pattern. An early British cohort study – the Scottish Mental Health Survey, a sample of children born in 1932 – found that the correlation between IQ and age of leaving school was comparatively weak, at around 0.3, and the comparable correlation with social class background was closer to 0.4 (Deary *et al.* 2005b). This suggests that, in the late 1940s, ability had only a moderate impact for school leaving and social class was a stronger influence.[17] In later studies, the correlation with ability was stronger and then subsequently declined as secondary school education expanded. For the 1958 NCDS cohort, the correlation (among men) between ability and age leaving school was –0.43 (–0.44 for women) but lower for the 1970 BCS birth cohort: –0.38 for men and –0.39 for women (Schoon 2008). Bynner and Joshi (2002: 412, 417) also found that the effects of both reading and mathematics test scores for leaving school at age 16 were weaker in the 1970 than in the 1958 birth cohort study. For Australia, Marks and McMillan (2003) found decreasing effects of ability (test scores) for school completion when comparing youth cohorts born between 1961 and the early 1980s, although its effects remained strong. Fullarton *et al.* (2003: 21) reported an odds ratio of 2.9 for a standardized measure of achievement (literacy and numeracy) on school completion, net of other influences including parental occupation and education, for a cohort born in 1961, but decreasing to an odds ratio of 2.0 for a cohort born in the mid-1980s.

College and university

Entrance to college or university is also strongly related to ability. In an analysis of college entry among a cohort of US high-school seniors in the early 1970s, academic factors – ability, college track and class rank – were much stronger predictors of college entry than social factors. Net of academic factors, the impact of a composite measure of socioeconomic background was weak (Thomas *et al.* 1979: 144, 147). Using data collected from 1972 and 1980 longitudinal studies of high-school graduates, Alexander *et al.* (1987: 72, 75) found "evidence for the preeminence of academic factors in facilitating four-year college attendance" and that socioeconomic status disparities are quite small once academic factors are taken into account. According to the 1997 NLSY, more than 80 percent of those in the highest ability quartile attended college and nearly 70 percent of those in the highest achievement quartile and who were also in the lowest family income quartile (Belley and Lochner 2007: 48). Multivariate analysis of the 1997 NLSY indicated a 52-percentage point gap in college entry between the highest and lowest ability quartiles, net of family income quartile, mother's education and a number of sociodemographic factors. This compares with gaps of 16 percentage points between the highest and lowest family income quartiles (Belley and Lochner 2007: 50). Korenman and Winship (2000) found strong positive effects of ability for obtaining a Bachelor of Arts (BA) degree, net of socioeconomic background. A one standard deviation increase in ability increased the odds of obtaining a BA degree (rather than not obtaining a BA) by about six times. This compares to an odds ratio of around 2 for a one standard deviation difference on their composite measure of socioeconomic background.[18]

The relationship between (SAT and similar tests) test scores and college grades is only marginally attenuated when controlling socioeconomic background. Sackett *et al.* (2009) conclude that the test score–college grade relationship is largely independent of socioeconomic background. Academic factors – ability, track and curriculum – dominate over social factors in college *completion* among college students (Alexander *et al.* 1982). Ability, measured by test scores, also has a strong impact on enrolment in doctoral and professional graduate programs (Mullen *et al.* 2003). A one standard deviation difference in test scores increased the odds of enrolling in a doctoral program about 2.8 times and 2.2 times for a professional program, net of parents' education.[19]

Ability is also a strong predictor of the status of the institution attended. The correlation between tested ability and Hearn's (1984) measure of institutional selectivity (based on the SAT scores of entering students) was around 0.44. This compares with correlations of 0.24, 0.20 and 0.21 for father's and mother's education and total family income. Later, Hearn (1988: 71) also found that ability has a substantially stronger correlation

(0.31) with the cost of the college institution attended – high-status colleges tend to be more expensive – than parental education (0.16) or family income (0.12). A later study on selectivity using the NELS data reported a correlation of 0.49 between tested ability and college selectivity (Karen 2002: 208).

In the Canadian YITS longitudinal study, the average PISA test scores of students at university was 594 compared with the (country) mean score of 534 (OECD 2010b: 55). Of those students who scored in the highest PISA proficiency level (level 5, 16 percent of the sample), 76 percent went to university compared with ten percent at level 1 or below (OECD 2010b: 80–1). Of those Australian students born in 1975, 69 percent of the top year-nine test score quartile had participated at university by the late 1990s compared to 6 percent in the bottom quartile (Marks *et al.* 2000: 17). Khoo and Ainley (2005) reported a (tetrachoric) correlation of 0.46 between year-nine mathematics test score and university entrance compared with correlations of 0.28 and 0.24 for parents' university education and occupational status. As was the case for the US, socioeconomic background made little or no difference to university entrance among students in the top three deciles of tertiary entrance performance (Marks and McMillan 2007: 371–2). A one standard deviation increase in year-nine achievement score increased the odds of university entry by 2.2 times compared with 1.4 times for a similar increase in socioeconomic background, net of each other and school type (Marks 2010b). Of those New Zealanders in the Christchurch birth cohort study with IQs greater than one standard deviation above the mean (115+) assessed at ages eight to nine, by age 25, 59 percent had gained a university degree compared with 34 percent of those with IQ scores between 105 and 114, and only 2.1 percent of those with IQs below 85. This strong relationship remained when taking into account other influences, such as socioeconomic disadvantage and behavioral problems during early childhood (Fergusson *et al.* 2005: 855).

Changes over time

Comparing IQ scores of US high-school graduates who did and did not enter college, Taubman and Wales (1972: 17–24, 19) found "a very pronounced upward trend" in the role of ability between 1921 and the early 1960s. In the 1920s, about 60 percent of the most able students (the top decile) went to college, while in the 1960s, the comparable figure was over 90 percent. Herrnstein and Murray (1994: 35) updated this analysis for the 1980s and found no change between the 1960s and 1980s. Comparing the 1979 and 1997 NLSY studies, Belley and Lochner (2007: 50) noted that the gap in college attendance between top and bottom ability quartiles had declined slightly from 55 to 52 percentage points. However, over time, ability had become a more important influence for college attendance towards the bottom end of the ability distribution (2007: 51–2). For enrolment in any college and enrolment in a four-year college degree, the effects of belonging to the two middle ability quartiles (compared to the bottom quartile) were stronger for the 1997 cohort than for the 1979 cohort. For the highest ability group there was no change (2007: 73).

For Australia, effects of test scores on participation at university decreased for LSAY cohorts born between the early 1960s and 1980s, although there was no significant decline if the analyses are restricted to school completers (Marks and McMillan 2003, 2007: 368–371). A later study found that the impact of ability was slightly greater for the PISA cohort born in 1985 than for an older cohort born around 1980 (Marks 2009a: 33). However, the measure from PISA has less measurement error, which may account for the difference.

Educational attainment

In a comprehensive review of the US data collected between the 1920s and 1960s, Jencks and his colleagues concluded that the correlation between test scores collected in elementary school and educational attainment (measured by years of formal education) was between 0.5 and 0.6 (Jencks *et al.* 1972: 144). For cohorts completing their schooling in the 1940s, Duncan *et al.* (1972: 84, 89) conclude that the correlation between ability and years of education was 0.5 to 0.6. In the WLS, the correlation was lower, at 0.45 (Sewell and Hauser 1975: 93). Jencks *et al.* (1979: 101–10) analyzed nine longitudinal studies that collected data on test scores and educational attainment. Although the sample sizes were small and only one study was conducted outside the US, their results are illustrative of the strong influence of test scores for educational attainment. The raw correlations again ranged from 0.4 to 0.6. Analyses of the 1979 NLSY reported a correlation of 0.53 between mathematics test scores and total years of schooling (Duncan *et al.* 2005: 52). For 1979 NLSY respondents in 2007, the correlation between adolescent ability and years of education had increased to 0.62 (Zagorsky 2007: 493). Strenze's (2007) meta-analysis of data from over 50 samples from mostly US studies estimates an average correlation of about 0.56 between ability and educational attainment, again measured by years of education.

Strong relationships have also been found in other countries. In the Scottish Lothian Birth 1936 Cohort study, the correlation between IQ measured at age 11 and total years of education was 0.42 (Johnson *et al.* 2010a: 275) A stronger relationship was observed for the 1958 NCDS study; Schoon (2008: 77) reported correlations of around 0.55 between general cognitive ability and educational attainment measured by highest qualification (which ranges from no qualifications to a university degree). The comparable correlations for parental social class were 0.35 for men and 0.30 for women. For New Zealand, the correlation between IQ at age eight or nine, with a measure of educational attainment at 25 years of age (a seven-point scale ranging from no high school qualification to the completion of a university bachelor degree), was 0.54 (Fergusson *et al.* 2008: 285). This compares with correlations of 0.38 for average family income (over five years) and 0.43 for a summary measure of socioeconomic status. For Sweden, the correlation between general intelligence and educational attainment was 0.56 (Sorjonen *et al.* 2011: 279). A study of Norwegian twins presented correlations of above 0.5 between IQ and both years of education and educational level attained (Tambs *et al.* 1989: 215).

The correlations between literacy scores in IALS and linear measures of educational attainment are 0.35 for Germany, 0.40 for Sweden, 0.45 for the Netherlands and 0.56 for the US (Devroye and Freeman 2001: Table 2, Panel B). These estimates can be questioned, since literacy is measured at the same time as educational attainment, but the magnitudes of the relationships are comparable with those observed in longitudinal studies where ability is (usually) measured several years prior to the completion of formal education.

Multivariate analyses show substantially stronger effects of ability on educational attainment than those of socioeconomic background. Sewell and Hauser (1975) found that adding test scores to a model of predicting educational attainment by socioeconomic background variables almost doubled the variance explained to 28 percent. The standardized effect for test scores was 0.37, much stronger than that for father's education (0.08), mother's education (0.10), father's occupational status (0.11), and parental income (0.11). Less than one-fifth of the effect of ability could be attributed to its correlation with socioeconomic background (1975: 100, Model 22, 102).[20] Analyzing educational attainment in the WLS, Project Talent, and Explorations of Equality of Opportunity (EEO) studies, Jencks *et al.* (1983: 8) report standardized effects of academic aptitude test scores between 0.37 and 0.46 compared with effects below 0.15 for father's occupation and education, mother's education and income, with some of these socioeconomic background variables having statistically insignificant effects. With the addition of academic aptitude, the variance in educational attainment accounted for doubled from 15 to 30 percent. Duncan *et al.* (1972: 90), using synthetic data (based on correlations from several data sources), estimated the net effect of intelligence for educational attainment at 0.44 compared with 0.22 and 0.24 for father's education and occupational status. Korenman and Winship (2000: 147), analyzing years of education, report a much stronger standardized effect of 0.62 for ability compared to 0.2 for a composite measure of socioeconomic background. Correcting for measurement errors and taking into account the reciprocal relationship of early schooling influencing ability (as well as the other way round), Winship and Korenman's (1999: 61–2) preferred causal estimate was 0.53 (a standardized effect).

In an exercise using a variety of techniques designed to show weaker effects of ability vis-à-vis socioeconomic background than those published in

The Bell Curve, Korenman and Winship (2000: 154) found the standardized effect of ability for educational attainment (years of education completed) was between two and three times that for socioeconomic background. Ability remained a stronger influence against a composite of measure of social background, which included socioeconomic background and other aspects of social background, family structure and the number of siblings (Korenman and Winship 2000: 155–9). Although correcting for measurement error increased the effect of socioeconomic background for years of schooling by up to 50 percent from 0.20 to 0.24 or 0.29, depending on the amount of measurement error assumed, ability remained a substantially stronger influence with a standardized effect of 0.61 (2000: 153–4). It was only with a fixed-effects sibling analysis that the effects of ability and family background were comparable (2000: 160). But this analysis rests on differences between siblings in both AFQT scores and educational attainment, since the fixed effect for family background controls for all time-invariant unobserved differences between families, which includes ability. Recall that the correlation in ability among siblings is about 0.5, indicating that 50 percent of the variation in ability is between families. The coefficient for AFQT is thus net of all ability differences between families.

Similarly, the impact of ability for educational attainment can only partially be attributed to socioeconomic background. Jencks *et al.* (1979: 104), analyzing several data sets, concluded that only 12 to 21 percent of the effect of ability on educational attainment could be attributed to measured family background variables, such as father's occupation, father's education, and mother's education. Using sibling studies to control for the total effect of family background, they found that unmeasured family characteristics could explain another 15–20 percent of the correlation between test scores and educational attainment. They conclude that a large "57 to 68% of the observed correlation between test scores and education is independent of family background". This estimate of the influence of "family background" includes both social and genetic components since it is derived from studies of brothers and twins. Based on some simple assumptions, Jencks *et al.* (1979: 106) conservatively conclude that, for educational attainment, 54 percent of the effect of test scores is because the tests are proxies for native intelligence. Sewell *et al.* (2004: 27) conclude that "less than one-fifth of the association between ability and schooling could be attributed to the mutual dependence of these variables on socioeconomic background".

The impact of ability for educational attainment is also relatively strong in other countries. In the 1958 NCDS cohort, the likelihood of a male student in the top ability quintile of obtaining an A level or higher level of educational attainment was 70 percentage points greater than students in the bottom ability quintile, net of family income, class background, and other background factors (Galindo-Rueda and Vignoles 2005: 343). Thienpont and Verleye (2004) reported a standardized coefficient of 0.7 for test scores predicting educational attainment (corrected for measurement error) compared to 0.4 for parents' education with little effect for social class. The addition of ability increased the explained variance from 30 to 50 percent in Chevalier and Lanot's (2002: 172–3) analyses of age completed formal schooling. They conclude that "early ability tests have a large positive effect on schooling achievement" (2002: 174). Connelly (2012: 111) reported standardized effects for childhood ability scores of 0.35 and 0.38 for the NCDS and BCS on educational attainment, net father's class and father's education. In a large study of over 140,000 Norwegian males born between 1961 and 1971, the (standardized) impact of general ability for educational attainment was relatively large: 0.46 compared to 0.15 for parents' education and 0.10 for parental income (Kristensen *et al.* 2009: 809).

Changes over time

Jencks *et al.* (1979: 86) conclude that the correlation of test scores with educational attainment (at around 0.55), had remained more or less stable since World War I. There is some indication that correlations have increased slightly since the 1970s. Several recent studies have reported correlations around 0.6 (Ganzach 2000: 426; Neisser *et al.* 1996: 82; Zagorsky 2007: 493). Jensen (1998: 279) provides a slightly higher range: between 0.6 and 0.7, and Hauser *et al.* (2000: 207) report a correlation of 0.66 between AFQT score and educational attainment among non-black men born between 1961 and 1964.

For the UK, there is evidence suggesting that the impact of ability for educational attainment increased between cohorts born in the early 1920s and the late 1950s. Analyzing longitudinal data from a Scottish cohort born in 1921, Johnson *et al.* (2010b: 60) found a moderate effect of ability (β = 0.31) measured at age 11 on educational attainment and a strong effect of father's social class (β = 0.59). Analyzing the 1946 birth cohort study, Richards and Sacker (2003) reported more or less equal effects of ability (β = 0.45) and father's occupation (β = 0.42), although regional and national studies are not really comparable. For the 1958 NCDS cohort, Thienpont and Verleye (2004, see above) reported much stronger effects for ability than socioeconomic background.

Comparison of the national birth cohort studies suggest that the impact of ability on educational attainment has declined slightly. The correlation between ability and educational attainment in the 1946 birth cohort was 0.54, 0.55 for both sexes in the 1958 cohort, and for the 1970 cohort substantially lower at 0.43 for men and 0.40 for women (Richards and Sacker 2003: 617; Schoon 2008: 77).[21] The effect of ability for educational attainment, net of other factors, has also declined. In Schoon's (2008) structural equation analysis, the direct effects of ability for educational attainment, net of class background and motivation, were weaker in the younger (1970) cohort. The decline was fairly small: from 0.24 to 0.20 for men and from 0.22 to 0.19 for women. Galindo-Rueda and Vignoles (2005) also found a decline in the impact of ability between the 1958 and 1970 birth cohorts. The likelihood of students in the top ability quintile compared with the bottom ability quintile of obtaining an A level qualification or higher declined from a 70 percentage point difference in the 1958 cohort to a 60 percentage point difference in the 1970 cohort, net of social background factors. The reduced importance of cognitive ability was observed across other educational branching points. According to the authors, the major reason for the decline was the increase in educational attainment among lower-ability students from higher socioeconomic backgrounds. Echoing the findings for the US and Australia for university entrance referred to above, they note that an unintended consequence of less selective schooling is greater progress by low ability students from higher socioeconomic backgrounds. Similarly, Chevalier and Lanot's (2002) analyses of the age at which young people left formal education predicted by family income, parental education, ability and other factors show smaller marginal effects for ability for the 1970 cohort compared with the 1958 cohort.

Educational transitions

The educational transitions literature conceptualizes educational attainment as a series of successive transitions from educational level to the next. Examples are the transitions from primary school to secondary school, from lower secondary school to middle school, from middle school to school graduation, and from school to college. Only students who made the previous transition are "at risk" of successfully completing the next transition. The model is primarily focused on changes in socioeconomic inequalities in education: over the school career and between cohorts. Much of the critique and debate about the transitions model has centered on "unobservables", unobserved variables which are believed to have strong effects on the transition but not included in the analyses. Also the "unobservables" affects the population at risk, since each population at risk differs because of the role of "unobservables" in survival (Cameron and Heckman 1998: 263). In addition, the absence of "unobservables" in the analysis upwardly biases the coefficient for socioeconomic background.[22] The principal "unobservable" is ability, with "motivation" less frequently mentioned.

In the educational transitions models, the addition of an ability measure substantially increases the explanatory power of the model, especially for the transitions occurring during school, doubling or tripling the pseudo R square measure used (Mare 1980: 303). Ability also substantially reduces the effects of socioeconomic background for educational transitions, especially father's occupational status. Like socioeconomic background, the impact of ability weakens substantially across transitions. For the transition from college to successfully completing the first year of post graduate study, the effect of ability was not statistically significant; in contrast, its effects for the earlier transitions were strong (Mare 1980: 303). The decline in the impact of ability with the educational career is likely, at least in part, due to selection effects because, with each successive transition, there is less variation in ability in the population analyzed.

Subsequent research has confirmed that the impact of ability on educational transitions is substantial. Holm and Jæger (2011: 219) showed strong effects of cognitive ability for the transition from successfully completing A levels to entering higher education in the UK. A one standard deviation change in ability score increased the odds of a successful transition by 2.26 times, net of father's and mother's education.[23] Holm and Jæger (2009) using data from the US, the UK, Denmark, and the Netherlands, reported estimates for socioeconomic background for educational transitions with and without ability measures. They conclude that cognitive ability accounts for about 40 percent of the unobserved characteristics in transitions models and that cognitive ability is very important for transitions models (2009: 22).

However, much of the literature on educational transitions does not include measures of cognitive ability. It was rarely included in the country-specific chapters in the edited books based on the Mare model (Shavit and Blossfeld 1993; Shavit *et al.* 2007a). This is because most of the data sets analyzed do not include ability measures, or, if they do, the focus is not on ability but socioeconomic background and hypotheses surrounding persistent socioeconomic inequality. Some of the more recent studies have included GPA and test scores to reduce the bias in estimates of the effects of socioeconomic background variables (Breen and Jonsson 2000; Lucas *et al.* 2011).

Non-cognitive attributes

There is little doubt that non-cognitive factors play some role in educational performance. It is very plausible that motivation, diligence and effort are rewarded by the education system and disruptive and other negative behaviors penalized. However, the effects for non-cognitive factors for education are generally weaker than for cognitive ability. Using data from a high-income New York high school, Bowles and Gintis (1976: 136) present significant partial correlations for non-cognitive factors with GPA, net of cognitive ability: 0.42 for "perseverant", 0.35 for "punctual" and 0.39 for "consistent" and "emphasizes orders" and negative correlations for "creativity", "aggressiveness" and "independence" (1976: 136). In a larger study, Olneck and Bills (1980) find weak effects on grade-10 test scores: for "appearance" (β = 0.08), "cooperativeness" (β = 0.10) and "industriousness" (β = 0.31), net of prior test scores (β = 0.26) and sociodemographic factors. Similarly, there were quite weak effects of non-cognitive attributes on educational attainment – "executive ability" (β = 0.09) and "industrious" (β = 0.10), net of academic and demographic factors. Lynn *et al.*'s (1983) study of students in Ulster found that "psychoticism" (β = –0.09) and "status aspiration" (β = 0.11) had significant effects on examination grades, although their effects were much weaker than those for intelligence (β = 0.30). Analyzing educational attainment of mothers in the 1979 NLSY, Duncan *et al.* (2005: 53–5) report weak effects for non-cognitive traits (measured during adolescence), locus of control (β = 0.06), self-esteem (β = 0.09), shyness at age six (β = –0.03) and substantially larger effects for mathematics (β = 0.31) and reading (β = 0.24) test scores. Rumberger (2010) finds significant but weak effects of non-cognitive skills – locus of control and educational expectations – on completion of a college degree. The addition of these two variables increased the explanatory power of the model marginally, from 43 percent to 46 percent. It is doubtful that "educational expectations" constitutes a non-cognitive skill. Covay and Carbonaro (2010) found that a composite measure of non-cognitive skills indexing students' approaches to learning reduced the effect of socioeconomic background on reading test scores by only 16 percent and by 18 percent for mathematics (2010: 35, 38). They also included extracurricular activities (sports, music, etc.) as enhancers of cognitive skills. However, they "did not find strong mediating mechanisms between SES and test scores" (2010: 41).

There are non-cognitive factors seemingly unrelated to schooling that have unexpectedly strong effects on education. A large study of over 950,000 Swedish men found that height at age 18 had a strong positive association with attaining higher education, net of year of birth, parental socioeconomic position, other shared family factors and cognitive ability (Magnusson *et al.* 2006). They found that a "2- to 3-fold difference in the probability of achieving higher education among tall (> 194 cm), compared with short (< 165 cm) men." (2006: 661).

Conclusions

This chapter shows that cognitive ability is important for educational outcomes. It exhibits sizable correlations with performance at school, educational aspirations and expectations, school completion (and its converse dropping out), school track, within-school educational differentiation, entry to college and university, and completion of university degrees. These correlations are typically substantially stronger than the comparable correlations with measures of socioeconomic background.

The common response to the conclusion that ability is important for educational outcomes is that ability is largely a function of social class or socioeconomic background. However, socioeconomic background does not account for the influence of ability. Indeed, ability has sizable effects, net of socioeconomic background, whereas, in many contexts, the inclusion of ability in the analysis reduces the impact of socioeconomic background considerably and in some cases to statistical insignificance. Kingston (2006: 114) also makes this point that test scores cannot be simply dismissed as manifestations of socioeconomic background or elite culture, since there are sizable effects of ability on educational outcomes, net of family socioeconomic status (and race). For the same reason, it is also a mistake to conclude that ability measures developed over the last 100 years or so – with all the careful research on its conceptualization and measurement – are nothing more than manifestations of socioeconomic background.

Another response to be found in the literature is that ability is unimportant once other factors are taken into account. It is relatively simple to show that the effects of ability on educational outcomes are smaller when including other predictors highly correlated with ability, such as educational and occupational aspirations, school track or school program and prior student performance (e.g. marks or grades).

Although the central argument of this chapter is that cognitive ability is important to educational outcomes, it should not be read as arguing that the environment has no role. A point made frequently is that the environment is important for the expression of a human trait. To be a good musician, it is not just a matter of talent: instruction and learning are required and it helps to have a decent instrument. Similarly, physically stronger and highly coordinated people are more likely to play sport and develop their skills. For intelligence to exert an influence it needs to be recognized, nurtured and rewarded by families, schools and institutions of higher education. The point is that in contemporary developed societies, to a considerable extent, it is.

Notes

1 Kingston (2006) makes a similar point that, for the US, ability is not decisive but is consequential and is more important than ascribed characteristics.

2 Although much of the literature points to tracking as maintaining socioeconomic inequalities in education, using test scores as the selection mechanism for the allocation to different school tracks should lower the impact of family background since the scope for social influences is reduced (Tieben *et al.* 2010).

3 Writing in the early 1970s, Bell (1973: 410–17) observed that the meritocratic ideology was being replaced by demands for equal outcomes for particular disadvantaged social groups rather than equality of opportunity.

4 This is similar to the Maximum Maintained Inequality thesis.

5 In a number of disciplines including education, economics, statistics and medicine, and often in reference to policy making and cost-benefit analysis, there are large literatures on "effect sizes" which try to quantify the importance of a factor. A good example is Hattie's (2009) extensive meta-analysis of effect sizes for various predictors of student achievement.

6 The socioeconomic status measure comprised mother's and father's educational levels, mother's and father's occupation, and family income.

7 This evidence is from calculating the standardized effects from the published coefficients and standard deviations.
8 Barron *et al.* (2000: 414) present t ratios for ability of 8.59 and 10.90 for the 1972 NLS and 1979 NLSY. These were converted to comparable standardized regression coefficients.
9 This could be due to a better measure of ability being used in the later study.
10 According to Ganzach (2000: 426), educational expectations and educational aspirations are highly correlated around 0.85.
11 The respective odds ratios for being in the academic track for a one standard deviation difference (calculated from the paper) were 1.4 for ability, 1.6 for educational aspirations, 1.4 for grades and 1.3 for socioeconomic status. Socioeconomic status was a composite of father's education; mother's education, father's occupation; and the average score for the presence of eight household items, such as newspapers, books and a typewriter.
12 The odds ratios are the exponents of the estimates presented in Herrnstein and Murray (1994: 597). The socioeconomic status measure comprises father's and mother's education, parental occupational status and family income.
13 These figures are calculated from the exponents of the (negative of) coefficients for "HS drop out" (from Korenman and Winship 2000: Table 7.2, 147).
14 These percentages were calculated from the effects of quantitative and verbal scores per one unit increase 0.6 and 0.9 (the estimates of 0.006 and 0.009 multiplied by 100), and multiplied by the respective standard deviations, 7.83 and 8.62 (from Bratti 2007: 26, 35).
15 Hobcraft (2001: 27) analyses of not having obtained any O levels show that compared to the highest ability category (two or three scores in highest quartile in several tests) the odds ratios was 13 for the next ability group (fewer than two high quartile measures), 31 for the third ability group (any low quartile measure) and a very large 52 for the lowest ability group (two or three low quartile measures). He notes that "The most striking set of associations in Table 8 are clearly for test scores: the association with low qualification levels in adulthood is extraordinarily strong" (2001: 16).
16 The odds ratio obtained from taking the exponent of the logistic coefficient of 0.82 in Table 5 (from Fergusson *et al.* 2005: 82).
17 Age at leaving school will have a weaker relationship with ability than years of education, since the measure does not include university study and includes older students in the same grade level.
18 Odds ratios calculated from the coefficients presented by Korenman and Winship (2000: 147).
19 Calculated from the coefficients of 0.530 and 0.416 in Model 2 in Table 2 and the standard deviation (191.252) presented in appendix B (from Mullen *et al.* 2003: 152, 165).
20 Sewell and Hauser (1975: 102) comment "Clearly, the effect of measured ability on schooling is not merely a reflection of an individual's socioeconomic status, the assumptions of some social scientists to the contrary notwithstanding".
21 The correlations for class background and highest qualification were also lower: 0.35 for men and 0.33 for women for the 1958 cohort, and 0.32 and 0.29 for the 1970 cohort (Schoon 2008: 77). By contrast, for the 1946 birth cohort, the correlation was 0.42 for father's occupation and highest qualification (Richards and Sacker 2003: 617).
22 There are also issues in comparing coefficients with different outcome variables across different populations: "outcome incommensurability" and "population incommensurability" (Xie 2011).

23 The authors (Holm and Jæger 2011: 315, 319) report the effects for father's and mother's years of education and the standard deviations allowing calculation of the comparable odds ratios for a one standard deviation increase in father's and mother's education. They are 1.14 and 1.09, respectively.

Chapter 6

Cognitive ability III

Labor market outcomes

There is little argument that one of the major controversies in social science is the importance of cognitive ability for labor market outcomes. The most prominent, and controversial, position is that cognitive ability is very important. This position is exemplified by Eysenck (1979: 85), who claimed that intelligence "determines a person's socio-economic status to a considerable extent, through this, it determines his general earning capacity and position in society". Similarly, Gottfredson (1997a: 14) makes the similarly strong contention that: "IQ is strongly related, probably more so, than any other single measurable human trait, to many important educational, occupational, economic and other social outcomes". Sternberg *et al.* (2001: 29) are more measured, "IQ is a relatively good predictor of many kinds of childhood and adult outcomes". Although outside the scope of this book, there is evidence that intelligence is important not just for educational and labor market outcomes, but also for a range of social outcomes, such as single motherhood, poverty, divorce, welfare dependency and crime (Fergusson *et al.* 2005; Herrnstein and Murray 1994: 127–253; Jensen 1998: 294–301; Korenman and Winship 2000).

The aim of this chapter is to demonstrate that cognitive ability is relevant to a variety of labor market outcomes. Labor market outcomes include participation in the labor market, hours worked per week, weeks worked per year, unemployment, exiting unemployment, occupational class, occupational status, and earnings. Owing to its strong relationship with education, ability has moderately strong associations with labor market outcomes, but its effects are mainly indirectly mediated by education. Cognitive ability also has smaller direct effects on labor market outcomes, net of educational attainment, and less importantly, socioeconomic background. This chapter documents the direct and indirect associations between cognitive ability and labor market outcomes. The last section discusses the role of non-cognitive attributes, some of which also influence labor market outcomes, but generally have weaker effects than cognitive ability.

Theoretical issues

Cognitive ability is important to the modernization thesis. This thesis contends that developed societies are becoming more meritocratic, since, in a meritocracy, access to privileged and important social positions are based on ability rather than socioeconomic background. Strong effects of cognitive ability for labor market outcomes – consistently and substantially stronger than that of ascribed attributes – would be evidence in support of modernization theory.

For labor force outcomes, modernization theory would imply that ability has overall become more important. This theory predicts that ability and competence will increasingly govern access to important social positions, not social background. The logic of industrialization means that private organizations competing for profits will employ and reward the most productive workers. More productive workers are thus more likely to gain higher status and higher earnings. There is evidence that cognitive ability is associated with job performance (see Gottfredson 1997a, 1997b; Jensen 1998: 282–92; Kingston 2006; Schmidt and Hunter 2004). In the professions, the most lucrative professions often select applicants at the very highest performance levels. In the state sector, where employment and promotion has long (purportedly) been based on bureaucratic and objective criteria, the pool of applicants from an increased range of social backgrounds means that cognitive ability becomes more important than when applicants came from a limited social pool. However, organizations almost never assess their employees' cognitive ability and allocate rewards accordingly. As Goldthorpe (1996b: 281) points out, "Markets do not reward merit but simply according to the value of goods and services offered".

Ability becomes more important for labor market outcomes for two reasons. First, many employing organizations recruit employees on academic criteria, since it is an efficient way of distinguishing potential employees from a large number of applicants. Applicants who performed at the highest level in gaining their qualification were likely to be looked on more favorably than other applicants. Educational expansion, together with the decline in unskilled manual work, means that educational qualifications are important to entry to an increasing proportion of occupations. Second, employing organizations promote and reward employees on criteria relating to cognitive ability, such as ability to reason, plan, solve problems, and comprehend complex ideas: skills often useful in modern workplaces.

The importance of cognitive ability for labor market outcomes is often dismissed or viewed as minimal. Bowles and Nelson (1974: 44) conclude, "the effect of socioeconomic background on each of the three adult status variables – schooling, income, and occupational status – is greater than the effect of childhood IQ". Nearly 30 years later, Bowles and Gintis (2002a: 12) claimed that "IQ is just not an important enough determinant of economic success".

Empirical evidence

Higher ability is associated with better labor market outcomes: higher levels of participation in the labor market, less unemployment, higher occupational class and status, and increased earnings. The following discussions focus on the associations between measures of ability and a variety of labor market outcomes.

Labor force status

For the US, Kirsh *et al.* (1993: 63) used the 1992 national adult literacy study to compare labor market participation rates across five levels of literacy. The differences were large. Of the group with the highest (prose) literacy skills only 11 percent were not in the labor force, compared with 52 percent in the lowest literacy skill group. Over 70 percent in the highest literacy skill group were employed full-time compared to 30 percent in the lowest skill group. Similarly, unemployment showed a strong association with literacy skills. The unemployment rate among the group with the highest skill levels was three percent compared with eight and ten percent in the two lowest cognitive skill groups. Rivera-Batiz (1992) found that higher scores in quantitative literacy – arithmetic skills for practical problems encountered every day – substantially increased the probability of full-time employment, net of education and social background.

Analyzing Australian data from IALS, Miller and Chiswick (1997: 74) concluded that literacy and numeracy skills were "inextricably linked to labor market outcomes". Labor force participation rates declined substantially from around 90 percent in the highest literacy group (varying slightly with the literacy measure used) to 60 percent in the lowest (fourth) literacy group. As in the US, there was also a strong effect of literacy skills for unemployment. For the highest literacy skill group on the prose scale, unemployment rates were around three to four percent, rising to about 20 percent for the lowest skill group. In a second study, about 94 percent of adults at the highest level (level 5) in quantitative literacy were in the labor force, compared to 46 percent of those at the lowest level. Similarly, the unemployment rate (defined only among those in the labor force) was 1.6 percent among adults at the highest level (level 5) compared with over 18 percent for adults at level 1 (Lee and Miller 2000: 54).

In countries participating in IALS, there were large differences by literacy level for labor force participation. About 30 to 40 percent of adults aged 25 to 65 with low literacy levels (below level 2) were not participating in the labor force compared with 10–20 percent of adults with higher literacy levels (Table 6.1). The differences were particularly large in Australia, Ireland, the Netherlands, and the UK, but sizable in all the countries examined. Even larger differences are found for unemployment. Unemployment rates for the low literacy group were about twice that for the higher literacy groups.

Table 6.1 Labor force participation, unemployment and adult literacy

Literacy	Not in the labor force		Unemployment	
	Low (level 1 or 2) (%)	High (level 3, 4/5) (%)	Low (level 1 or 2) (%)	High (level 3, 4/5) (%)
Australia	36.0	14.3	11.3	4.8
Belgium (Flanders)	39.9	17.2	20.3	6.6
Canada	32.8	18.4	17.7	6.6
Chile	36.0	15.9	14.5	7.2x
Czech Republic	29.5	20.0	8.3	5.1
Denmark	30.5	15.4	11.5	5.4
Finland	30.7	14.6	19.1	10.0
Germany	43.3	28.7	16.1	8.6
Hungary	41.8	22.0	18.2	11.4
Ireland	46.4	24.7	24.2	10.4
Netherlands	48.3	22.5	10.3	5.1
New Zealand	31.3	16.5	15.0	4.1
Norway	27.7	12.3	5.8	3.0
Poland	35.1	18.5	17.3	12.1
Portugal	29.1	14.1	16.0	8.8
Slovenia	30.6	10.4	14.6	7.8
Sweden	27.8	14.3	11.2	7.5
Switzerland	24.5	18.0	5.4	3.1
UK	32.3	13.5	17.0	8.0
US	27.2	15.7	7.4	3.3

Sources: IALS; for not in the labor force (OECD and HRDC 1997: Table 2.6C, 163); for unemployment (OECD and Statistics Canada 2000: 151, quantitative scale)

Within countries, literacy level is also strongly associated with labor market participation and number of weeks worked (OECD and HRDC 1997: 47–8, 162–3).

Similar findings are found for the later ALLS study. In the US, Canada and Italy, the odds of being unemployed for six months or more in a given year, rather than employed all year, for adults with low literacy (levels 1 and 2) were about twice that of the comparable odds for adults with higher literacy levels 3 to 5 (OECD 2005: 114). Adults with higher literacy levels are also more likely to exit from unemployment (OECD 2005: 115).

Findings from adult literacy studies may be challenged, since literacy and labor force outcomes were measured at the same time. It is possible that unemployment and non-participation in the labor force reduces literacy: "the use it or lose it" adage. This criticism cannot be directed at longitudinal studies, in which the respondents are recruited during adolescence, with tests of literacy (and numeracy) typically administered well before respondents enter the labor force. In Australia, achievement in literacy and numeracy at age 14 has strong positive effects for employment at age 19. Using data from four LSAY cohorts, Marks and Fleming (1998: 9) found that, for respondents in their 20s, unemployment rates were two to three times higher in the group with the lowest test scores compared with the group with the highest test scores. Furthermore, higher test scores substantially shortens the duration of unemployment, net of educational qualifications, and other influences including prior unemployment (1998: 21–8, 43–4). Analyzing the New Zealand Christchurch Health and Development Study, Fergusson *et al.* (2005: 855) reported that, among 18–25-year-olds with an IQ score above 115, the mean duration of unemployment was 4.5 months compared with 9.3 months for those with IQ scores below 85. The relationship between IQ and unemployment is still evident, net of measures of childhood social and family disadvantage, individual characteristics and behavior. The Dunedin Cohort Study showed that low IQ scores significantly increased the risk of unemployment, net of socioeconomic background and other influences (Caspi *et al.* 1998).

Occupational group and social class

There is an association between intelligence and occupational class. Eysenck (1979: 71) reported an IQ difference of 15 points between the working and middle classes. Analyzing US data from the 1992 national literacy study, Kirsh *et al.* (1993: 67) report that, of adults with the highest levels of adult literacy in prose, 70 percent were in the highest occupational group (professional, managerial and technical) compared with just two percent working as laborers, assemblers or farmers. For adults at the lowest literacy level (level 1), only five percent were in the highest occupational group and 80 percent were working in service, craft, laboring, assembler, or farm occupations.

The pattern of higher mean scores for managerial and especially professional workers and lower mean scores for manual occupations is found for other countries participating in IALS (Table 6.2). Associate professionals and managers tend to have the next highest mean scores followed by clerical and sales workers. For these data, there is a strong tendency for the average literacy scores for other occupational groups to correspond with occupational status.

There are surprisingly strong relationships between ability measured at a young age and social class 30 or so years later. In this literature, class is usually analyzed as an ordinal variable ranging from unskilled laboring to higher professional and managerial work.[1] According to the 1921 Scottish Mental Survey birth cohort study, the correlation between IQ measured at age 11 and mid-life social class was 0.52 (Deary *et al.* 2005b: 464). In the 1936 Lothian birth cohort study, the correlation between IQ measured at age 11 and class destination was 0.38 (Johnson *et al.* 2010a: 275). In the 1946 birth cohort study, the correlation between cognitive ability at age eight and occupation group at age 43 was 0.41 (Richards and Sacker 2003: 617). When the NCDS 1958 cohort was 33 years of age, the correlation between ability and class destination, 22 years after taking the test, was 0.37

Table 6.2 Mean score in quantitative literacy by occupational group

Country	*Legislators, senior officials and managers*		*Professionals*		*Technicians and associate professionals*		*Clerks*		*Service, shop and market sales workers*		*Skilled agricultural and fishery workers*		*Craft and related trades workers*		*Plant/machine operators and assemblers*		*Elementary occupations*	
	Avg. score	*Row (%)*	*Avg. score*	*Row (%)*	*Avg. score*	*Row (%)*	*Avg. score*	*Row (%)*	*Avg. score*	*Row (%)*	*Avg. score*	*Row (%)*	*Avg. score*	*Row (%)*	*Avg. score*	*Row (%)*	*Avg. score*	*Row (%)*
Australia	299	8	323	14	296	9	296	18	279	15	272	3	272	10	252	10	256	12
Belgium (Flanders)	303	9	–	–	306	5	303	18	299	39	–	3	269	26	–	–	–	–
Canada	306	8	327	17	318	11	291	15	281	16	273	3	257	11	256	12	272	8
Chile	249	3	282	6	268	6	251	11	218	18	178	7	215	15	215	11	191	23
Czech Republic	299	9	316	10	301	20	290	6	275	10	–	2	277	21	270	15	263	8
Denmark	307	10	322	6	309	21	299	10	287	19	281	3	278	10	280	9	274	12
Finland	308	9	320	18	301	16	304	10	290	13	259	5	278	13	282	7	279	9
Germany	304	5	316	13	303	15	288	18	285	14	–	2	285	19	266	7	265	6
Great Britain	298	13	314	15	295	7	284	17	275	16	–	1	262	13	255	7	240	11
Hungary	–	3	294	10	281	20	269	5	261	16	–	2	255	24	251	6	231	12
Ireland	297	6	308	13	292	9	293	13	273	14	244	9	266	14	258	9	241	11
Italy	277	4	288	8	281	17	276	16	242	17	232	6	228	13	236	6	226	13
Netherlands	295	12	314	15	306	22	294	11	288	12	–	2	278	10	276	6	272	8
New Zealand	301	11	314	11	302	10	289	14	276	17	266	9	270	9	257	13	247	6
Northern Ireland	286	12	308	13	294	7	295	16	271	20	–	1	263	14	256	7	243	10
Norway (Bokmal)	310	12	321	10	316	18	307	9	289	20	279	5	292	9	281	8	267	7
Poland	279	4	281	8	264	14	252	6	247	11	200	14	229	22	219	11	205	10
Portugal	229	10	308	5	279	10	268	11	212	16	–	6	202	17	–	10	179	15
Slovenia	275	6	288	9	278	13	263	12	252	14	181	6	219	12	219	22	206	5
Sweden	322	4	322	26	314	22	311	6	302	14	297	3	295	13	299	7	284	4
Switzerland	287	8	303	13	293	22	289	12	267	13	253	3	260	14	245	5	244	10
US	307	15	322	16	316	4	288	17	267	25	–	2	249	10	244	13	–	–

Note: Author's analysis from IALS database from Statistics Canada (www.statcan.gc.ca/pub/89-588-x/4067697-eng.htm). Scores range from 0 to 500.

compared with a correlation of 0.24 between ability and class of origin (Saunders 1996: 50). At 42 or 43 years old, the correlation was slightly higher at around 0.4 (Nettle 2003: 557; Thienpont and Verleye 2004: 337). Schoon (2008: 77) presents correlations between cognitive ability and current social class (registrar general's) among men at around 0.35 in the 1958 NCDS and the 1970 BCS, and for women, at 0.45 and 0.38. A Swedish study of 30,000 men reported a correlation of 0.47 between attained social class (a five-level hierarchy) at mid-life and intelligence measured when the respondents were army conscripts (Sorjonen *et al.* 2011: 279). These correlations are substantially stronger than the correlations between father's occupational class and ability measured during childhood or adolescence, or between class of origin and class of destination (see section on "Socioeconomic background" in Chapter 4, page 58 and section on "The impact of socioeconomic background on occupational attainment", page 201).

Occupational mobility

Lipset and Bendix (1959) devote a whole, largely ignored, chapter to the roles of intelligence and motivation for occupational mobility. After reviewing a number of small scale studies in different countries they emphasize the importance of ability:

> There can be no doubt ... that the discrepancy between the distribution of intelligence in a given generation of youth and the distribution of social positions in the parental generation is a major dynamic factor affecting mobility in all societies in which educational achievement or other qualities associated with intelligence play an important role in status placement.
>
> (Lipset and Bendix 1959: 236)

Later, Eckland (1967) criticizes the common procedure of mobility researchers to compare the observed mobility pattern with that of perfect mobility, where there is no association between parents and their children's occupational classes. It assumes that ability is randomly assigned at birth and there are no class differences in cognitive ability. He argues this is an untenable research strategy, since it assumes that there is no more biological resemblance between a parent and a child than between the child and a complete stranger (1967: 189). Swift (2004) makes a similar point that some of the mechanisms that produce an association between the social position of parents and their children are largely unobjectable and would exist in a just society.

Lipset and Bendix (1959: 234) report on a mobility study conducted in Stockholm, where 80 percent of young men from working class origins with IQ scores of 119 or more had moved upward from the social class position of their fathers. Of those from upper class backgrounds with IQs of 118 or lower, only 16 percent remained in the upper class. They (1959: 254) conclude that differences between the social status of the parental generation and the intelligence of their offspring strongly contributes to the dynamics of occupational mobility. Saunders (1996: 59) found larger differences in mean ability scores in the destination classes (15 score points) compared with the origin classes (10 score points). Even as long ago as the 1940s, high ability was associated with upward social mobility. Johnson *et al.* (2010a: 273) report a mean IQ score of 110 for men mobile from the class of partly skilled or unskilled manual workers to the professional group, compared with a mean score of 97 for the immobile group. There was a general pattern of upward mobility being associated with progressively higher mean IQ scores and downward mobility associated with progressively lower mean IQ scores.

In response to Saunders's analyses of the Hope-Goldthorpe measure of occupational status, Breen and Goldthorpe (1999, 2001) analyzed the role of ability for occupational mobility employing log-linear modeling. They concluded that ability has only a modest impact on class destination. The log odds of the parameters specifying the pattern of associations between origin and destination classes did not decline to statistical insignificance when controlling for ability and motivation. Their conclusion of strong effects for class of origin and weak effects of ability are due to the methodological approach, which analyses the cell counts (the number of survey respondents) in a cross-tabulation of class of destination by class of origin. The cell counts are modeled by a levels model which assigns a particular pattern of relative mobility chances. This is a quite a different type of analysis to that used in regression-type analyses. If the cross-tabulation analyzed was class of destination by ability quintile (at age 11), or that matter educational level, then the addition of class of origin would have little impact.

Controlling for social background and education

Education is the major influence for labor market outcomes. However, ability influences occupational class, when controlling for education. This means that the effects of ability cannot be dismissed as simply attributable to education. Analysis of data from a Scottish birth cohort found that a one standard deviation increase in childhood IQ increased the probability of upward social mobility 33 percent, net of years of education, and significantly reduced the chances of downward mobility (Deary *et al.* 2005b). In a structural equation analysis of the 1921 Scottish Mental Survey birth cohort, Johnson *et al.* (2010b: 60–1) found a surprisingly large effect of ability measured at age 11 ($\beta = 0.38$) on occupational class, net of educational attainment, although the impact of educational attainment was stronger ($\beta = 0.44$). Analyzing the 1958 NCDS on being in a semi-skilled or unskilled manual occupation, Hobcraft (2001: 27) reported strong (negative) effects for test scores, net of class of origin, parental income, father's school leaving age and many other controls (not including education). In the presence of test scores, there were no significant effects for father's school leaving age and few significant effects of father's income and class. He comments that "associations of earnings or income and of occupational class with these test scores is also very strong indeed" (2001: 16). Analyzing a six-category measure of occupational class (unskilled, partly skilled, skilled manual, skilled non-manual, managerial and professional) at age 30 in the 1970 BCS by structural equation modeling, von Stumm *et al.* (2009: 336–7) reported path coefficients of 0.33, 0.18 and 0.13 for educational attainment, intelligence and parental social class, net of a variety of childhood behavioral and psychological measures. Jackson (2006: 193) reports significant effects of cognitive ability on class destination, net of qualifications, two personality measures and father's occupational class. A one standard deviation increase in cognitive ability increases the odds of entry to the service class rather than the working class about 1.9 times, net of the other predictors. This compares with an odds ratio of 2.6 for a one standard deviation difference in the measure of educational qualifications employed.

Occupational status

The correlation between IQ and occupational status – where occupations are assigned scores based on their status or prestige – is slightly less than that for educational attainment: between 0.4 and 0.5. In a study of US cohorts born between 1930 and 1943, the correlation of IQ measured at age seven or eight with job status was around 0.5 (McCall 1977). Duncan *et al.* (1972: 89) present a correlation of 0.43 between intelligence and first job. Eysenck (1979: 71) settles on a correlation of 0.5. Based on US studies up until that time, Jencks *et al.* (1972: 322) offer a summary correlation of 0.46 between test scores and occupational status. After correcting for measurement error, they arrive at a correlation of 0.50. Analyzing four longitudinal studies, the bivariate standardized regression coefficients associated with adolescent test scores on occupational status were between 0.35 and 0.48 (Jencks *et al.* 1979: 111). The correlation between ability and occupational status in the WLS was between 0.39 and 0.44 (Hauser 2000: 37–8).[2] After correction for measurement error, the correlations rise marginally to between 0.43 and 0.48. A simple ten-item vocabulary test from the General Social Survey (GSS) correlated at 0.40 with occupational prestige (Weakliem *et al.* 1995: 274). McCall (1977) reports correlations of between 0.4 and 0.6 between IQ measured during childhood and job status. Consistently, correlations of between 0.50 and 0.55 were reported by Hauser *et al.* (2000: 206–7) for non-black male cohorts born between 1961 and 1964 and their occupational status between 1989 and 1993. A more recent estimate of the correlation between ability and occupational status is 0.47 from the NLSY using occupational status scores averaged over a 28-year time span and ability measured in 1979. This compares with a correlation of 0.35 for socio-economic background (Judge *et al.* 2010: 97). Strenze's (2007) meta-analysis of 21 "best" studies reported the correlation between ability and occupational status at around 0.45. Jensen (1998: 292–4) computes a true score correlation of 0.7 (correcting for measurement error) between *g* and occupational status. He also maintains that the correlation increases with age and the higher the occupational status, the less variation in IQ scores. High IQ individuals are found in virtually every occupation but the lowest IQ within an occupational group rises with occupational status.

Net of social background

For occupational status, the effect of test scores can only be partially accounted for by socioeconomic or family background. Analyzing data from three studies, Jencks *et al.* (1983: 8) report standardized effects of academic aptitude on occupational attainment between 0.26 and 0.39 compared with much weaker effects for father's occupation and education, mother's education and family income.[3] According to Jencks *et al.* (1979: 110–12), socioeconomic background reduces the effect of adolescent test scores for adult occupational status by between 12 and 25 percent. Using sibling data – where siblings are a proxy for all the things that siblings have in common – the effect of test score is reduced by up to 40 percent. They conclude that "almost two-thirds of the test-score effect arises from causes independent of family background" (1979: 112).

For the UK, Saunders (1997: 274) analyzing the Hope-Goldthorpe measure of occupational status at age 33 in the 1958 NCDS, concluded that ability has a far larger impact than socioeconomic background. The standardized coefficient for ability was 0.25 compared with 0.06, 0.05 and 0.08 for mother's and father's education and parental class.[4] Analyzing the socio-economic status of students' expected occupation at age 30, Marks (2010a) found that the effects of PISA test scores were substantially stronger than that of a comprehensive composite measure of socioeconomic background in all but three of the 30 countries examined. In most countries, the effect of test scores was two to three times larger. Furthermore, the relative effect of test scores tended to be stronger in wealthier countries – countries with higher per capita gross domestic product – suggesting that students' occupational aspirations will be increasingly influenced by ability as countries become wealthier. This finding is consistent with modernization theory.

Net of education

The main reason why ability influences occupational status is because it influences education, which in turn influences occupational attainment: an indirect effect. One unambiguous conclusion from the Blau–Duncaninspired occupational attainment tradition is that educational attainment is a strong predictor of occupational status. However, early studies analyzing occupational status suggest that the residual effect of test scores, net of education, is noteworthy. This suggests that, among people with similar educational attainment, those with higher ability tend to be working in jobs with higher occupational status. This residual effect is not large. Duncan *et al.* (1972: 102) estimate that the direct effect of intelligence for occupational status is 0.08, while the indirect effect mediated through education is twice as large. Analyses of occupational status using the 1992 US adult literacy study produced standardized effects of 0.17 for cognitive skill and 0.56 for education among white men and comparable effects of 0.16 and 0.58 among white women (Kerckhoff *et al.* 2001: 17). For occupational attainment, Jencks *et al.* (1979: 112) conclude that over 60 percent of the influence of test scores on occupational attainment is due to educational attainment: in other words, higher-ability people get more schooling. That leaves 40 percent independent of schooling. Judge *et al.*'s (2010) analysis of occupational attainment in the 1979 NLSY found significant effects of general ability, net of education, and positive interaction effects between educational level and ability. The higher the educational level attained, the stronger the impact of ability on occupational status.

For the UK, in Saunders's (1997: 275) analysis of occupational prestige, the standardized effect of ability was 0.13, net of qualifications, examination scores, first job, and other predictors. In contrast, the effect for parental class was only half as large (0.06) and the effects for father's and mother's education were not statistically significant. In a later study using structural equation modeling, Bond and Saunders (1999) found that three measures of ability accounted for 17 percent of the variation in occupational status, net of other influences. This compares with three percent for class background and five percent for ambition. The total (standardized) effect for ability (direct and indirectly through other influences including qualifications) was around 0.41 and was greater than that for qualifications. The effects for social background variables were "surprisingly modest" (1999: 243). Connelly's (2012: 111) more recent path analysis of the NCDS and BCS reports standardized effects for childhood ability of 0.21 and 0.16, respectively, on occupational attainment (a measure based on social interactions), net of father's class (β = 0.12 and β = 0.15), father's education (β = 0.04) and educational attainment (β = 0.37 and β = 0.42). The total effects of cognitive ability both direct and indirect (mediated through education) were sizable, 0.34 and 0.32, respectively. Using structural equation modeling on data from the 1921 Scottish cohort, Deary *et al.* (2005b) found a direct effect of ability measured at age 11 (β = 0.43) for mid-life status (indicated by social class, deprivation and car ownership) net of the effects of education and father's class (β = 0.22). (An assessment of the effect of education is difficult, since the published model included first occupation.) Von Stumm *et al.*

(2010: 208), analyzing data from the 1950–1956 Aberdeen birth cohort study, indexed mid-life status slightly differently by occupational status, income per annum, housing tenure, and car ownership. Class status at origin was also indexed by several variables. They found similar effects for educational attainment (β = 0.32) and mental ability (β = 0.29) for mid-life status and a weaker effect of origin status (β = 0.20). For mid-life status, the total effects of ability and social class (including indirect effects via education) were 0.44 and 0.27, respectively (2010: 208–9). They conclude that "educational and social status attainments were influenced to a considerably greater extent by childhood intelligence than by social class of origin" (2010: 202).

The effects of ability for occupational status persist over the life course. The impact of ability on occupational status is fairly stable across the life course, whereas the impact of educational attainment declines. Hauser *et al.* (2000: 209) note that these findings suggest that there is something more to ability than "its validation through schooling". Multivariate analysis of sibling data from the WLS also suggest that, while the impact of education for occupational standing decreases over the life course, there are smaller but constant effects of adolescent ability: up to 37 years after ability was measured.[5] Throughout the occupational career, a ten-point increase in test score was associated with a 0.08 increase in occupational-education and a 0.11 increase in occupational-income.[6] Because the analyses are based on differences between siblings, these effects are net of all (stable) family background factors. The authors conclude "there *are* positive, direct effects of cognitive ability on occupational standing throughout the life course" although these effects are small (Warren *et al.* 2002: 450). It should be noted that the effects of ability (and education) are within-family effects, so their effects are net of sibling similarities in ability and education.

Earnings, income and wealth

The correlation between ability and earnings is around 0.35, although there is considerable variability in the estimates, depending on the age of the sample, the reliability of the test and various other factors. Based on reanalyzing data from a study of veterans, Jencks *et al.* (1972: 322, 328, 337) approximate a raw correlation of 0.31 between armed services test score and annual earnings, 0.35 after correcting for measurement error. Olneck (1977: 131) reports a correlation of 0.36 between test scores (measured in grade six) and adult earnings. This compares with correlations of 0.17 and 0.21 with earnings for father's occupation and father's education. Analyzing sibling data from the 1979 NLSY, Rowe *et al.* (1999b: 419) estimated a correlation of 0.34 between IQ and income. For NLSY respondents in 2007, the correlation between adolescent ability and income was around 0.30, but only 0.16 for wealth (Zagorsky 2007: 493).[7] A more recent estimate of the correlation between ability and earnings (averaged over a 28-year time span) is 0.38 from the NLSY. This compares with a correlation of 0.28 for a composite measure of socioeconomic background (Judge *et al.* 2010: 97). The estimates from meta-analyses comprising predominately US studies tend to be lower, ranging from 0.20 to 0.27 (Ng *et al.* 2005: 384; Strenze 2007: 412). The lower correlations probably reflect the inclusion of studies with less reliable measures, younger respondents and/or more homogenous samples.

Similar relationships between ability and earnings have been found in other countries. For Britain, according to the Aberdeen Mental Health Study, the correlation between score in reading and mathematics tests at around age 11 and earnings at mid-life (ages 46–51) was between 0.25 and 0.29. This compares with correlations of around 0.12 for father's and mother's occupational class and lower correlations for the number of rooms and housing tenure during childhood (von Stumm *et al.* 2010: 207). Analyzing data from the 1946 Birth Cohort study, Irwing and Lynn (2006) estimated the correlation between IQ measured at age eight and income at age 43 was 0.37 for men and 0.32 for women. In the city of Malmö, Sweden, the correlation between ability and earnings at age 43 was around 0.40 (calculated by Jencks *et al.* 1979: 117). Strenze's (2007: 415) meta-analysis concluded that the magnitude of the correlations between ability and earnings was no higher in the US than in other countries.

Another approach to understanding the impact of ability on earnings is to focus on the predicted percentage increase in earnings for a one standard deviation difference in test scores. Analyzing the 1972 longitudinal survey, Murnane *et al.* (2000: 556) report that among 31-year-old males, a one-point difference in mathematics test score was associated with a 0.02 difference in logged earnings. This converts to a percentage increase of 15 percent for a standard deviation difference in test scores. For women, the estimate was smaller (0.013), an effect of nine percent.

The relationship between ability and earnings increases with age. Analyzing a variety of studies, Jencks *et al.* (1979: 117) conclude that the correlation increases up to about age 35 and then stabilizes. Farber and Gibbons (1996) conclude that ability effects on wages increase with experience. Zax and Rees (2002: 606, 609), analyzing the WLS, estimated that, a one standard deviation difference in ability measured at age 26 increased earnings by 11 percent but by 21 percent at age 53.[8] Strenze's (2007: 413) meta-analysis suggests that the correlation increases from zero during the early 20s, peaks around the late 30s and thereafter declines. Judge *et al.* (2010) found that, over the occupational career, the earnings of individuals with high levels of general mental ability increased far more rapidly than for other individuals.

Net of social background

Little of the correlation between ability and earnings can be attributed to socioeconomic background. This is in part because socioeconomic background itself is only weakly correlated with earnings.[9] After discussing the findings from studies based on either adolescent or adult test scores, Jencks *et al.* (1979: 119) report standardized effects of around 0.26 for ability predicting earnings, net of home background factors. Korenman and Winship (2000: 153), analyzing the 1979 NLSY, estimated that a one standard deviation change in AFQT score translates to an earnings difference of US$4,866 net of socioeconomic background; equivalent to a standardized coefficient of about 0.30. This compares with an effect of US$1,531 ($\beta$ = 0.10) for a composite measure of socioeconomic background. Currie and Thomas (2001), analyzing the British 1958 NCDS, found that, net of parents' education and occupation, a one standard deviation difference in test scores at age 16 was associated with between 11 and 14 percent higher wages at age 33 among those from low and middle socioeconomic backgrounds. Zax and Rees (2002: 605) found that, when controlling for household income, parental education, parental white-collar occupation, absence of one or more biological parent and the number of siblings, the effect of a one standard deviation difference in test score in predicting earnings at age 35 declined from 11.2 percent to 8.6 percent.[10] The authors argue that the effects of ability are overestimated without controls for the child's and parental aspirations, a result they highlight. However, as noted in the previous chapter, aspirations are clearly and often strongly associated with ability.

Put in another way, the effect of ability on earnings can only be partially attributed to socioeconomic background. Sewell and Hauser (1975: 108–9) calculate that only 16 percent of the low correlation (0.16) between ability and the earnings of WLS high-school graduates ten years after graduation could be attributed to social background factors. Jencks *et al.* (1979: 118) conclude that, when controlling for social background factors, such as father's occupation, parental education, income and other factors, the effect of test score in predicting earnings decreases by between 11 and 27 percent. Even taking into account total family effects using sibling data, substantial effects of ability remained. They conclude that the effect of test score "appears to be substantively important" net of family background (1979: 119).[11] Comparison of the coefficients for ability in the Zax and Rees (2002: Table 2) study indicates that about three-quarters of the effect of ability is independent of the suite of family background factors incorporated in their study.

Net of education

The effects of ability on earnings *net of educational attainment* are generally much weaker than its effects, net of socioeconomic background. This is mostly because of the sizable correlations between cognitive ability and educational attainment and the importance of education for earnings. However, it is remarkable that cognitive ability still influences earnings even when taking into account educational qualifications. Analyzing log earnings in the PSID, the standardized coefficient for IQ was 0.14, net of education and other factors (Kiker and Condon 1981).[12] In Korenman and Winship's (2000: 147) analysis of the 1979 NLSY, including educational attainment reduced the impact of ability for earnings from US$4,866 to US$3,040 (β = 0.19). Using fixed-effects models with sibling data, the effect for AFQT score was actually larger than in standard analyses suggesting that sibling differences in ability are important for earnings (2000: 147, 149–50). Making adjustments for measurement error in a model of annual earnings that includes both a suite of social background variables and educational attainment reduces the impact of a standard deviation difference in AFQT score to US$2,842: still a non-trivial beta of 0.18 (2000: 153).[13] A meta-analysis of the impact of cognitive ability and education on earnings estimated a standardized coefficient of 0.15 for ability and 0.22 for education. The net impact of a standard deviation difference in ability on earnings (about nine percent) was about the same as an extra year of education (Bowles *et al.* 2001: 1154). Analysis of earnings in the 1992 US adult literacy study produced standardized effects of 0.16 for cognitive skill and 0.29 for educational attainment among white men and 0.17 and 0.31 among white women (Kerckhoff *et al.* 2001: 17). Mulligan (1999: S212–13), analyzing the hourly earnings of 1979 NLSY respondents in 1990 and 1991, found that a one standard deviation difference in test score was associated with an 11 percent difference in earnings, net of several educational measures – years of education, private school attendance, college preparatory track participation – and several contextual influences. Zagorsky (2007: 489) concludes that "each point increase in IQ test scores raises income by between US$234 and US$616 per year after holding a variety of factors constant", equivalent to a standardized effect of between 0.07 and 0.19. Judge *et al.* (2010: 103), analyzing the 1979 NLSY, found steeper increases in earnings for high-ability individuals over the occupational career compared to low-ability individuals with the same education: the difference was about US$23,000 per annum (in 2008 dollars). Over the long time-periods of labor force careers, this amounts to a considerable difference in lifetime earnings.

Although much of the impact of cognitive ability on earnings is mediated by education, more than half of its influence is a direct effect, independent of educational attainment. Jencks *et al.* (1979: 119) conclude that the fact that academic ability influences educational attainment accounts for between 36 percent and 47 percent of the effect of ability on earnings. According to Korenman and Winship's (2000: 147, 153) analyses of annual earnings, the impact of ability (net of socioeconomic background) declines by between 35 percent and 45 percent with the addition of educational attainment. Murnane *et al.* (2000: 558) conclude that, for males graduating from school in 1972, about one-third of the impact of ability on earnings at age 33 is mediated through education, and two-thirds is a direct effect; that is, differences in earnings for individuals with the same educational level but with different ability scores.

Net of experience and education

According to the 1994–1995 IALS, there are substantial effects of ability for earnings net of gender, parent's education, educational attainment and employment experience across industrialized nations. Table 6.3 presents the standardized effects. Only in Poland were the effects of literacy of no consequence. Typically, the effects of literacy were substantial, although generally less than the effects of educational attainment. It is noteworthy that, in all countries except Portugal, parent's education has very small (often negative) net effects for earnings. In a multi-country study using IALS data, the effects for a one standard deviation difference in literacy skills, net of education and experience were surprisingly large: ranging between five percent for Germany, Norway, Hungary and Sweden, and 20 percent in the US (Denny *et al.* 2004). In analyses of earnings in 19 countries using IALS data, van de Werfhorst (2011: 1083) found that a one standard deviation increase in cognitive ability as measured by adult literacy score is associated with a six percent increase in earnings, net of age (a proxy for experience) and educational level.

Changes over time

There is evidence, at least in the US context, that for earnings, ability has become a stronger influence. Comparing the earnings of 24-year-olds in two longitudinal studies, larger effects for basic cognitive skills were reported, net of family background, education and experience, on earnings for the 1982 HS&B cohort than for the older NSL72 (Murnane *et al.* 1995: 258–9). Similarly, Grogger and Eide (1995: 292–4) found that the increase in the wage premium for a college degree among women could partially be attributed to increases in the returns to ability. In 1978, a one standard deviation increase in mathematics ability increased wages by about two percent. By 1987, this effect had grown to five percent for men and 7.5 percent for women (1995: 292). The returns to ability for men also increased but could be attributed to men's preference for college courses associated with higher-paying occupations. A later analysis by Murnane *et al.* (2000: 556–7) comparing the returns to ability at around age 30 (31 percent for the NLS72, 27 percent for the HS&B) was not so clear cut. For men, the percentage effect was actually larger in the older NLS72 cohort (14.7 percent compared with 11.1 percent). For women, there was a marginal increase from 9.4 percent to 11.8 percent. The authors were able to conclude that "basic cognitive skills are more important in predicting subsequent earnings for females in the high school class of 1982 than they were for females who graduated from high school a decade earlier." (2000: 557). So there is limited evidence that the impact of cognitive ability on earnings, net of education, is increasing.

Table 6.3 Effects of literacy score and other influences for earnings

Country	*Gender*	*Parents' education*	*Language (native vs. other)*	*Education*	*Literacy score*	*Labor market experience*	*R square*
Australia	0.41	–0.02	0.06	0.28	0.25	0.12	0.40
Belgium (Flanders)	0.48	–0.04	0.04	0.44	0.15	0.16	0.49
Canada	0.52	–0.09	0.05	0.28	0.32	0.20	0.48
Chile	0.55	0.06	–0.01	0.40	0.10	0.13	0.54
Czech Republic	0.47	0.05	0.06	0.38	0.09	0.23	0.41
Denmark	0.44	–0.02	–0.03	0.33	0.19	0.27	0.42
Finland	0.26	0.05	0.07	0.31	0.29	0.34	0.27
Germany	0.50	–0.21	0.06	0.36	0.08	0.20	0.39
Hungary	0.19	0.08	0.01	0.40	0.19	0.08	0.33
Ireland	0.36	0.05	0.03	0.31	0.21	0.11	0.35
Netherlands	0.48	–0.00	0.06	0.30	0.16	0.21	0.41
New Zealand	0.45	0.00	0.14	0.29	0.26	0.16	0.47
Norway	0.43	0.01	0.02	0.17	0.28	0.22	0.35
Poland	0.29	0.11	0.01	0.35	0.00	0.16	0.22
Portugal	0.35	0.21	0.06	0.23	0.20	0.35	0.41
Slovenia	0.24	–0.01	–0.03	0.46	0.18	0.05	0.37
Sweden	0.41	0.07	0.02	0.23	0.10	0.37	0.30
Switzerland	0.39	–0.06	0.01	0.40	0.12	0.29	0.39
UK	0.37	–0.06	0.03	0.38	0.29	0.17	0.48
US	0.36	–0.02	–0.04	0.38	0.24	0.11	0.43

Notes: From OECD and Statistics Canada (2000: 175) IALS 1994–1998. 25–55-year-olds. Presented are standardized regression coefficients from structural equation modeling. Educational attainment is a latent variable constructed from both years of education and formal qualifications in some countries and only one of these in others. Literacy score is a latent construct based on the prose, document and quantitative scales. Experience (in the labor force) is estimated by age minus years of education minus 5. "Earnings" is measured on an interval scale based on quintiles since some countries did not collect or release continuous wage data.

Non-cognitive attributes

A variety of non-cognitive attributes influence labor market outcomes although their impact is usually small. Jencks *et al.* (1979: 126–52) report smallish effects for self-assessed non-cognitive factors measured during adolescence on occupational status, net of test scores and education: "social sensitivity" (β = –0.08), "culture" (β = 0.10) and "leadership" (β = 0.10). Their addition to a model comprising background and test-score measures raised the explained variance very marginally from 26 to 27 percent. When controlling for grades at school, only leadership had a significant but weak effect (β = 0.09). They conclude that "self-assessed personality is far less important than either background or cognitive skills in determining eventual occupational status." (1979: 130). In contrast, self-assessed leadership had a stronger effect (β = 0.19) for (logged) hourly earnings than test scores and grades (combined β = 0.12) (1979: 131). "Leadership" effects appeared to be stronger towards the top of the income distribution. High-school behaviors had weak or no effects on occupational status and earnings. Most of the measures did not have significant effects on occupational status after controlling for social background, test scores and education. Measures that had significant effects included "study habits" (β = 0.07), "leadership roles" (β = 0.08), and dating behavior (1979: 138–42). Surprisingly, submitting one's "best work" when at school was negatively associated with occupational status. For earnings, "leadership roles" had the largest positive impact (β = 0.08) and "never gone steady" (β = –0.10), intellectual reading (β = –0.10) and "best work" (β = –0.09) were all associated with significantly lower earnings (1979: 142–5). Combining the large number of self-assessed and behavioral effects into a sheaf coefficient, Jencks *et al.* (1979: 146–51) concluded that non-cognitive factors have sizable effects for occupational status (β = 0.22), net of family background, test scores (β = 0.21) and grades at school (β = 0.09), but not education. For earnings, non-cognitive traits (β = 0.24) had a much larger impact than test scores (β = 0.09). Test score was no longer statistically significant when controlling for education whereas the effect for non-cognitive traits was unchanged. These later findings are cited to support the argument that non-cognitive traits are more important than cognitive ability, at least, for earnings (Bowles and Gintis 2002b: 15). However, the non-cognitive sheaf variable includes a large number of diverse components, few of which are skills in the conventional sense, and are only weakly associated with socioeconomic background. Furthermore, the effects of some non-cognitive attributes on earnings are in the opposite direction to that expected.

In an analysis of current occupational status, Olneck and Bills (1980: 48–50) found a significant effect for "industriousness" (β = 0.12), net of educational attainment (β = 0.50) and test score (β = 0.14). "Executive ability" (leadership) and "cooperativeness" had no impact. For earnings, they (1980: 51–3) found significant effects for "executive ability" (β = 0.11), net of educational attainment (β = 0.35) and test score (β = 0.14), but no significant effect for "industriousness", or measures of socioeconomic background. Importantly, the addition of non-cognitive attributes to the analysis did not appreciably reduce the strong effects of education. Furthermore, there was little "correspondence" between non-cognitive attributes associated with "success" in the labor market to those relevant for educational attainment, that is, no support for Bowles and Gintis's correspondence principle. These findings lead them to also reject Bowles and Gintis's claim that non-cognitive attributes explain the association between education and socioeconomic success.

Analyzing "extrinsic career success" – a combination of occupational status and income – Judge *et al.* (1999: 640) found sizeable negative effects for childhood neuroticism (β = –0.21) and agreeableness (β = –0.32), and positive effects for extraversion ($\beta = 0.27$) and consciousness ($\beta = 0.44$), net of cognitive ability ($\beta = 0.41$). Educational attainment was not included as a control variable. Osborne Groves (2005b: 218–19) reports that the Rotter measure of locus of control had a negative effect on logged earnings among father–son pairs in a 1960s longitudinal study, net of father's permanent income, job tenure, education and cognitive ability (i.e. children who felt they were less in control of their lives earned lower incomes as adults, other things being equal). It contributed to explaining some of the earnings correlation between fathers and sons. Net of education and tenure, it had a stronger impact than cognitive ability. She (2005a: 837) also found that, among young women, a one standard deviation increase in Rotter score decreased wages by almost seven percent, net of education (its effect was plus 17 percent for a one standard deviation increase), IQ quintile (plus eight percent), work experience (plus three percent), socioeconomic status (no significant impact), and the number of children.

In the US, non-cognitive skills were relevant in explaining why high-school dropouts who successfully obtain a high-school equivalency qualification have lower wages than dropouts without that qualification. The explanation is that high-school equivalency graduates were seen as less reliable and were more likely to have participated in illicit, violent or illegal activities (Heckman and Rubinstein 2001). A later analysis of non-cognitive attributes found that low self-esteem and low scores on the locus of control measure were associated with lower wages (Heckman *et al.* 2006). However, cognitive skills had stronger standardized effects on log hourly wages, with and without controls for education. Among men, a standard deviation increase in cognitive ability increased wages by 12 percent and non-cognitive skills by four percent, net of education. For women, the comparable estimates were 17 percent and three percent (2006: 418). Excluding education, cognitive skills account for nine percent of the variance in wages for men and non-cognitive skills only 0.9 percent. For women, the comparable estimates are 12 percent and 0.4 percent. (2006: 416). A subsequent complex latent variable analysis concluded that the effects of cognitive and non-cognitive skills for wages were comparable (2006: 437), although it appears that several of the non-cognitive attributes do not constitute skills but illicit behaviors.

For the UK, Saunders (2002: 568) found a significant but small effect of "motivation" ($\beta = 0.08$) on occupational status, net of class background, a range of social advantages and disadvantages, cognitive ability ($\beta = 0.16$) and educational qualifications, providing limited support for the meritocracy thesis (ability plus motivation). Analyzing entry to higher-status occupational groups in the UK, Jackson (2006) concluded that outgoingness (non-withdrawn) is important for managerial occupations, while being passive (non-aggressive) is important for higher technical occupations. Both non-cognitive traits were measured at age 11 and the effects were net of qualifications and cognitive ability. However, the effects are rather small and apply to only small proportions of the sample, since the measures of "withdrawal" and "aggression" were very highly skewed. An analysis of women's hourly wages at age 33 with the same data also found negative effects for "aggression" (a seven percent decrease in wages for a one standard deviation increase in aggression) and "withdrawal" (three percent) net of education, O level examination grades and IQ (Osborne Groves 2005a: 839). The addition of these two non-cognitive attributes only marginally increased the explanatory power of the model. Silles (2009) found negative effects of passive aggressiveness but positive effects for non-passive aggression for wages at age 33, net of cognitive ability and a large number of sociodemographic background variables and school type (but not educational qualifications). Heineck and Anger's (2010) analysis of the five personality traits on wages produced mixed results. There were no effects on wages for "neuroticism", net of cognitive ability, education and other controls. "Agreeableness" was negatively associated with wages among women and had no impact among men. "Openness" had a positive impact on wages among women – a two to six percent increase in wages for a standard deviation increase in openness, but a negative impact among men (a two to four percent decrease). "Consciousness" was associated with higher wages among men, but not among women. "Extraversion" was positively associated with wages among men but not (or negatively) among women. "External locus of control" had the strongest and most consistent effects, decreasing wages by between four and ten percent for a one standard deviation increase. For the Netherlands, Nyhus and Pons (2005) found effects for personality factors net of human capital variables. However, the effects were small and often not significant. "Emotional stability" was positively associated with wages among both men ($\beta = 0.09$) and women ($\beta = 0.12$). "Agreeableness" had a negative effect among women ($\beta = -0.10$). "Extraversion", "conscientiousness" and "autonomy" had no effects on wages, controlling for human capital variables.

There are also non-cognitive attributes that are not prominent in theoretical accounts of labor market outcomes but nevertheless have non-trivial effects. Deary *et al.* (2005b: 464) found that height correlated at 0.26 with destination class but only at 0.13 with class-of-origin. Multivariate analyses found that a one-centimeter increase in height increased the chances of upward social mobility by five percent, net of education and IQ. It also reduced the chances of downward mobility (2005b: 464). Judge and Cable's (2004) meta-analysis found that height was related to both intrinsic and extrinsic career success, although they did not control for education. Height was also correlated with non-cognitive attributes more commonly linked to labor market outcomes: self-esteem, leadership and performance. "Attractiveness" is also associated with labor market outcomes. Hamermesh and Biddle (1994) concluded that "plainness" was associated with an earnings penalty of five to ten percent, with effects just as large for men as for women. They suggest that employers actively discriminate against less-attractive employees. Analyzing the UK's NCDS, Harper (2000) concluded that, regardless of gender, workers assessed as unattractive or short experience a significant earnings penalty. Also, tall men enjoy an earnings premium, and obese women experience a wage penalty. Analyzing the wages of young people who had completed school only (all had the same level of education), Fletcher (2009) concluded that attractive or very attractive individuals earn five to ten percent more than average-looking individuals, and "plainness" was associated with a three to five percent penalty, net of ability, age, race, health status, and socioeconomic background variables. The results were remarkably robust after further fixed-effect controls for school attended and occupational group.

Conclusions

There is a recurring theme throughout the literature that cognitive ability is really not that important for labor market outcomes, and that non-cognitive abilities are more important. Cognitive ability influences labor market outcomes. There are medium to strong associations of cognitive ability with labor market status, occupational group or class, occupational attainment and weaker associations with earnings. These relationships cannot be attributed to socioeconomic background. Both upward and downward occupational mobility are associated with cognitive ability. Because of the importance of education on labor market outcomes, the impact of cognitive ability on labor market outcomes is mainly indirect, but there are substantial direct effects as well. Although, it cannot be concluded that Western societies are meritocracies, they are more meritocratic than generally believed; cognitive ability is important for education, education is the strongest predictor of labor market outcomes, and, in addition, cognitive ability influences labor market outcomes, net of educational attainment.

Non-cognitive attributes also impact on labor market outcomes. However, it cannot be argued that non-cognitive skills are just as important for socioeconomic stratification as cognitive ability. Non-cognitive factors have only weak effects on education, and education is the major determinant of subsequent labor market outcomes. The sheer diversity of non-cognitive factors that have been shown to affect labor market outcomes – personality traits, adolescent behaviors, physical attributes and fatalistic attitudes – undermines any parsimonious theoretical explanation of their importance. Most of the effects of individual non-cognitive factors for labor market outcomes are weak and only a handful show consistent effects in the literature (e.g. locus of control, leadership, height and appearance). Few are "abilities" that could be developed through schooling. Some non-cognitive attributes could be considered as aspects of merit (e.g. industriousness, study habits, motivation), and thus their impact on socioeconomic outcomes could be viewed as supporting the meritocracy thesis. Furthermore, no non-cognitive factor or group of non-cognitive factors strongly link socioeconomic background to adult occupational and economic outcomes.

Notes

1 In the Johnson *et al.* (2010a) study, the class groups comprised: I (professional occupations), II (managerial and technical occupations), IIIN (skilled nonmanual occupations), IIIM (skilled manual occupations), IV (partly-skilled occupations) and V (unskilled occupations).
2 The correlation is weaker at younger ages. In the WLS, the correlation among men ten years after graduating from high school was only 0.23 (Sewell and Hauser 1975: 92).
3 From the Jencks *et al.* (1983) paper, Roberts *et al.* (2007: 334) report standardized coefficients of 0.15 for father's occupation, 0.09 for mother's education, 0.11 for parental income and 0.35 for ability on occupational attainment.
4 The model included a large number of other predictors besides socioeconomic background and ability: motivation, school type, parental interest and work attitudes.
5 The data on achievement were collected in 1957 and occupational status was measured in 1970, 1975/1977 and 1992/1994.
6 Ability score had a standard deviation of about 15 points and occupational-education and occupational-income had standard deviations of 1.7 and 1.2. Very roughly, the standardized coefficients are in vicinity of 0.10–0.15. Occupational education is based on the percentage of incumbents in an occupational group with one or more years of college, and occupational income is based on the percentage of incumbents earning more than US$10,000 (in 1969 dollars).
7 Obtained by taking the square root of the R square value for the model (Zagorsky 2007: 493).
8 Calculated from Zax and Rees (2002). Standardized coefficients (β) were calculated from the unstandardized coefficients (b) in Table 5 and from the ratios of the standard deviations of the dependent (s_y) and independent variables (s_x) presented in Table 2.
9 There are claims that the family-of-origin's earnings and adult earnings are highly correlated. See Chapter 9 for discussions on intergenerational income elaticities and correlations.
10 Calculated by multiplying the standard deviation for IQ (14.9) by the elasticities in the first row of the first two columns in Table 3 (Zax and Rees 2002: 605).
11 Comparing the coefficients with and without "ALL BKG" in Jencks *et al.* (1979: Table 4.7).
12 Calculated by the author. The coefficient of 0.034 (from Table 1, 1st Model for logged earning) is multiplied by 2.41/0.60, which equals 0.14.
13 Calculated by dividing the coefficient (US$2,842) by the standard deviation of annual earnings (US$16,083) presented in Korenman and Winship (2000: 153, 142).

Chapter 7

Socioeconomic inequalities in education I

The strength of the relationship

Socioeconomic inequalities in education are a major concern for academics in the field, policymakers and politicians. The basic assumption is that educational outcomes very strongly relate to socioeconomic background. White provides the following examples from the literature:

- The family characteristic that is the most powerful predictor of school performance is socioeconomic status (SES): the higher the SES of the student's family, the higher his academic achievement. This relationship has been documented in countless studies and seems to hold no matter what measure of status is used (occupation of principal breadwinner, family income, parents' education, or some combination of these).
- To categorize youth according to the social class position of their parents is to order them on the extent of their participation and degree of success in the American Educational System. This has been so consistently confirmed by research that it can now be regarded as an empirical law ... SES predicts grades, achievement and intelligence test scores, retentions at grade level, course failures, truancy, suspensions from school, high school dropouts, plans for college attendance, and total amount of formal schooling.

(quotes from White 1982: 461–2)

To take a more recent example, Buchmann (2002: 183–4) writes about "the central importance of family background in *determining* student achievement" [my emphasis] and later "the strong correlations between aspects of family background and student achievement". The single underlying assumption in all theoretical explanations of socioeconomic inequalities in education is that class or socioeconomic background differences in educational outcomes are strong and it is the task of theory to explain these strong relationships.

The purpose of this chapter is to demonstrate that socioeconomic inequalities in education are not nearly as strong as often assumed by theorists and policymakers. The chapter discusses the magnitude of socioeconomic inequalities for student achievement, participation and performance at college or university and overall educational attainment. The second part of the chapter discusses a variety of issues that relate to socioeconomic inequalities in education. These issues are sometimes cited in arguments that the relationship is actually considerably stronger than that observed. These are subject type (e.g. literacy, numeracy), stage of educational career, choice of indicator for socioeconomic background, the role of income and wealth, aggregate data and school-level measures of socioeconomic status, the use of proxy measures, measurement error, the total effect of family background on education found in sibling studies, and the relative contributions of genetics and the environment to socioeconomic inequalities in education.

Student achievement, test scores

Occupational group and occupational class

The strength of the association between parental social class (or occupational group) and student achievement is much lower than is commonly assumed. In 30 countries participating in PISA, a six-category EGP-type measure of social class explained 7 to 15 percent of the variance in student performance (Marks 2005).[1] Focusing on occupational group rather than class background with PISA data from nearly 30 countries, Marks (2011) found that, in many countries, the children of teachers showed the highest mean scores which is unexpected if economic resources were the primary explanation for socioeconomic differences. Generally, the next highest scoring groups (in rough order) were children of professionals, managers and administrators, paraprofessionals and clerks. The children of farmers and laborers showed the lowest average scores. To varying degrees, all countries exhibited this general socioeconomic gradient. However, the differences were not particularly large, in most countries between 60 and 90 PISA test score points – one standard deviation was set to equal 100 score points – separated the mean scores of students whose parents belonged to the highest scoring occupational group from those belonging to the lowest scoring occupational group.

Single indictor continuous measures of socioeconomic background

Continuous measures of socioeconomic background, such as parental occupational status and parental education, show only moderate associations with student achievement. In the US among white northern sixth graders, the correlation between father's education and verbal test scores was 0.28 (cited by Bowles and Nelson 1974: footnote h). White's (1982) meta-analysis of over 200 mainly US studies found a mean correlation between socioeconomic background, measured in various ways, and academic achievement of only 0.22. In other words, on average, socioeconomic background could account for only about four percent of the variation in student achievement. A later study by Sirin (2005), with better measures of socioeconomic background, calculated an average correlation of 0.27, equivalent to about nine percent of the variance.

In cross-national studies of student achievement, the relationship between measures of father's occupational status and student achievement is also moderate. In the first international mathematics study of 12 countries conducted in 1964, the overall correlation between father's occupational status and mathematics achievement was 0.22 (Husen 1967: 206). For the first reading literacy study conducted in the mid-1960s, the median correlation between father's occupational status, constructed using the criterion scaling method, and reading achievement among ten-year-olds across 15 countries was 0.28 (Thorndike 1973: 76). In the first international science study, the average correlation between father's occupational status, constructed by criterion scaling, and science achievement was 0.23 (Comber and Keeves 1973: 258).

Multiple and composite measures of socioeconomic background

Multiple and composite measures comprising several indicators of socioeconomic background show stronger correlations with socioeconomic background but rarely account for more than one-fifth of the variation in student achievement.

For the first international reading literacy study, an index of socioeconomic status comprised father's occupation, father's education and mother's education. Father's occupation was criterion scaled.[2] The median correlation between reading achievement and the composite measure of socioeconomic status among 14-year-olds was 0.31 (Thorndike 1973: 76–7). In the first international science study, the composite "home circumstances" (comprising father's occupation, father's education and mother's education, the use of a dictionary, the number of books in the home and family size) explained on average about ten percent of the variation in science test scores (Comber and Keeves 1973: 261).

The OECD (2007b: 333) PISA study routinely constructs very broad composite measures of socioeconomic background denoted as the PISA index of Economic, Social and Cultural Status (ESCS). For the 2006 PISA study, the composite comprised the highest of father's or mother's occupational status, father's or mother's educational attainment, and data from approximately 20 wealth, educational and cultural items. There were similar broad (but not identical) composite measures for the other 2000, 2003 and 2009 PISA studies. Among OECD countries, this composite measure accounted for, on average, 15 percent of the variation in student achievement in science in 2006 and 14 percent in reading in 2009 (OECD 2007b: 184; 2010c: 55). These are equivalent to multiple correlations just below 0.4.

Socioeconomic background and demographic variables

Together, measures of family background and indicators of socioeconomic background also do not account for much of the variation in test scores. Mare (1980: 298) found that among US army veterans born between 1930 and 1945, social background variables comprising father's occupation and education, family type, from the South, and a farm background, could only account for ten percent of the variation in AFQT scores among army veterans. This declined to five percent when restricted to those who had completed at least 12 years of schooling. In a later study, only ten percent of the variation in test scores was accounted for by a swag of family background variables: family income (averaged over several years and obtained from tax records), father's occupation, father's and mother's education, coming from a "broken" family, and the number of siblings (Sewell *et al.* 1980: 566).

Analysis of the UK's 1958 NCDS found that social class (plus gender and parents' reading behavior) could only account for 15 percent of the variation in reading achievement and about 11 percent for mathematics score at age 11 (van de Werfhorst *et al.* 2003).

University and college

Socioeconomic background is only moderately associated with attendance at college or university. Academic factors are substantially more important, and the effects of socioeconomic status are very weak once academic performance is taken into account. Studies on entry to university or college are typically conducted on samples of high-school students, so are more selective than general population samples. The more selective samples mean that the effects of socioeconomic background and ability are less than they would be if the sample was initially selected before compulsory education ends, because lower socioeconomic status students and lower-ability students are more likely to have left school. However, even in less-selective samples, the impact of socioeconomic background, net of academic variables, on university or college entrance is surprisingly weak.

The US

For the US, Rumberger (2010: 252), analyzing college completion with data from the NELS sample of eighth graders, reported a pseudo R square of around 0.24 for a composite measure of socioeconomic background (comprising father and mother's educational attainment, father's and mother's occupational status, and family income). Adding test scores and grades almost doubled the explanatory power of the model to 43 percent and effectively halved the effects of socioeconomic background. Analyzing simply obtaining or not obtaining a college degree within 11 years of entering tenth grade, Reisel (2011: 270) reported a pseudo R square value of 13 percent for a model comprising several categorical measures of parental education and income. Thomas *et al.*'s (1979: 144) analyses of college attendance in the US among a more restrictive sample of high-school seniors found that a composite measure of socioeconomic background – comprising father's and mother's education, father's occupational status and an index of household possessions – together with gender and race accounted for only 13 percent of the variation in college attendance. Adding academic variables more than doubled the explained variance to 33 percent. The standardized effect of the composite measure of socioeconomic background was 0.19, net of test scores, curriculum track and class rank.

One response to these findings that socioeconomic status is not a strong influence on attendance at *any* college is that socioeconomic background is important for entry to four-year, as opposed to two-year, college programs and for entry to high-status institutions. However, socioeconomic background has only weak effects on college selectivity. Alexander *et al.* (1987: 76) concluded that "access to four-year schools as a higher education port of entry is affected very little by student background" among senior high-school students. The initial socioeconomic differences were greatly reduced once academic performance was taken into account. A more recent analysis found that socioeconomic quartiles could only account for about five percent of the variation (pseudo R square) on entry to two- and four-year non-selective and selective colleges, using data from three cohorts of high-school graduates (Alon 2009). Hearn (1984), analyzing college selectivity among college freshmen (measured by the average of students' SAT scores), found that ascribed and socioeconomic characteristics could only account uniquely for four percent of the variance in students' college selectivity (which accounted for 11 percent of the explained variance). This compares with 33 percent for academic factors (which accounted for 89 percent of the explained variance). Using another measure of college selectivity – costs – Hearn (1988: 72) found no significant effects for father's education and family income and only a very weak effect of mother's education, net of academic factors (tested ability, grades, within-school track and educational aspirations).

Similarly, performance at college is only weakly related to socioeconomic background. Buchmann and DiPrete (2006: 532) reported no significant effects of mothers having had some college education and only weak effects of father's college education on college grade point average (GPA) scores, net of high-school academic factors. Similarly, net of SAT scores, socioeconomic background only weakly relates to grades in college. The authors conclude that the "vast majority of the test-academic performance relationship was independent of SES" (Sackett *et al.* 2009: 1).

Other countries

The effects of socioeconomic background on entry to university are also weak in other countries. For the UK, Halsey *et al.* (1980: 141) note that the percentage of students obtaining a higher school certificate or taking A (Advanced) levels did not vary strongly by the class backgrounds of the examinees. For the higher A level examinations, success rates did not differ at all by class background. A more recent study found that there was no additional effect of socioeconomic background on university entrance in the UK, net of performance at the General Certificate of Secondary Education and A levels (Marcenaro-Gutierrez *et al.* 2007). For class differences in the transition to A levels, Erikson *et al.* (2005: 9731) concluded that primary effects (i.e. differences in previous academic performance) accounted for 70–80 percent of the total effect of class, leaving around one-quarter due to secondary effects (class effects independent of academic performance). A similar analysis on the NCDS data concludes that secondary effects account for only one-quarter of class differences in taking A levels (Jackson *et al.* 2007).

For Australia, Marks and McMillan (2007: 366), analyzing obtaining a bachelor degree with data from general population surveys, reported a pseudo R square of eight percent for class, gender and cohort. An earlier study found that a composite measure of socioeconomic background (incorporating father's and mother's education and occupation and students' cultural participation) could only account for 11 percent of the variation in tertiary entrance performance (Marks and McMillan 2003: 461). Analyzing data from Canadian General Social Science surveys, Sen and Clemente (2010: 150) found that only about ten percent of the variation in attending university was accounted for by father's and mother's education and a suite of sociodemographic controls. In an analysis of grades at Norwegian universities, a sociodemographic model comprising parent's occupational class, family income, gender, degree of urbanization and university returned a pseudo R square of 0.0048, which increased substantially to 0.0638 with the addition of grades at secondary school. In the model excluding secondary school grades, the predicted probabilities of obtaining an A or B grade was second highest for students from farming backgrounds (Hansen and Mastekaasa 2006: 284). However, the authors interpreted the estimates as supporting cultural capital theory. In a later Norwegian study, only 12 percent of the variation in degree completion could be accounted for by gender, parental education and family income in analyses of national registry data (Reisel 2011: 270). This figure increased to 23 percent after the inclusion of a measure of high school program (stream).

Educational attainment

In the US, the association between socioeconomic background and educational attainment (measured by years of education) is generally stronger than the relationship between socioeconomic background and test scores; with correlations around 0.4. According to analyses of the 1962 Occupational

Changes in a Generation (OCG) data, the correlations of educational attainment with father's education and father's occupational status among men were 0.42 and 0.43. Excluding men with farm backgrounds, the correlations declined marginally to 0.39 and 0.42 (Duncan *et al.* 1972: 263). In the WLS, Sewell and Hauser (1975: 51) report that 13 percent of the variation in educational attainment is accounted for by father's education and occupation. They (1975: 100–2) also report that about 15 percent of the variation in years of education can be attributed to measured aspects of socioeconomic background: father's and mother's education, father's occupation and family income. Adding the test score measure of mental ability doubled the variance explained to 28 percent and the effects of the socioeconomic background variables declined by between 15 and 40 percent.

For the UK, Johnson *et al.* (2010a: 275) report a correlation of 0.35 between social class origin and educational attainment for a Scottish birth cohort born in 1936. For Australia, the correlations of years of education (before entering work) with socioeconomic background variables were only moderate: father's education (0.36), father's occupational status (0.22), mother's education (0.37) and wealth (0.35). These variables together with family size (which is invariably negatively related to educational attainment) could then account for only 26 percent of the variation in educational attainment (Broom *et al.* 1980: 26, 28).

A cross-national study of educational attainment based on data collected in the 1960s and 1970s analyzed the effects of father's education and father's occupational prestige on educational attainment in 19 countries (Treiman and Yip 1989). Father's education had substantially stronger effects than father's occupational prestige in most countries. The amount of variation in educational attainment explained by these two variables was low in Ireland (16 percent); moderate in Germany (23 percent); the US (24 percent); England and Wales (20 percent); and unexpectedly high in Northern European countries: Finland (26 percent), Denmark (35 percent), Norway (29 percent), the Netherlands (38 percent) and Sweden (37 percent). The socialist countries, Hungary (27 percent) and Poland (28 percent), did not show particularly low associations between socioeconomic background and educational attainment during the 1970s (1989: 387).

More recent studies indicate that father's education and father's occupation account for about 20 percent of the variation in educational attainment for cohorts born in the twentieth century. The edited book, *Persistent Inequality*, reports R square values for a number of countries: the US (20 percent), England and Wales (18 percent), Italy (35 percent), Switzerland (19 percent), and the Czech Republic (between 13 and 25 percent), (Shavit and Blossfeld 1993: 34, 112, 165, 187, 262).[3] The figures are not strictly comparable across countries, owing to differences in the birth cohorts analyzed and the measurement of educational attainment and the predictor variables. However, these R square values indicate that, apart from Italy, these two measures of socioeconomic background account for less than a quarter of the variation in educational attainment.

Issues in the strength of the relationship

Subject type

There are plausible arguments that the associations with socioeconomic background differ by subject type or domain. Cultural capital theory would imply that subjects with a higher level of cultural content – literature and other humanities – would be more closely associated with socioeconomic background than mathematics or science. Lee and Bryk (1989: 179) justify their focus on mathematics by claiming that performance in mathematics is more influenced by schooling and least influenced by the home. Dronkers and Robert (2008: 295) claim that reading performance is less dependent on schools and more on parents than performance in mathematics.

The influence of socioeconomic background is not consistently stronger for one type of achievement test compared with others. Using Coleman's achievement measures, White (1982: 469) reported similar correlations with socioeconomic background for reading and mathematics. With a larger number of studies, the correlations were stronger for reading than for mathematics tests. In contrast, Sirin's (2005: 433) meta-analysis reported a larger mean correlation for mathematics (0.35) than for literacy (0.32) or science (0.27). Analyzing student achievement in 30 countries, Marks (2008) found similar amounts of variance explained for reading and mathematics scores (for most countries) for models comprising differing combinations of father's and mother's educational attainment and occupational status.

According to Sirin's (2005: 433) meta-analysis, the correlation of socioeconomic status with general achievement (GPA or combined achievement measures) tended to be substantially lower than that for reading or mathematics, at about 0.22. This pattern of lower was not evident in White's (1982: 469) earlier meta-analysis, although the correlations between GPA and socioeconomic background were similar, averaging about 0.24.

Grade level and age

There are two reasons why the impact of socioeconomic background may decline over the school career. Mare (1980) pointed out that the effects of socioeconomic background will be largest in the early school transitions, when almost the entire cohort is "at risk" of making the transition. For the subsequent transitions, the impact of social background will be smaller, since those students from lower status social backgrounds will have already exited the education system and so are no longer "at risk". For higher-level transitions, only high-ability students from low socioeconomic backgrounds are "at risk" of making the transition, so that the impact of socioeconomic background will be even smaller. In the other words, the relationships at each higher transition level are successively attenuated, due to attrition (Mare 1981: footnote 5). An alternative or additional explanation is the life-course hypothesis: older children are less dependent on their parents both economically and socially than younger children, so the effects of socioeconomic background progressively weaken through the educational career (Lucas 2001: 1646; Müller and Karle 1993: 3). The implication of the life-course hypothesis is that overall socio-economic inequalities will decline with educational expansion, since increasing proportions of students successfully complete the early transitions and the later transitions are more weakly influenced by socioeconomic background.

In a cross-national study of reading achievement conducted during the early 1960s, there was little difference in the socioeconomic status–achievement correlations between 10- (0.28) and 14-year-olds (0.31). The correlation among senior students (about 17 years of age) was considerably lower at 0.16, which is probably due to attrition (Thorndike 1973: 77). Analyzing longitudinal data with late and early measures of socio-economic background, Alwin and Thornton (1984) concluded that socioeconomic background measured during the early school career has a potentially stronger role than socioeconomic background measured later in the school career, although the differences were not large. According to White (1982: 469), using data from the Coleman report, the socioeconomic status–achievement correlations were progressively weaker for students in grades nine and six compared with students in grade three. However, a later meta-analysis found little difference by grade level; the correlation between SES and academic performance rose between elementary to middle school and then declined for senior high school students (Sirin 2005: 435).

The pattern of "waning coefficients" coefficients for each successive transition was evident in 12 of 13 countries in the *Persistent Inequality* collection (Blossfeld and Shavit 1993: 17). However, Lucas (1996) found that the effects of socioeconomic background on the transition from school to college entry in the US are greater than those for the transition to high-school graduation. Later, in a more methodological piece adjusting for threats to statistical inference from the classical transitions model, Lucas *et al.* (2011: 263) showed that the effects of socioeconomic background variables are much the same for college entry as those for school completion. They claim that "late stage educational egalitarianism in the United States" is disproved and their study shows that the waning coefficient pattern does not always hold.

Choice of indicator of socioeconomic background

For analyses of student achievement, it also makes little difference to the strength of the relationship if socioeconomic background is measured by single indicators based on father's occupational status, or mother's or father's education. The correlations with student achievement for these single indicators among developed countries mostly range between 0.20 and 0.30. Sirin's (2005: 433) meta-analysis reported similar-sized correlations (averaged across studies) between student achievement and parental education (0.30), and parental occupational status (0.28). Analyzing the correlations in 30 countries, Marks (2011) found similar-sized correlations for father's occupational status, father's education and mother's education. Only mother's occupational status showed generally weaker correlations and this may be due to the smaller variance in mother's occupational status and the lower labour market participation rates of mothers. For each single indicator of socioeconomic background, the correlations are slightly stronger if criterion scaling is used, and stronger again if missing data are included, since students who do not provide information on their parents' occupations or education tend to have low (often the lowest) mean achievement scores (Marks 2011).

In contrast to the findings for student achievement, Treiman and Yip (1989: 386–7) found that father's education is much more important than father's occupational attainment for *educational attainment*. On average, the ratio of the standardized coefficients was about eight to one. Citing a number of studies, Shavit *et al.* (2007b) conclude that parents' education typically has stronger relationships with educational attainment than parental occupational class.

A recent cross-national study of socioeconomic inequalities in gaining a bachelor's degree in European countries employed four indicators: father's and mother's education and occupations. In the 1950s and 1960s, father's education had the strongest impact and had declined since then. There were smaller declines in the effects of father's occupation and mother's education. There was a slight increase in the effects of mother's occupation from a much lower base (Koucký *et al.* 2010: 28). At the most recent time point, all four measured aspects of socioeconomic background had similar-sized effects.

Income and wealth

Bowles (1972) argued that social class is a considerably more important determinant of educational attainment than that indicated at that time by analyses by prominent sociologists such as Duncan and associates. He pointed out that the measurement of socioeconomic background suffers from at least two sources of error: the exclusion of "important dimensions of social class" (specifically family income and wealth) and errors of measurement in the standard indicators of social class (1972: S222).

It is quite plausible that not including family income and wealth would substantially weaken the influence of socioeconomic background. However, the extent that socioeconomic background accounts for variation in test scores or educational attainment, it is not substantially increased by the inclusion of family income. Responding to the criticism that in previous analyses of the WLS, socioeconomic background was inadequately measured, Sewell *et al.* (1970: 1018) obtained occupational and family income data from state tax returns. The correlation between a composite measure of socioeconomic status – comprising father's education, mother's education, father's occupation, and average annual parental income for three years – and student achievement was around 0.3, equivalent to an explained variance of nine percent. A later study using family income, obtained from tax records averaged for up to four years, together with father's education and occupational attainment, could only account for 14 percent of the variation in educational attainment and less than ten percent for mental ability (Sewell and Hauser 1975: 18, 73, 76). More generally, the effects of family income (and wealth) on educational outcomes are generally weaker than the effects of other socioeconomic background factors, and its addition does not substantially increase the extent that socioeconomic background accounts for variation in educational outcomes.[4]

Aggregate-level relationships[5]

The ecological fallacy has been well known for over 60 years – that aggregated data show much higher correlations than the same variables at the individual level and, furthermore, relationships at the aggregate level cannot be used to make assertions at the micro-level (Robinson 1950; Snijders and Bosker 2012: 15). The reason is that aggregating individual-level data, typically by calculating the school or area mean, removes the individual-level variation within aggregated units. For example, aggregation of students' scores at the school-level removes the considerable variation among students in their achievement scores within schools. Aggregation also removes the within-school variation in socioeconomic status.

The correlations between measures of socioeconomic status and student achievement aggregated by school or region are very much stronger than at the student level. These much larger correlations are sometimes offered as evidence that socioeconomic background is strongly associated with student achievement or other educational outcomes. White (1982: 467) and Sirin's (2005) meta-analyses calculated mean correlations of 0.60 and 0.73, respectively, between aggregated measures of socioeconomic background and achievement. White *et al.* (1993: 328) conclude that aggregate measures of socioeconomic status overstate the relationship by a factor of four. In the Australian PISA study, the OECD's ESCS measure correlates at 0.8 with the PISA test score both aggregated at the school level, whereas the correlation at the student level was around 0.4 (Marks 2010c: endnote 1).

Contextual effect of school-SES

School socioeconomic status, which is simply the school-level average of the students' socioeconomic status scores, usually has a strong association with individual-level student outcomes and again this is sometimes interpreted as evidence of the powerful role of socioeconomic status on educational and thus societal inequalities. The argument is that the contextual effects of socioeconomic status further advantage high-status students and disadvantage students from low socioeconomic status households. In addition, the strong effects for school socioeconomic status suggest that students from a low socioeconomic background benefit by attending high socioeconomic status schools and high socioeconomic status students attending low socioeconomic status schools, have poorer outcomes than if they attended a high socioeconomic status school. Because of the apparently large effects of school socioeconomic status, Willms (2010) and Perry and McConney (2010) call for policy responses to the effects of school socioeconomic status.

School socioeconomic status can also "explain" school sector differences. Analyzing differences in student achievement between private (government independent), other private (government dependent) and government schools in 16 countries, Dronkers and Robert (2008: 260) conclude that the "explanation of the gross differences in mathematical achievement is the better social composition of private schools". Similarly, school sector (independent, Catholic and government) differences in PISA test scores in Australia were not statistically significant when controlling for school socioeconomic status, allowing the authors to claim that school-sector differences can be entirely attributed to socioeconomic status (Thomson *et al.* 2010: 61–3). It is doubtful that the higher scores of students at independent and government-funded independent schools are due to the socioeconomic context of schools, through some type of contagion effect or some other mechanism rather than the provision of teaching and learning.

Analyzing PISA data, Willms (2010: 1017) finds a strong relationship between average school socioeconomic status and average school achievement in the US. For Australia, Perry and McConney (2010) conclude that the socioeconomic composition of the school matters greatly in terms of students' academic performance. Analyzing PISA data from 57 countries, Willms (2010: 1024) finds that the school socioeconomic status effect (at 62 score points) is much larger than the student-level socioeconomic status effect (at 17 score points), although they together account for *only* 4.4 percent of the student-level variation in science scores. In countries with large between-school variation in achievement, the effects of school socioeconomic status are large and, net of school socioeconomic status, the effects of individual student socioeconomic status are surprisingly small. For example, in the 2009 PISA study, the effects of school ESCS – ESCS is the OECD's broad composite measure of socioeconomic status mentioned earlier – and student-level ESCS on achievement were 111 and 13 score points, respectively, in Belgium, 123 and 14 in the Czech Republic, 122 and 10 in Germany, and 93 and 5 in the Netherlands. These effects compare with bivariate effects for student-level ESCS of 47, 46, 44 and 37, respectively (OECD 2010c: 186–7). Although, within a country, there is less variation in school-ESCS than student-ESCS, these very large effects for school-ESCS should not be interpreted as evidence of very strong socioeconomic inequalities in student achievement.[6]

The mechanisms for the contextual effects of socioeconomic status are unclear (Dumay and Dupriez 2008). Bourdieu (cited by Nash 2003b: 443) postulates that if the proportion of working class students exceeds a certain threshold, school classes become more disordered thus impeding learning. (This argument could imply that only working class students disrupt classes.) Alexander *et al.* (1979: 223) offer two mechanisms for the contextual effects of SES: a change in the academic climate of the school (academic press) or educational benefits produced by changes in peer networks. Rumberger and Palardy (2005) posit three mechanisms: alterable school characteristics (resources, structures and practices); peer effects; and through schools' responses to the student composition (i.e. "dumbing down" the curriculum to cater for low SES students, reduced teacher morale and efficacy). However, for any of these mechanisms to be viable they would need to involve student achievement; inadequate resources or poor administration affecting overall achievement, the influence of high or low-achieving peers, or changing the curriculum or expectations in accordance with the students' general level of achievement. Therefore, the effects of school-SES must be indirect and involve student achievement.

An important policy and research question is: Are the large effects for school socioeconomic status simply a methodological artifact? Hauser (1970: 659, 1974) argues that contextual effects of socioeconomic status relate to the ecological fallacy in that residual differences between groups (in this case schools) are interpreted as social processes. Such differences should disappear once relevant individual student-level predictors (correlated with schools) are included. Nash (2003b) makes a similar point, suggesting that the contextual effects of school socioeconomic status may be due to unmeasured non-cognitive or family factors that affect school performance. Gorard (2006: 91) suggests that the school-composition effect may be spurious because there is measurement error for socioeconomic status at the student level, but measurement error for socioeconomic status aggregated at the school level is lower, since the errors cancel out. Thrupp *et al.* (2002) suggest that the effects of school socioeconomic status may not survive controls for prior achievement and they advocate a full set of entry level variables.

There is an even simpler explanation for school socioeconomic status effects; school socioeconomic status is acting as a proxy for the contextual effects of prior achievement. As Thrupp *et al.* (2002: 486) point out, school-level prior achievement is rarely entered as a variable in these studies. The theoretical reasons for a contextual effect of achievement are more direct than parallel arguments for school socioeconomic status. Students in a high-achieving school perform better, over and above that expected by their prior achievement, for a variety of reasons: the curriculum and the teaching are delivered at a higher level, the schools' and teachers' expectations are higher, students' norms regarding the usefulness of academic work are more conducive to learning, and possibly there is less disruption to teaching and learning. For converse reasons, students in low-achieving schools perform lower than that expected.

The correlations at the school-level between socioeconomic status and prior achievement or ability are surprisingly large, suggesting that high multi-collinearity may be a problem in analyses that include both school-level variables. For New Zealand, Harker and Tymms (2004: 188) report a correlation of 0.87 for mean school prior achievement and mean school socioeconomic status. For Belgium, Opdenakker and van Damme (2001: 414) report a correlation of 0.82 between school mean prior ability and school mean father's education. The multicollinearity problem would be exacerbated by the addition of school-level measures for other contextual effects (e.g. race and ethnicity) and school-process variables (e.g. academic press, teacher morale, disciplinary climate). The high intercorrelations among school-level variables undermines researchers' ability to conclude on what school-level factors are important for student performance.[7]

Once school-level prior achievement is included in multivariate (including multilevel) analyses, the effects for school socioeconomic status disappear or, in some studies, become negative. Zimmer and Toma (2000) found strong effects for academic context in four school systems using data from a 1981 cross-national mathematics study which collected both pre- and post-test scores. Later studies also show that the effects for school socioeconomic status tend to disappear after controlling for school mean prior achievement or school mean student ability (Marks 2010c; Opdenakker and van Damme 2001: 417). Scheerens *et al.* (2000: 136) conclude that it is the contextual effects of IQ (or prior achievement) rather than contextual effects of socioeconomic status that predominate for student achievement. Snijders and Bosker (2012: 83–6) provide an example from a study of reading literacy in Dutch grade-eight students in which the effects of mean school socioeconomic status are negative on literacy score in the presence of mean school IQ and student-level measures of IQ and socioeconomic status. The negative coefficient indicates that students perform at a lower level in higher SES schools.

The very large effects for school socioeconomic status in PISA at first appear puzzling. Why should the effects of school socioeconomic status be so strong in countries such as Belgium, the Czech Republic, Germany and the Netherlands? It is because these countries have tracked school systems – at a younger age students are allocated to different school types largely based on their performance in primary school or early secondary school – and school socioeconomic status becomes a proxy for prior achievement aggregated at the school level. Similarly, the reason why school socioeconomic status explains differences between non-government and government schools – the Dronkers and Roberts (2008) and Thomson *et al.* (2010) studies – is also because it is highly correlated with school-level prior achievement. To explain differences in school-level achievement, the focus should be on the provision of teaching and learning between schools rather some type of contagion effect involving socioeconomic status.

Proxy data and measurement error

Socioeconomic background is most often measured by respondents recalling their father's occupation and education at some specified time point during their adolescence. Proxy measures of father's and mother's socioeconomic characteristics would be less accurate than obtaining that information directly from the individuals concerned. However, proxy measures are not particularly inaccurate. Hauser *et al.* (1983: 22) report several validation studies and conclude that proxy reports are not overly error prone. More recent studies on proxy reports make the same conclusion. There is generally a high correspondence between proxy and direct reporting in the US (Borus and Nestel 1973; Kerckhoff *et al.* 1973; Massagli and Hauser 1983). The correspondence found in other countries is also high (Lien *et al.* 2001; Looker 1989; West *et al.* 2001). Recent comparisons of child and parent reports from 10 countries in the PISA and PIRLS studies concluded that occupational data is reliable, measures of books in the home are not, and for parental education the findings were mixed (Jerrim and Mickelwright, 2012).

There is also measurement error in surveys when respondents provide unclear responses to questions about their occupation or education. Logically, proxy reports would contain even more measurement error. Measurement error attenuates the observed association between indicators of socioeconomic background and educational outcomes. The "true" correlation is a function of the observed correlation corrected by the reliabilities.[8] The less reliable the two measures, the more attenuated the correlation. Bowles and Nelson (1974) assigned reliabilities of around 0.8 for father's occupation, father's education, and 0.84 for family income, and concluded that socioeconomic background had a much larger effect than IQ for schooling, occupational status, and income. They reported relatively large standardized coefficients for socioeconomic background, close to 0.6, which were much larger than the standardized coefficients reported elsewhere (1974: 44). These estimates were derived from synthetic analyses from published correlations and reliabilities.

Other studies do not report such strong associations after correction for measurement error. Jencks *et al.* (1972: 78) estimate that, after accounting for measurement error, the correlation between father's occupation and achievement is 0.35. Jencks *et al.* (1979: 36) claim that the standardized regression coefficients will increase by between two and nine percent after correcting for reliability of the measures (random error in the dependent variable does not affect the estimates). Bielby *et al.* (1977) found that correcting for measurement error did not affect the estimates for parental education, but the effects of father's occupational status were underestimated by 16 to 22 percent and parental income by ten percent when not taking into account measurement error. They conclude that ignoring measurement error results in modest biases of 10 to 20 percent in the effects of father's occupational status and parental income. In the analysis of educational attainment, the uncorrected model overestimated the residual variation by about ten percent. A subsequent analysis using multiple indicators, Hauser *et al.* (1983: 32) concluded that, even after correcting for measurement error, the correlation between socioeconomic background and schooling is 0.42 which implies that 83 percent of the variance in schooling is, casually or coincidently, unrelated to socioeconomic background. For Australia, correcting for measurement increased the variance accounted for in years of education from 26 percent to 36 percent, although Broom *et al.* (1980: 28, 37) admited that the very low reliabilities assigned to socioeconomic background variables were probably unwarranted. So even assuming what Broom *et al.* (1980: 28, 37) refered to as "drastically different reliabilities" for the measures of socioeconomic background, 64 percent of the variation in educational attainment was not accounted for by socioeconomic background. Using three different approaches for correcting for measurement error in the analysis of educational attainment, de Vries and de Graaf (2006) found that the standardized effect of father's education increased from 0.31 to between 0.40 and 0.45. However, the effects of father's occupational status declined to statistical insignificance.[9] The two socioeconomic background variables explained 18 percent of the variance in educational attainment, without correcting for measurement error, and 25 percent after accounting for measurement error. The bottom line is that the weak to moderate associations between socioeconomic background and educational outcomes are not due to measurement error.

Measurement error will not transform a moderate association to a strong one. A correlation of 0.3 cannot become a correlation of 0.8 or even 0.6 by simply adjusting for measurement error. For example, if the observed correlation was 0.3, and the reliabilities for socioeconomic background and educational attainment were 0.6 and 0.9,[10] the true correlation would increase to 0.41. Moderate correlations could only be transformed into large correlations only if the measurement errors for the socioeconomic indicators are so large that the measures should be abandoned.

Sibling studies and the total effect of family background

Siblings have much more similar educational outcomes than do non-related individuals of the same age. The similarity between siblings' outcomes compared with individuals from different families provides a measure of the total impact of family (as opposed to socioeconomic) background. Family background includes not only parents' socioeconomic characteristics, but also a host of other factors that siblings have in common. It includes both environmental and biological factors. Jencks *et al.* (1979: 9–10) defined "family background" as "everything that makes men with one set of parents different from men with a different set of parents". So "family background" includes readily measurable characteristics, such as father's occupation, father's and mother's education, income, race, ethnicity and religion, but also factors typically unmeasured, such as values, norms and goals, interests, personality and, of course, cognitive ability. It represents the upper limit of the influence of family of origin, since it includes aspects of the family that are independent of parents, such as the influence that siblings have on one another's attitudes and aspirations (Benin and Johnson 1984). Because sibling analyses are based on comparing the between- and within-sibling pair variances, sibling analyses are generally restricted to continuous variables such as test scores, educational attainment, occupational status and earnings.

The sibling (or intraclass) correlation is the expected correlation for a randomly selected pair of siblings (Snijders and Bosker 2012: 18). The expected correlation for two unrelated individuals is zero. In the case of grouped data such as sibling data, the Pearson correlation coefficient is equal to the intraclass correlation. The intraclass correlation is also the proportion of within-group variation as a proportion of the total variation. Assuming that siblings do not influence each other, the intraclass correlation should be the same as the R square value obtained by regression of the outcome variable with all influences that siblings have in common, both genetic and environmental (Corcoran *et al.* 1976; Olneck 1977). For example, if the sibling correlation is 0.4, 40 percent of the variation is between families and 60 percent is within families.

The correlations in siblings' years of education are typically between 0.4 and 0.6 (Hauser and Mossel 1988: 657; Hauser and Sewell 1986: S99; Olneck 1977: 132).[11] Sieben and de Graaf (2003: 54) estimated the average sibling correlation of 0.45 in data from 11 nations. The total effects of family background on educational attainment (and on other outcomes) are much greater than those for single-indicator or composite measures of socioeconomic background. Analyzing survey data on brothers in England, Hungary, the Netherlands, Scotland, Spain and the US, Sieben and de Graaf (2001) found that about 52 percent of the variation in educational attainment can be attributed to differences between families. The explained variation of over 50 percent is very much higher than that typically observed in standard analyses where a maximum of about 35 percent of the variation in educational attainment is accounted for by measured aspects of social, not only socioeconomic, background. Of this explained variance, three measured characteristics (parental education, father's occupational status, and the number of siblings) accounted for approximately half. This pattern of families accounting for about half the variation in educational attainment and about half of that variation attributed to measured aspects of the family of origin is consistent across sibling studies (de Graaf and Huinink 1992; Dronkers 1993; Hauser and Wong 1989).

The high sibling correlation has led to claims that socioeconomic background has a much stronger influence than indicated by the effects of measures of socioeconomic background on educational outcomes. The lack of strong effects could be attributed to the omission of key influences in most studies, such as family wealth (Bowles 1972; Corcoran 1992). Although, part of the unmeasured aspects of family background are ascriptive in nature, it is a mistake to assume that the bulk of the unmeasured component is unmeasured aspects of socioeconomic background or other social characteristics. Siblings also are much more similar in cognitive ability than randomly selected similar-aged pairs of unrelated individuals with a correlation around 0.5 (see section on "Biology and genetics" in Chapter 4, page 60). According to Kingston (2006: 121):

> Predictably enough, this total effect is greater than the effect attributable to the measured SES-related dimensions of family background. Yet it is far from clear that this unspecified extra advantage represents unmeasured ascriptive influences. Indeed, it seems likely that much of this "family advantage" is attributable to genetic endowments that favor success, as well as environmental reinforcement of cognitive development, work-oriented values and the like. By excluding sibling analyses, then, some small part of the ascriptive aspects of background may be missed; but the far greater likelihood is that the total family effect incorporates substantial merit (and matters unrelated to ascription). It is therefore highly problematic to link the difference between the total family effect and the measured family effect to ascriptive processes.
>
> (Kingston 2006: 121)

Biology and genetics

Adoption studies suggest that about half of the correlation in educational attainment between parents and children is due to biological factors. For Sweden, Björklund *et al.* (2006: 1013) found that, among adopted children, the correlations between years of education and their (non-biological) father's and mother's education was 0.11 and 0.08, respectively, compared with correlations of around 0.24 for biological children. The correlations in years of education for adoptees and their non-residential biological parents were around 0.11. This suggests that about half of the intergenerational correlation in education is due to biological factors and the other due to half social factors. For university education, the biological component appeared stronger since the effects for adoptive mothers and fathers are weaker than those for biological mothers and fathers. A larger Swedish study on educational attainment found substantial effects for totally (or mostly) absent *biological* parents. For child's years of education, the effect of mother's years of education (0.17) among single-parent families was comparable to that of the absent biological father's years of education (0.17). Where there was an adoptive father, the effect of an adoptive father was weaker (0.09) than that for the absent biological father (0.13) and that for the resident biological mother (0.13). In the less common situation of families where the biological mother is absent, her years of education has a moderate impact on the child's years of education (between 0.10 and 0.15) but resident step-mother's years of education has little impact (0.03 to 0.05). The authors conclude there is a substantial role of pre-birth factors in educational attainment (Björklund *et al.* 2007: 9–10, 15).

Twin studies also indicate a sizable genetic component to educational attainment. In the US, the correlations for educational attainment among identical twins are considerable at about 0.75, and 0.55 among fraternal (dizygotic) twins (Behrman and Taubman 1989: 1436; Taubman 1976b: 452). Nielsen (2006: 202) reported correlations of about 0.65 among identical twins for GPA and college plans compared with 0.36 and 0.33 for full siblings and 0.10 and 0.18 for non-related (same family) siblings. In Sweden, the correlations in educational attainment for monozygotic twins reared together were between 0.6 and 0.7 compared with around 0.5 for dizygotic twins (Lichtenstein *et al.* 1992: 22). In Australia, the correlations for educational attainment among monozygotic twins were around 0.70 or higher, compared with around 0.40 for dizygotic twins (Baker *et al.* 1996: 97; Miller *et al.* 1995: 590). These correlations are strong evidence that a sizable proportion of the family influence on educational attainment is genetic rather than environmental.

Based on correlations among twins and siblings, the contributions of genes (heritability), the shared environment and non-shared unique factors can be estimated. Taubman (1976a: 867–8) estimates that 40 percent of the variation in years of education is due to genetics (not just cognitive ability), and 30 percent for the common environment and 24 percent for the unique (non-common) variance, although these estimates changed under different assumptions. For an older cohort born between 1917 and 1927, Behrman *et al.* (1980: 206–7) estimate that genetics contributes to 30 percent of the variation in schooling, 40 percent to the common environment and about 30 percent to unique effects not attributable to family background or genetics. In more recent studies, there is a weaker contribution by the shared environment. Rowe *et al.* (1999b) estimate that genes account for 52 percent of the variation, the shared environment for around 18 percent and the non-shared environment for about 14 percent. Nielsen (2006: 204) calculated very high heritabilities for GPA (67 percent) and college plans (60 percent), and almost zero for shared environmental factors. There was considerable unique variation not associated with genes or the shared environment: 33 percent for GPA and 37 percent for college plans. Within this approach, "ascription" is the variance in educational attainment attributed to the environment that siblings share. He concludes that "These results do not suggest strong impacts of shared environmental factors on the schooling process for these adolescents in US schools at the end of the twentieth century" (2006: 205).

For other countries, the heritabilities for student achievement and educational attainment are at least 50 percent. For Norway and Finland, the genetic heritability in educational attainment was around 50 percent (Silventoinen *et al.* 2000; Tambs *et al.* 1989). Among Norwegian men born after World War II, Heath *et al.* (1985) estimated that genes contributed to 70 percent of the variation in educational attainment, and the environment only ten percent. For Australia, Baker *et al.* (1996) concluded that 57 percent of the variance in educational attainment was due to genetic factors and, after adjustments, proposes that the true level heritability is above 80 percent. Later Australian studies concluded that, at least as much as 50 percent, but possibly up to 65 percent of the variation in educational attainment is due to genetic endowments and as little as eight percent is due to environmental factors (Le *et al.* 2011: 132; Miller *et al.* 2001). For the Netherlands, Bartels *et al.* (2002b) estimate that 60 percent of the variability in test scores among 12-year-olds is due to genetic factors.

Conclusions

The relationships between socioeconomic background and educational outcomes – test scores, educational attainment and transitions – are far from maximal. Single indicators of socioeconomic background typically have correlations of around 0.3, with educational outcomes and composite indicators around 0.4. The correlations tend to be weaker for student achievement than educational attainment. Groups of family background variables, including measures of socioeconomic background, rarely account for more than a quarter of the variation in the educational outcome. In developed countries, the effects of socioeconomic background for entry to college and university are usually quite weak after taking into account student performance, which more strongly relates to ability than socioeconomic background. The moderate-sized effects of socioeconomic background undermine theories which assume that socioeconomic background has strong, almost deterministic, overwhelming relationships with educational outcomes. They also indicate that privileged socioeconomic groups have not been all that successful in manipulating education systems for their own benefit. The absence of strong associations between socioeconomic background and educational outcomes is directly counter to the claims of reproduction theories.

Attempts to demonstrate the importance of socioeconomic background by school-average socioeconomic status are flawed because the considerable within-school variation in socioeconomic status is removed, and in some analyses, the within-school variation in performance. If school context is important, it is more likely to involve the contextual effects of school-average ability than school-average socioeconomic status. Given that there is a strong relationship between childhood ability and later school performance (and childhood ability has a substantial biological component) and the stability of cognitive ability over the life course, it is not plausible that average school ability is a consequence of average school socioeconomic status. Furthermore, studies on adoptees, siblings and twins show that much of the relationship between family background and educational attainment is due to biological rather than social factors, so it cannot be assumed that the relationship between socioeconomic background and education is only due to social factors.

Notes

1 The EGP-based class measure comprised an upper service class, a lower service class, routine white collar, skilled and supervisory manual workers, semi-skilled and unskilled manual workers, and farm workers. For details on the EGP measure (see section on "Social class" in Chapter 3, page 35).
2 For the composite measure of socioeconomic status, father's occupation, father's education and mother's education were assigned weights of 0.25, 0.06 and 0.12, respectively (Thorndike 1973: 74).
3 The models for West Germany, the Netherlands, England and Wales, Japan, Hungary, Poland and Israel included birth cohorts or were by cohort so are not comparable.
4 This literature is documented in the next chapter in the section evaluating economic explanations for socioeconomic inequalities in education (Chapter 8).
5 Parts of this section are from Marks (2012).
6 In PISA, a one standard deviation difference in student achievement is standardized at one hundred score points (calculated from OECD countries). The meaning of a one-unit change in school socioeconomic status differs between countries dependent on the distributions of socioeconomic status across schools within a country.
7 Alexander *et al.* (1979: 235) also cautions against the use of school-level variables due to their high collinearity (intercorrelations of variables).
8 This literature is documented in the following chapter in the section evaluating economic explanations for socioeconomic inequalities in education (also see section on "Social class" in Chapter 3, page 35).
9 The true correlation between two variables x and y can be calculated from the reliabilities of the two variables. A reliability closer to 1 indicates a more reliable measure:

$$r_{xy}^{true} = \frac{r_{xy}^{observed}}{(\sqrt{\rho_x})(\sqrt{\rho_y})}$$

10 They interpreted this result as further evidence that economic resources matter little for socioeconomic inequalities in the Dutch education system.
11 The reliability for educational attainment is probably higher at around 0.95 (Osborne Groves 2005b: 225–6). Jencks *et al.* (1972: 337) offer a reliability of

0.82 for father's education, 0.77 for father's occupation and 0.98 for son's educational attainment.

12 A more recent study reports sibling correlations in educational attainment as high as 0.7 for sisters in the US (Conley and Glauber 2008).

Chapter 8

Socioeconomic inequalities in education II

Theoretical explanations

Although there is much agreement that socioeconomic background influences education, there is little consensus on how socioeconomic background matters. It is implausible that socioeconomic gradients in education exist because high-status parents are better at directly teaching their children the school curricula. Parents may be able to provide some direct assistance, but very few parents, no matter their education, occupation or income can effectively instruct their children across the range of subjects in senior or even middle secondary school. Invariably, explanations of socioeconomic inequalities in education posit indirect mechanisms, involving combinations of economic, cultural and social factors, usually emphasizing particular influences and social processes.

Theoretical explanations for socioeconomic inequalities in education incorporate, to varying degrees, economic, cultural and social resources, schools and student ability. Economic resources include money and wealth. Richer (or wealthier) families are able to purchase a better education or alternatively poorer families cannot meet the costs associated with an adequate education for their children. More common are cultural explanations: highly educated parents value education more, engender higher educational aspirations and are more involved in their children's schooling. Like the economic resources approach, there are both deficit and surfeit theories. Particular socioeconomic (or social) groups lack or possess the appropriate cultural resources for a successful educational career. Social networks are a third type of explanation. According to socioeconomic position, students participate in family or peer networks that may facilitate or hinder their education. Schools are also often involved in explanations for socioeconomic inequalities in education: only high-income or wealthy families can afford the best schools or tutors, highly educated parents better understand school systems so can manipulate the system to the advantage of their children. Although, most explanations incorporate aspects from two or more approaches (e.g. wealthy parents sending their children to expensive private schools), there is usually a primary focus. Most theoretical discussions tend to favor a particular approach and are sometimes critical of other approaches.

The purpose of this chapter is to evaluate the various theoretical explanations for socioeconomic inequalities in education.

General issues

In some discussions, economic, cultural and social resources constitute different forms of "capital", since they can be "converted" into human capital (education)[1] and eventually into "real" money capital.[2] This approach is an extension of the concept of human capital in economics and with it the notion that individuals rationally choose to invest in education in the expectation of receiving higher (monetary) returns later, in much the same way as investors invest money.[3] Although sociologists tend to reject this view of education as a rational investment decision and would argue that educational attainment has more to do with social influences, the idea that various forms of "capital" – social, cultural, human and economic – are interchangeable is common in the sociological literature (Bourdieu 1986; Coleman 1988; Ishida 1993: 66–9; Teachman *et al.* 1997).

Of the theoretical approaches to socioeconomic inequalities, some are more policy relevant. It is easier to address socioeconomic inequalities generated by economic and school factors rather than by cultural or social factors. Governments can provide financial support in the form of scholarships, stipends, allowances for textbooks and other educational materials. Similarly, governments can address school-based educational inequalities by increasing the funding of schools deemed as socioeconomically disadvantaged, providing incentives for high-quality teachers to teach in such schools and directly funding specific educational resources such as classrooms, libraries, laboratories and specialist teachers. They can also restrict public resources to schools serving students from privileged backgrounds. Governments can, and have, reformed school systems by replacing school tracks with more comprehensive systems, limiting within-school educational differentiation and increasing the flexibility of educational pathways. However, policies focusing on the costs of schooling and schools themselves will be ineffective in reducing socioeconomic inequalities in education, if economic factors and schools are not (or no longer) substantially involved in generating socioeconomic inequalities.

Either implicitly or explicitly "ability" figures in explanations for socioeconomic inequalities in education. If socioeconomic inequalities were removed then the only influences on educational performance would be ability and motivation, the two classical components of merit. High-ability students from low socioeconomic backgrounds do not reach their full potential, owing to a variety of social processes: not identified by the system as capable, lacking the appropriate cultural understandings or rationally opting for financial independence rather than further education. Alternatively or additionally, lower-ability students from high socioeconomic backgrounds are more successful than they otherwise would be, because their parents can use monetary and/or other resources to facilitate their educational careers.

The sociology of education literature is not unaware that cognitive ability is relevant. According to Nash (2001: 195), the dominant approach to class differences in educational outcomes in the 1950s was IQ. In a study of sixth graders published as long ago as 1962, Curry (1962) concluded that an above-average intellectual ability is likely to overcome deprived social and economic conditions but, as ability decreases, the effects of deprivation become serious. Nash (2001: 195–200) understood Bernstein's thesis on elaborated and restricted codes of speech as a response to the observation that working-class students performed less well at school than middle-class students did, even though they were probably just as bright. Goldthorpe's (2000: 188, 190–1) relative risk aversion thesis explicitly assumes that classes differ in average ability and thus influences the family's expectation of success. Jackson *et al.* (2007: 225) also acknowledge the importance of ability: "the results ... indicate that ability that is demonstrated by children from less advantaged backgrounds in their earlier academic careers is still often not exploited as fully as it could be at later stages". Lucas (2009: 507) contends that the task of theory is to understand how high-origin, middle-achieving youths "deploy non-meritocratic resources to secure opportunity, and thus may crowd deserving middle origin youth out of advantageous curricula". Not all theories on socioeconomic inequalities involve ability. According to Nash (2001: 190), Bourdieu utterly rejects the concept of intelligence in both its biological and social aspects.

Economic explanations

Income

Economic explanations of socioeconomic inequalities of education focus on economic resources, most commonly parental income, and, more rarely, household wealth. According to the economic-resources approach, economic inequality is the prime generator of differences in student performance. The essence of this economistic approach is that parents either can or cannot afford to "buy" educational success for their children. They can do this by sending their child to a high-fee private school or buying (or possibly renting) a house or apartment in the catchment area of a high-performing public school, which tend to be located in more expensive neighborhoods. In some countries, parents commonly employ personal tutors to improve their child's performance. At the other end of the economic spectrum, poorer families cannot buy the essentials: textbooks, reading books and other educational resources, and possibly their crowded living areas do not provide enough space for focused productive study. In reference to college education in the US, which can be very costly, the economic argument focuses on credit constraints; poorer families are unable to borrow the money necessary for a good education for their child (Becker 1975; Carneiro and Heckman 2002). Such credit constraint arguments do not apply as well, or not at all, in countries where university education is largely free or has relatively low upfront costs.

Empirical evidence

Family income

Family income is significantly related to student achievement and other educational outcomes. In Sirin's (2005) meta-analysis of mainly small studies conducted in the US between 1982 and 2000, it was found that the average-effect size (adjusted correlation coefficient) for the bivariate relationship between family income and student achievement was around 0.29, comparable with effect sizes of 0.30 and 0.28 for parental education and father's occupational status. This contrasts with White's (1982: 470) earlier meta-analysis, which found that family income showed stronger correlations (0.32) than parental occupation (0.20) or education (0.19). Ganzach (2000) reports a correlation of 0.30 between household income and educational attainment in the 1979 NLSY, although the correlations with father's or mother's education were larger (at about) 0.45.

However, for educational outcomes the impact of family income, net of other socioeconomic background factors, tends to be weaker than economic explanations of socioeconomic inequalities in education would predict. In the WLS, family income was obtained from state tax records and averaged over four years (Sewell and Hauser 1975: 18). It displayed surprisingly weak correlations with mental ability measured by test scores (0.18) and educational attainment (0.28). In a regression analysis of educational attainment, the standardized effect of family income (β = 0.12) was smaller than that for father's education (β = 0.22) and father's occupational status (β = 0.14) (Sewell and Hauser 1975: 72–3). In an earlier publication, Sewell and Hauser (1972: 101) comment, "there may be little merit in the efforts of some social scientists to interpret all social inequalities in terms of income differences". Analyzing mathematics scores in the 1988 NELS study, Fejgin (1995: 24) reported a standardized effect of 0.07 for family income, compared with 0.32 for parents' education. An even weaker standardized effect (β = 0.05 for family income) was found for reading achievement. Analyzing mathematics achievement scores in the children of NLSY 1979 study, Orr (2003: 291, 293, model 2) reported no effect for family income (averaged over five years) on mathematics achievement, net of father's occupational status, mother's education, mother's AFQT score and other variables (not including wealth).

In Olneck's (1977: footnote 1) analysis of educational attainment using sibling data, the addition of average family income over three years did not increase the explained variance beyond that provided by father's and mother's education, and father's occupation. According to an early analysis of the PSID, family income averaged over five years had no effect on young men's educational attainment, net of a crude measure of ability and father's education (Kiker and Condon 1981: 102). In a review article, Haveman and Wolfe (1995: 1856) conclude changes in family economic resources, however, are associated with relatively small changes in educational attainments. They cite Hill and Duncan's (1987) analysis of the PSID where a ten percent increase in family income (averaged over three years) was associated with an increase in educational attainment by only 1.4 percent, less when controlling for other social background factors. Similarly, Belzil and Hansen (2003: 694) conclude that for educational attainment, father's and mother's education have much stronger effects than family income. A one-year increase in parental education, on average, increases years of education by 0.3 of a year. To obtain a similar increase requires a difference of US$30,000 in income; a large difference given the average family income in that study (conducted in 1990) was US$37,000. For school completion, Belley and Lochner (2007: 51) found only a seven or eight percentage point difference in school completion rates between the top and bottom family income quartiles, net of measured AFQT quartile and mother's education.

In the US, going to college is often expensive, so income should have stronger effects for college entry than school completion. However, economic factors play a minor role compared with academic and social factors. Hearn's (1988) analysis of factors that influence the cost of the institution attended concludes that the relatively minor effects of socioeconomic status and ascriptive factors that matter are more "social" than "economic". Cameron and Heckman (2001: 485) concluded that family income has an important role in explaining grades at age 15, a modest role in high-school continuation decisions but "no role in college entry decisions"; and contrary to prevailing economic theory, they concluded that credit market constraints are not a strong determinant of college choices. Belley and Lochner (2007: 51–2) found modest effects for family income in the 1979 cohort; the difference in college attendance at age 21 between the top and bottom income quartiles, net of measured ability, was nine percentage points. For the 1997 NLSY, the difference had risen to 16 percentage points. This analysis included ability quartile but the only "social" background factor included was mother's education.

For enrolment in US graduate programs, family income has only weak effects. Net of grade point average (GPA) and other factors, a US$10,000 rise in income increases the probability of graduate school enrolment by only 0.37 percent (Zhang 2005: 324). Morgan and Kim (2005: 177) also found small effects. They conclude "that giving the average family US$6,000 per year in family income would increase the college enrollment rate among their adolescents by an additional two-thirds to one full percent".[4] In addition, they do not regard this effect as causal, since other home background and academic performance measures were not included.

Furthermore, family income has only weak effects on social, cognitive and behavioral outcomes among children (Aughinbaugh and Gittleman 2003; Blau 1999). Mayer's (1997) analysis of the PSID and the 1979 NLSY also concluded that the influence of family income on social and economic inequalities is, at best, modest when taking into account other family characteristics.

It is not only in the US where the effect of income on educational outcomes is weak. Bratti (2007: 36–7) finds significant negative effects of household income on dropping out of school in England and Wales, but concludes "the magnitude of the effect is relatively small". From an analysis of the age of finishing formal education, using data from the 1958 and 1970 NCDS and BCS studies, Chevalier and Lanot (2002: 179) concluded that "the effect of family income on a child's schooling attainment is rather limited". In their regression equation, family income was often not statistically significant, especially when controlling for ability. In the UK, Blanden and Gregg (2004) identified a small effect of income in the 1970 BCS, controlling for unmeasured differences between families using a fixed effect model; a decrease of one-third in household income reduced the probability of obtaining a degree by between one and six percent. The effect of household income may have increased when compared with the British Household Panel Survey (BHPS). According to their analysis of the BHPS, the comparable effect was between three and seven percent, although the BHPS does not include comparable measures of childhood ability.

In Canada, the association between dropping out of school and family income is weak (Foley *et al.* 2009). The effect of family income on university participation is very weak with R square values less than four percent, and in some years less than one percent (Corak *et al.* 2003). For New Zealand, Fergusson *et al.* (2008) conclude that the family's economic resources (and the socioeconomic level of the school) do not mediate the relationship between socioeconomic background and educational achievement. Much of the relationship was mediated by children's cognitive ability (35 percent) measured at age 8, 9 and 13 years, followed by educational aspirations. For Sweden, Erikson and Jonsson (1996: 21–2) conclude that "background factors other than economic resources are important in explaining the association between social origins and educational decision", although they suggest that economic resources may be important for the transition to university. For Denmark, Jæger (2007: 546) found no significant effects on completing secondary school for family income, home ownership, car ownership, or summer house ownership for the younger generation, and only family income mattered for the parental generation. He concluded, "economic capital has largely ceased to predict educational attainment" (2007: 546). In Germany, income plays a much smaller role than parental education in the allocation of students to different academic tracks (Schneider 2004). For Poland, the impact of income on educational attainment is generally weaker than that for other aspects of socioeconomic background, such as parent's education (Beblo and Lauer 2004). For the Netherlands, the effect of monthly income on education level was about one-third that of parental education (Vollebergh *et al.* 2001). Less direct evidence is provided by de Vries and de Graaf (2006: 226), who found no effect for father's occupational status (which is indexed by each occupational group's mean income and education), and concluded that "the economic dimension does not matter in the Dutch Education system". This conclusion was consistent with earlier research, which found that financial resources were important in the Dutch education system before 1950 but not since then. The change is attributed to policies which removed financial barriers to education (de Graaf 1986). In Norway, family income had no effect on grades at university when controlling for secondary school grades (Hansen and Mastekaasa 2006: 284). Japan is a possible exception to the general pattern of family income having limited effects. The impact of family income on continuing education beyond the minimum school leaving age and academic qualifications was higher in Japan than in either Britain or the US (Ishida 1993).

Wealth

A further argument concerning economic resources is the role of family wealth. Bowles (1972) argues that the effects of a family background on education are severely understated, since most studies do not include a measure of family wealth. It is arguable whether wealth is theoretically more important than income; both enable the securing of credit.[5]

Wealth does not strongly influence educational outcomes, Alwin and Thornton (1984: 795) report measurement error-corrected correlations of family assets with several educational outcomes. They were small: less than 0.14 for verbal ability, less than 0.05 for GPA, about 0.20 for a college-preparatory high school program and less than 0.25 for overall educational attainment. Family's economic position – a combination of family assets (measured on three occasions) and income (measured on four occasions) – had no significant effects on students' test scores or GPA, net of parental occupation and education. There were significant but weak effects for early economic position (β is less than 0.2), but not later economic position on college track and years of education (1984: 796). Analyzing data collected in 1966, Rumberger (1983: 763) found no wealth effects on ability (scores in a knowledge of the working world test). For years of education, the effect for wealth was significant, net of the ability measure, but quite moderate: a 100 percent increase in wealth was associated with an increase of 0.1 of a year of schooling. Pfeffer (2011: 126–31) presents sizable correlations from the PSID of around 0.37 between wealth and educational attainment, around 0.30 for the 1979 NLSY and 0.21 for the German GSOEP. The standardized effects of wealth on educational attainment in a structural equation model were 0.13 in the NLSY and 0.15 in the PSID, net of father's education, father's occupational status and family income. These are moderate effects, considering that the model did not include ability measures. The inclusion of wealth substantially reduced the impact of family income. A drop in the impact of income on college attendance with the inclusion of family wealth was also noted by Belley and Lochner (2007: 57–8). They found slightly stronger effects for wealth than income. Youth from the highest wealth quartile were 24 percentage points more likely to attend college than students from the lowest wealth quartile, not controlling for income, and 20 percent when controlling for income. The analyses did not control for father's education or occupation. Even Conley's (2001: 68) article trumpeting the importance of wealth on college enrolment shows weak effects of wealth: *a doubling* of parental assets increases the predicted years of education by 0.12 years and increases the probability of attending college by eight percent. There were no controls for student ability or other "academic" measures. Orr's (2003: 292) analysis of mathematics achievement included mother's ability measured by AFQT test scores. The study found that household wealth (averaged over five years) had larger standardized effects than parental education and occupation, net of mother's ability score. However, the standardized effects for all three background factors were weak: 0.08, 0.06 and 0.06, respectively. By contrast, the standardized effect for mother's ability was around 0.30.[6] The addition of the household wealth increased the explained variance very marginally from 0.239 to 0.242 (2003: 293).

Rational choice

A variant on economic explanations to socioeconomic inequalities in education focus on rational choice. This approach uses the jargon of economics; students and families make rational choices in order to maximize their "utility": their most satisfactory outcome. Boudon (1974) proposed the seemingly useful distinction between primary and secondary effects. Primary effects are class or socioeconomic differences in academic ability or student performance, which are due to mainly cultural factors, "the cultural effects of the stratification system" (1974: 36). Secondary effects are class differences in educational attainment given differences in academic ability or prior performance. Working-class students tend to have lower educational attainments than middle-class students with the same level of ability. Secondary effects stem from rational decision making based on subjective evaluations of the costs and benefits of remaining in education for families from different socioeconomic strata. For students from low socioeconomic backgrounds, their economic interests are arguably best served by choosing less academic pathways while at school, post-school vocational training, or leaving full-time education altogether and gaining employment. There is a general view that primary effects are more important than secondary effects (Erikson *et al.* 2005; Jackson *et al.* 2007; Nash 2003a).

Goldthorpe's (1996a) Relative Risk Aversion (RRA) thesis purports to explain class differences in educational attainment in terms of rational evaluations of the costs and benefits of pursuing further education by families from different classes. According to RRA, the primary aim for families is to avoid downward mobility in occupational class. This approach largely rejects the notion that cultural or normative factors are involved (1996a: 485; Breen and Goldthorpe 1997: 278). Resources and constraints account for class and gender differences. The calculation of continuation decisions is based on the costs of continuing education, the probability of success and the value placed on educational and other outcomes, formally expressed by a series of mathematical statements (Breen and Goldthorpe 1997: 279–81; Goldthorpe 2000). Another version of the rational choice approach is the "diversion" thesis; students (or their families) make choices that reduce their risk of failure, and since working class students are more likely to fail, they are less likely to choose higher level academic pathways (Becker and Hecken 2009; Gabay-Egozi *et al.* 2010).

The RRA thesis rests on several questionable assumptions. It is doubtful that families are overly concerned with class mobility. Aspirations are usually about a particular job (e.g. doctor, lawyer, teacher), a type of job (e.g. white collar, the trades) or a job in a particular industry (e.g. car maintenance, tourism, finance). If parents are concerned about downward mobility, it is more likely to be in terms of occupational status or income rather than the occupational-class categories that advocates of this approach have in mind. What is more likely is that families weigh up a range of factors: the parents' and the student's educational and occupational aspirations; the student's performance at school and occupational interests; probable job earnings; tastes for security, status and types of jobs; and "guesstimates" of what is likely or possible. Often parents do not express specific occupational aspirations for their child, indicating that they will go along with whatever their child wants to do, "as long as they are happy". Furthermore, RRA-type explanations assume that families in a particular class think and behave in one way and families in other classes homogenously act in a different way. Given the literature on class differences in attitudes and behaviors, it is likely that the variation within classes on any factor related to RRA, and similar approaches, is considerably greater than the between-class variation.

Furthermore and not surprisingly, families do not have the same understanding of class as class theorists. Substantial proportions of the population are puzzled by survey questions about what social class they belong to, or do not accept that social classes exist. Among those that accept that social classes exist, they have varying conceptualizations of the class structure and their location in it (Evans *et al.* 1992; see Jackman and Jackman 1983: 14). Few parents would conceptualize class in terms of the EGP eleven-, seven- or even five-fold class structures. The irony is, of course, there is little consensus among sociologists on the class structure of modern societies (see Sørensen 2000).

Finally, the common criticisms of rational action theories also apply to RRA theorizing: incomplete and erroneous information, emotions, differential weighting of different factors, and the difficulty in making accurate predictions. People have different tolerances of risk and there is no reason to suppose that these tolerances are associated with occupational class, with the notable exception of entrepreneurs. Nash (2003a) points out that most people act in such a way that it is difficult to separate rational and habitual behavior. Is it rational or simply sentiment for parents to encourage their child to join the family business, or become a doctor or lawyer?

Social capital

Social capital is defined as a complex set of beneficial relationships that involve shared norms based on trust. According to Bourdieu (cited by Jæger 2009: 532), social capital is defined as a set of social networks that can be used to promote an individual's interests. Social capital exists both within the extended family and the community (Coleman 1987). For understanding differences in student outcomes, the social capital argument is attractive, since it is plausible that families in more closely knit communities can use their social connections to enhance their children's educational outcomes. According to Coleman (1988), social capital works through social norms that support and provide effective rewards for success and prohibit detrimental and inappropriate behaviors. Erikson and Jonsson (1996: 30) suggest that social capital facilitates educational attainment through networks, by a variety of processes: accessing information; exchanging knowledge about educational strategies (this is difficult to disentangle from cultural resources); and students' friendship networks since students can help one another. Social capital arguments have been used to explain the superior performance of students attending religious, especially Catholic, schools.

Social capital theory could also explain the superior educational outcomes of some ethnic communities, such as Jewish and Asian groups, although it is less useful in accounting for the weaker educational performance of students from other ethnic minorities (logically there are negative forms of social capital, social networks which undermine educational success). However, social capital theory is not particularly valuable in explaining socioeconomic inequalities in education. It may have been once possible to argue that upper middle class students have the "right" social connections (e.g. for entry to a prestigious college or university), or that low socioeconomic background students have the "wrong" social connections (e.g. peer groups that are disparaging about education or even gangs). However, such arguments do not apply to the great bulk of students not from either end of the socioeconomic spectrum.

Measurement

Very often, variables that purport to be measures of social capital have little to do with a theory emphasizing networks with supportive social norms. Parcel and Dufur's (2001) very broad definition of social capital included school's disciplinary climate, mother's marital status and family size. Bassani's (2008) measures of "school social capital" include school type (public versus private), the proportion of students from single-parent families, classroom disruption and teacher encouragement. Although social capital theory was originally used to explain the higher performance of students attending Catholic schools, attending a Catholic school has also been used an indicator of social capital (Sandefur *et al.* 2006).

Family structure, family size,[7] disciplinary climate, teacher encouragement, school type, etc. are conceptually very distant from the theoretical definition of social capital defined by Teachman *et al.* (1997: 1344) as "represented by the density and consistency of educationally-focused relationships that exist among parents, children, and schools". The schooling variables often feature in the school effects literature with no reference to social capital theory. Similarly, concepts such as family size, family structure and school type have their own intellectual traditions, largely independent of the concept of social capital.

Empirical evidence

One of the most prominent pieces of evidence for social capital theory is the much lower proportion of dropouts in Catholic schools than in US public schools. Coleman and Hoffer (1987) attribute this to the strong church-based community centered on Catholic schools. Coleman's empirical basis for social capital theory is questionable, since when controlling for prior achievement differences between Catholic and public-school students' test scores are trivial, less than 0.1 of a standard deviation in test performance (Alexander and Pallas 1985: 115).

The general thrust of the social capital argument is that supportive parents and communities enhance student performance. However, cross-national studies of student achievement show that parental involvement is negatively associated with student performance. Thorndike (1973: 75) notes that the relationship between parental help for homework was consistently negative. In combination with two other indicators of home help, "helping with speaking" and "helping with writing", the correlations with reading achievement were negative. The size of the correlations was not large with a median correlation of –0.08. However, in some countries, the negative correlation between home help and reading achievement was stronger: up to –0.20 in the US and –0.17 in New Zealand (Thorndike 1973: 76–7). The most obvious reason for these negative relationships is that parents are more likely to be involved in their child's school work when they are performing poorly.

The second international mathematics study defined the concept of "home support" as the extent that parents provided encouragement and assistance for mathematics (as perceived by students). This concept avoids the idea of the parents directly "helping" with the student's work, and instead encompasses notions of encouragement, interest and involvement. The measure of "home support" comprised whether the student's father and mother: enjoy doing mathematics; are able to help the student's work in mathematics; are very interested in helping; think that mathematics is important; encourage the student to learn as much mathematics as possible; and want the student to do very well in mathematics (Kifer and Robitalle 1989: 189–90). According to social capital theory, this measure should be positively associated with mathematics achievement, since it taps positive pedagogical relationships between students and their parents. However, the scalar measure was either negatively associated or had no relationship with mathematics achievement in the countries participating in the study (Schmidt and Kifer 1989: 224–5).

In the PISA 2000 study, an index of *family educational support* was constructed from questions on the extent that the student's mother, father, and brothers and sisters "worked with" the student on the student's schoolwork. Again, the relationship was negative. For reading achievement the average correlation between family educational support and reading achievement was –0.11, although it was weakly positive in Korea and Japan.[8] Similarly, Dronkers and Robert (2008: 287, 292) report negative effects on mathematics achievement for "family educational support".

Sandefur *et al.* (2006), examining post-school education, found significant effects parental expectations, parent/adolescent discussion of school activities, Catholic school attendance, school changing, parental involvement in school activities, and parent-school academic contact, controlling for tests scores and GPA. Many of these effects could also be evidence for cultural factors. There was no effects for parents knowing the students' friends' parents. Huang's (2009) two measures of social capital, positive parent–child and teacher–parent interactions, were associated with higher achievement scores. However, very little variation in these two measures was explained by his measures of socioeconomic background. He also reported that support from teachers was negatively associated with student achievement, and this probably again reflects academically weaker students obtaining greater help from teachers. Jæger (2007) found few significant effects for indicators of social capital on educational attainment, only for parents finding a job (among the parental generation), and providing help if the child wants to study abroad. Jæger and Holm (2007) found that social capital was associated with entry into vocational education, but this was on a measure simply indexing knowing people who could get their child a job or an apprenticeship.

Schools

There is a commonly held image of a "bad" school, characterized by crumbling and inadequate infrastructure; populated by students who are disruptive, rude and aggressive, and uninterested in school work; and poor teachers who fail to motivate the students, are unqualified or inexperienced, and cannot teach properly or keep order. In contrast, a "good" school is characterized by clean and modern facilities, quiet and orderly classes, with students attentive and eager to learn taught by enthusiastic well-qualified and experienced teachers. Characteristically, bad schools serve students from low socioeconomic backgrounds while good schools are in prosperous neighborhoods. There is no doubt that there are schools that fit these stereotypes, but they are in a minority. The great bulk of schools are in the middle of the distributions of resources, infrastructure, teacher quality and school climate. Most schools have both disruptive and enthusiastic students, a share of good, poor and average teachers, and teach students from a variety of socioeconomic backgrounds. Therefore, the correlations between individual-level measures of student socioeconomic background and indicators of school quality, and the provision of teaching and learning, are typically quite low.

It is not clear how schools contribute to socioeconomic inequalities. The quality of schools may co-vary with the socioeconomic backgrounds of the students attending, with the best schools attended by the most privileged students and the worst schools attended by the most disadvantaged students. Other mechanisms include the presence of high-quality schools only being available to parents who can afford the fees or the housing in the catchment area, strong socioeconomic biases in the allocation of students to different school tracks (in school systems where there is tracking), or the allocation of students to different curricula pathways within schools, which lead to different educational outcomes. However, there is evidence that schools reduce rather than increase socioeconomic inequalities in education. Socioeconomic and racial/ethnic gaps increase during the summer months and decrease during the school term (Downey *et al.* 2004).

Between-school variation

The problem with school-based explanations is that there simply is not that much variation between schools in student performance compared with within-school variation. One of the most startling findings of the Coleman report (Coleman *et al.* 1966: 297), *Equality of Educational Opportunity*, was that, in the US, the variation in student performance is much greater *within schools* (about 80 percent) than between schools. The report concludes "that schools bring little influence to bear on a child's achievement that is independent of his background and general social context" (1966: 325). This undermined the argument that schools and differences in school resources are responsible for racial and socioeconomic differences in student outcomes. In other Anglo-Saxon countries also with largely comprehensive school systems – Australia, Canada, New Zealand and the UK – the between-school variation in PISA test scores (as a percentage of the total variation) is between 16 and 30 percent. These percentages divided by 100 produce the intraclass correlation, which can be interpreted as the expected correlation in student achievement between two randomly selected students from the same school (in this example between 0.16 and 0.22). In some countries – Finland, Iceland, Norway and Sweden – the between-school variation is even lower, around ten percent of the total variation. In countries with tracked schools, where the students are allocated to different school types at a young age, the between-school variation can be very high: 50 percent or more in Austria, Belgium, France, Germany, Greece, the Netherlands and Poland (Marks 2006: 36). In this group of countries, the between-school differences are very large because students are allocated to different school tracks largely by ability, which is highly correlated with student achievement (see section on "Tracking and streaming" in Chapter 5, page 75).

Where there are larger differences between schools in average student performance and other student outcomes, much of the difference can be attributed to differences in the intake characteristics of students rather than what schools do. When taking into account individual students' socio-economic background and other aspects of their social backgrounds, schools contribute less than ten percent of the variation in student performance in the US (Coleman *et al.* 1982: xxvi). Hauser (1969) concluded that school differences in educational outcomes are small and may be largely an artifact of compositional differences. Scheerens and Bosker's (1997: 77) meta-analysis concluded that schools account for about 19 percent of achievement differences between students and eight percent when adjusting for the intake characteristics of students. They later argue that these moderate differences are large enough to be important. Jencks *et al.* (1972: 93) concluded that "differences between high schools contribute almost nothing to the overall level of cognitive inequality" (i.e. inequality in test scores). They point out that, if all schools were equally effective in raising student achievement during the final years of secondary school, inequality among twelfth graders would fall by less than one per cent (1972: 90).

The most important student intake characteristic is prior achievement usually measured by test scores. The correlation between prior achievement and student performance is typically above 0.7, often higher (Dumay and Dupriez 2008: 451; Hemmings and Kay 2010; Reynolds and Walberg 1992). According to Thrupp *et al.* (2002: 485), "An uncontroversial finding from the school effectiveness literature is that measures of 'ability' or prior achievement are the best predictors of future outcomes". It could be argued that schools contribute substantially to the initial levels of student achievement. However, test scores are very stable across the school career (see section on "Stability" in Chapter 4, page 55), and prior ability has stronger effects on student achievement than home factors and the bulk of school and teacher factors (Hattie, 2009). Therefore, the role of schools in raising or lowering student outcomes, independent of students' prior performance, is quite limited. That is not to say that there are no schools that raise or lower student performance beyond that expected by student characteristics, only that these constitute a minority of schools. This means that school characteristics such as resources,[9] disciplinary climate, teacher qualifications, student morale and academic press will have an even more limited impact on student outcomes. Therefore, schools and school characteristics will not feature largely in explaining socioeconomic inequalities in education.

Private and other school types

In countries where private schools exist, they charge high fees and their students have superior educational outcomes; they are part of the explanation for the socioeconomic gradient in educational outcomes. There is no doubt that students attending one of the greater English public schools are far more likely to enjoy an Oxbridge education and a successful career than students at a local comprehensive school. However, the existence of private schools is not a sufficient explanation for socioeconomic inequalities in education, since high-fee private schools typically serve only a small proportion of students. Similarly, the existence of schools not always exclusively funded and administered by the state – religious, ethnic, selective, international, bilingual, charter schools and specialist schools orientated toward the arts or sports – does not easily explain socioeconomic inequalities. For such schools to account for socioeconomic inequalities in education several conditions must be satisfied; they serve a large proportion of the student population, the socioeconomic profiles of the schools' students is substantially higher than that of state-administered (public) schools and they deliver superior student outcomes. These three conditions are rarely satisfied.

School tracks

In many European and other educational systems, different types of government schools (tracks) are associated with particular educational and occupational pathways. Academic gymnasiums are the first step in a pathway that leads to high-status, post-school education and eventually to well-remunerated administrative or professional positions. In contrast, vocational schools prepare students for early exit from school to the labor market or post-secondary vocational study. In some countries (e.g. Austria and Germany), school tracking begins as young as age 10 or 11, and in most others around age 15 or 16. National educational systems differ in the number of tracks and the proportion of students in vocational, academic or general tracks (OECD 2004: 262). Although the official position is that school tracks facilitate learning by catering to students with different abilities and interests, it is argued that the allocation of students to school tracks is considerably influenced by social origins (see Buchmann and Park 2009; Müller and Karle 1993). Therefore, tracked school systems are understood as maintaining existing, or even enhancing, socioeconomic inequalities. Socioeconomic inequalities associated with school tracks are intensified by early tracking at an early age, the number of tracks and inflexibility in moving between tracks (Horn 2009; van de Werfhorst and Mijs 2010).

The counter argument is that tracking decreases the reproduction of socioeconomic inequality. Tieben *et al.* (2010: 82) point out that using test scores as a selection mechanism for the allocation to different school tracks was intended to lower the impact of family background, since it is a more objective criterion than teacher, principal or school recommendations, or other mechanisms that allow family input. Arguably, school tracks facilitate social mobility by providing recognized pathways for high-ability students from low or middle socioeconomic backgrounds. Furthermore, tracking provides occupational pathways for non-academic youth from disadvantaged backgrounds who otherwise would have difficulties in securing careers (Brunello and Checchi 2007). Ayalon and Shavit (2004: 117) note that, in Israel, school tracking keeps students in the school system who otherwise would have felt excluded from an academically orientated curriculum. Abolishing school tracks may not reduce socioeconomic inequalities. In Japan, de-tracking public schools had the unintended consequence of encouraging parents to opt for private schools (Kariya and Rosenbaum 1999).

There are countries with tracked school systems which, according to PISA, exhibit moderate or low socioeconomic inequalities in student achievement: the Netherlands, which has four tracks beginning at age 12; Italy, which has three tracks at age 15; and Korea, which has three tracks beginning at age 14. New Zealand, the US and the UK have largely comprehensive systems but socioeconomic inequalities in education (as measured by PISA) are similar to the OECD average (see section on "Cross-national studies" in Chapter 9, page 177). In addition, there is little evidence that school tracks are closely associated with socioeconomic background. Analyzing between-school differences using PISA data, Marks (2006: 35–7) found that the between-school variation in student achievement is only marginally reduced when controlling for comprehensive composite measures of socioeconomic background that included cultural and economic aspects of the home as well as parental education and occupation.

Socioeconomic background has become less important for track placement in the Netherlands. Fasse *et al.* (1987) found that the secondary effects of social class (its effect net of ability) on teachers' advice and school track attended had declined to almost zero. The effects of father's occupational status on entry to different educational tracks declined for cohorts born between 1917 and 1987, although the effects of parental education were mostly unchanged. Father's occupational status was almost irrelevant for entry to school tracks in the youngest cohort (Tieben *et al.* 2010).

Within-school streaming

For countries with largely comprehensive education systems, the parallel argument to school tracking is that schools maintain socioeconomic inequalities by within-school streaming (or curriculum placement). Like school tracks, the criticism is that socioeconomic background and other ascribed characteristics (usually gender and race) figure far too strongly in the allocation of students to different streams or curriculums (Abraham 1995; Hout and Garnier 1979: 55; Oakes 1985).

Although there have been reforms to delay curriculum differentiation and increase flexibility in most developed countries, educational differentiation at senior secondary school will continue, owing to the requirements of post-school educational institutions and the labor market. For example, engineering courses will always require higher-level mathematics and science subjects as prerequisites, while medical faculties often require higher-level sciences, such as chemistry. Furthermore, school systems endeavor to cater for a diverse range of student interests especially for students at risk of not completing school.

Within-school streams are not inflexible pathways to post-school destinations. Lucas (2001), who incorporates within-school streaming in his theory of Effectively Maintained Inequality, notes that, in the US, the classic model of rigid assignment of students to academic and non-academic streams with no mobility between tracks is not borne out empirically. Students make subject choices at several points of their school career; there are no overarching streams that govern subject choice; upward mobility is common, and the role of counselors in student placement has diminished (2001: 1649). Furthermore, increasing proportions are in the college-orientated academic track: 85 percent in the early 1990s compared with 61 percent ten years earlier (Karen 2002: 200). Reisel's (2011: 267–8) flow charts show that less than half (47 percent) of US high-school graduates in the academic track complete a four-year college degree. Furthermore, the same outcome is possible, but far less likely, for high-school graduates who were in the general track (25 percent). In the UK, Australia and other countries with largely comprehensive systems, it is not a simple matter to distinguish between university-bound and non-university-bound subject pathways. Typically, entry requirements for university are less prescriptive and increasing proportions of school completers are eligible for university.

Curriculum location is only weakly linked to socioeconomic background.

Socioeconomic background has only small effects for within-school curriculum placement, net of ability or prior performance. Analyzing track placement, the direct effect of a block of socioeconomic status variables – father's education, father's occupation, mother's education and size of house – was small (β = 0.16), net of ability (Alexander *et al.* 1978: 55). Alexander and Cook (1982: 632) report a standardized effect of 0.14 for socioeconomic status on senior high-school curriculum placement compared with 0.36 for fifth-grade ability test scores. The standardized effect for SES declines to a very small 0.07 when controlling for ninth-grade GPA. They conclude that "inequalities of access linked to social background were small overall" (1982: 633). Citing a paper by Gamoran and Mare (1989), Kingston (2006: 124) concludes that, for the US, "track placement is most significantly determined by prior performance (grades and test scores)", and the net impact of socioeconomic background is relatively minor. Acland's (1973: 151) study of English primary schools concluded that, net of ability, "stream assignment decisions do not appear to be influenced by social background differences, and that the effect of stream position on achievement is small". For France, analyzing curricula type, Hout and Garnier (1979: 154) report a stronger effect for a quintile measure of academic performance than father's occupational status.

Cultural explanations

Cultural explanations of socioeconomic inequalities in education argue that particular social groups have distinct cultures that either facilitate or hinder their children's education. One type of cultural explanation sees working-class (or ethnic) cultures as detrimental in themselves: "deficit" theories (they are sometimes criticized as blaming the victim). It is argued that, compared with middle-class families, working-class families do not value education, have much lower educational aspirations for their children and generally are not nearly as involved in their children's education as middle-class families. Hyman (1966) concluded that class differences in student outcomes could largely be attributed to class differences in parents' attitudes to the value of education. Bernstein (1971) theorized that elaborated and restricted codes of speech, respectively, enhance and undermine the academic achievement of middle- and working-class students (at least in England). Willis (1977) emphasized that the subcultural norms of working-class youth (including misbehavior) were not conducive to success in the education system and were largely responsible for the (assumed) lack of intergenerational mobility.

Alternative explanations focus on the benefits that advantaged groups obtain from education. Collins (1971: 1008) argues that status groups use education "to monopolize or dominate jobs by imposing their cultural standards on the selection process". According to him, the main purpose of education is not to impart knowledge but to impart particular status cultures;

schools "primarily teach vocabulary and inflection, styles of dress, aesthetic tastes, values and manners" (1971: 1010). Subsequently, education serves as an indicator of ascribed characteristics for selection by employing organizations, and the skills gained are of secondary importance. This disparaging and radical (and highly cited) view of schooling presupposes very strong links between socioeconomic background, students' behaviors and attitudes which are "learnt" at school and labor force outcomes which simply do not exist. It is also implausible that privileged status groups act unilaterally to control the education system. Similarly, it is doubtful that the ideologies surrounding education systems strongly reinforce social inequality. If anything, the education industry tends to attract those with a reformist, sometimes radical, left-of-center political orientation.

Bowles and Gintis (2002b: 1) argue that "schools prepare people for adult work rules, by socializing people to function well, and without complaint, in the hierarchical structure of the modern corporation". Apparently, schooling does more than just reproduce the reward structures of modern society, but promotes the spread of cultural traits (e.g. acceptance of authority) that would not otherwise spread. Schooling also promotes those traits that are advantageous to the privileged group that determines the structure of schooling (2002b: 19). Again and implausibly, this view assumes very strong relationships between socioeconomic privilege, "cultural traits" and educational outcomes, and politically powerful and activist elites.

Cultural explanations are based on the idea that there are distinct and enduring subcultures linked to class or socioeconomic groups. Goldthorpe (2007) and van de Werfhorst (2010: 158–9) point out that, if cultural based explanations of socioeconomic inequalities were correct, educational expansion should increase socioeconomic inequalities because working-class children would not have the cultural know-how to increase their level of participation. In response to the high proportion of working-class students who achieved an acceptable academic standard for entry to A level courses in the UK, Jackson *et al.* (2007: 224) conclude that their findings "can scarcely bear out the idea of static and homogenous class subcultures in which prevailing values and norms are powerfully inimical to educational aspirations". If there were a dichotomy in cultural norms between middle- and working-class families or between elite and non-elite social groups then educational outcomes should reflect these dichotomous distinctions. Instead, almost everywhere a social gradient is observed (for test scores in PISA, see Marks 2011). Furthermore, there is little evidence that there are strong distinct class cultures. Class is a weak predictor of attitudes, values and behaviors (Davis 1982; Kingston 2000). Analysis of the PISA data show that in developed countries, occupational aspirations are only weakly linked to students' socioeconomic background, especially when controlling for students' test scores (Marks 2010a).[10]

Cultural capital theory

The most well-known theory that focuses on cultural factors in explaining socioeconomic differences in education is Bourdieu's theory of cultural capital. Bourdieu (1977) argues that the success of students from high-status backgrounds, who are naturally adept in the dominant culture, is enhanced because teachers and other gatekeepers judge and assess students by the implicit criteria of the dominant culture, so they are almost invariably successful. Therefore, the curricula, the methods of assessment and the organization of the education system itself create hurdles, which those not from elite backgrounds find almost impossible to overcome. Bourdieu's argument is an adaptation of Marxist theory; the very way in which education is organized and the ideologies surrounding education function to maintain existing social class inequalities.

Bourdieu's theory of cultural capital has generated an enormous amount of literature. Goldthorpe (2007) distinguishes two cultural capital literatures. The "domesticated" variety treats the theory within the context of normal science, in which concepts are operationalized, hypotheses generated and tested. This contrasts with the "wild" version, where Bourdieu's theory of cultural capital is a new paradigm where normal science does not apply. In the "wild" version, cultural capital theory accounts for any aspect of social life that relates to student performance. For example, the strong influence of cognitive ability on educational outcomes documented in Chapter 5 becomes "cultural capital", enabling and legitimizing the success of students from privileged backgrounds (Lareau and Weininger 2003: 569). Sullivan (2007: 3.2) points out that, if cultural capital cannot be distinguished from student ability, the cultural capital arguments about social class differences in achievement become circular. Similarly, Jæger (2009: 1948–9) points out that cultural capital and cognitive ability are conceptually distinct. Cultural capital is about "knowing the rules of the game", and cognitive ability is about "being smart", involving quite different processes. According to the Lareau and Weininger perspective, test scores are at once an important and consequential educational outcome, and an indicator of cultural capital. So test scores become synonymous with cultural capital and a strong relationship between test scores and later educational outcomes is evidence for cultural capital theory. Subsuming cognitive ability under the concept of cultural capital substantially strengthens its explanatory power, but ultimately undermines cultural capital theory because there is a sizable genetic component to cognitive ability and cultural capital theory is exclusively a socialization theory.

Bourdieu's theory of cultural capital has plausibility in some areas of the curriculum, such as literature and history, where prior cultural knowledge is beneficial. However, it is difficult to understand how the dominant culture is important to mathematics and science. Calculus, molecular physics and organic chemistry, to take several of many examples, do not have strong cultural components, so the cultural "signals" transmitted from students to gatekeepers would not be particularly relevant.

Measurement

Although cultural capital is about elite culture, it is not uncommon for cultural capital to be measured by parental education or occupation. Bourdieu and Passeron (1977: 497) measure family cultural capital by the academic achievements of previous generations. Erikson and Jonsson (1996: 25) contend that a good indicator of cultural capital is simply the effect of parental educational qualifications, net of social class. Jæger (2007) measures cultural capital by father's and mother's education, and subscription to a newspaper. Jonsson (1987: 231) takes the parental level of education as an indication of the cultural standing of the family. Sullivan (2001: 896) points out that equating cultural capital with parental education is highly questionable, since it begs the question of whether parental education actually reflects the possession of cultural capital. It is contradictory that a very prominent theoretical *explanation* for socioeconomic inequalities in education, cultural capital, should be measured by a commonly used *indicator* of socioeconomic background, parental education. This logic also means that children's cultural capital could be measured by their educational attainment.

Less commonly, the cultural capital of an individual student is indicated by parental social class. Hansen and Mastekaasa (2006: 283) equate social-class origin with level of cultural capital: the "Professional and higher level cultural occupations" class having the highest level of cultural capital followed by the class of "Engineers and Administrators", and for other occupational groups assumptions are made about their relative levels of cultural capital. The problem here is that the theory of cultural capital is apparently supported simply by differences in educational outcomes by class of origin, admittedly net of family income. Cultural capital theory is supposed to explain these differences.

More commonly, cultural capital is measured by interest in or engagement with "high culture". In DiMaggio's (1982) much-cited study on the effects of cultural capital on high-school grades, cultural capital was measured by interest in attending symphony orchestras, performing music, attendance of artistic events, reading literature and a cultivated self-image. de Graaf (1986) measures cultural capital by the number of visits per month to museums, galleries, concerts, theatres and historical buildings. Other studies have also measured cultural capital by participation in such culturally elite activities (Katsillis and Rubinson 1990; Crook 1997; de Graaf *et al.* 2000). Flerea *et al.*'s (2010) measure of cultural capital combines parental education, cultural participation and other cultural indicators.

Bourdieu's theory of cultural capital includes the nebulous and broad concept of "habitus". Habitus could be understood as a person's unacknowledged preferences, behaviors, dispositions, values and tastes. In standard sociology textbooks, "preferences, behaviors, dispositions, values and tastes" would be understood as products of "socialization". Summarizing Bourdieu, Goldthorpe (2007: 5) defines habitus as "the system of socially constituted dispositions that the individual acquires, most effectively in early life, and that determines his or her entire orientation to the world and modes of conduct within it". Lamont and Lareau (1988: 158) describe habitus as "dispositions" acquired through family socialization. According to Dumais (2002: 45), habitus is "one's view of the world and one's place in it", but oddly enough, it was measured by occupational aspirations (2002: 51).

In several international studies of achievement, students have been asked the simple question, "Approximately, how many books are there in your home?". Although this item was probably intended as a predictor of reading achievement (it was included in the first international reading study), it is increasingly used as an indicator of cultural capital. Surprisingly, it is correlated with mathematics and science achievement just as strongly as parental occupational status. In the first international science study, the overall correlation between books in the home and science achievement was 0.21 compared with 0.23 for the criterion-scaled measure of father's occupational status (Comber and Keeves 1973: 259). In the first and second international science studies, "Books in the home" tended to have stronger correlations with test scores than parental occupation (Keeves *et al.* 1991: 75).

Cultural capital theory's contentions and empirical evidence

For cultural capital to be important to the reproduction of socioeconomic inequalities, it needs to be strongly associated with socioeconomic background. Within the same generation, there is some association between cultural activities and socioeconomic position. Analyzing two Dutch cohorts, de Graaf (1986: 245) reports sizable correlations of 0.65 and 0.59 between composite measures of socioeconomic status and participation in formal culture, respectively, for older and younger cohorts. The raw correlations for single measures are much lower. The correlations between the frequency of museum visits and indicators of socioeconomic background ranged from low (0.16 for family income) to moderate (0.40 for father's education) for the younger cohort, but was more substantial for the older cohort: (0.29 for family income to 0.50 for mother's education) (de Graaf 1986: 241). After noting the low correlations between parental education and students' cultural capital in data from high-school students in the US, DiMaggio (1982: 198–9) concluded that cultural participation is "less strongly tied to parental background traits than Bourdieu's theory or similar discussions of class and culture in the US would predict" (see also DiMaggio and Mohr 1985: 1232). Dumais (2002: 65) reports a correlation of 0.4 between a composite measure of socioeconomic status and students' cultural capital. Analyzing data from a representative sample of Australian adults, Crook (1997: 81) reported correlations of 0.3 to 0.4 among adults between cultural participation and their father's occupation and their parents' education. Sullivan's (2001) study of English high-school students reported a significant difference in students' cultural activities between students from higher service and unskilled manual backgrounds, but no statistically significant differences between other class backgrounds and an unskilled manual background. The significant difference in students' cultural activities between upper service and unskilled manual backgrounds disappeared when controlling for parents' cultural activities. For Denmark, Jæger (2009: 1963) found that family socioeconomic status and two measures of parental education had weak effects on cultural participation. In Slovenia, there was only a correlation of 0.19 between cultural capital and self-perceived economic status of the student's family (Flerea *et al.* 2010: 53). For France, Germany and Switzerland, measures of cultural and social capital could only partially account for socioeconomic differences in PISA test scores (Jungbauer-Gans 2004). In a 30-country study, a measure of cultural resources comprising "books in the home" and cultural possessions in the home, such as works and art and classic literature, accounted for about 25 percent of the effect of socioeconomic background on students' test scores (Marks *et al.* 2006). Similarly, Barone's (2006) analysis of 25 countries using the PISA data concluded that in no country does his two indices of cultural capital account for more than 30 percent of the effect of socioeconomic background. (These studies could not include student ability.) Therefore, the link between cultural participation and socioeconomic background is substantially weaker than generally supposed by cultural capital theory. Kingston (2001: 92) observes that, since cultural capital is so weakly associated with family status, it "cannot unlock the puzzle of why privilege is linked to academic success".

There is a much stronger association between parents' and children's cultural activities. Sullivan (2001) reported a correlation of over 0.6 between parents' and students' cultural activities. Regression analyses led her to conclude that parents' cultural capital is "by far the most important factor in accounting for pupils' cultural activities". Similarly, Crook (1997: 81) reported a correlation of 0.6 between parents' and child's participation in "high" cultural activities. In a regression analysis of cultural participation, the standardized coefficient for parental cultural participation was 0.54, dwarfing the effects of parental education and father's occupation. Nagel and Ganzeboom (2002) report substantially stronger effects of parents' cultural participation than parental education on their children's cultural participation, so it appears that the intergenerational reproduction of cultural preferences and practices is fairly strong, but such practices are only moderately related to socioeconomic status.

There are relationships between participation in high culture and student performance. DiMaggio (1982: 195) shows that cultural participation among US high-school students was positively associated with school grades in English, history, mathematics, and grades in all subjects. This finding is impressive, since these effects were net of measured cognitive ability and father's education. The effects of cultural participation were only moderate with standardized coefficients of around 0.15–0.20 on grades in English, history, and all subjects, and it had weaker effects on grades in mathematics. In a follow-up study, DiMaggio and Mohr (1985) established that cultural participation was also associated with years of education, college attendance and college graduation. However, other US studies found weaker effects. Analyzing the 1988 NELS study, Dumais (2002: 55) found that cultural capital had only a weak effect on grades at school among boys and a very limited effect among girls. The impact of *ability* on grades was ten times that of cultural capital among boys and 13 times greater among girls. Bourdieu's concept "habitus", measured by occupational expectations, had sizable effects for grades. However, occupational expectations are more strongly shaped by ability than socioeconomic background (Marks 2010a). Although without the theoretical pedigree of cultural capital theory, participation in sports had a substantially stronger impact on grades at school (for both sexes) than cultural capital or, for that matter, socioeconomic status or occupational expectations, but not ability. Dumais and Ward (2010) found no link between cultural capital and GPA while at college.

In other countries, the effects of cultural capital on educational outcomes are generally weak or nonexistent. de Graaf (1986: 245), analyzing Dutch sibling data collected in 1977, found that the effect of formal culture on educational attainment was nil and concluded that "families who participated more in formal culture than other families did not provide a better education climate for their children" (1986: 245). For Germany, grades are the dominant influence on the transition to the prestigious gymnasium track, and grades could only be partially explained by family factors (de Graaf 1988: 219). For the UK, Sullivan (2001) found that although students' cultural participation was significantly related to students' performance in the General Certificate of Secondary Education, the effect was not significant after controlling for students' linguistic ability and vocabulary. Analyzing applicants to Oxford University, Zimdars *et al.* (2009) found no effect for participation in the *beaux arts*, but scores on a test of cultural knowledge had a significant effect for entry to arts subjects but not science, net of "meritocratic" controls (i.e. academic performance in the final years of schooling which appears to have the strongest effects). "Books in the home" had significant effects for entry to sciences, but not for the arts. The cultural-capital measures only very partially mediated the relationship between class of origin and successful admission to Oxford.

For Greece, Katsillis and Rubinson (1990) found no effect of students' cultural participation on grade point average. Similarly, Crook's (1997:

86–108) Australian study did not find significant effects of students' cultural participation on most educational outcomes. de Graaf *et al.* (1989), who constructed two dimensions of parental occupational status (cultural and economic), found that, although the cultural dimension had a stronger effect on children's education, its effect could only be described as moderate (with a standardized effect of 0.19). They concluded that this supports a probabilistic version of Bourdieu's thesis, but note that it does not confirm the main contentions of cultural capital theory. Jæger (2009: 1963) concluded, from analyses of longitudinal data from the Danish PISA 2000 study, that "cultural capital only to a very limited degree explains the effect of SES on secondary school choice".

Reading behavior may explain the different conclusions of DiMaggio and others regarding the importance of cultural practices on educational outcomes. DiMaggio's (1982) measure of cultural capital included reading as well as participation in cultural activities. In contrast, Crook (1997: 86–104) created separate measures and found significant effects for students' reading behavior on educational outcomes but no significant effects for students' cultural participation. Similarly in West Germany and the Netherlands, the effects of *parental* reading behavior on educational outcomes were stronger than the effects of parental participation in cultural activities (de Graaf 1988; de Graaf *et al.* 2000). de Graaf (1988), analyzing data from West Germany, found effects of parental reading on grades at school and the transition to the more prestigious academically Gymnasium school track. In contrast, financial resources had no effect.

Another criticism of cultural capital theory is that part of the observed effects of cultural capital can be attributed to "ability". As documented in Chapter 5, there is no doubt that ability plays an important role in student performance and thus socioeconomic inequalities in education. As early as 1972, Jencks *et al.* (1972: 140) noted that middle- and working-class students with the same prior test scores received much the same grades, undermining the contention that cultural differences between social classes are important to performance. Apart from the pioneering studies by DiMaggio (1982) and DiMaggio and Mohr (1985), ability is conspicuous by its absence in studies of cultural capital. Barone (2006: 1051) attributes the effects of his two indices of cultural capital on student achievement as indirect effects of "*cognitive* resources". Similarly, Kingston (2001: 93–4) notes that student ability is often missing from studies of cultural capital, and effects purported to reflect cultural capital are more likely to reflect academic ability. Dumais (2002) reports a correlation of 0.29 between her measure of cultural capital and ability. The effects of parents' reading behavior on their child's reading and mathematics test scores, net of social class ($\beta = 0.23$ for reading and $\beta = 0.19$ for mathematics),[11] reported by van de Werfhorst *et al.* (2003: 53), could be understood as evidence for the importance of cultural capital, but is also consistent with parental reading behavior being a proxy measure of parental ability. The effect for parental reading behavior on students' O-level grades in humanities and science subjects declined by about 75 percent when students' reading and mathematics test scores were added to the analysis (van de Werfhorst *et al.* 2003: 54). This is consistent with the argument that part of the effect of cultural capital indictors on educational outcomes can be attributed to ability.

Some of the empirical work on cultural capital leads to conclusions directly contradictory to what cultural capital theory purports to explain. Instead of explaining why students from lower-class backgrounds have lower educational outcomes, a common conclusion is that cultural capital serves as a mechanism for upward mobility for working-class children – the cultural mobility model – rather than maintaining the reproduction of socioeconomic inequalities (Aschaffenburg and Maas 1997; de Graaf *et al.* 2000; DiMaggio 1982; Kalmijn and Kraaykamp 1996). There is a variety of other criticisms of cultural capital theory: its vague and changing definitions of cultural capital by Bourdieu (Goldthorpe 2007; Lamont and Lareau 1988); the lack of evidence that teachers act as gatekeepers discriminating against students from lower socioeconomic backgrounds (Sullivan 2001);[12] and the assumption that there are distinct class cultures in developed countries (Kingston 2001).

Scholarly culture and books in the home

Although there are problems with cultural-capital theory, there is evidence that cultural factors contribute to inequalities in education. Using data from 27 countries in the International Social Science Project, Evans *et al.* (2010: 25) found that, net of other influences, books in the home had a standardized effect of 0.27 on educational attainment (years of schooling), compared with standardized effects of 0.14 and 0.16 for father's education and occupation. A fairly unreliable measure of academic ability decreased the standardized effect for books in the home to 0.20. The authors argue that that their analysis is consistent with the social mobility hypothesis for cultural capital and is contrary to the predictions of cultural capital theory. Scholarly culture is a means of social mobility, not of social exclusion. One explanation is that the number of books in the home is an indicator of the intellectual environment of the home, or "scholarly culture", where learning and intellectual pursuits are valued and encouraged. Reading and books in the home are parts of a "toolkit" comprising competencies, skills and sources of knowledge, which all enhance learning and student performance (Evans *et al.* 2010: 25). This is consistent with the conclusion from the cultural capital literature that reading behavior is a much stronger influence on educational outcomes than participation in elite cultural practices.

Jæger's (2011) double fixed-effect analysis focused on the causal impact of cultural factors. The data analyzed included siblings and was longitudinal for individual students. A fixed effect was specified for family of origin to control for all unmeasured family influences on student performance. A second fixed effect was included for individual students to control for unmeasured differences between students (ability, personality, etc.) that impact on achievement. He was also able to include controls for socioeconomic background, mother's AFQT score, race and other factors. In the fixed-effect analyses of the entire sample, there was no significant effect of aspects of high culture (taken to museums, concerts), but significant effects for the number of books in the home, reading for enjoyment and engaged in extracurricular activities (an odd measure comprising extracurricular participation in sport or music as well as outside school tutoring) (2011: 291). However, the significant effects for the number of books in the home and reading for enjoyment were small, too small to support theories of cultural capital.[13] Disaggregated analyses by socioeconomic background provided evidence for both the cultural reproduction and cultural mobility models: being taken to museums and reading behavior had stronger effects among higher socioeconomic status families, supporting cultural reproduction arguments; and the effect of the child's number of books and parental encouragement for hobbies had stronger effects among lower socioeconomic status families, supporting the cultural mobility model (2011: 292–4). However, these differences were not strong.

Conclusions

Theoretical accounts of the reproduction of socioeconomic inequalities in education fare poorly when assessed by empirical work. Economic explanations, which contend that the family's economic status is an overwhelming influence on education and subsequent socioeconomic attainments, are not supported. Relative to other aspects of the family of origin, father's or family income has only weak effects on educational outcomes (and early childhood cognitive outcomes). The general idea that those from lower socioeconomic backgrounds have lower educational and socioeconomic attainments owing to credit constraints is not sustainable. This is not to say that money does not matter at all, but its role in education is not as large as is commonly believed. The rich can buy a superior education, but they also often have labor market options for their children which are not dependent on success in the education system. The weak effect of family income is a problem for policymakers, because providing money to poorer schools and families is their most readily available policy lever.

Social capital theory was never intended to account for socioeconomic inequalities in education but rather school-type differences in student achievement. Unfortunately, the measures often used in studies incorporating social capital theory do not really tap the concept and often have quite different intellectual pedigrees. One problem with explanations of social capital is that greater parental or other family involvement in a child's schooling is often because the student is performing below expectations, so measures of social capital are negatively associated with student outcomes.

School-based explanations for socioeconomic inequalities are also not sufficient. There are high-performing schools that cater for high socioeconomic status families and low-performing schools serving low socioeconomic status families, but there is only a weak link between family SES, the school that the children attend and their performance. There are sometimes sizable differences in performance between school types (for example, private, religious), and schools belonging to different tracks. However, much of the between-school differences are due to differences in the intake characteristics of their students. Expect for highly differentiated school systems, which allocate students to different school tracks on the basis of prior achievement, the great bulk of the variation in student outcomes is within schools, not between schools. The allocation of students to different school tracks and streams within schools are much more strongly based on prior performance or ability than socioeconomic background.

It is true that students who are intellectually curious, who immerse themselves in science or literature, or who simply read a lot are more likely to have superior educational outcomes compared with students who do not have these interests, other things being equal. However, this is a long way from cultural capital theory, which involves a clear distinction between elite and non-elite culture, a strong relationship between participation in elite culture and the family's socioeconomic position, pervasive and strong cultural biases in the school curriculum, teachers and other gatekeepers unwittingly favoring students from elite backgrounds, and a strong relationship between participation in elite culture (by either the family or the student) and substantially superior educational outcomes. There are not strong relationships between cultural participation or other cultural aspects and families' socioeconomic standing. "Culture", unless it is defined by test scores, has only weak to moderate effects on educational outcomes. There is scant evidence that teachers and other gate keepers reward elite cultural knowledge or even treat students differently according to their socioeconomic backgrounds.

Notes

1 Human capital is not just education, but the "skills, knowledge, and character traits that influence a worker's potential earnings" (Harding *et al.* 2005: 107). In other words, it is more or less a worker's market value. The concept of "human capital" lends itself to the argument that, if more were invested in human beings (in their education, health and welfare) rather than other forms of investment (of capital), productivity would increase and many societal problems would be alleviated (Schultz 1977).

2 For example, "Social capital mediates the relationship between parents' financial and human capital and the development of human capital in their children" (Teachman *et al.* 1997: 1343–4).

3 However, it is doubtful that adolescents do make these calculations (Manski 1993).
4 The median and mean monthly incomes were around US$2,500 and US$3,000.
5 Contrary to popular perceptions, the inheritance of wealth has little to do with income inequalities. Jencks *et al.* (1972: 214), citing the findings from a 1960 survey, point out that inheritance plays an extremely limited role: 80 percent of families inherited nothing, a further 14 percent inherited very little and only one percent inherited enough to substantially boost their income. More recent estimates are reported by Harding *et al.* (2005: 108).
6 Standardized effects were calculated by the author from the standard deviations of child's test score (12.97) and mother's AFQT (193.80) and the coefficient for mother's AFQT (0.02). Therefore, 0.30=0.02*(193.80/12.97).
7 It is plausible to argue that larger families have more social capital, since there are more intimate social relationships, or that single-parent families have more social capital, since they are more likely to be involved in community networks. However, theoretical arguments are usually in the opposite direction to explain the weaker educational outcomes of children from larger or single-parent families.
8 Author's own analyses.
9 School resources do not seem to be important (Hanushek 2006).
10 For 30 countries, the standardized effects range from 0.03 to 0.08, not controlling for test scores.
11 Calculated by the author from Wolf (1986: 35).
12 Hauser (1969) points out that teachers are unlikely to consciously treat students differently according to their socioeconomic background.
13 Calculation of the standardized effects from the published standard deviations suggests that the standardized effects were often substantially less than 0.10, and sometimes as low as 0.03.

Chapter 9

Socioeconomic inequalities in education III

Changes over time

The ultimate aim of much educational policy over the twentieth century was to reduce socioeconomic inequalities in education and thus the intergenerational reproduction of socioeconomic inequalities. It was a means to a fair and just society. Talented boys from disadvantaged backgrounds (and the focus was usually on males) who worked hard could succeed in the education system and thereby rise in social standing. The education system was fairer than any previous system of selection to high-status positions. It was theoretically "fairer" because power and money could not influence students' grades, nor could friends and relations in education bureaucracies make a student successful. The curriculum and assessment procedures were rational, guided by a neutral centralized bureaucracy. Ideally, students' performance in the education system reflected merit. Although few believed that education systems would suddenly become meritocratic, the expectation was that the role of social background in educational outcomes would dissipate and merit would ultimately govern educational success.

Reducing inequalities in educational opportunity has considerable support from both sides of politics. The left, which by the mid-twentieth century had mostly given up on the possibility of a radical transformation of capitalist society, saw a meritocratic education system as a way of dismantling the reproduction of privilege and disadvantage from one generation to the next. Advocating equality of opportunity was certainly more politically palatable and realistic than advocating equal social and economic outcomes. Providing greater educational opportunities for students from low socioeconomic backgrounds was, and still is, a major policy plank of left-of-center political parties. The parties of the right could not oppose this admirable goal, although their focus was not so much on social equity; the right viewed education as a mechanism for ensuring that those with ability or talent would be rewarded and thus would lead to a more efficient and productive society. The most talented people available, rather than the offspring of the rich and powerful, would secure the most important (and well-paid) positions in society. Ultimately, we would all be better off. Goldthorpe (1996b: 255–6) traces this position to nineteenth-century liberal critiques, which argued that positions of societal responsibility should be based on "competence rather than through nepotism, patronage, bribery or purchase". Few adhered to the aristocratic notion that the reproduction of inequality is uncontroversial because families with the expertise and appropriate social networks, in particular trades or professions, provide the best possible training environments for the next generation.

In the context of the social and political upheavals of the late 1960s, the academic and political left became very skeptical of the argument that educational reforms could reduce the reproduction of socioeconomic inequality. They pointed out that education was not a fair competition since children from advantaged backgrounds were more likely to succeed. The education reforms of the early post-war period did not clearly reduce social inequalities in education. The "social gradient" – where each rise in children's socioeconomic background is associated with superior outcomes – was ubiquitous and seemingly insensitive to policy. Ability tests that were designed to identify high-ability students from disadvantaged backgrounds, to provide them with a pathway for upward social mobility were under attack, and often abandoned, since students from higher socioeconomic backgrounds tended to perform better. Rewarding students because of merit or ability was simply part of the ideology that reinforced the status quo and perpetuated social disadvantage. Education, it was argued, rather than providing working-class children with the means for upward social mobility, simply prepared them for factory and laboring jobs (Bowles 1972; Willis 1977).

Few other social science research questions have confused policymakers, undergraduates, postgraduate students and interested laypersons as much as the simple question "have socioeconomic inequalities in education declined?". The general answer from the academic community has been "no". Goldthorpe (1996a) regarded persisting education differentials as so established empirically that it should drive a major redirection in theory to explain these enduring inequalities. In a review of socioeconomic and other inequalities in US education, Gamoran (2001: 135) asserted that socioeconomic inequalities in education are "maximally maintained" and are expected to persist at their present level throughout the twenty-first century. In a major and often-cited cross-national study, *Persistent Inequality*, Shavit and Blossfeld (1993: 19) concluded that, with the exception of Sweden and the Netherlands, there has been little change in the relationship between socioeconomic background and educational attainment in industrialized countries.

"Maximally maintained" and "persisting class differentials in education" are surprising conclusions given the huge increases in prosperity over the last 60 years in Western countries, the virtual eradication of grinding poverty, the rise of the welfare state (including the provision of free education), the massive expansion of education at all levels, and the implementation of specific policies to reduce socioeconomic inequalities in education. However, there is no denying of the often-unacknowledged caveat to the persistent inequality position, the absolute chances of children from lower socioeconomic backgrounds completing school or entering higher education have increased dramatically simply because of educational expansion.

Given the amount of research on socioeconomic inequalities in education, there is surprisingly little consensus. Breen and Jonsson (2005: 223) conclude that "unambiguous conclusions about trends and ranking of countries have proven elusive", which they attribute to issues about comparability of measures in analyses over time and between countries. Added to this is the variety of statistical procedures used which can produce seemingly contradictory conclusions.

Theoretical issues

Modernization theories

A central contention from modernization theory is that the link between socioeconomic origins and educational attainment will decline over time. A further contention is that at the same time point the most "modern" countries will show weaker socioeconomic inequalities in education. Two processes stand out as responsible: educational expansion and the implementation of policies specifically aimed at reducing socioeconomic inequalities in education.

Educational expansion

The expansion of education means that there are more opportunities for students from lower socioeconomic backgrounds. A moderate- to high-ability student from a low socioeconomic background would have little or no likelihood of a university education when less than ten percent of the cohort attends university. In contrast, they are much more likely to attend with participation rates of 30 percent, or, as is common in many industrial countries today, around 50 percent. Educational expansion means that students from low socioeconomic backgrounds are still in the competition for high-status post-school education at upper secondary school, whereas in previous generations most would have already left school so would not have been eligible. Collins (1971), better known as a reproduction theorist, maintains the expansion of education in the US as primarily a response to minority-group demands for greater opportunities for social mobility. According to Hout and Dohan (1996: 210), as education expands, socioeconomic background becomes less important for academic selection at the earlier points as increasing proportions of successive cohorts make the education transition, so decreasing the overall association between socioeconomic background and educational outcomes. Focusing on higher-level transitions, Treiman *et al.* (2003: 25) argue that educational expansion reduces socioeconomic inequalities because it moves the bulk of students into later points in the educational career where the dependence on social origins is weaker.

There are knock-on effects from educational expansion that should also reduce socioeconomic inequalities. Increasing educational participation is likely to engender changes in student, family and community norms and expectations in regard to education. As education expands, working-class communities increasingly view college or university education for their young people as a realistic goal. Similarly, schools and teachers are more likely to encourage students from lower socioeconomic backgrounds to further pursue education and provide facilities for them, if the expected probability of success is high enough.

Educational expansion in industrialized countries has been substantial. Around 1900, it was not uncommon for as few as ten percent of men and even fewer women to have had any secondary education and high proportions had no schooling at all (Treiman *et al.* 2003: 1). By the middle of the twentieth century, completion of primary school had become universal, and by the end of the twentieth century, participation and completion of secondary school. Mean years of education increased in most industrialized countries from about eight or nine in 1910 to about 11 or 12 in 1965. There was no universal pattern to changes in inequality in the distribution of education, indexed by its standard deviation, increasing in some countries (e.g. England and West Germany), decreasing in others (e.g. the US), and no clear pattern in others (Rijken 1999: 150–1). For industrialized countries, Hertz *et al.* (2007: 10, 12) report an increase of about three years in the average years of education across cohorts born 50 years apart. According to the OECD (2009a), 22 of the 25 OECD countries with comparable data have school graduation rates in 2008 of over 70 percent. In several countries (Finland, Germany, Greece, Ireland, Japan, Korea and Norway) the graduation rates exceed 90 percent.

Educational expansion is characteristic of almost all countries, with expansion accelerating after 1950 for secondary education and after 1960 for tertiary education (Meyer *et al.* 1992; Schofer and Meyer 2005).

In some countries, the expansion in school completion has been particularly rapid. In Britain in 1960, only 12 percent of the cohort stayed past the school leaving age (then 15), but in the early 2000s, about 70 percent stayed on past the compulsory school leaving age of 16 (Galindo-Rueda and Vignoles 2005: 336). In Australia, school completion rose from about one-third of students in the early 1980s to over three-quarters in 2005 (Marks 2007: 430). In Denmark, only 14 percent of the cohort born in 1954 completed upper secondary school, compared with 44 percent of their children (Jæger 2007: 535). In contrast, in the US, school completion has been high for a long time: around 83 percent in 1972, increasing only six percent to 89 percent in 2007, 35 years later (Cataldi *et al.* 2009: 36).

University education has expanded from elite to mass participation, and later towards universalistic participation. Elite systems are loosely defined as having less than 15 percent of the cohort participating at university, and universalistic systems over 50 percent of the cohort. Before World War II, typically three to five percent of the cohort participated in university education (Trow 2006: 244–5). For the US, the proportion of the population of 23-year-olds with bachelor degrees increased from two percent in 1900 to over 30 percent in 1990 (Herrnstein and Murray 1994: 32). Between 1960 and 2005, the proportion of high-school graduates enrolling in college increased from 45 percent to 65–70 percent (Alon 2009: 788). For Canada, McIntosh (2010: 458) observes that post-secondary education increased by a factor of six between 1961 and 1997. Arum *et al.* (2006: 15–16) show a doubling of higher education *participation* across developed countries from 20 percent in the 1960s to 40 percent in the 1990s. In most countries, graduation from university – what the OECD (2009a: 62) refers to as tertiary type A education – has increased to around an average of 40 percent in OECD countries, with substantial increases in many countries over the period 2000–2007. According to the European Social Survey, the proportion of university degree graduates of the relevant age cohort in European countries increased from about 12 percent in the 1950s to nearly 40 percent in the decade, 2001–2010 (Koucký *et al.* 2010: 10). University participation rates for the decade 2001–2010 were highest in Ireland, Denmark, Spain and Norway, approaching 60 percent or more. With such high levels of participation the analytical focus has somewhat changed from vertical stratification, differences in the level of educational attainment, to horizontal stratification, differences in the status of the area of study and institution attended.

Policies

In addition to educational expansion, specific policy initiatives have been implemented and explicitly designed to reduce socioeconomic inequalities in education. These include abolishing school fees for government schools, raising the school leaving age, abolishing, reducing and/or delaying educational differentiation (tracking and streaming), opening access to university to students without a traditional academic background and providing scholarships and other monetary incentives for children from low socioeconomic backgrounds (Ambler and Neathery 1999; Treiman and Yip 1989). Specific policy initiatives include the replacement of grammar schools by comprehensive schools in Britain in the late 1960s (Halsey *et al.* 1980; Paterson and Iannelli 2007), similar reforms in Sweden and Finland (Hout and Dohan 1996; Pekkarinen *et al.* 2009), and the limitation of subject choice and elimination of selective examinations in Scotland (Gamoran 1996; Paterson and Iannelli 2007). At university level, there has been an expansion in the sector (to differing extents) mainly by converting lower tier tertiary institutions – technical, nursing and teaching institutions and colleges of advanced or adult education – into universities, so they too can offer degree courses, as well as the expansion of places at existing universities (see various chapters in Shavit *et al.*

2007a). In addition, university entrance has become more flexible, allowing the admission of applicants from non-academic school-tracks or with lower levels of achievement. Examples are the 1968 reforms in the Netherlands and later reforms in Sweden (Faasse *et al.* 1987; Ringdal and Birkelund 2001).

Other reasons for declining inequalities

There have also been other changes that arguably should reduce socio-economic inequalities in education. More generally, the expansion of the welfare state means that children from disadvantaged backgrounds have adequate levels of health and nutrition (Jonsson *et al.* 1996). The assessment of student performance is often centrally administered through objective examinations purportedly minimizing social biases, at least the obvious ones, which result from school and family involvement. No longer is there an emphasis on the "classics". In many countries, the school curriculum has been democratized – some would say "dumbed down" – to be more accessible to students from a diverse range of social backgrounds. There has been a movement away from rote learning and memorization. University entrance is largely based on performance, not on the recommendation of teachers or the school principal, largely removing the direct influence of family, friends or family connections. Often higher-education institutions have implemented quotas, endeavoring to reduce the proportion of students from privileged backgrounds and to actively recruit high-ability students from underprivileged backgrounds. Tuition costs for university education have generally declined. In Scandinavian and several European countries, university education is mostly free (CESifo 2011). Many countries have scholarship and extensive loan schemes. However, more recently, governments are endeavoring to reduce the costs to taxpayers by cost sharing (Johnstone 2004). Although there are other significant costs associated with university education, such as accommodation, educational resources, and foregone earnings, the economic barriers to university education have declined over the long term.

Breen *et al.* (2009) present a number of arguments for why both Boudon's primary and secondary effects have declined. Reasons for declining primary effects include: general improvements in health and nutrition for working class children; improvements in the financial situation of poor families; reductions in family size; growth in the public provision of childcare and preschool education; development of full-day rather than part-day schooling; expansion of remedial education; and reforms to the timing, extent and manner of school tracking. Reasons for declining secondary effects include: abolishing or substantially reducing school fees; more schools, so greater access to education for children living in non-urban areas; increases in real family income; declines in other costs of education; increases in the length of compulsory schooling; and expansion of welfare cushioning financial problems caused by unemployment and illness (2009: 1479–80).

Reproduction theories

Although a large number of social processes can be argued as supporting the case for declining socioeconomic inequalities in education, most of the theoretical work focuses on persistent socioeconomic inequalities. Collins (1971) argues that the expansion of education (in the US) is best understood by conflict theories, where competing status groups are able to control the education system to secure well-remunerated employment for their children. This argument is in opposition to what was then characterized as functionalist theories, attributing educational expansion to the technological and skills requirements of industrialized society. His argument implies that high-status social groups successfully maintain their relative advantage through setting the educational requirements for jobs that maintain their interests.

Maximally maintained inequality

Shavit and Blossfeld's (1993) conclusion of persistent inequality is based on the Maximally Maintained Inequality (MMI) thesis, which posits that relative socioeconomic inequalities in education will not change with the expansion of education. It sits within the educational transitions approach to educational inequalities. It hypotheses that only when participation rates for a given educational level approach saturation levels among the most privileged socioeconomic group, will the impact of socioeconomic background on the transition to that level decline. Otherwise, socioeconomic inequalities in education will remain unchanged (Raftery and Hout 1993). The analogy is with a queue ordered by socioeconomic background, with the most privileged groups first making the transition to the next educational level. With the expansion of education, participants further down the queue make the transition (see Hout 2007: 12–13). Only when almost every student from a privileged background makes the transition (the saturation level) will the impact of socioeconomic background begin to decline.

MMI rests on the notion that class barriers "keep pace" with educational expansion so that relative inequality remains constant (Hout 2007: 1). To explain MMI, a rational choice explanation is proposed, arguing that continuation decisions are based on the weighing up of costs and benefits, where the costs outweigh the benefits for lower-class families. The explanation is economic, with an emphasis on the actual momentary costs and benefits (Raftery and Hout 1993: 57–9). For some reason, although the cost–benefit calculations must change with educational expansion, the relative differences are unchanged. Since the costs of education have declined substantially, arguably more so for disadvantaged families, and there is no evidence that the benefits have declined, it is difficult to understand how rational choice leads to MMI.

There are recent variants on MMI. These variants postulate no change or even increasing socioeconomic inequalities in education. Effectively

Expanding Inequality (EEI) maintains that the class divide for post-secondary education is maintained in the face of educational expansion (Alon 2009). Lucas's (2001) Effectively Maintained Inequality (EMI) thesis argues that socioeconomic inequalities are no longer maintained by vertical inequality in the level of attainment reached, but by horizontal inequalities among students in the same year level, typically between academic and vocational-orientated tracks or streams (Lucas 2001). EMI includes stratification within the schools (streaming) and the transition out of school. According to Ichou and Vallet (2011: 168), "Lucas's hypothesis states that when a level of education becomes almost universal – and therefore quantitative inequality in attaining this level is likely to decrease – class inequality is primarily expressed through qualitative differences between academically and socially stratified tracks".

Mechanisms

The literature on persistent inequality, MMI, EEI and EMI is replete with references to privileged classes or higher socioeconomic status families able to easily manipulate education systems for the benefit of their children. Goldthorpe *et al.* (1987: 328) lamented that educational reformers were unaware of "the flexibility and effectiveness with which the more powerful and advantaged groupings in society can use the resources at their disposal to preserve their privileged positions". According to Heath *et al.* (1992), they adopt "strategies" so they succeed, and such families are pictured as "outmaneuvering" reformist legislation. Barone (2009: 106) concludes that post-secondary education was a "forced option" for the upper classes if they wished to maintain their educational advantage in the face of educational expansion. Duru-Bellat (2008: 88) speaks of "actors' strategies to preserve their advantage with the complicity of politicians". Shavit *et al.* (2007b: 2–3) cite other researchers who argue that professional organizations support selectivity in the education system, and that teachers and educational administrators favor educational selection since it increases their prestige and power. Pfeffer (2008: 546) emphasizes parents' strategic knowledge that "translates into differential educational outcomes". The implication is that these strategies change in order to maintain existing levels of socioeconomic inequalities between social classes. Alon (2009: 750) states that the "vicious cycle of adaptation and exclusion" practised by the most privileged classes are the reasons why US colleges place more weight on students' test scores. According to Lucas (2001: 1680), "class conflict" involves not only obtaining advantageous positions for children for different classes in the education system, but is also about securing or dismantling the stratified curriculum.

It is not credible that socioeconomically privileged families *en masse* are especially aware of the specific implications of educational reforms or expansion and have successfully implemented "strategies" that maintain (but somehow not increase) their relative advantage as measured by odds ratios.

It is more plausible that such families are concerned about the educational and occupational futures of their own children (to varying degrees), but not at all concerned about maintaining relative class inequalities. For many wealthy families, and not-so-wealthy families involved in business, their children's success in the education system is not a particularly high priority. In addition, it is not at all obvious what political strategies privileged families have employed to maintain their relative advantage. If they had the power, wouldn't they "increase" rather than "maintain" their relative advantage? Furthermore, arguments about the stratified curriculum in schools (which in most countries is becoming less rigid) and the use of test scores for university admission cannot be simply reduced to "class conflict". This literature resonates with the neo-Marxist literature of the 1970s and 1980s, where dark unseen class forces move mysteriously to successfully maintain existing class differentials.

From the social reproduction perspective, there is a general consensus that educational reforms enacted by industrialized countries have not reduced socioeconomic inequalities in education. The educational reforms introduced in the Netherlands in the late 1960s did not alter the primary effects of class background although the secondary effects declined (Faasse *et al.* 1987). Kerckhoff and Trott (1993) note that their analyses suggest that the educational reforms implemented in England and Wales in the late 1940s did not reduce socioeconomic inequalities in education. Stemming from their book, *Persistent Inequality*, Blossfeld and Shavit (1993: 19–20) concluded that educational reforms "did not lead to a reduction of the association between social origins and any of the educational transitions". In addition, in the countries where declines occurred, the Netherlands and Sweden, the declines could not be attributed to educational reforms. Shavit and Westerbeek (1998: 36) later claim more generally, without referring to educational transitions, "In none of the thirteen countries studied did educational reforms lead to more equality of educational opportunity". The 1990s reforms designed to increase access to matriculation in Israel appeared to have increased socioeconomic inequalities in obtaining the university qualifying diploma (Ayalon and Shavit 2004). Ichou and Vallet (2011: 187), summarizing studies from France and other countries, concluded that educational reforms have limited or unintended consequences, especially in regard to class inequalities. For Europe, Ambler and Neathery (1999) concluded that educational expansion produced a modest decrease in class inequalities in education, with no evidence that the introduction of comprehensive education reduced socioeconomic inequalities.[1] Paterson and Iannelli (2007) concluded that policy differences between England, Wales and Scotland had not yielded differences over time in the association between class origins and educational attainment.

It is surprising that the extensive educational reforms that have been implemented over the last half century, or in some countries longer, have had little or no impact on reducing socioeconomic inequalities in education.

Methodological matters

Log-linear models

A major problem with the log-linear approach is that the focus is on the cell counts in a contingency table. This is quite different from regression-type approaches that focus on predicting the values of the measure of educational attainment. The focus on the particular bivariate association between socio-economic background and educational attainment means that other important influences (e.g. ability) cannot be included. Even if they were, they are unlikely to have much impact on the association between the two variables that, in part, contributes to the cell counts in the cross-tabulation. In addition, log-linear models are very restrictive in the number of variables that can be considered. A large data set soon produces very small cell counts if the contingency table for class and educational attainment is broken down by gender, cohort and other variables.

There are also issues in the substantive interpretations of the estimates from the log-linear model. Ringen (2006) shows that the decline in educational inequality indicated by the Gini coefficient is not mirrored by declines in the odds ratios. He reports a decline in educational inequality in the UK, indicated by the Gini coefficient decreasing from 0.24 in the 1930s to 0.11 in 1960 (2006: 476–80). However, the odds ratios remain stable and are suggestive of a much higher level of inequality. He (2006: 487) also questions whether it is really possible to distinguish structural changes from association. Odds ratios being invariant under row or column multiplications are one thing, but claiming that association parameters in the log-linear model capture the true association independent of educational expansion is quite another.[2] He notes there is also a problem with the logic. Education expansion is hypothesized to decrease inequality, but any decrease in inequality attributable to educational expansion does not count as reducing inequality. Furthermore, the log-odds estimates are not stable under different models of the association of class origins and educational attainment. Even different parameterizations of the same model (e.g. effect or dummy coding) will produce different (but mathematically equivalent) estimates. Because these and possibly other considerations, there has been an unheralded trend away from log-linear analyses of educational attainment by class contingency tables, to analyses based on Boudon's primary and secondary effects (e.g. Erikson *et al.* 2005; Jackson 2013).

Educational transitions

The educational transitions literature focuses on the transition from one educational level to the next. Introduced to the field by Mare (1980, 1981), the educational transitions approach to analyzing socioeconomic inequalities in education involves the analysis of a series of logistic regression equations for each important educational transition. Students who do not continue schooling at a transition point are not included in the analysis of the next transition: statistically they are not "at risk" of undergoing the next transition. Mare argued that standard Ordinary Least Squares (OLS) regression estimates of the effects of social background for over-time analyses on an ordinal measure of educational attainment (e.g. years of education) are sensitive to changes in the distribution of educational attainment (due to educational expansion) as well as the parameters that link socioeconomic origins to each transition (Hout *et al.* 1993: 35; Mare, 1993). However, Mare (1993: 353) agrees that linear effects of measures of socioeconomic background on educational attainment "remain valid and parsimonious summary statistics for inequality of educational opportunity". The logic is as follows. Educational expansion reduces the impact of socioeconomic background for lower transitions completing primary school, and later for middle secondary school and school graduation – because in progressively younger cohorts higher and higher proportions make each transition. Also with expansion, the effects of socioeconomic background for higher-level transitions supposedly increase because of greater socioeconomic variation in the population "at risk". Together these two processes result in generally stable effects of socioeconomic background.

The coefficients obtained in logistic regression analysis for a series of educational transitions from one grade to the next relate to the overall effects of socioeconomic background on educational attainment. This is demonstrated by Mare (1981: 78), who summarizes "The linear effects of background on highest grade completed are weighted sums of the logistic response-model parameters for grade progression, where the weights are functions of the grade-progression proportions". However, this equivalency requires the parameters and weights for all transitions. Focusing on a few and finding no change in the impact of socioeconomic background for a couple of transitions does not necessarily mean persistent inequality. It is very likely that the effects of socioeconomic background for earlier transitions have declined. A second important point is that estimates of the effects of socioeconomic background in educational transitions models are substantially upwardly biased when cognitive ability is not included (see section on "Educational transitions" in Chapter 5, page 85).

The educational transitions model has been severely criticized by economists (Cameron and Heckman 1998). The methodological issues surrounding the educational transitions model have been well documented by Lucas *et al.* (2011). The first criticism is that the parameters are unidentified. Since the predictor variables are the same for each respondent at every transition, the only parameter that changes is the error term. Therefore, it is not possible to test for differences in the effects of predictor variables across transitions. A second issue is unobserved heterogeneity which increases the likelihood that the estimates for the observed variables are spurious. A third is "selection" bias. At each transition, the population at risk of the transition differs and the selection of the at risk students is dependent on unobserved factors, mainly cognitive ability. A fourth issue is that the dependent variable has different variances at each transition. The solutions include a suite of time-varying covariates, such as GPA to reduce unobserved heterogeneity, a standardized dependent variable and additional variables to take into account selection biases. The authors provide evidence undermining the waning coefficients hypothesis but at a severe cost: the parameter estimates are not readily interpretable. Their analyses provide no indication of the extent that socio-economic background, test scores and other factors influence high school and college transitions. The interpretation is not helped by the severe multi-collinearity evident by including several measures of test scores. The estimates for "reading", "vocabulary" and "arithmetic" make little substantive sense. There are also questions surrounding the suitability of the "instruments" to take into account sample selectivity (see Lucas *et al.* 2011: footnote 12).

Logistic regression in transitions and other analyses

A more basic statistical issue is the use of logistic regression in transitions models or indeed any analysis of categorical outcomes. The estimates of the effects of independent variables are distorted even when unobserved variables *are uncorrelated* with the independent variables (Mare, 1993: 353). In logistic regression, the residual variance is fixed and any increases in the explained variance forces the total variance of the dependent variable to increase and thus its scale (Mood, 2010: 68–9). In contrast, in OLS regression the estimates are only affected if the unobserved variables are correlated with the predictor variables. This means that in the logistic model with an additional predictor variable uncorrelated with the original predictor, the estimates for the coefficient for the original predictor will increase because the scale increases to accommodate the fixed error variance. Mood (2010) demonstrates this with models for the transition to university predicted by IQ and sex which are uncorrelated with each other. The effect for IQ is larger in the model that includes sex since the unobserved heterogeneity is less in the model that includes sex but the fixed error variance is the same. This technical point is important because it undermines conclusions from studies that have used logistic regression that do not include relevant unobservables. The solutions involve using continuous dependent variables where possible, or if this is not possible ensuring properly specified models that include all important predictors not just those correlated with the predictor variable of interest, and presenting the estimates several ways (Mood, 2010: 79–80). Mood is also surprisingly positive about the linear probability model (OLS regression for dichotomous dependent variables) which had become an unacceptable methodological approach (for journal publication), although it does not produce biased estimates of linear probabilities.

Student achievement

There is evidence that socioeconomic differences in achievement as measured by test scores are declining in the US. White's (1982: 468) meta-analysis of largely American studies employed widely differing measures of socio-economic status and school achievement and identified an over-time trend of lower correlations. He suggests that the increased availability of television, movies and preschools to children from families of all socioeconomic status levels and the efforts of compensatory education have reduced the effects of socioeconomic status on achievement. Sirin (2005: 442) concurs that the correlations have declined slightly which "may reflect social and overall policy changes over time". Social changes postulated include increased access to learning materials and increased availability of compensatory education.

The US National Assessment of Educational Progress (NAEP) studies have been examining student performance in reading, mathematics and science since 1972 for students aged nine, 13 and 17. The gap in achievement between students from the most highly and least educated households has declined. The average scores in mathematics for nine-year-olds with parents who have the lowest education levels (not completing high school) increased by 17 score points between 1979 and 1992, and for 13-year-olds by over ten points. In contrast, the scores of comparable students with college-educated parents remained much the same (NCES 1996: 73; Tate 1997). This narrowing continued to occur according to the 2008 trend report (NCES 2008: 41). Among 13-year-olds, the gap in mathematics achievement between the lowest and highest parental education groups was 39 points in 1978 compared with 23 points in 2008: a substantial decline. Among 17-year-olds, the decline was from 37 points in 1978 to 23 points in 2008. Although it may be argued that the college-educated (parents) group is now less selective (comprising approximately 40 percent of the sample), the increase in achievement among students with parents with a less than high school education is unmistakable.

A second measure that used to be available in the NAEP studies was community type. This measure distinguished between students living in disadvantaged rural and urban areas, advantaged urban and other. Between 1977 and 1990, the science scores for nine-year-olds from "disadvantaged" urban areas rose by 30 points, whereas there was no change among students from "advantaged" urban areas. For 13-year-olds, the increase was about ten points, with no rise among students from advantaged communities. There was no narrowing of the gap for science among 17-year-olds. For reading and mathematics, declines were also found. For mathematics among 13-year-olds, the mean scores for students from disadvantaged urban communities rose by 20 points, compared with a two-point increase among students from advantaged communities. For reading among 17-year-olds, there was a distinct narrowing of the gap, with smaller declines for nine- and 13-year-olds (Mullis *et al.* 1991: 31, 68, 116). The measure of community type was discontinued in the 1990s.

For the UK, McNiece *et al.* (2004) compared social class differences in mathematics and reading achievement between the 1958 and 1970 British birth cohort studies. The authors conclude that class differences have declined over time for mathematics, but not for reading (2004: 125). In their repeated measures model (model 1.1), class differences in both reading and mathematics appear to be smaller for the more recent cohort (2004: 135). In Australia, Rothman (2003) found a decline in class differences in achievement in reading and mathematics among secondary school students between 1975 and 1995. In the Netherlands, the effects of social class, father's and mother's education on achievement were no different for the 1964 cohort compared with the 1940 cohort (Faasse *et al.* 1987). However, the effects of all three measures were quite weak with standardized coefficients of 0.10, 0.14 and 0.06, respectively.

Cross-national studies

According to the PISA study, between 2000 and 2006, the relationship between socioeconomic background and test scores weakened in many countries, most notably in reading (OECD 2007b: 190). In no OECD country had the relationship between socioeconomic background and science performance strengthened between 2000 and 2006. Countries with notable declines in the effect of their composite ESCS measure of socioeconomic background on *mathematics* achievement include Australia (a decline of 5.6 score points), the Czech Republic (–4.7), Germany (–7.2), Hungary (–12.2), Mexico (–4.5), Poland (–6.3), Portugal (–5.1), and the US (–7.8). Considering that the average effect was around 40 score points for a one standard deviation change in the composite measure of socioeconomic background, these declines over a period of six years are notable. The coefficient had increased markedly in France by over 12 score points and there were smaller declines for Korea and Finland (OECD 2007a: 130). For reading, the decline in the effects of ESCS measure of socioeconomic background was large in Australia (–9.0), the Czech Republic (–8.5), Denmark (–10.3), Germany (–11.6), Hungary (–12.0), Mexico (–5.0), Spain (–4.8), and Switzerland (–11.0) (OECD 2007a: 132).

According to the OECD's (2010a: 78, 163) 2009 PISA study, there were statistically significant declines in the relationship between the composite ESCS measure of socioeconomic background and reading test scores between 2000 and 2009 in the Czech Republic, Germany, the US, Canada, Chile and Mexico. Its effects had significantly increased in Sweden, Finland, Korea and Iceland: the last three had exhibited unusually weak effects in 2000. The data for France, Japan, the Netherlands and the UK were incomplete or withheld.

Table 9.1 presents the percentage of variance explained in student achievement in the primary domain by the ESCS measures of socioeconomic background from published tables in OECD reports for the four PISA studies between 2000 and 2009. They are suggestive of declines in about 16 of

Table 9.1 Percentage of variance explained in student achievement by the ESCS measures of socioeconomic background

	2000 Reading	2003 Mathematics	2006 Science	2009 Reading	Decline?
Australia	17	13.7	11.3	12.7	✓
Austria	14[a]	16.0	15.4	16.6	
Belgium	21	24.1	19.4	19.3	?
Canada	11	10.5	8.2	8.6	✓
Czech Republic	20	19.5	15.6	12.4	✓
Denmark	15	17.6	14.1	14.5	
Finland	9	10.8	8.3	7.8	
France	22	19.6	21.2	16.7	✓
Germany	22	22.8	19.0	17.9	✓
Greece	15	15.9	15.0	12.5	?
Hungary	26	27.0	21.4	26.0	
Iceland	5	6.5	6.7	6.2	
Ireland	13	16.2	12.7	12.6	
Italy	11[a]	13.6	10.0	11.8	
Japan	6[a]	11.6	7.4	8.6	
Korea	9	14.2	8.1	11.0	?
Luxembourg	24	17.1	21.7	18.0	✓
Netherlands	15	18.6	16.7	12.8	✓
New Zealand	16	16.8	16.4	16.6	✓
Norway	13	14.1	8.3	8.6	✓
Poland	14	16.7	14.5	14.8	
Portugal	20	17.5	16.6	16.5	✓
Slovak Republic	–	22.3	19.2	14.6	✓
Spain	16	14.0	13.9	13.6	✓
Sweden	11	15.3	10.6	13.4	
Switzerland	19	16.8	15.7	14.1	✓
Turkey	–	22.3	16.5	19.0	?
UK	19	19.7	13.9	13.7	✓
US	22	19.0	17.9	16.8	✓
OECD average[b]	20	20.3	14.9	14.0	✓

Notes:
[a] Questionable estimate, owing to sample or missing data issues.
[b] Number of OECD countries increased between 2000 and 2009.

Source: OECD (2001: 308; 2004: 399; 2007a: 184; 2010c: 55)

the countries listed and possible declines in three more over the relatively short time frame of nine years. Although there are technical issues regarding sampling and missing data for some countries, and there is an issue regarding comparability of the ESCS composite measure of socioeconomic background across the different waves (the measures are not exactly the same), the findings suggest a trend towards weaker socioeconomic inequalities in student achievement.[3]

Adult literacy

One source of international comparative data is the adult literacy studies. Table 9.2 shows the standardized effects of parents' education on performance in the adult literacy tests in 15 Western countries by age cohort using IALS data. In ten of 15 countries, the effect of the standardized measure of parents' education on performance is substantially smaller in the younger age group aged 16 to 25 years compared with the older group aged 26 to 55. Two more countries show marginal declines. In the much smaller second ALLS study, the gradient for parental education and literacy score were shallower in younger cohorts (aged 16–25) than older cohorts in Canada, Norway and Italy, but not in Switzerland or the US (OECD 2005: 235, 244–5). Although, these findings from adult literacy studies are again subject to the criticism that adult literacy is confounded with education and age (which it is) and socioeconomic background is indicated by only a single variable, parental education, these findings suggest a decline in socioeconomic inequalities in literacy has occurred in many Western countries.

Table 9.2 Effects of parental education on literacy by age cohort

Country	*Young adults (16–25)*	*Older adults (26–55)*	*Decline?*
Australia	0.25	0.38	✓
Belgium (Flanders)	0.39	0.33	
Canada	0.34	0.47	✓
Denmark	0.29	0.31	?
Finland	0.18	0.40	✓
Germany	0.27	0.17	
Ireland	0.32	0.39	✓
Netherlands	0.32	0.35	
New Zealand	0.27	0.33	✓
Norway	0.24	0.34	✓
Portugal	0.32	0.48	✓
Sweden	0.23	0.39	✓
Switzerland	0.30	0.41	✓
UK	0.18	0.28	✓
US	0.48	0.40	

Source: OECD and Statistics Canada (2000: 142–3)
Note: Standardized coefficients

School completion and university

Baker and Vélez (1996: 82) reviewed US studies of college entry and persistence conducted between the early 1960s and early 1990s and found a "generally declining importance of socioeconomic advantage, as compared to academic ability". Belley and Lochner (2007) examined the effects of income and ability on both high-school graduation and college entrance by comparing the 1997 NLSY with the 1979 NLSY. They found that, for school completion, ability has become less important and income more important for low-ability students. For the top-ability quartiles, family income makes no or very little difference to high-school graduation. The rise in high-school completion between the two cohorts comes from the bottom of the ability distribution (2007: 47). The effects of social background declined somewhat because almost all youth in the younger cohort complete high school (2007: 50–1). For college entry, they find a similar pattern with lower levels of participation. For the top-ability quartile, family income makes little difference but has a successively larger impact for lower-ability students. The impact of income for college entry was substantially higher for the 1997 cohort than for the 1979 cohort, especially in the low-ability quartiles. They conclude that the increased impact of income is difficult to reconcile with arguments about borrowing constraints because family income has its weakest effects among the most-able (2007: 81).

Contrary to declining socioeconomic inequalities, Alon (2009) argues for an increasing class divide in the US. Analyzing a five-category measure of college attendance distinguishing two-year, four-year and selective colleges,[4] she found the odds of attending selective colleges between low and high socioeconomic status seniors narrowed between 1972 and 1982 but increased between 1982 and 1992. However, socioeconomic background (based on the available composite measures available in the data sets divided into quartiles) poorly explains the pattern of college entry (and non-entry) accounting for only five percent of the (pseudo) variance. Adding class rank and test scores increased the variance accounted for to 16 percent (2009: 741). The decrease in socioeconomic inequalities (between 1972 and 1982) and the subsequent increase (between 1982 and 1992) was explained entirely by test scores (2009: 742–3). In this very different take on the meritocracy thesis, she attributes the increasing class divide to privileged groups adapting to the greater weight placed on test scores for college admission, which she views as an exclusionary practice. The problem with this argument is that it assumes that class has a very much stronger relationship with college entry than it actually has, and that performance in test scores is largely determined by class background which it clearly is not. Furthermore, she argues that the increasing use of test scores for selection is an exclusionary class practice. The use of SAT and ACT test scores for college selection is not the result of political actions by some undefined social class or classes, but it is simply an exclusionary practice by college administrators to select the most able students. A much more effective exclusionary practice for privileged groups would be substantially increased fees.

Analyzing college selectivity, Karen (2002) found increasing effects of socioeconomic background. Comparing the early 1970s and early 1980s, the standardized effect for father's education increased from 0.13 to 0.21, declined slightly for mother's education and increased from 0.11 to 0.16 for family income. The variance explained by social background factors increased from ten percent to 17 percent. Including test scores and other academic variables increased the explained variance further to around 30 percent, and reduced the effects for parental education and income. One explanation for the increase in the small effects of socioeconomic background factors is the greater variation in the samples, which is restricted to high-school graduates who had attended a post-secondary educational institution in the next year. A more heterogeneous population means that the effects of socioeconomic background variables are less attenuated.

For the UK, socioeconomic inequalities in school completion and university participation appear to have declined. Heath (2000) calculated the odds ratios from the observed counts in cross-tabulations of educational qualifications by class of origin. The odds ratios of obtaining an O level for students from a salariat (the service class) background compared with a working-class background declined from 11.6 for the oldest cohort to 5.1 for the youngest cohort. For A levels or above, the odds ratio declined from 15.5 for the oldest cohort to 4.3 for the youngest cohort (2000: 318–19). Bynner and Joshi's (2002: 412–16) analysis of leaving school at age 16 shows smaller odds ratios for father's occupational class for the younger 1970 birth cohort than the 1958 birth cohort. There were also weaker effects for the age at which each parent left school. Between the 1980s and 2002, Iannelli (2008) found a reduction in social class differences in participation in higher education. For England and Wales, the odds ratio for entry to higher education for the professional class compared with the working class had declined from 6.8 in 1989 to 3.7 in 2001/2002. For Scotland, the comparable odds ratio declined from 7.1 in 1987 to 5.6 in 2001/2002. She (2008: 14) found "a clear decline in social class inequalities in England, which seem to have occurred at A-level and HE [higher-education] level" and notes that this conclusion is contrary to that of other studies which used income to measure socioeconomic background. Boliver (2011) found no changes across enrolment year cohorts (1960 to 1993) in class differences for entry to degree programs or for entry to degree programs at an "old" university. There was some convergence in participation in higher education between the service and intermediate class groups. There has been concern in the UK that the reintroduction of (contingent loan) fees in 1998 would increase socioeconomic inequalities. However, a 2007 study concluded that "over the full period of 1994–2000 there is no consistent evidence of a widening in the HE participation gap between higher and lower socio-economic groups" (Marcenaro-Gutierrez *et al.* 2007: 352).

For Canada, analyzing data collected between 1973 and 1993, Christofides *et al.* (2001) report a relative increase in participation in post-secondary education of students from low-income households, resulting in a convergence between income groups. (Post-secondary education includes university, technical and community colleges.) The impact of family income on *university* participation has also decreased since the mid-1990s (Corak *et al.* 2003). Sen and Clemente (2010) found that the effects of both father's and mother's (post-secondary) education on attending university were weaker in 2001 than in 1986. There was also an unambiguous decline in the effects on post-secondary education.

For Australia, Marks and McMillan (2003) found statistically significant declines in the effects of socioeconomic background on school completion and university entrance in youth cohorts born between 1961 and around 1981. A subsequent study found narrowing class differences and declining effects for father's education on school completion and obtaining a bachelor degree, in data covering cohorts born between 1890 and 1981 (Marks and McMillan 2007: 364–6).

For the Netherlands, the effects of socioeconomic background on leaving school unqualified have lost much of their impact over time (Gesthuizen *et al.* 2005). There were declines in the effects of father's occupational status, parental financial resources (indexed by possessions) and parental education. The (weaker) impact of cultural capital (measured by participation in cultural activities) did not decline. For the cohort born in the 1970s, the effect of socioeconomic resources on leaving school without qualifications had declined to insignificance.

Jæger (2007) concludes that inequality of educational opportunity has declined substantially in Denmark over the post-war period. Comparing the cohort born in 1954 and their children, the effects of both father's and mother's social class, family income, home ownership, father's education, and mother's education have all declined for completion of upper secondary education. He also concludes that parents' economic, cultural and social capital, are becoming less important in determining children's educational success. The decline was particularly striking. The effects of father's and mother's social class, family income, and father's education were not significant in the second generation. There were no significant effects for indicators of social capital. The change is attributed to government policies, specifically the rise of the welfare state since the 1960s.

Cross-national studies

A multi-country study on changes over time in socioeconomic inequalities in obtaining a bachelor degree used a methodology similar to the Gini index for income inequality. The index can be understood as the percentage of correct predictions in access to university education given gender and father's and mother's occupation and education (Koucký *et al.* 2010: 20). The index of inequality declined from 54 from the early 1950s to 49 for the period 2000–2010, leading the authors (2010: 26) to conclude that "the level of inequality in access to tertiary education in Europe has been gradually decreasing", but they note that the trend is not particularly strong. The results are summarized in Table 9.3. There were clear declines in socio-economic inequalities in obtaining a bachelor degree in eight of the 15 countries (Austria, Finland, France, Greece, Ireland, the Netherlands, Portugal and Spain) and smaller declines in four others (Belgium, Denmark, Norway and Sweden). There were no declines evident using this methodology for Germany, Switzerland and the UK.

Table 9.3 Effects of inequality index on obtaining a bachelor degree

Country	*1950s*	*1960s*	*1970s*	*1980s*	*1990s*	*2000–07*	*Decline?*
Austria	54	50	49	43	44	38	✓
Belgium	56	58	54	52	54	51	?
Denmark	44	47	43	40	41	40	?
Finland	59	46	39	32	35	32	✓
France	62	56	52	53	53	51	✓
Germany	47	41	43	41	47	48	
Greece	62	60	51	44	45	49	✓
Ireland	57	56	51	49	43	34	✓
Netherlands	51	50	50	44	48	45	✓
Norway	45	49	49	41	46	43	?
Portugal	81	78	63	56	55	57	✓
Spain	71	64	60	52	56	53	✓
Sweden	45	45	40	35	39	41	?
Switzerland	50	46	50	46	46	51	
UK	38	44	40	48	48	44	

Notes: From Koucký *et al.* (2010). Index ranges from 0 to 100. High values mean more socioeconomic inequality in obtaining a bachelor degree.

Educational attainment

Identifying changes over time in socioeconomic inequalities in educational attainment is very sensitive to the methodology used. Correlations and linear regression analyses tend to identify declines, as do more complex regression procedures for ordinal outcomes. However, log-linear modeling and the transitions approach tend to conclude there has been no change or even increases in socioeconomic inequalities in educational attainment.

Correlations

The raw correlation between single indicators of socioeconomic background and ordinal measures of educational attainment appear to have declined. For the UK 1946 Birth Cohort Study, the correlation between father's occupation and highest qualification was 0.42 (Richards and Sacker 2003: 617). For the 1958 cohort, the correlations were 0.35 for men and 0.33 for women, and 0.32 and 0.29 for the 1970 cohort (Schoon 2008: 77). Hertz *et al.* (2007) document clear declines in the correlation between parental and child's years of education in Denmark, Finland, the Netherlands and Switzerland. For Ireland and Norway the correlation declined only marginally and not at all in Belgium, Italy, New Zealand and the US. For the UK, the correlation may have increased. In some of these countries – Ireland, Italy, Norway, Sweden – the regression coefficient for parental education declined but not the correlation. This discrepancy is explained by the larger variance in education of the parental generation relative to the children's generation.[5]

Linear regression-based analyses

Studies from Persistent Inequality

The *Persistent Inequality* collection included regression analyses of the effects of socioeconomic background (usually indicated by father's occupational class and father's education) for a country-appropriate measure of educational attainment. There were linear declines in either the effect of father's education or father's occupation in five of the seven Western capitalist nations in the study (Blossfeld and Shavit 1993: 16). Treiman and Ganzeboom (2000: endnote 9) note that there were declines in the explained variance in six of the eight countries for which cohort analyses were reported.

Several of the declines reported in *Persistent Inequality* were quite steep. For the US, the effect of father's occupational status on years of education completed was about three times stronger in the oldest cohort compared with the youngest cohort, declining from 0.62 for the cohort born between 1905 and 1914 to 0.22 for the cohort born between 1955 and 1964. The effect for mother's education for the oldest cohort was nearly three times its effect for the youngest cohort. There was also a decline for the effect of father's education from the oldest to the second youngest cohort, but it increased for the youngest cohort. The explanatory power of the model, which also included gender and farm background, declined from 24 percent for the oldest cohort to 15 percent for the youngest cohort (Hout *et al.* 1993: 34). For Italy, among both men and women, the effects of father's schooling on years of education was about one-third less for the cohort born between 1948 and 1961 than the oldest cohort born between 1920 and 1933. The effects of one year of father's education on son's years of education had declined from 0.70 to 0.41. The impact of father's occupational status may have increased slightly. Among both men and women, father's education and occupation explained much less variation in the youngest cohort (born between 1948 and 1961), 28 percent for men and 26 percent for women, than in the oldest cohort (born between 1920 and 1933), 39 percent and 46 percent, respectively

(Cobalti and Schizzerotto 1993: 165). For the Netherlands, there were substantial declines in the effects of father's occupation and father's education on educational attainment for both men and women. For men the effect of father's socioeconomic status declined from 0.21 for the cohort born between 1890 and 1900 to 0.07 for the cohort born between 1951 and 1960. The variance explained in educational attainment declined substantially from 35 percent in the oldest cohort to 11 percent in the youngest cohort. Similar declines were found for women. There was also a substantial decline in the explained variance from 45 percent in the oldest cohort to 12 percent in the youngest cohort, with models that substituted class background for father' occupational status (de Graaf and Ganzeboom 1993: 84). For Sweden, the effects of both social class and father's education also declined significantly (Jonsson 1993: 111–12).

Declines were also identified for non-Western countries. For Taiwan, the explanatory power of the model comprising father's occupational status and father's education declined from 33 percent for the 1919–1928 cohort to 25 percent for the 1959–1968 cohort. For Japan, Treiman and Yamaguchi (1993: 237) found strong declines in the effects of parents' schooling on educational attainment. The effect for the 1946–1955 cohort was 0.36 compared with 0.48 for the 1926–1935 cohort and 0.98 for the oldest (1906–1915) cohort. The effects of father's occupational prestige also declined linearly in the three youngest cohorts. Again, the variation in educational attainment explained declined substantially from 46 percent in the oldest cohort to 24 percent in the youngest cohort.

In contrast, there was no clear decline for Switzerland, Germany and the UK. For Switzerland, father's occupation and father's education accounted for 15 percent of the variation in educational attainment for men born in 1950 which declined to 12 percent for men born in 1960. In contrast, there was an increase in the variation accounted for among women from 12 percent to 14 percent (Buchmann *et al.* 1993:187). Blossfeld (1993: 63–4) found no cohort differences in the effects of father's education and father's occupational status on educational attainment in German birth cohorts born between 1916 and 1965 for both men and women. However, the sample was small and the interaction effects with the cohorts were quite volatile. For the UK, Kerckhoff and Trott (1993: 145) found no decline in the effects of father's education and father's occupation on educational attainment. Instead, the effect father's occupation increased slightly.

Similar linear regression-type studies

The great majority of similar studies of the linear relationship between indicators of socioeconomic background and educational attainment have also found declines. For the US, Grusky and DiPrete (1990) found substantially weaker effects of father's occupation and education. The effects of father's occupation and education declined by 16 percent and 20 percent, respectively, between 1972 and 1987 (DiPrete and Grusky 1990: 128). For the UK, Bynner and Joshi (2002: 412, 416–7), after comparing the 1958 and 1970 birth cohorts in the UK, concluded that there was no change in class-based inequalities in educational qualifications. For Canada, Wanner (1999: 426–9) found declining linear effects for father's education, mother's education and father's occupational status on total years of schooling for cohorts born between 1905 and 1969. Similarly, Nakhaie and Curtis (1998) found that the effects of parental class position and parental education on their children's educational attainment decreased in the post-1960 period compared with earlier periods. For Australia, Graetz (1988: 371), analyzing total years of education, found declines in the effects of father's and mother's education and "books in the home", but increases in the effect of family wealth (measured by household possessions) and subjective assessment of ability. Marks (2009b) concluded that the effects of father's occupational status on years of education declined by about eight percent per decade and for a composite measure of socioeconomic background, by about 22 percent. For France, Duru-Bellat and Kieffer (2000: 344) reported a decline in the explanatory power of father's socioeconomic category, and father's and mother's education on highest qualification. The R square value decreased from 26 percent for men and women born before 1939 to 18 percent for the youngest (1964–1973) birth cohort. The coefficient for father's education declined precipitously whereas the effects for father's socioeconomic group and mother's education remained much the same.

de Graaf (1986) concluded that, in the Netherlands since 1950, financial resources had disappeared completely as an influence on educational attainment. Furthermore, the small influence of cultural resources became even smaller after 1950. For Greece, Daouli *et al.* (2010: 87) document strong declines in the effects of parental education for daughters' education. The effect of father's education declined from 0.45 for the cohort born between 1940 and 1944 to 0.16 for the cohort born between 1975 and 1979. The decline in the effect of mother's education was less pronounced. Together, father's and mother's education explained nearly 40 percent of the variance in daughter's education for the oldest cohort (1940–1944), declining to about 20 percent for the youngest cohort (1975–1979). For Norway, Ringdal and Birkelund (2001) found a general decline in the effects of social background on children's education between 1973 and 1995.

Ganzeboom and Treiman (1993) analyzed the effects of father's occupational status and father's education on (adult) child's years of education for 29 countries. For the bivariate relationships, there were declines in 19 of the 26 countries for father's education, and in 14 of the 29 countries for father's occupational status. Significant declines were found in 11 countries for father's education and in seven for father's occupation. They conclude that there is a dominant but not universal pattern of decline (1993: 482). Rijken's

(1999: 52) cross-national study, using updated data from the Ganzeboom and Treiman study, concluded that, among men, the effect of father's occupation on years of education had declined in many countries – Australia, Canada, France, Italy, Japan, the Netherlands, Sweden and the US – but not in West Germany. The declines among men were particularly evident for Canada, Sweden and the US, with less steep declines observed for Australia and the Netherlands (1999: 204–5). For women, declining socioeconomic inequalities in the effects of father's occupation tended to be weaker in the earlier decades of the twentieth century than that for men, but in many countries, the effects of social origin among women had also declined over time (1999: 52).

In a study on the impact of mother's characteristics on educational inequalities in the Netherlands, West Germany and the US, Korupp *et al.* (2002: 31) concluded that the "the importance of social origin, be it the father's or the mother's SES, is becoming less and less determining for the educational attainment of children". They describe the decline in the effects of socioeconomic status as rapid. Including mother's occupation and education made no difference to the trend of declining effects.

Hertz *et al.*'s (2007) analyzed the relationship between parental and their (adult) child's education in 42 countries, identified declines in the regression coefficient for Denmark, Finland, Ireland (but not Northern Ireland), the Netherlands, Norway, Sweden and Switzerland. In these countries, coefficients linking parents' and their children's years of education in the youngest cohorts were small, around 0.2 (2007: 39–41). However, there was no change for New Zealand, the UK or the US (2007: 24–5).

Table 9.4 presents more recent analyses of the Ganzeboom and Treiman data. For each country, it shows the average correlation between son's educational attainment and father's occupational status (ISEI scores) for the time period in which data were collected, and estimates of the correlation at the beginning and end of the period, based on a regression analysis of the year of data collection. Declines are evident in many countries, especially in countries where the initial correlation was relatively large. Among Western countries, there unambiguous are declines for Austria, Belgium (Wallonia), Canada, Denmark, England and Wales, France, West Germany, Ireland, Italy, the Netherlands, New Zealand, Northern Ireland, Norway, Scotland and Sweden; but not for Australia, Finland, Greece, Portugal, Spain or the US. Such an analysis is only illustrative, since father's socioeconomic background is the only indicator of socioeconomic background and the effects of this indicator have not been separated from the effects of cognitive ability. Declines are also apparent for a number of non-Western countries; for example, Argentina, Brazil, Russia, South Africa, Taiwan and several east European countries.

Table 9.4 Correlations between father's occupation (ISEI) and son's education

Country	*Studies (n)*	*Cases (n)*	*Initial year*	*Most recent year*	*Average correlation*	*Estimate of initial correlation*	*Estimate of most recent correlation*	*Decline?*
Argentina	6	3,617	1973	2009	0.537	0.645	0.501	✓
Australia	14	14,793	1965	2009	0.372	0.374	0.368	
Austria	16	25,439	1969	2009	0.430	0.519	0.323	✓
Belgium (Flanders)	12	6,595	1971	2010	0.390	0.361	0.409	↑
Belgium (Wallonia)	13	4,954	1971	2010	0.444	0.512	0.386	✓
Brazil	5	18,754	1972	1999	0.511	0.545	0.423	✓
Bulgaria	6	4,798	1991	2010	0.393	0.336	0.466	↑
Canada	8	25,599	1965	1999	0.399	0.454	0.338	✓
Chile	4	11,460	1998	2009	0.497	0.501	0.487	?
China	3	4,858	1996	2009	0.294	0.273	0.316	↑
Croatia	4	1,592	2008	2010	0.411	0.409	0.415	↑
Cyprus	6	3,781	1999	2010	0.408	0.385	0.424	↑
Czech Republic	14	12,769	1984	2010	0.374	0.379	0.371	
Denmark	11	9,027	1972	2010	0.347	0.426	0.307	✓
England and Wales	14	19,778	1969	2010	0.393	0.442	0.331	✓
Estonia	8	4,534	1991	2010	0.286	0.327	0.274	✓
Finland	13	9,562	1972	2010	0.347	0.337	0.354	
France	15	15,876	1958	2010	0.410	0.537	0.367	✓
Germany (East)	20	7,742	1991	2010	0.316	0.275	0.362	↑
Germany (West)	43	38,322	1959	2010	0.423	0.485	0.397	✓
Greece	6	6,358	2002	2010	0.384	0.381	0.390	
Hungary	22	63,603	1973	2010	0.424	0.440	0.403	✓
Iceland	4	1,591	2004	2009	0.296	0.255	0.346	↑
India	3	5,734	1967	1971	0.438	0.421	0.448	
Ireland	10	8,565	1973	2010	0.364	0.394	0.345	✓
Israel	11	10,603	1974	2010	0.273	0.223	0.333	↑
Italy	34	79,691	1963	2009	0.425	0.533	0.398	✓
Japan	9	10,187	1955	2009	0.438	0.445	0.429	
Latvia	6	3,133	1999	2009	0.285	0.256	0.301	↑
Lithuania	3	2,302	2005	2010	0.279	0.294	0.241	✓
Luxembourg	4	3,370	2002	2008	0.449	0.402	0.502	↑
Malaysia	2	5,798	1967	1976	0.311	0.307	0.330	
Mexico	2	6,052	2006	2006	0.370	0.370	0.370	
Netherlands	62	51,526	1958	2011	0.371	0.446	0.338	✓
Northern Ireland	9	8,621	1968	2010	0.397	0.428	0.221	✓

Table 9.4 continued

Country	*Studies (n)*	*Cases (n)*	*Initial year*	*Most recent year*	*Average correlation*	*Estimate of initial correlation*	*Estimate of most recent correlation*	*Decline?*
New Zealand	5	3,387	1976	2009	0.324	0.365	0.252	✓
Norway	14	9,929	1957	2010	0.364	0.394	0.355	✓
Poland	26	63,659	1972	2010	0.392	0.398	0.381	
Portugal	9	7,240	1999	2010	0.450	0.434	0.462	
Quebec	9	11,359	1960	1999	0.380	0.381	0.389	
Romania	3	1,552	2006	2008	0.370	0.385	0.362	
Russia	11	7,932	1991	2010	0.317	0.338	0.293	✓
Scotland	15	5,837	1963	2010	0.344	0.361	0.323	✓
Slovakia	13	10,951	1984	2010	0.357	0.380	0.350	✓
Slovenia	19	11,309	1967	2010	0.358	0.393	0.336	✓
South Africa	2	3,593	1991	2009	0.488	0.522	0.353	✓
Spain	15	22,298	1990	2010	0.430	0.423	0.442	
Sweden	18	9,465	1960	2010	0.395	0.505	0.351	✓
Switzerland	11	7,823	1972	2010	0.438	0.442	0.439	
Taiwan	28	27,188	1970	2009	0.401	0.454	0.373	✓
Turkey	5	6,597	1978	2009	0.339	0.345	0.327	
Ukraine	6	3,314	2004	2010	0.284	0.230	0.320	↑
US	46	65,959	1947	2010	0.413	0.414	0.410	
Summary	686	790,376			0.384	0.402	0.369	

Note: Analyses by the author on the International Social Mobility File supplied by Ganzeboom.

Ordinal logit and probit models

Studies that employ ordinal logit or probit models also tend to show declining socioeconomic inequalities in education.

For the UK, Heath (2000) reported a decline in the (logistic) effects of class of origin on an ordinal measure of educational qualifications. For the the oldest (1900–1920) cohort, the estimates for the salariat and intermediate class backgrounds compared to a working class background were 2.4 and 1.0, respectively. For the youngest (1960–1967) cohort, the comparable effects were 1.6 and 0.5, although the estimates for the youngest cohort were only marginally smaller than those for the 1920–1927 cohort (2000: 322). For Canada, McIntosh (2010: 457), using an ordered probability model with an ordinal measure of educational attainment and allowing for unobserved heterogeneity, concludes that "educational attainments depend significantly less on family background variables for younger cohorts". The effects for father's and mother's educational level were substantially smaller in the younger cohort. He claims that much of the decline can be attributed to educational policies, most notably increasing participation and the public funding of post-secondary education.

In a cross-national analysis focusing on Ireland, Hout (2007) found weakening socioeconomic inequalities in educational attainment in many nations. Analyzing the relationship using an ordinal logit model and socio-economic background measured by father's and mother's education, and books in the home, Hout (2007) concludes that the effects of family background declined faster among cohorts born after 1950 than older cohorts: declining by about 0.5 percent per single-year cohort before 1950 and by 1.1 percent after 1950. He was not able to distinguish the trends in individual countries.

Using ordered logit models, Breen *et al.* (2009) found widespread declines in educational inequality by social origin among men in eight European countries: Britain, France, Germany, Ireland, Italy, the Netherlands, Poland and Sweden. Using EGP class categories, they find that the most disadvantaged classes improved their position during the first two-thirds of the twentieth century, and suggest that post-war economic growth was important to the decline in inequality (2009: 1496). These declines in class inequality were large, halving the initial extent of inequality (2009: 1511). In addition, there was a decline in the effects of parental education in all countries except Ireland (2009: 1504), although the decline was less pronounced than that for class background. Their analyses indicate that class inequalities in educational attainment were initially largest in Germany, Italy, France and Poland, and weaker in Britain, Sweden and the Netherlands (2009: 1510). A second study focusing on women also found large declines, with class inequalities in educational attainment declining 30 percent or more from the oldest to the youngest cohorts. The central finding of declining class inequality in educational attainment for both men and women directly contradicts the "persistent inequality" thesis (Breen *et al.* 2010: 39).

Log-linear modeling

Log-linear analyses of the relationship between class of origin and educational attainment tend to show no change. It was such log-linear analyses that led Goldthorpe (1996a) to call for a reorientation in theory from trying to explain decreasing socioeconomic inequalities, as in modernization theories, but persisting socioeconomic differences in education which led to the development of the Relative Risk Aversion (RRA) hypothesis.

Using data from representative surveys conducted in the UK in 1949, 1972, 1983, and 1987, Heath and Clifford (1990) found no decline in the association between class background and educational attainment. Similarly, Paterson and Iannelli (2007) found no decline in the association for the cohorts born between 1927 and 1976 in England, Wales or Scotland. For Italy, Barone's (2009) log-linear analyses show no decline in the association between class background and educational attainment. The only evidence of equalization was among students from agricultural backgrounds. Pfeffer's (2008) 20-nation log-linear analysis of the relationship between parents and their children's educational attainment concluded that the association "has remained stable across the second half of the 20th century in virtually all countries" (2008: 543).

There are studies using log-linear techniques that have found declines in the association between socioeconomic background and education. Jonsson's (1987) log-linear analysis concluded that, in Sweden, education is allocated according to social origin to a decreasing extent. He also found that the impact of cultural capital, measured by parental education, is decreasing at a faster rate than class background. Jonsson *et al.* (1996: 199) conclude that, in Germany and Sweden (but not Britain), there has been a long-term and decelerating attenuation of class differentials in educational attainment for individuals of both sexes born between 1900 and 1950. The change was not trivial. They calculated that overall, five percent more children from unskilled manual backgrounds reached senior secondary school, owing to a reduction in class barriers. The chances of students from unskilled working class backgrounds attaining university education improved by about 70 percent (1996: 196–7). Vallet's (2002) log-linear analyses of educational attainment in France found that, over 60 years, the strength of the association between social origins and educational destination declined by about 35 percent. The downward trend was less marked for parental education than parental occupation, which is supposedly evidence that the cultural dimension of socioeconomic background is more important than the economic dimension. The decline appears to be largely independent of educational reforms introduced in the late 1950s which were designed to promote equality of opportunity. Vallet (2002: 29) concludes that the results do not conform to the persistent inequality thesis and that France is the fourth country – after Sweden, the Netherlands and Germany – where the trend is declining socioeconomic inequalities in education rather than persistent inequalities.

Using log-linear models on data collected between 1962 and 2006, Ichou and Vallet (2011) confirm that there was a decline in socioeconomic inequalities in holding or not holding a baccalauréat, the final examination in French secondary schools. Class inequality in holding a baccalauréat declined by more than one-quarter between 1962 and 1995. However, no change was found if finer distinctions are made between academic, technological and vocational baccalauréats, providing some support Lucas's (2001) EMI thesis. It should be remembered that these are models of the association between socioeconomic background and education and do not include any other influences on education.

Educational transitions

The most prominent evidence for the contention that socioeconomic inequalities in education are not declining is Shavit and Blossfeld's (1993) edited volume, *Persistent Inequality*. They concluded that, with the exception of Sweden and the Netherlands, there has been little change in the relationship between social background and educational attainment in industrialized countries. Countries where there was no change in socioeconomic inequalities were Czechoslovakia, West Germany, England and Wales, Hungary, Israel, Italy, Japan, Poland, Switzerland and the US. This often-cited conclusion is based on the changes over time in the effects of measures of socioeconomic background on the odds of making the transition from one level of education to the next.

One important set of findings largely overlooked in the educational transitions literature is the very weak or non-existent effect of socioeconomic variables on the higher-level transitions, which are arguably the most important. The reason for the weak or non-existent effects of socioeconomic background on the transition from school to university or college observed in cohorts born in the first 50 or 60 years of the twentieth century is that there is little variation in socioeconomic background (and ability) for students "at risk" of the transition to the university. Students at risk of a successful transition from the final year of school to university typically were higher-ability students. The minority of students from low socioeconomic backgrounds were probably of even higher ability. The emergence of stronger and significant effects for socioeconomic background among younger cohorts on university entry among high-school graduates, reported in more recent studies, can be attributed to greater heterogeneity in the population at risk. In the populations at risk, there is much greater variation in terms of socioeconomic background and ability.

The US

For the US, the effects of mother's and father's education and father's occupational prestige on the transitions from high school to higher education, and from higher education to completing a degree, were very small and sometimes negative (reported by Hout *et al.* 1993: 40–1). This finding is consistent with Mare's (1980: 303) original paper on educational transitions, in which socioeconomic background factors had weak effects on the transition from school graduation to the first year of college, and for the transition from college entry to college completion. Analyzing more recent youth cohorts, Roksa *et al.* (2007: 183) found significant effects for parents' education in the expected direction with high-school completers with more highly educated parents being more likely to enter a bachelor degree-granting institution.[6] However, the effects for father's occupation did not follow the expected pattern. Students whose fathers worked in a professional or managerial job were no more likely to enter such institutions than were students whose fathers worked in unskilled manual jobs. In addition, several of the coefficients for non-manual groups were negative and significant, indicating that students belonging to these occupational class groups were *less* likely to enter such institutions than the unskilled manual group. When controlling for academic performance and subjects taken during high school, the effect for parents with a college education declined by 30–40 percent, and the effect for father's professional or managerial occupation was no longer statistically significant (2007: 186). Buchmann and DiPrete (2006: 530) reported significant effects of father's and mother's education (some college) on enrolment in a four-year college degree among high-school graduates and those holding a high-school equivalency. When controlling for academic performance and subjects taken during high school, the effect of having parents with some college education declined by about 40 percent.

Despite the high costs of *elite* university education in the US, the influence of socioeconomic background is also weak. For entry to an elite institution – defined by the top ten percent of institutions, indicated by first-year students' mean SAT or ACT test scores – there were few significant effects for parental occupational and educational categories.[7] There were some significant differences in entry to elite colleges for parents with college or higher education versus high-school completion in all three cohorts (1970s, 1980s and 1990s), and parents with some post-secondary education versus high-school completion in the 1970s cohort. For parental occupational categories, there were even fewer significant differences: for professional and managerial occupations versus unskilled manual (in the 1970s and 1990s cohorts) and self-employed versus unskilled manual (in the 1990s cohort). *However, there were no other significant differences for parental education and father's occupation for the remaining 17 comparisons.* Subsequently, controlling for academic performance reduced the coefficients for a parent with a college degree by 10–40 percent and the effect for (father's) professional and managerial occupation became not statistically significant in all three cohorts analyzed (reported by Roksa *et al.* 2007: 184, 185).

For the next transition from college entry to graduation, socioeconomic background has even weaker effects. In a sample of 1952 freshmen, Eckland (1965: 740) found that father's occupation had only a weak correlation with college graduation (0.13) compared with academic performance at school (0.35) measured poorly by high-school rank. Alexander *et al.* (1982) found that academic variables – test scores, track and high-school class rank – were each more strongly associated with degree completion than a composite measure of socioeconomic background (comprising family income, father's and mother's education, father's occupational status and household possessions). They conclude, "The predominant influence of academic resources relative to other factors is inescapable". College completion rates did not reach ten percent among advantaged groups – the example given was high socioeconomic status white males – if their academic credentials were uniformly low (1982: 326). Socioeconomic background has no effect on further education among college graduates (Stolzenberg 1992). Mullen *et al.* (2003) found no effects of parental education on entry to master of business administration programs, but strong effects of parent's education on entry to professional and doctoral programs mediated entirely through academic performance, undergraduate institution and other factors. Academic performance was again the strongest influence.

Other countries

The influence of socioeconomic background on entry to university is also weak in the UK. For England and Wales, the effects of father's education and father's occupation on the transition from secondary school to some tertiary qualification or obtaining a degree was either minuscule or not statistically significant among cohorts born between 1913 and 1952 (Kerckhoff and Trott 1993: 146–7). Analyzing data from the 1958 and 1970 birth cohort studies, Cheung and Egerton (2007: 212–13) report stronger effects for father's education and class of origin on entry to a degree-granting institution and entry to university conditional on eligibility for higher education. They note that, since their analyses were performed on a less restrictive definition than that used in previous studies, it gave the "family of origin variables some purchase" (2007: 216). Their analyses did not include controls for performance or test scores, which would have substantially reduced the influence of family background variables.

For Australian cohorts born between 1890 and 1981, parental education and father's occupational class accounted for less than four percent of the variation in university entrance conditional on school completion. For younger cohorts born between 1961 and 1975, father's occupational class accounted for six percent of the variation. The addition of school sector increased this figure to nine percent and grade-nine test scores increased it to 23 percent (Marks and McMillan 2007: 366, 371). Recent studies indicate that university entrance in Australia does not differ by socioeconomic background, net of performance in the final year of schooling (Cardak and Ryan 2009; Marks and McMillan 2007). For Ireland, Raftery and Hout (1993: 52–3) found no effects of class origins for the transition from secondary school to higher education. A later study on data from younger cohorts found significant effects, but they were much weaker than those for the earlier transitions (Whelan and Hannan 1999).

For West Germany, the effects of social background on the transition from intermediate school to upper-secondary school and from upper-secondary school to professional college and university were small and often not statistically significant (Blossfeld 1993: 70). A later analysis on a much larger data set found significant effects of both class background and father's education for entry to upper university study relative to non-tertiary vocational training among men who had attained an *Abitur* degree (academic track school completion). However, there were far fewer significant differences among comparable women or the contrast between lower tertiary education and non-tertiary vocational education (Mayer *et al.* 2007: 259–61). For Switzerland, father's occupation had no significant effects on the transition from the Gymnasium to university for Swiss German men or women born in 1950 or 1960, and only a statistically significant effect of father's education among men born in 1960 (Buchmann *et al.* 1993: 188–9). For the Netherlands, de Graaf and Ganzeboom (1993: 97) comment that, for the transition from secondary to tertiary education, "the effects of social background are significant, but quite small". A more recent analysis of university education, given participation at the previous level, also shows fairly weak effects for class background and stronger effects for parental education, which the authors attribute to increased heterogeneity in the cohort "at risk" of university education (Rijken *et al.* 2007: 284–5). For Italy, Shavit and Westerbeek (1998: 40) reported statistically insignificant effects for father's occupation, father's education, and father's self-employment on the transition from the "Matura" to university.

Part of the argument for the transitions model was that the stability in the overall relationship between socioeconomic background and educational attainment can be disaggregated into two components: educational expansion, which decreases the overall association, and increases in the impact of socioeconomic background at higher-level transitions. The *Persistent Inequality* book found no evidence of an increase in the impact of socioeconomic background on the transition from one level to the next (Blossfeld and Shavit 1993: 18). In a later publication, Shavit *et al.* (2007b) are less confident and conclude that a strong version of the persistent inequality thesis is probably wrong, since there are declines on the effects of social origin during the early decades of the twentieth century. However, they maintain that a weaker version of the persistent inequality thesis is credible, since the reduction in socioeconomic inequality is only moderate, and that socioeconomic inequality at the higher transitions, where it counts, persists.

Given the weak effects of socioeconomic background in higher transitions, it is not surprising that there is little evidence that socioeconomic inequalities in the transition from one educational level to the next decline *only* when participation by the most privileged group reach saturation. Marks and McMillan (2003) found socioeconomic inequalities in university education declining, although participation by the most privileged group was nowhere near saturation. Ayalon and Shavit (2004) conclude that the MMI thesis is not supported, since socioeconomic inequalities declined in response to an educational reform without participation by the privileged group reaching saturation. One of the originators of the MMI thesis, Hout (2007), notes that his findings from ordinal logit modeling, not an educational-transitions approach, are inconsistent with the strong version of the MMI thesis. Contrary to the MMI thesis, Bar Haim and Shavit (2013) found that the effect of reaching saturation levels had no impact on socioeconomic inequalities in education. They also found that expansion did reduce inequality of educational opportunity for tertiary education but not for secondary education.

Sibling and twin studies

Sibling studies tend to find declines over time in the importance of the family of origin. In the US, Kuo and Hauser (1995) were unambiguous, concluding that "the global secular decline in inequality of educational attainments cuts across all sources of variation in schooling – measured and unmeasured common family characteristics and unmeasured individual characteristics". Similarly for West Germany, de Graaf and Huinink (1992) found that the total effect of family background lost some of its predictive power on educational attainment for the youngest (1950) of the three cohorts studied. The intraclass correlation for educational attainment in a West German sibling study declined from 0.53 to 0.41 percent (1992: 103, 108). They also found declines in the effects of father's occupational status but not father's or mother's education. They attribute this finding to a weakening of economic factors on educational attainment with an increase in the relative importance of cultural factors. For the Netherlands, Dronkers (1993) found an increase in the variation in educational attainment unexplained by the common family factor and a decline in the effect of parental social class on the common family factor. Sieben and de Graaf's (2003) sibling analysis of 11 countries found that, although the measured aspects of socioeconomic background had declining effects on educational attainment, the overall impact of family background had not declined. They suggest that cognitive ability may be involved in explaining the difference (2003: 58).

Twin studies also suggest weaker effects for environmental factors over time. Nielsen (2006) argues that disadvantaged social contexts are characterized by low (genetic) heritability and higher "environmentality"; increased heritability can be understood as the realization of genetic potential as socioeconomic barriers are reduced. Analysis of data from Norwegian twins concluded that the impact of family background on educational attainment declined among men but not among women (Heath *et al.* 1985). The heritability of educational attainment, that is the impact of genes, was stronger for the post-1940 cohort. Similarly, the Tambs *et al.* (1989) Norwegian study concluded that that genetic heritability for educational attainment was only about ten percent for the oldest cohort born between 1931 and 1935, but around 50 percent for younger cohorts. Also, the variation attributed to the shared family environment was much higher in the oldest cohort. For Sweden, Lichtenstein *et al.* (1992) found stronger genetic heritabilities in younger cohorts compared with older cohorts and a weaker environmental component. This pattern of increased role of genetics vis-à-vis the environment was also found among Australian twins (Baker *et al.* 1996). A more recent Australian study found, after adjusting for assortative mating, that "environmentality" contributed to as little as eight percent of the variation in educational attainment in the younger (1964–1971) cohort (Le *et al.* 2011: 132).

Between-country differences and modernization

Endeavoring to explain differences between countries by various societal characteristics (including measures of modernization) Treiman and Yip (1989) concluded that educational attainment is more dependent on socio-economic background in more unequal countries, but found no relationship with the degree of industrialization (measured by energy consumption per capita and the percentage of the population employed in agriculture). This study did not support modernization theory in that more industrialized countries did not show weaker effects for socioeconomic background nor did countries with larger welfare sectors. Hout's (2007) cross-national analyses showed that socioeconomic inequalities in education were strongest in Brazil, Portugal, West Germany, Chile and Ireland; weaker in Norway, France, Israel, and Sweden; and weaker again in Australia, Japan, Canada and New Zealand. The US showed one of the weakest associations.

There is recent evidence that modernization reduces socioeconomic inequalities in education. Using the transitions approach, Müller and Karle (1993) rejected the hypothesis that industrial development is associated with reduced class differences in educational outcomes. They concluded that differences between nations can be attributed to their individual historical, institutional and political characteristics, although these are strongly associated with modernization. Although Rijken (1999: 75–6) found substantial declines in inequality of educational opportunity, she concluded that the declines did not coincide with the level of modernization. However, Sieben and de Graaf's (2001) sibling analysis of six countries – England, Hungary, the Netherlands, Scotland, Spain and the US – found that the effects of parental social class on educational attainment are weaker in the more technologically advanced societies. In a second study with sibling data from 11 countries, Sieben and de Graaf (2003: 52) also found that the effects of parent's socioeconomic characteristics were smaller in the more technologically advanced societies. They concluded that indicators of modernization, individualization and socialism negatively influenced the measured effects of parents' socioeconomic position on educational attainment. Treiman *et al.*'s (2003: 21–3) multilevel analysis of 42 countries found that the level of education reached in a society (and its gender gap) depends heavily on the level of modernization. Furthermore, educational expansion strongly reduced the effects of father's education. Each extra (average) year of schooling in society reduced the impact of father's education by nearly ten percent of its average effect. In addition, reducing the level of educational inequality (indicated by the standard deviation for years of education) reduced the impact of father's education for educational attainment. Similar declines were found for father's socioeconomic status. The authors emphasized that these are large declines. Additional evidence for the modernization thesis in regard to education has been reported by van Doorn *et al.* (2011) in an analysis over time of the effects of parental education in 28 countries using data from three waves of the International Social Science Project. They found that the effects of parental education were inversely associated with per capita gross domestic product (GDP), higher female labor force participation, and expenditure on education as a proportion of GDP; and were positively associated with higher growth rates of (tertiary) service sector employment (2011: 108–11). The authors concluded that "the industrialization thesis is the most important explanation of the variation in the relationship between parents' education and their children's educational achievements across countries and cohorts" (2011: 113). In contrast, Bar Haim and Shavit (2013) concluded that inequality of educational opportunity does not decline with GDP or educational expansion.

Conclusions

The bulk of the evidence indicates that socioeconomic inequalities in student achievement (test scores) have declined. In many countries, smaller amounts of the variation in PISA test scores is accounted for by comparable composite measures of socioeconomic background in 2009 than in 2000. There is indirect evidence of declining socioeconomic inequalities from the adult literacy studies. For higher education most studies suggest a weakening of socioeconomic inequalities. For more elite types of higher education, the evidence is mixed, although the majority of countries show declines. Several studies suggest that socioeconomic inequalities in university and more elite educational destinations are not declining. Since these studies almost invariably do not include ability, it is difficult to speculate why this should be the case. One possibility is that the overall effects of socioeconomic background are not changing because, with the expansion of university education, there is increased participation of middle- and low-ability students from higher socioeconomic backgrounds.

Conclusions on whether socioeconomic inequalities in educational attainment are declining depend, to some extent, on the method used. Linear regression-type analyses of some measure of socioeconomic background and a continuous measure of educational attainment tend to find declines. In addition, more complex linear models, such as ordered logit and probit, also tend to find declines. In contrast, analyses of educational transitions most often tend to support the persistent inequality thesis, as do log-linear analyses of class differences in educational attainment. Log-linear analyses focus on the counts in a cross-tabulation of educational attainment by class or some measure of socioeconomic background. They give theoretical primacy to socioeconomic background when other factors are involved which are often just as, or more, important. The extent that the association between educational attainment and class background accounts for the observed counts is not at all equivalent to explaining the variation in educational outcomes among individuals. In higher-level transitions the impact of socioeconomic background has typically been small, especially net of student performance or ability.

Further evidence that socioeconomic inequalities in education are declining comes from twin studies, which show that the shared family environment has only a limited impact and a weaker impact among younger than older cohorts. The genetic heritability, which includes both cognitive and non-cognitive traits, of educational attainment appears to have increased.

Notes

1 Breen (2010) concluded that educational expansion increased social mobility in the three countries he analyzed: Britain, Sweden and Germany.

2 For a critique of the log-linear model for educational research, see Hellevik (2013); and for a critique of log-linear models in mobility research, see Kelley (1990).

3 The ESCS measures of students' socioeconomic background for the different PISA cycles are detailed in the appropriate OECD publications (OECD 2007b: 333; 2010c: 131). There are differences in the measures across cycles, but arguably the more recent measures are stronger measures. For example, the 2000 measure does not include books in the home and does not distinguish between parents' university and vocational tertiary education. The correlation between the 2003 and 2006 measures was very high at 0.96 (OECD 2007b: 334).

4 Her five-category dependent variable distinguished non-attendance, two-year non-selective, four-year non-selective, four-year selective colleges (median SAT scores between 900 and 1050), and four-year highly selective colleges (median SAT scores above 1050).

5 In bivariate regression, the correlation (r) or the standardized coefficient (b_1^*) is the unstandardized coefficient (b_1) multiplied by the ratio of the standard deviation of the x variable to the standard deviation of the y variable:

$$r = b_1^* = b_1 \left(\frac{s_x}{s_y}\right)$$

6 The effect of parents with a college education on entry to a degree-granting institution declined by about one-third when controlling for academic achievement at high school (Roksa *et al.* 2007: 185).

7 Significant differences in parents' occupational group for entry to elite colleges were: professional and managerial occupations versus unskilled manual (in two of the three data sets analyzed); self-employed versus unskilled manual (in the most recent cohort); and for parental education: parents with college or higher education versus high school completion in all three cohorts (reported by Roksa *et al.* 2007: 184–5).

Chapter 10

Occupational attainment

Research on the process of occupational attainment can be traced to the pioneering work of Blau and Duncan (1967), to whom the term "status attainment research" is attributed. This model links causal pathways from socioeconomic origins to adult socioeconomic outcomes. The pathways are arranged in a temporal sequence; socioeconomic background influences educational attainment, which in turn influences occupation and earnings. Therefore, the relationships between factors that are temporally most distant, such as socioeconomic origins and earnings, are weaker than the relationships between more proximal factors, such as socioeconomic background and educational performance. An important component of the Blau–Duncan model is the conceptual distinction between ascription and achievement. Ascription includes all ascribed characteristics, socioeconomic background, gender and race, although the main focus is on socioeconomic background factors, while achievement is the level achieved in the education system. According to Coser (1975: 694), the model allows for the first time an assessment of the precise details of the process of occupational attainment. It also permits comparison of the contributions of social inheritance and individual effort in the attainment of socioeconomic status. A major variant of the status attainment model is the Wisconsin model, based on WLS high-school seniors in 1957. This psychosociological model includes measured ability, high-school grades, the influence of significant others (i.e. teachers and peers), and educational and occupational aspirations (Sewell *et al.* 1969, 1970, 2004).

Occupational status research provides a vehicle that allows examination of some questions about the modern world. These include which is the stronger influence, ascription or achievement? Are achieved characteristics more important in Western Europe than in the New World societies such as the US? Are ascriptive characteristics weaker under countries with greater social democratic incumbency or socialist histories? Importantly, the status attainment research paradigm approach allows the examination of changes over time in the influence of ascribed and achieved characteristics.

The impact of socioeconomic background on occupational attainment

Contrary to common perceptions, the correlations for occupational status across generations are not particularly strong. If there was little mobility in Western countries, the intergenerational correlations for occupational status would be at least 0.7, possibly around 0.8. The raw association between parental and their (adult) children's occupations is only moderate. For the US, Blau and Duncan (1967: 104) present a Cramer's V coefficient of 0.34 for the association between father's and son's occupational group, crudely measured with three categories: non-manual, manual and farm.[1] The observed correlation from the large 1962 OCG study was around 0.40 (Blau and Duncan 1967: 169; Duncan *et al.* 1972: 263; Featherman *et al.* 1975: 343). For occupational attainment, father's education tends to have weaker correlations than father's occupational status (see Broom *et al.* 1980: 26; Featherman *et al.* 1975: 343; Halsey 1977: 179). Reviewing studies up until that time, Jencks *et al.* (1972: 179) note that the role of father's occupational status in determining his son's occupational status is surprisingly small, contrary to most people's preconceptions. In the early 1960s, a substantial proportion of US men had farm backgrounds: more than one in four (Blau and Duncan 1967: 60). Excluding men with a farm background reduces the correlation with father's occupational status only slightly to 0.37 (Duncan *et al.* 1972: 264). This indicates that, in the early 1960s in the US, about 16 percent of the variation in men's occupational attainment could be accounted for by father's occupation. A recent estimate for the intergenerational correlation for socioeconomic status is 0.35 for men and less than 0.30 for women. The correlation was zero among college graduates (Torche 2011: 785–6).

Weaker correlations are observed using measures of occupational prestige – based on respondents' evaluations of the relative standing of occupations – compared with socioeconomic measures. These prestige measures suggest that the US is a very open society. Treiman and Terrell (1975: 573) report an intergenerational correlation of 0.26 for occupational prestige, which Treas and Tyree (1979) compare with correlations of 0.32 for the socio-economic scale. Featherman *et al.* (1975: 343) report an intergenerational correlation of 0.24 for occupational prestige compared with 0.38 for Duncan's socioeconomic measure. Similarly, prestige scales return weaker correlations than socioeconomic measures in Australia (1975: 344). Kelley (1990: 344) shows that the intergenerational correlations for prestige measures are weaker than those for socioeconomic indices of occupation in developing countries as well as for the UK and the US.

There is little direct influence of socioeconomic origins on occupational attainment. Analyzing the 1962 OCG, only 16 percent of the variation in occupational attainment could be accounted for by father's education and occupation. The addition of educational attainment increased the explained variance substantially to 44 percent. For occupational status, the standardized effects for father's education and father's occupation, net of educational attainment, are very weak (0.07 and 0.08), compared with a much stronger effect for educational attainment (0.59; Sewell and Hauser 1975: 61). Featherman and Hauser (1978: 258–259) concluded that the net direct effect of social background accounted for ten percent of the variance in occupational attainment and 20 percent of the variance in educational attainment.

For the UK, Treiman and Terrell (1975: 573) report an intergenerational correlation of 0.31 for occupational prestige. Using the BHPS, Ermisch and Francesconi (2004) found that the intergenerational correlation in occupational status using the Hope–Goldthorpe scale, depending on the method used, ranged from 0.20 to 0.31. Among the British birth cohort studies, the strongest correlation reported was 0.45 between father's class and respondent's class in the 1921 Scottish mental survey (Deary *et al.* 2005b: 464). Another study reported correlations between father's and respondent's social class of only 0.29, and 0.28 between the social classes of respondents and their children (Johnson *et al.* 2010b: 60). Studying the three generations associated with the Lothian 1936 cohort in Scotland, Johnson *et al.* (2010a) report correlations of 0.23 between father's and participants social class and 0.26 between participant's and offspring's social class. The correlation between social class of origin and destination was only 0.26 in the 1958 NCDS (Nettle 2003: 554) and 0.31 in the 1970 BCS (von Stumm *et al.* 2009) (these measures of class cannot be easily compared with the measures used in the earlier birth cohort studies). Using a different measure of class, Erikson and Goldthorpe (2010) report correlations of 0.34 between father's and son's class for the 1958 cohort and 0.31 for the 1970 cohort. Therefore, only about 11 percent of the variation in class destination, at best, can be attributed to class of origin. For Sweden, Sorjonen *et al.* (2011: 279) report a correlation of 0.30 between social class of origin and attained social class. These moderate correlations are lower than the correlations between ability and attained class destination (see section on "Occupation group and social class" and in Chapter 6, page 95) and are not substantially higher than other non-sociological associations. For example, physical height and destination class are correlated at around 0.26 (Deary *et al.* 2005b: 464).

In Britain, as in the US, education has a substantially greater influence on occupational attainment than social background. According to Halsey's (1977: 179) simple path model of the 1972 Oxford mobility study data, the effect of education (0.46) on occupational attainment among men was over twice that of social background (0.18). After analyses of several more complex models, Halsey (1977) concludes that the effects of social origins are relatively small compared to education. Later, Marshall and Swift (1993: 202) note that among "males, high educational achievement guarantees equal chance of entry to service-class occupations, irrespective of social background".

A note on occupational mobility

The perceived wisdom is that there is little social mobility in modern societies. If there were limited occupational mobility, the amount of immobility in the most privileged and least privileged class groups would be very high. US data collected between 1988 and 2004 indicate that about 42 percent of sons from upper professional backgrounds were in the same class destination, and immobility in the lowest status class (unskilled and service) was 38 percent (Beller and Hout 2006: 24). Similarly, Britain is not a highly immobile society. According to the 1972 Oxford mobility survey, immobility in the service class (both upper and lower) was around 60 percent, and for the industrial working class was 66 percent (1979: 434–5). These figures are not indicative of social closure.

There is, of course, more mobility with more classes. Jonsson *et al.* (2009: 999–1000) found that immobility ranges from a high of 65–70 percent for a two-class manual and non-manual classification, 40–50 percent for five-class schema, 20–30 percent for a ten-class schema, and 10–20 percent for an occupational schema comprising 82 occupational groups.

The rates of mobility are higher than expected. Erikson and Goldthorpe (1992: 74–5), analyzing data from nine European countries with a seven-category class schema, indicated that 50–70 percent of cohorts born after 1925 experienced mobility out of their occupational class of origin. Breen and Luijkx (2004: 48–9) analyzed data from ten countries and calculated that the total mobility in a three-class schema[2] among men measured in the 1970s, 1980s and 1990s averaged around 66–68 percent. Approximately 45 to 50 percent was vertical mobility (either up or down) and about 30 percent was upward mobility, and less than 20 percent was downward mobility.

Issues in the strength of the relationship

Family income, wealth and socioeconomic background factors

Bowles (1972) argues that using parental education and occupation as indicators of socioeconomic backgrounds neglects the important role of family's economic resources. However, in the WLS, as noted earlier, family income (from tax records) had a weaker impact on occupational status (β = 0.09) than father's education (β = 0.18), and father's occupational status (β = 0.16). Together, the three variables could only account for ten percent of the variation in occupational status (Sewell and Hauser 1975: 73).

Pfeffer (200711: 126–31) presents correlations of between 0.17 and 0.29 between the household wealth of the family of origin and occupational status at mid-life of around 0.2 for the NLSY, 0.3 for the PSID and 0.16 the German GSOEP. These correlations are only slightly lower than the correlations for household income and father's occupational status, but substantially lower than that for father's education (which was close to 0.4). For Australia, a measure of the wealth of the family of origin derived from a principle component analysis of five items – home ownership, possession of a car, telephone, refrigerator and inside toilet – had a stronger correlation with respondent's present occupational status (β = 0.33) than father's occupational status (β = 0.26), father's education (β = 0.24) or mother's education (β = 0.25). However, the impact of this measure of wealth on the occupational status of the first job, net of education, was very small (β = 0.05) (Broom *et al.* 1980: 26, 28).

Broom *et al.* (1980: 36) created a composite measure of socioeconomic background from five indicators: father's occupational status, father's education, mother's education, wealth (based on possessions) and family size. Its standardized effect on the socioeconomic status of the current job was 0.5. However after adding education to the analysis, this effect declined to 0.27 and the variance explained increased from 25 to 35 percent. In a logistic regression analysis of entry to the salariat (or service class) in Britain, only 11 percent of the pseudo variation could be accounted for by father's and mother's education and occupation (Lampard 2012: 9).

Measurement error

Featherman and Hauser (1978: 258–9) summarize the criticisms of the basic occupational attainment models that: (i) measurement errors overstate the effects of education and understate the effects of social background; and (ii) the poor explanatory power of the models is because important social background variables have been left out, such as mother's education and occupation, and family income. They concede that measurement error reduces the magnitude of the estimates, but measurement error does not change the substantive conclusions that background affects occupational attainment through schooling, and schooling has a large impact on occupational attainment independent of background. Hauser and Sewell (1986: 99) report the disattenuated correlations (corrected for measurement error)[3] between father's occupation and father's education with respondent's occupational status at around 0.39 and 0.36, not much greater than the unadjusted correlations.

Sibling and twin studies

As discussed in earlier chapters, sibling studies can estimate the total effect of family background by comparing the between-family variation in a particular outcome (e.g. educational attainment, occupational attainment and earnings) and the total variation. The intraclass sibling correlations are much weaker for occupational status than for educational outcomes; around 0.31 compared with 0.47 for test scores and 0.55 for education (Olneck 1977: 132). About one-third of the variation in occupational status can be attributed to differences between families compared with about half for education (Hauser and

Mossel 1988: 650). Reviewing more recent data, Hauser (2000: 190) summarizes the sibling correlation for occupational status as between 0.24 and 0.29, much weaker than that for educational attainment. This suggests that family background, indexed by everything siblings have in common, has a much weaker impact on occupational status than on educational attainment.

Twin studies suggest that genes play a role in occupational attainment. The (intraclass) correlations in occupational status for Swedish male monozygotic twins reared together was reported at 0.82, and 0.44 for monozygotic twins reared apart. This compares with correlations of 0.44 and 0.36 for dizygotic twins (Lichtenstein *et al.* 1992: 24). For a white cohort born between 1917 and 1927, Behrman *et al.* (1980: 206–7) estimate that genetics accounts for 40 percent of the variation in mid-life occupational status, the common environment ten percent, and about 60 percent to unique effects not attributable to family background or genetics. Tambs *et al.* (1989) estimate heritabilities of 43 percent for post-war Norwegian cohorts, and the common-factor environmental within-family variances were generally small. For Sweden, Lichtenstein *et al.* (1992) concluded that the genetic component to men's occupational status was around 60 percent compared with nine percent for the shared environment and 31 percent for the non-shared environment. Similarly, a study of occupational status (occupations were ranked by average earnings) of twins in Australia concluded that the shared environment (i.e. family background) has a minor role (Miller *et al.* 1996: 233, 237).

As was the case for educational attainment, twin studies indicate that the environmental component in occupational attainment is substantially smaller in post-War than in pre-War birth cohorts, indicating that socioeconomic and other social impediments to educational and socioeconomic attainments have been reduced. The Tambs *et al.* (1989) study of Norwegian twins estimated that genetic heritability (which includes every trait that is inherited) of occupational status was very much lower in the oldest cohort (1931–1935) than in younger cohorts. Similarly, the contribution of the shared family components was substantially smaller in the younger cohorts. The authors speculate that the "lack of" an environmental family effect for younger cohorts is due to Norwegian sociodemocratic egalitarian policies (1989: 220). For Sweden, Lichtenstein *et al.* (1992) surmised that the shared environment had a declining impact on socioeconomic attainments, since the shared environment had only a weak impact on occupational attainment and its impact for education had declined over time.

Changes over time in the influences on occupational attainment

Modernization theory would hypothesize declining correlations and effects for socioeconomic background and increasing effects for educational attainment on occupational attainment, in other words, increasing effects of (educational) achievement and declining effects of ascription.

In a comparison of the 1962 and 1973 OCG surveys, Featherman and Hauser (1978: 103–4) summarize that, apart from some exceptions, the correlations between father's and son's occupational status were lower in 1973 than in 1962 for matched cohorts and two measures of occupational status. The correlations were also stronger in older cohorts in each study. The decline could not be explained by the decline in farming. In a multiple regression model, the effects of father's occupational status (but not father's education) were weaker in 1962 than in 1976, and the explanatory power of the model comprising a suite of explanatory variables declined from 25 percent to 20 percent (Featherman and Hauser 1978: 235, 259). With respondent's education in the analysis, the effects of father's occupation and father's education were weaker in 1973, and the effects of years of school and a college education were stronger (1978: 256). In an article on the importance of race in occupational mobility and attainment, Davis (1995) reported weak and declining effects for father's occupational prestige from 0.090 in the 1970s to 0.064 in the 1980s, and inconsequential effects for father's and mother's education. DiPrete and Grusky (1990) found that the effects of education on occupational attainment increased by nearly 30 percent between 1972 and 1987, but there was no increase for women. The much smaller effect of father's occupational status had declined for both sexes.

There is also evidence of more openness and an increasing influence of education in Britain. Comparing the 1949 Glass data with the 1972 Nuffield data, Halsey (1977: 178) reported that the overall correlation between father's and son's occupational status declined from 0.46 to 0.36, although he noted (correctly) that the data were not exactly comparable. Comparing age cohorts, Halsey (1977: 182–4) found a decrease in the effect of parental status and an increase in the influence of education on both first job and present job. Kerckhoff *et al.* (1982) found larger returns to occupational status from education for younger age cohorts. Comparing data collected at different times, Heath (1981: 168–78, 173) concluded that the influence of academic qualifications had increased at the expense of the influence of social origins. More recently, a stronger association between education and social class destination was found in the offspring generation than in the participant or parental generation (Johnson *et al.* 2010b: 60). Examining occupational attainment over a very long period of time (1800–2004), Lambert *et al.*'s (2007) meta-analysis concludes that Britain has steadily moved towards increasing equality in the relationship between occupational attainment and parental background. For sons, the correlation declined from about 0.6 to below 0.3, and for daughters from 0.5 to about 0.25.

For Canada, Goyder and Curtis (1977: 308) report declining correlations in occupational status across four generations. For grandfathers and fathers the correlation was 0.49, 0.38 between respondents and their fathers, declining to 0.22 between respondents and their sons. The same pattern is found when excluding farmers: 0.50, 0.33, and 0.22. The correlation between grandfathers and grandsons was only 0.22, and only 0.05 across four generations. They conclude that cumulative effects of family status ascription cannot be said to be large (1977: 311). A later study found that the effect of socioeconomic origins for occupational attainment declined considerably during the twentieth century, although the impact of education on occupation was constant (Wanner 2005).

Over time, Australia appears to have become more open. Comparing occupational attainment in two generations, Jones (1979) concluded that Australia had become more meritocratic during the post-War period compared to the pre-War period. Cohort analysis of data collected in 1965 shows that the relationship between education and occupational attainment is likely to become stronger (Broom and Jones 1976: 101–2). Marks (2009b) found declines in the effects of socioeconomic background on occupational attainment and an increasing effect of education among men, but not among women.

Cross-national differences and modernization

A cross-national study of occupational attainment, based on data collected in the 1960s and 1970s, analyzed the effects of respondent's education and father's occupational prestige on occupational attainment in 19 countries (Treiman and Yip 1989). Education had substantially stronger effects than father's occupational prestige in most countries; on average its effect was four times that of father's occupation. Only in Ireland was the impact of father's occupation comparable to that of education. Kelley (1990: 341), analyzing data from the 1960s to 1970s in 16 countries, found that the correlations ranged from a high of just over 0.5 to a low of 0.25. The highest correlations were in Brazil, Bolivia and the Netherlands (close to 0.5), followed by Northern Ireland, Denmark, Germany and Norway (around 0.4) and then, Sweden, Finland, Australia, the US and Taiwan (below 0.4). The country showing the lowest intergenerational correlation was Britain. In a study of 20 industrialized countries using data collected in the 1990s, the overall effect of father's occupational status on adult child's occupational status was 0.35. The countries exhibiting the lowest correlations included Australia, Canada, France, New Zealand, Sweden and the US and the highest correlations were for Portugal and Chile (Yaish and Andersen 2012: 530).

There is evidence for the modernization thesis in cross-country and over-time analyses: a tendency for the intergenerational correlations for occupations to be lower in more "modern" countries. Treiman and Yip (1989: 392) found that the effect of education on occupational status increased with industrialization, and that the effect of father's occupational status on son's occupational status decreased. Rijken (1999: 109) concluded that modernization promotes achievement – a stronger impact of educational attainment – but does this indirectly by reducing the variation in educational achievement. Indicators of modernization were found to have no direct effect on the effects of socioeconomic background. Ganzeboom and Treiman's (2007) analysis of occupational attainment, comprising over 370,000 men from 42 countries, concluded that achievement (the effect of education on occupational status) increases with economic development while ascription (the effect of father's on son's occupational status) decreases with economic development. A more recent study by Yaish and Anderson (2012) found systematic cross-national variation in the association between the occupational status of respondents and their fathers. They note that "Consistent with the industrialization thesis, this variation is positively associated with per-capita GDP, suggesting that more affluent nations are characterized by more open and fluid stratification structures" (2012: 533).

Table 10.1 presents the correlations between father's and son's occupational status and the correlations estimated for the initial and most recent studies. These are the same data analyzed for the correlations between father's occupational status and son's education presented in Chapter 9 (see Table 9.4). Substantial declines are found for the Anglo-Saxon democracies, most Western European countries, southern European countries, the Scandinavian countries, and Japan. In the Netherlands, the correlation has almost halved. Declines are also evident for South American countries: Argentina, Brazil and Chile. The exceptions to the pattern of declines over time are the formerly Eastern Bloc countries, China and Israel. In these countries, the correlation in the first study is generally lower than that in Western countries. It is noteworthy that the correlations are seldom below 0.25, which may represent the lower limit of the intergenerational correlations for occupational status, given genetic transmission of cognitive ability and to a lesser extent non-cognitive attributes.

Table 10.2 presents the (standardized) effects of education on occupational status among men in the same data. Contrary to modernization theory, not all Western countries show an increase in the impact of education. Increases are observed for Austria, Belgium (Flanders), Germany (East and West), Iceland, Ireland, Italy, the Netherlands, Norway, New Zealand, Portugal, Quebec, Scotland, Spain, Switzerland and the US. However, consistent with the modernization thesis are declines in the impact of father's occupational status. Table 10.3 shows declines in the much weaker (standardized) effects of father's occupational status on son's occupational status, net of education. Declines are apparent for almost all Western countries, indicating a continuing decline in the importance of ascription vis-à-vis educational achievement.

Table 10.1 Correlations between father's occupation (ISEI) and son's occupation (ISEI)

Country	*Studies (n)*	*Cases (n)*	*Initial year*	*Most recent year*	*Average correlation*	*Estimate of initial correlation*	*Estimate of most recent correlation*	*Decline?*
Argentina	6	3,617	1973	2009	0.453	0.689	0.363	✓
Australia	14	14,793	1965	2009	0.340	0.385	0.250	✓
Austria	16	25,439	1969	2009	0.425	0.506	0.336	✓
Belgium (Flanders)	12	6,595	1971	2010	0.345	0.465	0.295	✓
Belgium (Wallonia)	13	4,954	1971	2010	0.414	0.485	0.347	✓
Brazil	5	18,754	1972	1999	0.462	0.504	0.340	✓
Bulgaria	6	4,798	1991	2010	0.347	0.284	0.411	
Canada	8	25,599	1965	1999	0.334	0.414	0.233	✓
Chile	4	11,460	1998	2009	0.465	0.490	0.400	✓
China	3	4,858	1996	2009	0.338	0.340	0.337	No
Croatia	4	1,592	2008	2010	0.298	0.328	0.249	✓
Cyprus	6	3,781	1999	2010	0.362	0.418	0.327	No
Czech Republic	14	12,769	1984	2010	0.345	0.306	0.376	No
Denmark	11	9,027	1972	2010	0.334	0.401	0.297	✓
England and Wales	14	19,778	1969	2010	0.348	0.390	0.288	✓
Estonia	8	4,534	1991	2010	0.258	0.284	0.250	✓
Finland	13	9,562	1972	2010	0.298	0.385	0.269	✓
France	15	15,876	1958	2010	0.379	0.513	0.328	✓
Germany (East)	20	7,742	1991	2010	0.284	0.236	0.325	No
Germany (West)	43	38,322	1959	2010	0.393	0.482	0.343	✓
Greece	6	6,358	2002	2010	0.345	0.355	0.333	✓
Hungary	22	63,603	1973	2010	0.387	0.414	0.331	✓
Iceland	4	1,591	2004	2009	0.253			
India	3	5,734	1967	1971	0.514	0.573	0.491	✓
Ireland	10	8,565	1973	2010	0.355	0.452	0.281	✓
Israel	11	10,603	1974	2010	0.266	0.255	0.279	✓
Italy	34	79691	1963	2009	0.396	0.538	0.356	✓
Japan	9	10,187	1955	2009	0.415	0.480	0.293	✓
Latvia	6	3,133	1999	2009	0.275	0.239	0.290	No
Lithuania	3	2,302	2005	2010	0.285			
Luxembourg	4	3,370	2002	2008	0.407	0.368	0.449	No
Mexico	2	6,052	2006	2006	0.358			
Netherlands	62	51,526	1958	2011	0.330	0.497	0.243	✓
New Zealand	5	3,387	1976	2009	0.295	0.342	0.212	✓
Northern Ireland	9	8,621	1968	2010	0.404	0.446	0.146	✓

Table 10.1 continued

Country	*Studies (n)*	*Cases (n)*	*Initial year*	*Most recent year*	*Average correlation*	*Estimate of initial correlation*	*Estimate of most recent correlation*	*Decline?*
Norway	14	9,929	1957	2010	0.309	0.366	0.290	✓
Poland	26	63,659	1972	2010	0.357	0.365	0.337	?
Portugal	9	7,240	1999	2010	0.388	0.439	0.351	✓
Quebec	9	11,359	1960	1999	0.357	0.404	0.309	✓
Romania	3	1,552	2006	2008	0.361			
Russia	11	7,932	1991	2010	0.274	0.265	0.285	
Scotland	15	5,837	1963	2010	0.392	0.460	0.238	✓
Slovakia	13	10,951	1984	2010	0.308	0.299	0.313	
Slovenia	19	11,309	1967	2010	0.341	0.353	0.333	?
South Africa	2	3,593	1991	2009	0.459	0.476	0.374	✓
Spain	15	22,298	1990	2010	0.407	0.416	0.395	?
Sweden	18	9,465	1960	2010	0.325	0.462	0.261	✓
Switzerland	11	7,823	1972	2010	0.386	0.437	0.363	✓
Taiwan	28	27,188	1970	2009	0.396	0.383	0.404	
Turkey	5	6,597	1978	2009	0.364	0.392	0.306	✓
Ukraine	6	3,314	2004	2010	0.239	0.250	0.310	
US	46	65,959	1947	2010	0.352	0.397	0.302	✓
Summary	686	784,578			0.356	0.382	0.324	✓

Note: Analyses by the author on the International Social Mobility File supplied by Ganzeboom.

Table 10.2 Effects of education on occupation (ISEI), net of father's occupation (ISEI)

Country	*Studies (n)*	*Cases (n)*	*Initial year*	*Most recent year*	*Average std. effect*	*Std. effect for initial year*	*Std. effect for most recent year*	*Increase?*
Argentina	6	3,617	1973	2009	0.535	0.463	0.559	✓
Australia	14	14,793	1965	2009	0.477	0.470	0.491	
Austria	16	25,439	1969	2009	0.459	0.432	0.492	✓
Belgium (Flanders)	12	6,595	1971	2010	0.521	0.479	0.542	✓
Belgium (Wallonia)	13	4,954	1971	2010	0.521	0.594	0.455	
Brazil	5	18,754	1972	1999	0.512	0.513	0.513	
Bulgaria	6	4,798	1991	2010	0.551	0.527	0.581	✓
Canada	8	25,599	1965	1999	0.510	0.530	0.487	
Chile	4	11,460	1998	2009	0.527	0.527	0.525	

Table 10.2 continued

Country	*Studies (n)*	*Cases (n)*	*Initial year*	*Most recent year*	*Average std. effect*	*Std. effect for initial year*	*Std. effect for most recent year*	*Increase?*
China	3	4,858	1996	2009	0.395	0.376	0.416	✓
Croatia	4	1,592	2008	2010	0.530	0.504	0.577	✓
Cyprus	6	3,781	1999	2010	0.550	0.571	0.535	
Czech Republic	14	12,769	1984	2010	0.555	0.547	0.561	
Denmark	11	9,027	1972	2010	0.559	0.674	0.499	
England and Wales	14	19,778	1969	2010	0.467	0.463	0.473	
Estonia	8	4,534	1991	2010	0.520	0.560	0.508	
Finland	13	9,562	1972	2010	0.571	0.567	0.571	
France	15	15,876	1958	2010	0.455	0.444	0.459	?
Germany (East)	20	7,742	1991	2010	0.572	0.488	0.653	✓
Germany (West)	43	38,322	1959	2010	0.524	0.440	0.578	✓
Greece	6	6,358	2002	2010	0.534	0.608	0.450	
Hungary	22	63,603	1973	2010	0.545	0.528	0.596	✓
Iceland	4	1,591	2004	2009	0.463	0.422	0.521	✓
India	3	5,734	1967	1971	0.344	0.368	0.339	
Ireland	10	8,565	1973	2010	0.483	0.465	0.496	?
Israel	11	10,603	1974	2010	0.555	0.591	0.514	
Italy	34	79,691	1963	2009	0.524	0.485	0.534	✓
Japan	9	10,187	1955	2009	0.422	0.441	0.389	
Latvia	6	3,133	1999	2009	0.522	0.597	0.492	
Lithuania	3	2,302	2005	2010	0.525	0.516	0.553	✓
Luxembourg	4	3,370	2002	2008	0.577	0.616	0.532	
Mexico	2	6,052	2006	2006	0.526	0.526	0.526	
Netherlands	62	51,526	1958	2011	0.513	0.478	0.531	✓
New Zealand	5	3,387	1976	2009	0.449	0.412	0.515	✓
Northern Ireland	9	8,621	1968	2010	0.506	0.509	0.492	
Norway	14	9,929	1957	2010	0.485	0.358	0.536	✓
Poland	26	63,659	1972	2010	0.627	0.653	0.564	
Portugal	9	7,240	1999	2010	0.525	0.469	0.564	✓
Quebec	9	11,359	1960	1999	0.531	0.442	0.630	✓
Romania	3	1,552	2006	2008	0.488	0.529	0.464	
Russia	11	7,932	1991	2010	0.538	0.501	0.582	✓
Scotland	15	5,837	1963	2010	0.399	0.356	0.510	✓
Slovakia	13	10,951	1984	2010	0.586	0.562	0.601	✓
Slovenia	19	11,309	1967	2010	0.605	0.639	0.581	
South Africa	2	3,593	1991	2009	0.498	0.528	0.380	

Table 10.2 continued

Country	*Studies (n)*	*Cases (n)*	*Initial year*	*Most recent year*	*Average std. effect*	*Std. effect for initial year*	*Std. effect for most recent year*	*Increase?*
Spain	15	22,298	1990	2010	0.482	0.457	0.516	✓
Sweden	18	9,465	1960	2010	0.485	0.488	0.487	
Switzerland	11	7,823	1972	2010	0.528	0.405	0.588	✓
Taiwan	28	27,188	1970	2009	0.557	0.461	0.612	✓
Turkey	5	6,597	1978	2009	0.448	0.422	0.504	✓
Ukraine	6	3,314	2004	2010	0.555	0.496	0.598	✓
US	46	65,959	1947	2010	0.526	0.498	0.564	✓
Summary	686	784,578			0.513	0.500	0.524	✓

Note: Analyses by the author on the International Social Mobility File supplied by Ganzeboom.

Table 10.3 Effects of father's occupation (ISEI) on son's occupation (ISEI), net of education

Country	*Studies (n)*	*Cases (n)*	*Initial year*	*Most recent year*	*Average std. effect*	*Std. effect for initial year*	*Std. effect for most recent year*	*Decrease?*
Argentina	6	3617	1973	2009	0.160	0.386	0.085	✓
Australia	14	14793	1965	2009	0.161	0.209	0.070	✓
Austria	16	25439	1969	2009	0.229	0.281	0.173	✓
Belgium (Flanders)	12	6595	1971	2010	0.137	0.293	0.071	✓
Belgium (Wallonia)	13	4954	1971	2010	0.177	0.180	0.175	
Brazil	5	18754	1972	1999	0.198	0.226	0.120	✓
Bulgaria	6	4798	1991	2010	0.125	0.109	0.143	
Canada	8	25599	1965	1999	0.128	0.177	0.066	✓
Chile	4	11460	1998	2009	0.201	0.225	0.140	✓
China	3	4858	1996	2009	0.221	0.237	0.206	✓
Croatia	4	1592	2008	2010	0.080	0.127	0.010	✓
Cyprus	6	3781	1999	2010	0.136	0.198	0.096	✓
Czech Republic	14	12769	1984	2010	0.137	0.099	0.168	
Denmark	11	9027	1972	2010	0.137	0.118	0.146	
England and Wales	14	19778	1969	2010	0.162	0.185	0.131	✓
Estonia	8	4534	1991	2010	0.109	0.100	0.112	
Finland	13	9562	1972	2010	0.101	0.198	0.068	✓

Table 10.3 continued

Country	*Studies (n)*	*Cases (n)*	*Initial year*	*Most recent year*	*Average std. effect*	*Std. effect for initial year*	*Std. effect for most recent year*	*Decrease?*
France	15	15,876	1958	2010	0.192	0.278	0.161	✓
Germany (East)	20	7,742	1991	2010	0.099	0.104	0.094	
Germany (West)	43	38,322	1959	2010	0.167	0.266	0.111	✓
Greece	6	6,358	2002	2010	0.139	0.123	0.158	
Hungary	22	63,603	1973	2010	0.151	0.183	0.088	✓
Iceland	4	1,591	2004	2009	0.108	0.138	0.074	✓
India	3	5,734	1967	1971	0.359	0.418	0.337	✓
Ireland	10	8,565	1973	2010	0.174	0.270	0.106	✓
Israel	11	10,603	1974	2010	0.115	0.123	0.106	✓
Italy	34	79,691	1963	2009	0.171	0.279	0.143	✓
Japan	9	10,187	1955	2009	0.229	0.285	0.127	✓
Latvia	6	3,133	1999	2009	0.122	0.090	0.136	
Lithuania	3	2,302	2005	2010	0.141	0.164	0.088	✓
Luxembourg	4	3,370	2002	2008	0.149	0.118	0.183	
Mexico	2	6,052	2006	2006	0.164			
Netherlands	62	51,526	1958	2011	0.138	0.282	0.064	✓
New Zealand	5	3,387	1976	2009	0.149	0.190	0.079	✓
Northern Ireland	9	8,621	1968	2010	0.201	0.229	0.038	✓
Norway	14	9,929	1957	2010	0.131	0.226	0.098	✓
Poland	26	63,659	1972	2010	0.110	0.105	0.119	
Portugal	9	7,240	1999	2010	0.153	0.236	0.090	✓
Quebec	9	11,359	1960	1999	0.146	0.227	0.062	✓
Romania	3	1,552	2006	2008	0.179	0.186	0.175	
Russia	11	7,932	1991	2010	0.105	0.097	0.114	
Scotland	15	5,837	1963	2010	0.253	0.339	0.059	✓
Slovakia	13	10,951	1984	2010	0.097	0.088	0.102	
Slovenia	19	11,309	1967	2010	0.124	0.100	0.140	
South Africa	2	3,593	1991	2009	0.208	0.200	0.240	
Spain	15	22,298	1990	2010	0.200	0.223	0.169	✓
Sweden	18	9,465	1960	2010	0.129	0.225	0.087	✓
Switzerland	11	7,823	1972	2010	0.153	0.264	0.104	✓
Taiwan	28	27,188	1970	2009	0.173	0.171	0.174	
Turkey	5	6,597	1978	2009	0.212	0.246	0.141	✓
Ukraine	6	3,314	2004	2010	0.078	0.021	0.118	✓
US	46	65,959	1947	2010	0.135	0.190	0.071	✓
Summary	686	784,578			0.157	0.192	0.112	✓

Note: Analyses by the author on the International Social Mobility File supplied by Ganzeboom.

Conclusions

This chapter presents much evidence in support of modernization theory. The intergenerational correlations for occupational status are not strong and are most often declining. There is considerable occupational mobility in Western countries, and lower rates of immobility than those expected according to reproduction theories. The relative impact of educational attainment is much stronger than that for socioeconomic background, and with modernization the effects of education strengthen in many countries, and those for socioeconomic background weaken. Twin studies tend to confirm that shared the family environment has a very limited impact on occupational attainment and younger cohorts exhibit stronger genetic and weaker environmental effects.

Notes

1 The statistic is based on chi-square for contingency tables and ranges from zero (no association) to one (identical).

2 The three classes were:

 upper: EGP I and II (high- and lower-grade professionals and administrators);
 middle: EGP III, IV, V and VI (routine non-manual, small proprietors with and without employees including farmers, lower-grade technicians and supervisors of manual workers);
 working EGP VII (semi-skilled manual workers, including those in agriculture).

3 The attenuated correlations correct for measurement error by dividing the observed correlation by the square root of the products of the reliabilities of the two variables:

$$\text{Attenuated correlation} = \frac{\text{Corr}(x, y)}{\sqrt{r_x r_y}}$$

Chapter 11

Reproduction of economic inequalities[1]

Economists' interest in the reproduction of inequality focuses on earnings and income rather than occupational class or occupational status. They focus on the association between the earnings (or income) of the parental generation and that of their adult children. Sociologists have in general not contributed to this research literature. This is particularly surprising, given the body of research on the reproduction of educational and occupational inequalities, the literature on occupational mobility, and inconsistencies between the intergenerational income literature and the sociological literature. However, some sociologists have expressed doubts about the high intergenerational correlation observed in the US (Beller and Hout 2006; Hauser 2010).

A burgeoning subfield in economics is the intergenerational transmission of economic inequality. It is concerned with the statistical coefficient(s) linking parents' and their adult children's (logged) wages, earnings or incomes. The coefficient is referred to as the elasticity (or, if standardized, the intergenerational correlation), which indicates the degree of economic inequality transmitted across generations. Although the sociological status attainment literature includes both family income and earnings in the causal chain, there is no particular focus on the transmission of economic inequalities. Since adult earnings are temporally more distant from socioeconomic background than education or first occupation, it invariably shows weaker associations. Economists, using particular theoretical and methodological approaches, tend to conclude that the transmission of economic inequality is much higher than previously believed (especially in the US and the UK), although there is considerable variability in the estimates. These findings are often interpreted negatively as evidence of the strength and durability of socioeconomic inequality in those countries and the failure of social reforms.

Theoretical issues

In economics, the theoretical approach to the intergenerational reproduction of economic status focuses on borrowing constraints. Becker and Tomes (1986) begin their argument that parents transmit their endowments (both genetic and cultural) to their children and these endowments regress to the mean. Since parents are concerned about the welfare of their children, they engage in behavior to maximize their welfare. Parents from richer families use their financial endowments to reduce the tendency for regression to the mean. This involves investing in their education or other income-enhancing strategies. Poorer families have difficulty in financing such investments for their children. The transmission of income inequality may be exacerbated by increases in the returns to education, since richer parents have successfully invested in the higher educational attainments of their children.

In sociology, the theoretical background for the intergenerational income correlation is more an extension of the socioeconomic inequalities in educational and occupational attainment. The status attainment approach understands earnings, income and wealth distant in a sequence of causal pathways. Earnings are understood as dependent on occupation; in the "context of the allocation of occupational roles and related prerequisites" (Sewell and Hauser 1975: 3). In other words, earnings depends on jobs. The causal sequence begins with parents' characteristics, usually parental education and occupation but can include family income and more rarely family wealth. These factors influence educational attainment mediated by mental ability, grades at school, aspirations and expectations. In turn, educational attainment influences income in directly via occupation. Although father's earnings or family income are part of the causal sequence since parents can purchase schooling or other desirable goods for their children, economic background is given no special prominence in the causal pathway. The major focus is on the social forces that shape education and occupational attainment and, as a consequence, earnings.

Solon (1999: 1763–6) develops a theoretical model which proposes that the relationship between parents' and their adult children's economic situation is dependent on:

1) parental investment in the child's human capital. This depends partly on parental earnings but also on other background factors. Parents may prefer to consume rather than invest in their children's education. If there is a strong relationship between parental income and children's educational attainment then the intergenerational association is likely to be larger;
2) the efficacy of the transformation of the child's human capital into earnings;
3) the intergeneration transmission of ability; if ability is strongly transmitted across generations, the intergenerational association will be higher;
4) the degree to which government investment in a child's education tapers off with increasing family income. More to the point, if the state can provide a relatively high standard of education to low-income families then the intergenerational correlation will be weaker.

It is clear that, over time, changes in the intergenerational correlation occur in a number of ways:

- an increase (decrease) in the direct effect of family income on earnings, other relationships unchanged, would increase (decrease) the overall intergenerational correlation;
- an increase (decrease) in the indirect effects of parental occupation or parental education through education on earnings, other relationships unchanged, would increase (decrease) the overall intergenerational correlation;
- an increase (decrease) in the effects of parental ability on ability, other things being equal, would increase (decrease) the overall intergenerational correlation; and
- an increase (decrease) in the effects of education on earnings, other things being equal, would increase (decrease) the overall intergenerational correlation.

In the context of modernization theory, a decrease over time in the intergenerational correlation would be supportive evidence for modernization theory, but not if the decline is a result of a decline in the impact of ability on education and/or education on earnings. Similarly, an increase in the intergenerational correlation is not necessarily evidence against modernization theory, if it is a result of strengthening relationships involving parental ability, ability, education and earnings. Changes over time in the intergenerational correlation may also be entirely due to changes in the income equality between generations.

Conceptual and methodological issues

Intergenerational elasticities and correlations

Research on the intergenerational correlation for economic status focuses on the regression coefficient β_1 known as the "intergenerational elasticity" in the following equation:

$$\log(Y_{child}) = \alpha + \beta_1 \log(Y_{par})$$

where $\log(Y_{child})$ is the natural logarithm of child's earnings or income as an adult; α is a constant (or intercept) and $\log(Y_{par})$ is the natural logarithm of parental generation's earnings or income. Incomes are typically logged given their very skewed distribution. If $\beta_1 = 0.10$ then children who grew up in families where income differs by ten percent will typically have incomes that differ by one percent. If $\beta_1 = 0.40$ then the difference will be four percent. β_1 may or may not be larger than the coefficient obtained from standard OLS regression. The equation can include age to adjust for the age–earnings profile and other influences that impact on economic position (e.g. education, cognitive ability).

The literature moves between the elasticity measure and the intergenerational correlation. The correlation coefficient $r_{child.par}$ or the intergenerational income correlation is simply the standardized regression coefficient, which adjusts for the distributions of economic status in both generations:

$$r_{child.par} = \beta_1 \left(\frac{\sigma_{par}}{\sigma_{child}}\right)$$

σ_{par} is the standard deviation, of say, income, for the parental generation and σ_{child} is the standard deviation of incomes for the children's generation. The correlation ranges between −1 and +1, and 0 indicates no relationship. If the standard deviations are identical for the two generations, the correlation equals the elasticity.[2] However, if income inequality has decreased between generations then $(\sigma_{par}/\sigma_{child})$ is greater than one and the intergenerational income correlation is larger than the elasticity. In practice, there is not a huge difference between elasticities and correlations because the ratio of the income distributions is usually fairly close to one.

Strength of the relationship

Up until the early 1990s, the general consensus among both economists and sociologists was that the relationship between a person's income and that of their parents when they were growing up was much weaker than other intergenerational relationships (e.g. educational attainment, occupational class and occupational status). Becker and Tomes (1986) reported a widely cited correlation of 0.15 and concluded that, in the US, father's income has little influence on son's income. Weak correlations were also reported by in the sociological literature, below and around 0.20 (Jencks *et al.* 1979: 327; Sewell and Hauser 1975: 93). This low correlation is consistent with the idea that the influence of socioeconomic background on socioeconomic outcomes weakens with age (or time), since earnings are typically measured in mid-adulthood.

The conclusion of a weak correspondence between parental and children's incomes in the US was overturned by Solon (1992) and Zimmerman (1992), analyzing, respectively, the PSID and several longitudinal cohorts of the National Longitudinal Study (NLS). They concluded that the intergenerational correlation in income was much stronger than previously thought. The logic is that one year's income does not capture permanent income (stripped of income's transitory components), which apparently is the proper concept to use for economic status. Averaging incomes over a three- or five-year period increased the intergenerational correlation (or elasticity) to around 0.40. The correlation is also attenuated because of measurement error, and adjusting for measurement error with fairly dubious instruments, that is father's education, increases the estimate for the elasticity to well above 0.50. Although the conclusion of substantial intergenerational correlations was based on small samples in only two data sets,[3] later work using social security records over a 15-year period shows even higher correlations of around 0.60 (Mazumder 2001, 2005). The high intergenerational correlations in the US have made odd ideological bedfellows; Herrnstein and Murray (1994) cite them as evidence of the increasing importance of cognitive skills, whereas Bowles and Gintis (2002b) see them as support for their radical critique of American society and its school system.

Similarly, high intergenerational elasticities have been found for the UK. Using instrumental variable methods, Dearden *et al.* (1997) report very high elasticities: 0.57 for father's and son's wages, and an incredible 0.68 for father's and daughter's wages. Analyzing data from the BHPS, Ermisch and Francesconi (2004: 182) conclude that intergenerational correlations range from 0.45 to 0.75 for father–son pairs, and from 0.30 to 0.50 for mother–daughter pairs. After reviewing several studies, Corak (2006: 63) offers a preferred estimate for the UK of 0.50 with lower and upper bounds of 0.42 and 0.55. An OECD (2009b: 205) report places the UK at the top of the pecking order for intergenerational income elasticities. The finding that income inequalities in the UK are strongly reproduced across generations is readily believed, given the accepted wisdom that it is a highly stratified class-ridden society. The high intergenerational correlation in the UK enables Corak (2005: 9) to conclude that reforms to the British education system dating back to the 1980s have decreased, rather than increased, social mobility.

Issues in the strength of the relationship

It is expected that adult earnings, being most distal to socioeconomic background (in the temporal causal chain from socioeconomic background, via education and occupation to earnings) would show the weakest association with socioeconomic background. This expectation is supported by much of status-attainment research, with socioeconomic background accounting for less explained variance in earnings than in educational attainment or test scores. In twin studies, the contribution of the common environment is generally much less for earnings than for earlier socioeconomic attainments. Behrman *et al.* (1980: 207) show that the contribution of the common environment declines from 40 percent for education, 30 percent for first occupation, 13 percent for present occupation, and 12 percent for earnings. The estimation of elasticities and the intergenerational income and earnings correlation are not usually estimated with a single regression or correlation analysis with accurate data on both parents' and (adult) children's income or earnings. There are a number of data-related issues that cast doubt on the accuracy of the estimates.

Consistency

Although the consensus estimate for the intergenerational elasticity for the US is 0.4, there is great variation in the estimates. Mayer and Lopoo (2005) show that, in reports in 18 US studies, the elasticity of son's and father's earnings ranged from 0.13 to 0.53. Corak (2006: 52) reports elasticities from the published literature ranging from 0.08 to 0.60. Similarly, Grawe (2006) lists six US studies with estimated elasticities ranging from 0.13 to 0.42. There is even a lack of consensus on the extent of the intergenerational correlation in the same data sets. In the PSID, least squares estimates (not using instrumental variable techniques) reported correlations ranging between 0.13 and 0.48, while in the NLS the correlations are generally lower but ranging between 0.14 and 0.53 (Solon 1999: Tables 3 and 4). Admittedly, the studies vary in the ages of the respondents and the measures used. Such large variations are not encountered for the corresponding relationships in adolescent achievement, educational attainment or occupational attainment. The raw correlation between father's and son's earnings in the PSID, according to Björklund and Jäntti (1997), is between 0.26 and 0.31. This is about 25 percent less than the consensus estimate of 0.4. Torche (2011: 787) reports elasticities for hourly earnings from the PSID of 0.36 for men and 0.31 for women.

For the UK, there is also considerable variation in the estimates. Although the UK is supposed to show large intergenerational elasticities and correlations, those reported for the 1958 NCDS and 1970 BCS studies are quite low for sons, with elasticities between 0.18 and 0.25, and unexpectedly higher for daughters, between 0.31 and 0.32 (Blanden *et al.* 2004: 131–4). The low elasticities can be attributed to only having one observation for income in the 1958 cohort and only two for the 1970 cohort.

Unfortunately, different methods generate disparate estimates. Despite all the prominence given to the purportedly high intergenerational correlations between parent's income and child's income in the UK, Erikson and Goldthorpe (2010) report correlations of only 0.18 between father's and son's income for the 1958 NCDS cohort and 0.29 for the 1970 BCS cohort. These estimates have not been adjusted for permanent versus transitory components. As mentioned earlier, the correlation for 1958 is unusually low, since it is based on only one year's measure of parents' income. It is only after making statistical adjustments for permanent and transitory income components and instrumental variables for measurement error that the intergenerational income correlation approaches 0.5 or higher.

Gorard (2008) makes the simple point that these correlations are not particularly high, explaining less than eight percent of the variation in income (three percent for the older cohort). He also questions the reliability of the estimates, noting that the analyses were based on just 13 percent and 12 percent of the original NCDS and BCS samples, the remainder lost through attrition. Similarly, Hertz (2005: 170) points out that if the correlation is 0.4 – which is probably the most popular estimate for the intergenerational earnings correlation in the US – that means that 84 percent of the variation in long-range income is not explained by parental income.[4] For Norway, which has very reliable registry data for incomes with hundreds of thousands of observations, the effects of father's earnings or family's earnings (averaged over four or five years) on son's or daughter's income are very weak and, together with measures of father's age and child's cohort, explain very little of the variation in earnings, between three and six percent (Hansen 2010: 143–5).

Measure of economic status

There are choices in the measure of economic status: annual earnings or income, or hourly wage rate; or father's or family's earnings. For the US, elasticities and correlations tend to be higher, with measures of family income rather than father's earnings, presumably because family income is a more accurate measure of the family's economic position (Solon 1992: 403). The estimates tend to be lower using hourly wages. Eide and Showalter (1999: 258, 260) reported an elasticity of 0.45 for family income compared with 0.34 for father's earnings. Analyzing the PSID, Torche (2011: 787, 789) found that the intergenerational income association was 0.45 for men, compared with 0.36 for hourly earnings. For women, the respective coefficients were 0.53 and 0.31. Hertz (2005: 177) analyzed up to 30 years for parental earnings (average 11.5 years) and 28 years for the second generation's earnings (average 11.9 years). He reported age-adjusted elasticities for parental family's earnings on child's family earnings: 0.53 for the entire sample, 0.39 for whites, and 0.32 for blacks. These respective correlations are lower at 0.42, 0.32 and 0.21, which could be regarded as upper bounds given the long time periods involved.[5]

In contrast, Hobcraft's (2001: 10–11, Table 6) analysis of the UK's NCDS finds that, among males, the elasticity was lower for family income among sons than for father's earnings. He notes that the most challenging finding is that the elasticities between males and their partner's family's income (or father's earnings) were comparable to those between men and their own parent's income (or father's earnings), suggesting that assortative mating may play a substantial role in the intergenerational income correlation. The implication is that, for the economic standing of men, "assortative mating" is just as important as the family of origin's economic resources.

Permanent and observed incomes

Mazumder's (2005) estimates of 0.6 are obtained by estimating permanent income (which is not observed) from observed incomes over 15 years. The greater the number of instances (years) over which a variable is averaged, the greater the correlation it will have with other variables. The justification for this practice is that it minimizes measurement error since income has both permanent and transitory components. Beller and Hout (2006: 25) doubt the estimate of 0.6 for father–son earnings persistence. They argue that averaging earnings over a long period of time is a dubious practice, since it is difficult to believe there is one true value. Muller (2010) makes the point that simply averaging the years will lead to over estimates of the elasticity because there is a serial correlation in the measures of annual income. In other words, if the serial correlation of earnings (or income) is low – that is, there is much year-to-year volatility in earnings – then averaging earnings will produce a higher estimate of the intergenerational associations than if the year-to-year correlations in earnings were close to one.[6] Typically, the year-to-year correlations are about 0.8 for adjacent years declining to around 0.5 or less for observations which are ten or more years apart. Muller (2010) also makes the substantive point that averaging parental income is based on the questionable assumption that family income is equally important no matter the child's age. He found that family income is more important at younger ages, and his overall estimates from the PSID are considerably lower than 0.4.[7]

Hauser (2010) indirectly argues that the intergenerational income correlation is likely to be lower. He indexed occupations two ways: by the typical education of occupations and the typical income of occupations. The intergenerational correlations were much stronger for the education measure (at around 0.37) than for occupational-income (at around 0.21). Similarly, Hauser and Warren (1997: 222–4) found that the income-derived measures of occupational standing showed much lower intergenerational correlations (between 0.21 and 0.25) than occupational prestige (about 0.30), socioeconomic status (about 0.35) or education-based measures (0.30 to 0.38).

Instrumental variables

Instrumental variables (IV) are commonly used in the estimation of intergenerational elasticities and correlations. The estimates from instrumental variable are techniques almost invariably larger than conventional estimates. Sometimes, instrumental variables lead to extraordinary increases in the estimates of the elasticities. Normally, instrumental variables are used to counter "endogeniety" or, more sociologically speaking, "specification error". In the context of intergenerational income elasticities and correlations, instruments are used to purge the dependent variable of measurement error. The greater the error variance in the exogenous variable, the greater the downward bias in the estimate. The resulting purged regressor is uncorrelated with measurement error and error in prediction (Angrist and Krueger 2001). An ideal instrument is strongly correlated with the exogenous (predictor) variable but has no direct association with the endogenous (outcome) variable. In the first stage, the exogenous variable is regressed on the instrument or instrumental variables, and the predicted values are obtained, which are (of course) uncorrelated with the instrumental variables. These predicted values are then used as the regressor for the second stage. Instrumental variables do not work very well if the instruments are only weakly correlated with the exogenous variable (Bound *et al.* 1995) or are moderately correlated with the endogenous variable.

Solon (1992) used father's education as an instrumental variable, and Zimmerman (1992) used the Duncan socioeconomic index. The problem with these instruments is that they tend to have non-trivial correlations with the child's (adult) income. That is why predicted values of family income typically have stronger relationships with child's income than the original observed measures of family income. Also, parental education and occupational status have plausible causal relationships with child's income that do not involve family income. A well-educated parent or a parent in a higher-status job may have the "know how", cultural resources, social connections or whatever to land their child a higher-paying job. For estimating the returns (in earnings) to education, Card (1999: 1825) demonstrates that family background is not a legitimate instrument. Finally, instrumental techniques do not produce stable estimates. Blanden *et al.* (2004: 134) could not identify credible instruments and note that "limited experimentation here revealed that their use, especially in the cross-cohort context, seemed rather dubious, both on the basis of Sargan tests and on the sensitivity of IV estimates to choice of instrument".

Comparison with wealth

Some estimates of the intergenerational income elasticities and correlations are higher than those for wealth in the US. Since family wealth is a combination of returns to human capital, monetary gifts, (sometimes) inheritance, and luck, the intergenerational correlation for wealth should at least be comparable to that for income. Keister (2005) reports an intergenerational correlation of 0.5 for wealth.[8] Charles and Hurst (2003) calculated the age-adjusted (pre-bequest) elasticity of child's and parental wealth in the US at 0.37. This is the regression coefficient of child's logged wealth on parental logged wealth. They note that less than ten percent of the variation in child's wealth can be accounted for by parental wealth. Black and Devereux (2011: 1533) simply note that that the intergenerational wealth elasticity appears to be lower than the intergenerational earnings elasticity which raises questions for further work.

Net effects of economic background

The relationship between parents' and their adult children's incomes is not direct. The relationship must largely involve education and to some extent cognitive ability. Another consideration is that the relationship between family income and child's earnings is spurious in that family income is acting as a proxy for other socioeconomic background factors, such as parental education or occupation.

Net of other indicators of socioeconomic background

In contrast to the effects of various aspects of socioeconomic background on education where income has weaker effects, father's earnings or family income is relatively more important for their children's earnings. However, the net impact of family income on child's income is quite weak. In the WLS, the correlation of family income and child's income about a decade after graduation was, although small, at around 0.17 larger than the correlations for father's education with income (0.08), mother's education (0.06), father's occupational status (0.08) and ability (0.16) (Sewell and Hauser 1975: 93). Analyzing data from NLSY respondents collected when they were 29 years of age, Peters (1992) found that parental income accounted for 11 percent of the variation in earnings, rising only a few percentage points with the addition of other social background variables. Analyzing the WLS and Equal Employment Opportunity studies, Jencks *et al.* (1983: 8) found that, of the four social background variables, family income had the strongest impact, although the effect was fairly weak with standardized coefficients of 0.15 and 0.16.[9] Similarly, in the WLS, Sewell and Hauser (1975: 100, 107–10) found that, of the four indicators of socioeconomic background, only parents' average income (over four years) had a statistically significant effect on male earnings ten years after graduating.

Hertz (2006: 19) concludes that three-fifths of the effect of family income can be attributed to family characteristics other than income.[10] Jencks and Tach (2006) find a weak impact of family income (elasticity = 0.10) on daughters' earnings, which was no longer statistically significant when controlling for father's education and occupation. For sons' earnings, the bivariate relationship was stronger (elasticity = 0.21), but declined substantially (elasticity = 0.13) with the addition of father's occupation and education. From the WLS, the coefficient for parent's logged income (in 1957) on son's logged earnings (in 1991) declined from 0.21 to 0.13 when controlling for other family characteristics, including father's and mother's education and occupational status (2006: 30).

Net of ability and education

The impact of family background factors is much weaker after controlling for ability and education. In the PSID, the effects of family income decline by about 30 percent with the addition of education and by about a quarter for father's earnings (Eide and Showalter 1999: 259–63). Jencks and Tach (2006: 29–33) report the impact of family income on son's earnings, with declines from 0.21 to 0.13 when controlling for father's education and occupation, to 0.11 after the further addition of eleventh-grade IQ score, and to 0.09 after adding educational attainment. This means that only half of the initial impact of family income can be explained by obvious covariates and mediators and the net effect is small (0.09). Therefore, the family of origin's economic resources have only small direct impacts on earnings. Furthermore, the big-five personality traits explained almost none of the effect of family income on either sons' or daughters' earnings.

Biology and genetics

Adoptees

Intergenerational income correlations are much lower for adopted children than for biological children. Using the PSID, Liu and Zeng (2009) found that intergenerational elasticity for wages and earnings among adopted children were 0.113 and 0.096 compared with 0.345 and 0.369 for non-adopted children. These differences even applied to adopted and biological children in the same family. They concluded that a large proportion of the transmission of earnings inequality across generations could be attributed to genetic factors. For Sweden, Björklund *et al.* (2006: 1013, 1015) report earnings and income elasticities of 0.10 and 0.17 for adopted children (with their non-biological father) compared with 0.24 for biological children. The income and earnings correlations for children and their non-resident biological fathers' earnings were very low (around 0.05). A later Swedish study found a substantial impact for the absent biological parents' education on their child's earnings. Focusing on men's earnings, the effect of absent (but biological) father's years of education (0.016) on son's earnings was larger than that of the residential biological mother's years of education (0.011). Where there was an adoptive father, the effect of the absent biological father's years of education (0.023) was comparable to the resident adoptive fathers' years of education (0.021) and both effects were substantially stronger than that for the resident biological mother's years of education (0.009). The authors concluded that there are substantial effects of both nature and nurture on earnings (Björklund *et al.* 2007: 16).

Siblings

The intraclass sibling correlations are much weaker for earnings than for other socioeconomic outcomes, around 0.22 compared with 0.47 for test scores, 0.55 for education and 0.31 for occupation (Olneck 1977: 132). Similarly, Jencks *et al.* (1979: 340) report sibling correlations for earnings between 0.13 and 0.21 from three studies. In these studies the sibling correlations are much weaker than those for test scores (0.47 and 0.48), education (0.53–0.55) and occupation (0.31–0.37), indicating that family background overall has a much weaker impact on earnings than on earlier outcomes. The low sibling correlations suggest that family background is not a strong driver of earnings. Olneck (1977: 137–8) calculates that, even if all family background differences in earnings were eliminated, the variation in earnings would be only slightly smaller: at 87 percent of the original standard deviation.

Corcoran *et al.* (1976: 433) estimated the intraclass correlation for brothers at 0.23. This is equivalent to the variation accounted for (R square) by family background (i.e. everything that is common to brothers). As was the case for education, the measured characteristics explain about half of the variation accounted for by family background. They note that the unmeasured characteristics of brothers affect earnings independently of test scores and educational attainment. They suggest that these unmeasured characteristics may involve family preferences for monetary or non-monetary rewards. Mazumder (2008), using a different methodology that removed the transitory component in individual earnings, estimated the brother intracorrelation in earnings at around 0.5. If the transitory component was included (which is much closer to the observed earnings), the brother correlation would be much less, at 0.3 (2008: 693).

Unsurprisingly, educational attainment and ability are the major contributors to the brother correlations. Each of these "human capital" variables accounts for between 40 and 50 percent of the correlation. Only six percent of brother correlation is accounted for by parental income when controlling for education and AFQT score. Physical characteristics and psychological factors made little or no contribution to the sibling correlation in earnings when controlling for education and adolescent test scores (Mazumder 2008: 699).

Twins

The correlations of earnings among identical twins are surprisingly high. Taubman (1976b) collected data on the 1973 earnings of white male twins who had served in the American armed forces during World War II. Monozygotic twins' 1973 earnings correlated at 0.54, while dizygotic twins' earnings correlated at 0.30. Similarly, Ashenfelter and Krueger (1994: 1160) reported correlations of 0.56 for the wage rates of identical twins and 0.36

for fraternal twins. A later study found correlations (for hourly wage rates) of 0.63 and 0.37, respectively (Jencks and Tach 2006: footnote 15). The correlations among identical twins' earnings in Australia and Sweden are even higher, approaching 0.7, with correlations among fraternal twins being much lower (Solon 1999: 1774). A recent estimate for Sweden was a correlation of 0.49 for earnings among monozygotic twins compared to 0.29 for dizygotic twins (Cesarini 2013: 35).

The heritability of earnings is surprisingly high. Taubman's (1976b) estimate for the US was about 50 percent. For a white cohort born between 1917 and 1927, Behrman *et al.* (1980: 206–7) estimate that 45 percent of the variation in logged earnings was due to genetics, the common environment only ten percent, and nearly 45 percent to unique effects not attributable to family background or genetics. The genetic component for earnings was higher than that for education or occupation (30 percent). In a study of twins and other sibling types in Sweden, Björklund *et al.* (2005: 161) initially estimated that about 80 percent of the intergenerational earning correlation among twins and siblings could be accounted for by genetic factors. This assumed that the importance of the environment was the same for identical twins and non-identical twins or siblings (a reasonable assumption). When they relaxed the assumption that the correlation for the environment among monozygotic twins reared together was 1.0 but the environmental correlation for dizygotic twins and siblings was less than 1.0 and had to be estimated, they concluded that about 60 percent of the intergenerational correlation was due to genetics (2005: 161). Here the environmental component includes twins' *in utero* environment, and their treatment as infants and their schooling environments. These aspects are quite distinct from the family's socioeconomic resources. In a different type of analysis, Jencks and Tach (2006: 24) conclude that approximately half of the correlation of earnings across generations can be attributed to genes and individual values. These studies imply that genes, but not necessarily ability, are a major contributor to the similarity of earnings.

Changes over time

Intergenerational earnings correlation

There is no consensus on whether the intergenerational correlations for earnings have declined over time. There is little appropriate data. Fertig (2003) used the PSID to analyze trends in earnings mobility in the US. She found that the association between fathers' and sons' earnings weakened over time, although this was not true for mothers' earnings. She concluded that a rise in *equality* of opportunity accompanied the recent growth in income inequality. Levine and Mazumder (2007) also found an (insignificant) decline in the intergenerational elasticity of sons' earnings with respect to their parents' family income in the PSID. Mayer and Lopoo (2005) found a downward trend in the effect of parents' family income on both sons' family income and their wages at age 30 among those born after 1952, but the linear trend was no longer significant when they included sons born between 1949 and 1951. Harding *et al.* (2005) found that the multiple correlation of parent's characteristics with family income declined between 1961 and 1999. However, the brothers' correlations in earnings increased over time and this increase could not be attributed to an increase in the sibling correlations for education or increases in the economic returns to education (Levine and Mazumder 2007). Pistolesi (2009) concluded that the importance of inequality of opportunity for earnings inequality declined from about 40 percent in the late 1960s to about 18 percent in 2001.

In the UK, considerable attention has focused on the finding that income mobility appears to have declined. Comparing the 1958 and 1970 child cohort studies, the elasticity (β) increased from 0.20 to 0.29 and the intergenerational correlation increased from 0.17 to 0.29 (Blanden *et al.* 2005). These are very large changes in the space of only 12 years. For Finland, the intergenerational income correlation declined from 0.30 to 0.23 (Pekkarinen *et al.* 2009). This decline was attributed to Finland changing from a two-track education system to a one-track system between 1972 and 1977 and increasing the age that educational differentiation begins from 10 to 16. For Norway, Hansen (2010) identified a decline in the relationship between father's income and son's income but an increase in the relationship between family income and son's income. For Sweden, brothers' correlations in income declined from 0.49 for cohorts born in the early 1930s to 0.32 for cohorts born around 1950. Subsequently, the correlations increased to 0.37 (Björklund *et al.* 2009b).

Earnings returns to education

The impact of education on income is increasing in the US. However, there is little evidence that the returns to education are increasing elsewhere. Gottschalk and Joyce (1998) document strong increases in the impact of a college education on earnings in the US between 1979 and 1981 of around 1.6 percent per annum. There was a slightly weaker increase of 1.1 percent between 1986 and 1991. Kaymak (2009) concluded that the return to earnings from a one-year increase in education increased from 4.8 percent to 8.4 percent between 1964 and 2003, and argues that the increase in the education premium after 1990 was almost entirely due to ability.

In the Gottschalk and Joyce (1998) study, the countries with the next strongest increases in the returns to college education were Sweden and Finland, two countries that did not experience an increase in earnings inequality. There were weaker increases in the earnings returns to education for Canada, the UK, the Netherlands and Australia. More recent evidence for the UK is mixed. Silles (2007) found increased earnings returns to education among men but not among women, whereas Walker and Zhu (2008) found no evidence of increases in the college premium. In addition, there is little evidence from recent studies for increasing effects of education on earnings for countries other than the US, such as Australia, Canada, Norway and the UK (Burbidge *et al.* 2002; Coelli and Wilkins 2009; Haegeland *et al.* 1999). This is despite large increases in the proportion of the workforce with college degrees. In Ireland and Spain, the returns to education have declined (Voitchovsky *et al.* 2012).

Cross-national differences

Cross-national comparisons in earnings and income suggest that the UK and the US stand out as countries that strongly reproduce economic inequalities (Corak 2005: 9; OECD 2009b). Although, it may be tempting to argue that the high elasticities in the US and the UK have something to do with their liberal capitalist economies, their more limited social welfare provisions or Anglo-Saxon culture, the intergenerational correlations are much weaker in Australia and Canada. In the introduction to *Generational Income Mobility in North America and Europe*, the editor, Miles Corak, summarizes:

> In the US and the UK at least 40 per cent of the economic advantage high-income parents have over low-income parents is passed on to the next generation. The Nordic countries and Canada seem to be the most mobile societies, with less than 20 per cent of an income advantage being passed on between parent and child.
>
> (Corak 2005: 9)

The OECD's (2009b) report, *Growing Unequal?*, concluded that earnings elasticities were lowest (meaning more mobility) in Denmark, Australia, Norway, Finland and Canada and highest in Great Britain, Italy, the US and France (in that order).

The conclusion of high intergenerational income correlations in the UK and US, if correct, is not consistent with other literatures. It is not consistent with the general conclusion from social stratification research that the impact of socioeconomic background is fairly modest. The previous chapters have shown that the correlations between measures of socioeconomic background and student achievement, educational attainment and occupational attainment are around 0.3 and 0.4, and, together, indicators of socioeconomic background rarely account for more than 20 percent of the variation in these outcomes. The work on intergenerational income correlations led Bowles and Gintis (2002b: 4) to make the claim that, for the US, "knowing the income and wealth of someone's parents is about as informative about the person's own economic status as is the person's years of schooling or attained score in a cognitive test". This statement is true in the case of test scores but for education assumes that the zero order inter-generational correlation for income is well above 0.4. It is also misleading in that with the bulk of research evidence shows that education is clearly the primary influence on adult economic outcomes and that cognitive ability is the major influence on education. In the ascription versus achievement paradigm, the general conclusion is that ascription is much less important than ascribed characteristics (Blau and Duncan 1967; Grusky and DiPrete 1990). In light of high intergenerational correlations for income in the US, such a conclusion would appear unwarranted. Theoretically, the focus would switch from a range of sociological (including economic) influences to credit constraints among poor families. Finally, the high intergenerational income correlations in the US turn the American exceptionalism argument on its head. The country which was renowned for being more "open" than the old-world countries of Europe with their supposedly more rigid class structures is, if the conclusions are true, much more closed than Europe, with the notable exception of the UK and possibly Italy. The US is unique, since other "new-world societies" such as Australia and Canada exhibit low correlations. Nowhere in the cross-national comparative literature on student achievement, educational and occupational attainment and occupational mobility (discussed in previous chapters) has it been concluded that the reproduction of educational and socioeconomic inequalities is so much higher in the UK and the US than in comparable countries.

Issues with cross-national comparisons

Table 11.1 presents the estimates of intergenerational elasticities for different countries from several sources. Some estimates only use proxies for income. The estimate for Australia calculated by Leigh (2007) was not based on any measure of father's income but was estimated from respondents' reports of their father's occupation and education. Respondents' income was based on quite unreliable questions that asked them the income band of their or their family's income. Such indirect and very questionable measures are not unknown in studies conducted in other countries. Solon (2002: 63) notes that Dearden *et al.*'s (1997) estimate of an elasticity of 0.57 may be biased upward, since father's income was not used but was predicted by education and occupational class. An estimate for the intergenerational elasticity for Singapore was based on the weak association found for youths aged between 23 and 29, and then adjusted upwards by comparison with the PSID, taking into account the sample's youth and the limitation of only one year of earnings data (Ng *et al.* 2009). There must be much error associated with these quite substantial adjustments, which nearly double the magnitude of the original estimates (from 0.26 to 0.44). The analysis over time by Aaronson and Mazumder (2008) uses census data without any direct linkage between father's and son's earnings. Their analysis is more about the "importance of

Table 11.1 Estimates of intergenerational elasticities

Country	*OECD*	*Solon*		*Corak*	
			Lowest	*Highest*	*Preferred*
Australia	0.16				
Canada	0.19	0.23	0.13	0.23	0.19
Denmark	0.15		0.08	0.08	0.15
Finland	0.18	0.22	0.09	0.18	0.18
France	0.41				
Germany	0.32	0.11	0.10	0.34	0.32
Great Britain	0.50	0.57	0.22	0.58	0.50
Italy	0.48				
Norway	0.17		0.12	0.29	0.17
Spain	0.32				
Sweden	0.27	0.28	0.13	0.30	
US	0.47		0.09	0.61	0.47

Sources: Corak (2006); OECD (2009b); Solon (2002)

average family income in one's state of birth on children's economic success" (2008: 142).

Most often low elasticities are found with reliable data. The estimate of 0.2 for the intergenerational elasticity for Canada is based on longitudinal data from 400,000 father–son pairs (Corak and Heisz 1999). Hansen's (2010) estimate of around 0.3 for Norway is based on very reliable registry data for incomes with hundreds of thousands of cases.[11] The estimates for Sweden are also usually based on registry data (Hirvonen 2008). These reliable estimates are often included with estimates from other countries based on a small number of cases or in some cases proxies for income.

The higher intergenerational correlation for earnings in the US than that for other outcomes may be explained by regional labor markets. There are large regional differences in earnings between metropolitan and non-metropolitan areas in the US (Glaeser and Maré 2001; Jencks and Tach 2006). Jencks and Tach (2006: 40) cite personal communication with Kim, who controlled for the size of the community and the region in which a son was raised, and found that the father–son earnings elasticity in the PSID fell from 0.447 to 0.315. This adjustment suggests that the relative high reproduction of economic inequality in the US can be attributed somewhat to region. The same argument may apply to the UK, where wages are higher in London than in other regions. Although it is plausible that the high intergenerational correlations for earnings in the US and the UK, together with their unexceptional intergenerational associations for test scores, education and occupation, can be explained by more flexible labor markets or stronger regional differences, Occam's razor would suggest otherwise. If more flexible labor markets and stronger regional differences were the explanation then

Canada (and Australia) would exhibit similarly high intergenerational associations for earnings and income.

Conclusions

The reported high estimates for the intergenerational associations correlations for earnings and income in the US and UK cast doubt on the contention that the reproduction of socioeconomic inequalities in Western countries is only moderate. However, there are several reasons to doubt the accuracy of the high-end estimates. These high intergenerational elasticities and correlations are not consistent with cross-national comparisons in the intergenerational relationships for test scores, educational attainment, occupational status, and occupational mobility. Family income tends to have a much weaker relationship with test scores, educational attainment and other childhood outcomes than parental occupation and parental education. There are issues with the data; for some countries, the number of cases is low and earnings and income are not accurately measured. In some cases, the estimates do not involve actual data on income or the earnings of the older generation. There are doubts surrounding the concept of "permanent income"; the higher the assumed transitory component, the higher the intergenerational correlation. Theoretical estimates obtained from assumptions about permanent income are usually considerably higher than observed averages calculated over long periods. Instrumental variable approaches using social background variables are inappropriate, upwardly biasing the estimates. Finally, the net effect of family income on adult child's earnings or income is quite weak, when taking into account other family background variables and cognitive ability. This indicates that the observed association does not really reflect the direct impact of the family of origin's economic resources on the subsequent generation's economic situation, or even its indirect impact through education.

For earnings, changes in the intergenerational elasticities or correlations cannot test the modernization thesis. The intergenerational relationship is complex; mediated by cognitive ability, education, occupation and other factors. Even if the overall relationship between parental and adult child's earnings has increased, this may be due to changes consistent with modernization theory; stronger relationships between parental and children's cognitive ability, cognitive ability and education, and education and earnings.

Notes

1 Some parts of this chapter have been published in Marks (2013).
2 The intergenerational correlation can also be estimated by the square root of the R square value for the elasticity equation.
3 The well-cited estimates by Solon (1992) and Zimmerman (1992) are based on only 290 and 175 father–son pairs, respectively.

4 Hertz's (2005: 176) scatter plot show the extent of variation in the relationship. It appears that there is little downward mobility for children of family's with income at the highest levels.
5 The elasticities are higher because of the greater variance in earnings in the second generation.
6 This implies that unreliable measures of earnings/income will produce higher estimates of the intergenerational associations than highly reliable measures.
7 According to Muller (2010: 294):

> Applying these results to our estimates would put the range of the betas conservatively between 0.05 (in the late teens and early 20s) and 0.25 (in early childhood), so early childhood income may be four times as important as income in other periods.

8 There is again much variation in the estimates. Bowles and Gintis (2002b) report estimates ranging from 0.27 to 0.76 from nine studies.
9 Sewell and Hauser (1975: 111) noted that the most pertinent of father's characteristics had the strongest effect of the socioeconomic background variables: father's education on son's educations, father's occupational status on son's occupational status, and family income on son's income.
10 Parental characteristics with at least moderate effects include race, education and religion.
11 The estimate of 0.3 is the highest, based on family income including capital income limited to men. However, family income together with father's age and child's cohort explain little of the variation in sons' or daughters' income, 4.4 and 3.4 per cent, respectively (Hansen 2010: 144).

Chapter 12

Conclusions and discussion

The evidence from this book is clear: the reproduction of socioeconomic inequalities in Western societies is not nearly as strong as is so often assumed. The overall relationship between socioeconomic background and the range of educational, occupational and economic outcomes is best described as moderate, not strong. For educational outcomes, the direct effect of socioeconomic background, no matter what indicators are used or combined together, is even smaller after taking into account cognitive ability. For occupational and economic outcomes, the direct impact of socioeconomic background is even smaller, and smaller again after taking into account educational attainment and, to a lesser extent, cognitive ability.

There has been a general tendency for socioeconomic inequalities to decline over time. In many countries socioeconomic inequalities for educational outcomes are declining for student achievement (test scores), adult literacy, university entrance and educational attainment. Similarly, the bivariate correlations between father's socioeconomic status and both son's educational attainment and socioeconomic status have most often declined. The direct effect of father's socioeconomic status on son's socioeconomic status, net of education, is declining in almost all Western countries.

Despite years of contentious debate, it is well established that cognitive ability is a stable human trait, quite distinct from social class or socioeconomic background, with a substantial genetic component. There is also evidence that many non-cognitive traits have a genetic component. Cognitive ability has a considerably stronger influence than socioeconomic background on educational outcomes in many different contexts. Therefore, cognitive ability has substantial indirect effects on labor market outcomes mediated through education, and in addition, has direct effects, net of education. No single non-cognitive attribute or group of theoretically related non-cognitive attributes has a consistent impact on educational and labor market outcomes comparable to that of cognitive ability.

Sibling studies suggest that there are sizable effects of family background on education since siblings have much more similar educational attainments than non-related individuals. Similarly, siblings are more similar in their occupations and earnings than non-related persons. However, only about half the impact of family background is accounted for by measured family factors (e.g. socioeconomic background, ethnicity, race, region); the other half is due to unmeasured family characteristics that siblings have in common, and this includes cognitive ability and non-cognitive attributes. This suggests that genes play a role in sibling similarities in educational and labor market outcomes. Twin studies show that the environmental component to education, occupational status and earnings is much smaller than the genetic component and over-time studies indicate that the magnitude of the environmental component has declined.

There are two main criticisms likely to be directed at this book. First, the book is based on the existing, well-known literature and therefore adds nothing new to current understandings. The second, quite contradictory criticism, is that the conclusions made in this book are contrary to the established conclusions of the literature. It is true that this book does not include much new analysis, but it does use the existing literature to make arguments consistent with the evidence. In sociology and to a lesser extent economics, it is very rare for studies to conclude that: (i) socioeconomic inequalities are not as strong as commonly believed; (ii) cognitive ability plays an important role in social stratification, whereas non-cognitive attributes play a lesser role; and (iii) socioeconomic inequalities have declined or are declining. It is not the case at all that there is general agreement with each of these statements among social scientists. Much evidence was assembled to support these contentions. As for the second criticism, the book has incorporated most major studies relevant to the particular argument and avoided "cherry picking". There are instances where the findings are presented rather than the authors' conclusions but this should be clear. Critics would be hard pressed to find conclusive evidence that socioeconomic inequalities are strong and enduring or that cognitive ability has little or no role in socioeconomic outcomes, or evidence that refutes the many other contentions made in this book.

The arguments presented in this book break down if the concept of cognitive ability is rejected. This is why a considerable part of the book is devoted to demonstrating that cognitive ability is a valid concept, adequately measured by cognitive tests, is stable even over long periods, is basically unidimensional, cannot be dismissed simply as a function of socioeconomic background, and has a considerable biological component. It is not credible to argue that cognitive ability does not exist or that its effects are so weak that it should be dismissed in studies of educational and socioeconomic stratification.

Reproduction theories

The conclusions from this study strongly run counter to the contentions of reproduction theory. Reproduction theories assume that socioeconomic inequalities are strong and durable. Correlations of 0.2 and 0.3 between single indicators of socioeconomic background and education are evidence against reproduction theory. Stronger correlations are found if more indicators are used, combining parental education and occupation, family income, books in the home, etc., but the association remains moderate, explaining less than 20 percent of the variation in educational outcomes. Adjusting for measurement error only marginally increases the effects of socioeconomic background on education and other outcomes. Even if background is measured in sibling studies by the family of origin, it is not credible to argue that what siblings have in common is entirely social and does not include biological factors. There is little evidence that socioeconomic inequalities in education can be explained by economic factors, schools, or culture. Such theorizing needs to acknowledge that cognitive ability plays a substantial role in educational outcomes.

Modernization theories

How does modernization theory fare in light of more than half a century of studies? Modernization theory is supported by the generally weak and declining impact of socioeconomic background for education and subsequent socioeconomic attainments. Socioeconomic background still influences educational outcomes and, through education, indirectly impacts on adults' occupational outcomes. Western societies are not meritocracies, if the definition of a meritocracy is that educational and socioeconomic outcomes are entirely accounted for by cognitive ability and effort. However, it can be concluded that Western societies have strong meritocratic characteristics; the effects of cognitive ability for educational outcomes are invariably stronger than those for socioeconomic background. Cognitive ability also has direct and durable effects on occupational outcomes and earnings, in addition to its indirect effects mediated through education. If educational attainment was mainly the product of ability and effort, the correlation between ability and education would be much higher, rather than around 0.5. Ironically, if the correlation between ability and education was 0.8 and the correlation between parent's and child's ability was 0.5 (an accepted figure), then the intergenerational (parent–child) correlation for educational attainment would be much the same as that commonly observed, 0.3. Furthermore, there is evidence that, compared with pre-War cohorts, the contribution of the environment to cognitive ability and educational attainment has declined appreciably.

Other findings presented in this book tend to support modernization theory in a modified form. There is evidence for increasing effects of ability for educational aspirations and stronger effects of test scores on occupational aspirations in wealthier countries. For school completion, university and college entrance, the effects of ability have tended to increase over the twentieth century. This increase has been followed by a decline. For school completion and university entrance, the decline in the impact of ability is likely to continue as more and more students who are lower down the ability continuum complete high school and enter university. These changes also increase the effect of socioeconomic background on university entrance since a more socially heterogeneous group is "at risk" of university entrance, although the relative effect of socioeconomic background for university entrance is typically much smaller than that for cognitive ability. There is some evidence that the impact of ability on college selectivity and grades in the US has increased. Cross-nationally, indicators of modernization, including educational expansion and declines in the variation of education, as well as traditional indicators of modernization, are associated with declining effects for socioeconomic background.

Turning to the labor market, there are also good reasons to suppose that education and cognitive ability have become more important – increasing credentialism and the imperatives of employers to employ and promote the most productive applicants that maybe, but not necessarily are, the best and the brightest. There is evidence that the impact of educational attainment on occupational status has increased in most (but not all) Western countries, and the impact of socioeconomic background variables has declined. These changes are consistent with modernization theory. The genetic component of the variation for occupation and earnings is much higher than the environmental component. There is also substantial unique variation not attributable to either family background or genetics. However, there is little evidence that education has increased its effects for earnings, although increasing effects of education and ability have been offered as explanations for the increase in earnings inequality in the US.

Policy

Western societies have done a reasonable job in reducing socioeconomic inequalities in education. If they had done a poor job, then the correlations between socioeconomic background and educational and subsequent socioeconomic outcomes would be much higher than 0.4. First, the intergenerational correlations for education, occupational status and earnings are generally substantially lower than the intergenerational correlations for cognitive ability. Second, the intergenerational correlations for education, occupational status and earnings tend to be lower in Western countries than in non-Western countries. Third, the absolute chances of students born into lower socioeconomic backgrounds completing school and pursuing university education have increased dramatically.

Deliberations on education policy should not be based on the premise that the bulk of inequalities in education can be attributed to socioeconomic background. This leads to an emphasis on providing money to particular schools, regions, ethnic groups and low-income groups. By and large, such policies have not been successful. Governments spending money on programs purported to reduce socioeconomic inequalities may appear attractive to policymakers and politicians, but the answer to whether these programs work is not known until years after, if at all. A better strategy is to focus directly on those students who are struggling with school work and to take whatever remedial action that seems to work, no matter their social background or social characteristics. Similarly, policymakers should not work on the premise that educational outcomes are all about cognitive ability. Ability is a strong influence but the relationship is not deterministic. Governments should continue to try and remove the social impediments faced by high- and moderate-ability students from disadvantaged backgrounds. This was the philosophy of the early post-War educational reforms in the UK and elsewhere, where such students were "sponsored" by the system to obtain better educational outcomes than they would otherwise have had. The present strategy of delaying educational differentiation for as long as possible, say until the final years of secondary school, is a sound one because there is some socioeconomic bias in the allocation of students to tracks and streams and it keeps students' options open for as long as possible.

Unresolved issues

A variety of questions remain unresolved for modernization theory. Unfortunately, there are too few studies to reliably detect changes in the role of cognitive ability on social stratification over time. A second unresolved issue is identifying the social processes involved. It is not at all clear whether the moderate and/or declining impact of socioeconomic background can be attributed to specific educational policies (e.g. reducing education differentiation, implementation of free and low-cost schooling, better educational practices, improvements in remedial education and educational expansion), societal changes (e.g. the improvements in prenatal and early childhood health, the virtual eradication of grinding poverty, the expansion of the welfare state) or more glacial and difficult to discern factors (e.g. changes in the educational aspirations and attitudes to education by parents and students). A third unresolved issue is country differences. There is no obvious explanation why the intergenerational earnings correlations in the US and the UK are so high, although there are good reasons to doubt these estimates. These countries do not stand out as having much stronger socioeconomic inequalities in test scores, educational attainment and occupational attainment. There is much less consistency between countries than expected, when comparing socioeconomic inequalities in test scores, educational attainment, occupational mobility, occupational attainment and earnings. It may be that issues with data, measurement and the techniques used undermine consistency, or there could be good theoretical reasons why consistency across these distinct albeit related outcomes is not to be expected.

Theorizing socioeconomic inequalities

A striking characteristic of the social stratification literature is its disparate nature and very distinct schools and traditions. The literature does not present a clear coherent picture. In examining socioeconomic inequalities, there are traditions that focus (or focused) on social class and school sub-cultures, economic resources, cultural capital, cognitive ability, non-cognitive attributes, schools, school tracking and streaming, educational transitions and siblings and twins, to name a few. The traditions often link to particular statistical methods. In addition, there is a major division between researchers motivated by modernization and reproduction theories. Beyond quantitative work, there is a variety of non-quantitative research traditions that also focus on socioeconomic inequalities. This is akin to a postmodernist world, in that each tradition has its own narrative, literature, respected scholars and methods, and all assume they have a better understanding of socioeconomic inequalities in modern societies. Unsurprisingly, they produce quite different and often contradictory findings. This is all very confronting and confusing to anyone new to the field, and they must choose or fall into a particular tradition, largely disregarding traditions that are not very compatible with the one they have chosen. This pluralism may be viewed as positive with many different approaches to the same general set of research questions. However, a variety of quite separate and distinct research traditions that do not try to resolve their inconsistencies does not contribute to generating a knowledge base.

Below is the outline of a theory for educational and socioeconomic outcomes, incorporating education, social background and cognitive ability. The contentions in the theory are consistent with the bulk of empirical work referred to throughout this book.

A basic assumption is that cognitive ability is and has always been important for educational performance. Since ability involves the "ability to reason, plan, solve problems, think abstractly, comprehend complex ideas, learn quickly and learn from experience" (from Gottfredson 1997a: 14), high-ability students will always perform better in educational contexts. Ability will typically show strong correlations with student performance and will be important to educational outcomes within that context (certification, rank, honors, grades etc.). It does not matter what the context is, from Plato's Academy of classical Greece, learned religious institutions in medieval Europe, English public schools of the nineteenth century or schools in contemporary education systems. Outside the educational setting, ability may or may not impact on the social destinations of individuals. If the educational context is limited to social elites and the very act of participation in that education setting is the first step on the pathway to privileged social positions, then ability will have little impact. In this situation, entrance to privileged societal positions would be based almost exclusively on ascribed social attributes. If the situation changes slightly so that entrance to more privileged social positions is based on performance in that educational context, then ability will have some influence on subsequent occupational outcomes. But since entrance to educational institutions is limited to social elites, then in the context of society as a whole, ability would have only a very limited influence and social background would be the dominant factor.

With the expansion of education so that just about everybody receives some primary school education, ability is a strong predictor of performance but financial factors, social norms and other factors limit opportunities for moderate- to high-ability students from non-elite backgrounds to continue their education, although some very high-ability students from non-elite backgrounds proceed further. Overall, educational attainment would largely reflect socioeconomic background. With the expansion of secondary education, ability remains important to student performance and the allocation of students to different school tracks and streams. At the same time, the impact of socioeconomic background declines as the health, finances, welfare and schooling of students from lower socioeconomic backgrounds improve.

With further educational expansion so that high-school graduation is increasingly common, ability becomes a stronger predictor of school graduation since graduation is a function of student performance which relates strongly to ability. With this expansion the impact of socioeconomic background declines, as more higher-ability students from lower socioeconomic backgrounds complete school. If there is a further expansion of education so that school completion approaches universal levels, the influence of ability will begin to decline as nearly all high- and middle-ability students complete school along with increasing proportions (over time) of lower-ability students. However, ability remains a substantially stronger influence than socioeconomic background on test scores, grades and performance in examinations while at school and for university entrance.

For college or university education the pattern is similar to that for school completion. As university education changes from an elite to a mass system, ability becomes more important for entry and socioeconomic background becomes less important as barriers are removed for high-ability students from lower socioeconomic backgrounds. With a further expansion of university education, ability becomes less important as lower-ability students gain access. At the same time, the impact of socioeconomic background for university participation increases as lower-ability students from higher socioeconomic backgrounds gain entry. However, ability will again remain important for performance at university and for entrance to academically elite institutions and courses.

Declines in socioeconomic inequalities in education will be reflected in the labor market. The role of social background will decline and the increase in the genetic component implies that there are increases in the importance of cognitive ability and non-cognitive attributes. Such changes in process may not necessarily be reflected in declines in the raw correlations between socio-economic background and labor market outcomes, but the direct influence of socioeconomic background will have declined. It is true to say that human capital models in economics and status attainment models in sociology will not capture the great variation in labor market outcomes. There is a range of processes that cannot easily be included: businesses going bankrupt or new ones growing; slow changes in the size of employment sectors; changes in the influence of employers, trade union and professional organizations; government legislation on employment conditions; and just plain old "luck".

Conclusions

There are reasons why most theoretical explanations for changes over time and cross-national differences in socioeconomic inequalities are inadequate. One reason is fashion. For a decade or so, much of the research on social stratification was with log-linear modeling, a technique that now has gone out of fashion. This was followed by the Mare-type educational transitions models and after they were critiqued, more complex educational transitions models, and recently, Boudon's primary and secondary effects have been resurrected, which at least acknowledge the importance of student performance.

A second reason is that the prominence of log-linear modeling during the 1980s meant that many of the insights from the 1960s and 1970s based on Blau and Duncan-type analyses (and this includes Jencks *et al.* 1972) were discarded: that there is much unexplained variation in educational attainment and occupational attainment; socioeconomic background, schools, school resources poorly account for children's test scores; a certain amount of luck is involved in labor market outcomes; cognitive ability is important to educational attainment and thus social stratification; and, importantly, education has a much stronger impact on both occupational attainment and earnings than socioeconomic background.[1] The Blau–Duncan approach had largely been discredited for a variety of reasons: that modern societies were stratified by class not occupation; it was sexist since it focused mainly on men; it ignored the political machinations of interest groups; its preferred method of path analysis prioritized method over "substance" and the use of standardized coefficients and model fit was inappropriate and misleading. There is some substance to these criticisms but they are not strong enough to justify largely abandoning the approach. The Blau–Duncan approach was not perfect but it is was groundbreaking for its time and provided many important insights and most of its conclusions remain true today. The core reason for its rejection was that it gave a rather benign view of the reproduction of socioeconomic inequalities in the US[2] that was incompatible with a radical political agenda. Before then, a strongly reformist or even radical political ideology was quite compatible with a science of society. After the 1970s, such a position was much more difficult. It was very unfortunate that ideology trumped science.

A third reason for the inadequacy of theoretical explanations of socioeconomic inequalities is the prominence of non-explanatory theory. Such theory is useless for empirical work. If the findings from stratification studies were followed by constant interaction between hypotheses generated from explanatory theory and empirical work, we would have a much better understanding of socioeconomic inequalities in modern societies than we do today.

Notes

1 Ganzeboom *et al.* (1991) have made similar and additional points.
2 Jencks *et al.* (1972) were by no means conservative. At the end of the book, they were advocating policies to reduce inequality in earnings rather than inequality of opportunity since socioeconomic background, test scores, schools and education did not contribute much to income inequalities.

References

Aaronson, D. and Mazumder, B. (2008) 'Intergenerational Economic Mobility in the United States, 1940 to 2000', *Journal of Human Resources*, 43(1), 139–72.

Abraham, J. (1995) *Divide and School: Gender and Class Dynamics in Comprehensive Education*, London: Falmer Press.

Acker, J. (1973) 'Women and Social Stratification: A Case of Intellectual Sexism', *American Journal of Sociology*, 78(4), 936–45.

Acland, H. (1973) 'Streaming in English Primary Schools', *British Journal of Educational Psychology*, 43(2), 151–9.

Adey, P., Csapó, B., Demetriou, A., Hautamäki, J. and Shayer, M. (2007) 'Can We Be Intelligent About Intelligence? Why Education Needs the Concept of Plastic General Ability', *Educational Research Review*, 2(2), 75–97.

Alexander, K. L. and Cook, M. A. (1982) 'Curricula and Coursework: A Surprise Ending to a Familiar Story', *American Sociological Review*, 47(5), 626–40.

Alexander, K. L. and Eckland, B. K. (1974) 'Sex Differences in the Educational Attainment Process', *American Sociological Review*, 39(5), 668–82.

Alexander, K. L. and Pallas, A. M. (1985) 'School Sector and Cognitive Performance: When is a Little a Little?', *Sociology of Education*, 58(2), 115–28.

Alexander, K. L., Cook, M. and McDill, E. L. (1978) 'Curriculum Tracking and Educational Stratification: Some Further Evidence', *American Sociological Review*, 43(1), 47–66.

Alexander, K. L., Fennessey, J., McDill, E. L. and D'Amico, R. J. (1979) 'School SES Influences – Composition or Context?', *Sociology of Education*, 52(4), 222–37.

Alexander, K. L., Holupka, S. and Pallas, A. M. (1987) 'Social Background and Academic Determinants of Two-Year Versus Four-Year College Attendance: Evidence from Two Cohorts a Decade Apart', *American Journal of Education*, 96(1), 56–80.

Alexander, K. L., Riordan, C., Fennessey, J. and Aaron, M. P. (1982) 'Social Background, Academic Resources, and College Graduation: Recent Evidence from the National Longitudinal Survey', *American Journal of Education*, 90(4), 315–33.

Alon, S. (2009) 'The Evolution of Class Inequality in Higher Education: Competition, Exclusion, and Adaptation', *American Sociological Review*, 74(5), 731–55.

Alon, S. and Tienda, M. (2007) 'Diversity, Opportunity, and the Shifting Meritocracy in Higher Education', *American Sociological Review*, 72(4), 487–511.

Alwin, D. F. and Thornton, A. (1984) 'Family Origins and the Schooling Process:

Early Versus Late Influence of Parental Characteristics', *American Sociological Review*, 49(6), 784–802.

Alwin, D. F. and Otto, L. B. (1977) 'High School Context Effects on Aspirations', *Sociology of Education*, 50(4), 259–73.

Ambler, J. S. and Neathery, J. (1999) 'Education Policy and Equality: Some Evidence from Europe', *Social Science Quartely*, 80(3), 437–56.

Anger, S. (2012) 'The Intergenerational Transmission of Cognitive and Non-Cognitive Skills During Adolescence and Young Adulthood' in Ermisch, J., Jäntti, M. and Smeeding, T. M. (eds) *From Parents to Children: The Intergenerational Transmission of Advantage*, New York: Russell Sage Foundation, 393–421.

Anger, S. and Heineck, G. (2010) 'Do Smart Parents Raise Smart Children? The Intergenerational Transmission of Cognitive Abilities', *Journal of Population Economics*, 23(2), 1105–32.

Angrist, J. and Krueger, A. B. (2001) 'Instrumental Variables and the Search for Identification: From Supply and Demand to Natural Experiments', *Journal of Economic Perspectives*, 15(4), 69–85.

Aron, R. (1967) *Main Currents in Sociological Thought*, London: Weidenfeld and Nicolson.

Arrow, K., Bowles, S. and Durlauf, S. (eds) (2000) *Meritocracy and Economic Inequality*, Princeton, NJ: Princeton University Press.

Arum, R., Gamoran, A. and Shavit, Y. (2007) 'More Inclusion than Diversion: Expansion, Differientation and Market Structure in Higher Education' in Shavit, Y., Arum, R. and Gamoran, A. (eds) *Stratification in Higher Education: A Comparative Study*, Stanford, CA: Stanford University Press, 1–35.

Aschaffenburg, K. and Maas, I. (1997) 'Cultural and Educational Careers: The Dynamics of Social Reproduction', *American Sociological Review*, 62(4), 573–87

Ashenfelter, O. and Krueger, A. (1994) 'Estimates of the Economic Return to Schooling from a New Sample of Twins', *American Economic Review*, 84(5), 1157–73.

Aughinbaugh, A. and Gittleman, M. (2003) 'Does Money Matter? A Comparison of the Effect of Income on Child Development in the United States and Great Britain', *Journal of Human Resources*, 38(2), 416–40.

Ayalon, H. and Shavit, Y. (2004) 'Educational Reforms and Inequalities in Israel: The MMI Hypothesis Revisited', *Sociology of Education*, 77(2), 103–20.

Baker, L. A., Treloar, S. A., Reynolds, C. A., Heath, A. C. and Martin, N. G. (1996) 'Genetics of Educational Attainment in Australian Twins: Sex Differences and Secular Changes', *Behavior Genetics*, 26(2), 89–102.

Baker, T. L. and Vélez, W. (1996) 'Access to and Opportunity in Post-Secondary Education in the United States: A Review', *Sociology of Education*, 69(Extra Issue), 82–101.

Bar Haim, E. and Shavit, Y. (2013) 'Expansion and Inequality of Educational Opportunity: A Comparative Study', *Research in Social Stratification and Mobility*, 31(1), 22–31.

Barber, N. (2005) 'Educational and Ecological Correlates of IQ: A Cross-National Investigation', *Intelligence*, 33(3), 273–84.

Barone, C. (2006) 'Cultural Capital, Ambition and the Explanation of Inequalities in Learning Outcomes: A Comparative Analysis', *Sociology*, 40(6), 1039–58.

Barone, C. (2009) 'A New Look at Schooling Inequalities in Italy and Their Trends Over Time', *Research in Social Stratification and Mobility*, 27(2), 92–109.

Barron, J. M., Ewing, B. T. and Waddell, G. R. (2000) 'The Effects of High School Athletic Participation on Education and Labour Market Outcomes', *Review of Economics and Statistics*, 82(3), 409–21.

Bartels, M., Rietveld, M. J. H., van Baal, G. C. M. and Boomsma, D. I. (2002a) 'Genetic and Environmental Influences on the Development of Intelligence', *Behavior Genetics*, 32(4), 237–49.

Bartels, M., Rietveld, M. J. H., van Baal, G. C. M. and Boomsma, D. I. (2002b) 'Heritability of Educational Achievement in 12-Year-Olds and the Overlap with Cognitive Ability', *Twin Research*, 5(6), 544–53.

Bassani, C. (2008) 'Social Capital and Disparities in Canadian Youth's Mathematics Achievement', *Canadian Journal of Education*, 31(3), 727–60.

Baumert, J., Lüdtke, O., Trautwein, U. and Brunner, M. (2009) 'Large-Scale Student Assessment Studies Measure the Results of Processes of Knowledge Acquisition: Evidence in Support of the Distinction Between Intelligence and Student Achievement', *Educational Research Review*, 4(3), 165–76.

Beblo, M. and Lauer, C. (2004) 'Do Family Resources Matter? Educational Attainment During Transition in Poland', *Economics of Transition*, 12(3), 537–58.

Beck, U. (1992) *Risk Society: Towards a New Modernity*, New Delhi: Sage.

Beck, U. and Beck-Gernsheim, E. (2002) *Individualization: Institutionalized Individualism and Its Social and Political Consequences*, London: Sage.

Becker, G. S. (1975) *Human Capital*, 2nd edn., New York: Columbia University Press.

Becker, G. S. and Tomes, N. (1986) 'Human Capital and the Rise and Fall of Families', *Journal of Labor Economics*, 43(3), S1–S39.

Becker, R. and Hecken, A. E. (2009) 'Why are Working-Class Children Diverted from Universities? An Empirical Assessment of the Diversion Thesis', *European Sociological Review*, 25(2), 233–50.

Behrman, J. R., Hrubec, Z., Taubman, P. and Wales, T. J. (1980) *Socioeconomic Success: A Study of the Effects of Genetic Endownments, Family Environment, and Schooling, Contributions to Economic Analyses*, Amsterdam: North-Holland Publishing.

Behrman, J. R. and Taubman, P. (1989) 'Is Schooling "Mostly in the Genes"? The Nature–Nuture Decomposition Using Data on Relatives', *Journal of Political Economy*, 97(6), 1425–46.

Bell, D. (1973) *The Coming of Post-Industrial Society: A Venture in Social Forecasting*, New York: Basic Books.

Beller, E. and Hout, M. (2006) 'Intergenerational Social Mobility: The United States in Comparative Perspective', *Future of Children*, 16(2), 19–36.

Belley, P. and Lochner, L. (2007) 'The Changing Role of Family Income and Ability in Determining Educational Achievement', *Journal of Human Capital*, 1(1), 37–89.

Belzil, C. and Hansen, J. (2003) 'Structural Estimates of the Intergenerational Education Correlation', *Journal of Applied Econometrics*, 18(6), 679–96.

Benin, M. H. and Johnson, D. R. (1984) 'Sibling Similarities in Educational Attainment: A Comparison of Like-Sex and Cross-Sex Sibling Pairs', *Sociology of Education*, 57(1), 11–21.

Berger, P. L. (1992) 'Sociology: A Disinvitation?', *Society*, 30(November/December), 12–18.

Berger, P. L. (2002) 'Whatever Happened to Sociology?', *First Things*, 2002(October).

Bergman, M. M. and Joye, D. (2005) 'Comparing Social Stratification Schemata:

CAMSIS, CSP-CH, Goldthorpe, ISCO-88, Treiman, and Wright' in Blackburn, R. M., *Cambridge Studies in Social Research*, Volume 10, Cambridge: SSRG Publications.

Bernstein, B. (1971) *Class, Codes and Control*, London: Routledge and Kegan Paul.

Bielby, W. T., Hauser, R. M. and Featherman, D. L. (1977) 'Response Errors of Black and Nonblack Males in Models of the Inter-generational Transmission of Socioeconomic Status', *American Journal of Sociology*, 82(6), 1242–88.

Björklund, A. and Jäntti, M. (1997) 'Integenerational Income Mobility in Sweden Compared to the United States', *American Economic Review*, 87(5), 1009–17.

Björklund, A., Eriksson, K. H. and Jäntti, M. (2009a) 'IQ and Family Background: Are Associations Strong or Weak?', *B. E. Journal of Economic Analysis and Policy*, 10(1), Article 2.

Björklund, A., Jäntti, M. and Lindquist, M. J. (2009b) 'Family Background and Income During the Rise of the Welfare State: Brother Correlations in Income for Swedish Men Born 1932–1968', *Journal of Public Economics*, 93(5–6), 671–80.

Björklund, A., Jäntti, M. and Solon, G. (2005) 'Influences of Nature and Nuture on Earnings Variation' in Bowles, S., Gintis, H. and Osborne Groves, M. (eds) *Unequal Chances: Family Background and Economic Success*, Princeton, NJ: Russell Sage Foundation, Princeton University Press, 145–64.

Björklund, A., Jäntti, M. and Solon, G. (2007) 'Nature and Nurture in the Intergenerational Transmission of Socioeconomic Status: Evidence from Swedish Children and Their Biological and Rearing Parents', *B. E. Journal of Economic Analysis and Policy*, 7(2), Article 4.

Björklund, A., Lindal, M. and Plug, E. (2006) 'The Origins of Intergenerational Associations: Lessons from Swedish Adoption Data', *Quarterly Journal of Economics*, 121(3), 999–1028.

Black, S. E. and Devereux, P. J. (2011) 'Recent Developments in Intergenerational Mobility', *Handbook of Labor Economics*, 4(Part B), 1487–541.

Black, S. E., Devereux, P. J. and Salvanes, K. G. (2009) 'Like Father, Like Son? A Note on the Intergenerational Transmission of IQ Scores', *Economics Letters*, 105(1), 138–40.

Blanden, J. and Gregg, P. (2004) 'Family Income and Educational Attainment: A Review of Approaches and Evidence for Britain', *Oxford Review of Economic Policy*, 20(2), 245–63.

Blanden, J., Goodman, A., Gregg, P. and Machin, S. (2004) 'Changes in Intergenerational Mobility in Britain' in Corak, M. (ed.) *Generational Income Mobility in North America and Europe*, Cambridge: Cambridge University Press, 123–46.

Blanden, J., Gregg, P. and Machin, S. (2005) *Intergenerational Mobility in Europe and North America*, London: Centre for Economic Performance, London School of Economics.

Blau, D. M. (1999) 'The Effect of Income on Child Development', *Review of Economics and Statistics*, 81(2), 261–76.

Blau, P. M. and Duncan, O. D. (1967) *The American Occupational Structure*, New York: John Wiley.

Blishen, B. R. and McRoberts, H. A. (1976) 'A Revised Socioeconomic Index for Occupations in Canada', *Canadian Review of Sociology and Anthropology*, 13(1), 71–9.

Blossfeld, H.-P. (1993) 'Changes in Educational Opportunities in the Federal Republic of Germany: A Longitudinal Study of Cohorts Born Between 1916 and 1965' in Shavit, Y. and Blossfeld, H.-P. (eds) *Persistent Inequality: Changing Educational Attainment in Thirteen Countries*, Boulder, CO: Westview, 51–74.

Blossfeld, H.-P. and Shavit, Y. (1993) 'Persisting Barriers: Changes in Educational Barriers in Thirteen Countries' in Shavit, Y. and Blossfeld, H.-P. (eds) *Persistent Inequality: Changing Educational Attainment in Thirteen Countries*, Boulder, CO: Westview, 1–24.

Boliver, V. (2011) 'Expansion, Differentiation, and the Persistence of Social Class Inequalities in British Higher Education', *Higher Education*, 61(3), 229–42.

Bond, R. and Saunders, P. (1999) 'Routes of Success: Influences on the Occupational Attainment of Young British Males', *British Journal of Sociology*, 50(2), 217–49.

Bond, T. G. and Fox, C. M. (2001) *Applying the Rasch Model: Fundamental Measurement in the Social Sciences*, Mahwah, NJ: Lawrence Erlbaum Associates.

Borus, M. E. and Nestel, G. (1973) 'Response Bias in Reports of Father's Education and Socioeconomic Status', *Journal of the American Statistical Association*, 68(344), 816–20.

Bouchard, T. J. and McGue, M. (1981) 'Familial Studies of Intelligence: A Review', *Science*, 212(4498), 1055–9.

Bouchard, T. J., Lykken, D. T., McGue, M., Segal, N. L. and Tellegen, A. (1990) 'Sources of Human Psychological Differences: The Minnesota Study of Twins Reared Apart', *Science*, 250(4978), 223–8.

Boudon, R. (1974) *Education, Opportunity and Social Inequality: Changing Prospects in Western Society*, New York: Wiley–Interscience.

Bound, J., Jaeger, D. A. and Baker, R. M. (1995) 'Problems with Instrumental Variables Estimation When the Correlation Between the Instruments and the Endogenous Explanatory Variable is Weak', *Journal of the American Statistical Association*, 90(430), 443–50.

Bourdieu, P. (1977) 'Cultural Reproduction and Social Reproduction' in Karabel, J. and Halsey, A. H. (eds) *Power and Ideology in Education*, Oxford: Oxford University Press, 487–511.

Bourdieu, P. (1986) 'The Forms of Capital' in Richardson, J. E. (ed.) *Handbook of Theory of Research for the Sociology of Education*, New York: Greenwood, 241–58.

Bourdieu, P. and Passeron, J.-C. (1977) *Reproduction in Education, Society and Culture*, London: Sage.

Bowles, S. (1972) 'Schooling and Inequality from Generation to Generation', *Journal of Political Economy*, 80(3), S219–51

Bowles, S. and Gintis, H. (1976) *Schooling in Capitalist America: Educational Reform and the Contradictions of Economic Life*, New York: Basic Books.

Bowles, S. and Gintis, H. (1977) 'IQ in the US Class Structure', in Karabel, J. and Halsey, A. H. (eds) *Power and Ideology in Education*, New York: Oxford University Press, 215–32.

Bowles, S. and Gintis, H. (2002a) 'The Inheritance of Inequality', *Journal of Economic Perspectives*, 16(3), 3–30.

Bowles, S. and Gintis, H. (2002b) *Schooling in Capitalist America Revisited*, *Sociology of Education*, 75(1), 1–18.

Bowles, S. and Nelson, V. I. (1974) 'The "Inheritance of IQ" and the Intergenerational Reproduction of Economic Inequality', *Review of Economics and Statistics*, 56(1), 39–51.

Bowles, S., Gintis, H. and Osborne, M. (2001) 'The Determinants of Earnings: A Behavioral Approach', *Journal of Economic Literature*, 39(4), 1137–76.
Boyd, M. (2008) 'A Socioeconomic Scale for Canada: Measuring Occupational Status from the Census', *Canadian Review of Sociology/Revue Canadienne de Sociologie*, 45(1), 51–91.
Boyd, M., Goyer, J., Jones, F. E. and McRoberts, H. A. (1985) *Ascription and Achievement in Mobility and Status Attainment in Canada*, Ottawa: Carelton University Press.
Bratti, M. (2007) 'Parents' Income and Children's School Drop–Out at 16 in England and Wales: Evidence from the 1970 British Cohort Study', *Review of Economics of the Household*, 5(1), 15–40.
Brauns, H. and Steinmann, S. (1997) *Educational Reform in France, West Germany, the United Kingdom and Hungary: Updating the CASMIN Educational Classification*, Mannheim: Mannheim Centre for European Social Research (MZES).
Braverman, H. (1974) *Labor and Monopoly Capital: The Degradation of Work in the Twentieth Century*, New York: Monthly Review Press.
Breen, R. (ed.) (2004) *Social Mobility in Europe*, Oxford: Oxford University Press.
Breen, R. (2010) 'Educational Expansion and Social Mobility in the 20th Century', *Social Forces*, 89(2), 365–88.
Breen, R. and Goldthorpe, J. H. (1997) 'Explaining Educational Differentials: Towards a Formal Rational Action Theory', *Rationality and Society*, 9(3), 275–305.
Breen, R. and Goldthorpe, J. H. (1999) 'Class Inequality and Meritocracy: A Critique of Saunders and an Alternative Analysis', *British Journal of Sociology*, 50(1), 1–27.
Breen, R. and Goldthorpe, J. H. (2001) 'Class, Mobility and Merit. The Experience of Two British Cohorts', *European Sociological Review*, 17(2), 81–101.
Breen, R. and Jonsson, J. O. (2000) 'Analyzing Educational Careers: A Multinomial Transition Model', *American Sociological Review*, 65(5), 754–72.
Breen, R. and Jonsson, J. O. (2005) 'Inequality of Opportunity in Comparative Perspective', *Annual Review of Sociology*, 31, 223–43.
Breen, R. and Luijkx, R. (2004) 'Social Mobility in Europe Between 1970 and 2000' in Breen, R. (ed.) *Social Mobility in Europe*, Oxford: Oxford University Press, 37–76.
Breen, R., Luijkx, R., Müller, W. and Pollak, R. (2009) 'Non-Persistent Inequality in Educational Attainment: Evidence from Eight European Countries', *American Journal of Sociology*, 114(5), 1475–521.
Breen, R., Luijkx, R., Müller, W. and Pollak, R. (2010) 'Long-Term Trends in Educational Inequality in Europe: Class Inequalities and Gender Differences', *European Sociological Review*, 26(1), 31–48.
Bring, J. (1994) 'How to Standardize Regression-Coefficients', *American Statistician*, 48(3), 209–13.
Broom, L. and Jones, F. L. (1976) *Opportunity and Attainment in Australia*, Canberra: Australian National University Press.
Broom, L., Jones, F. L., McDonald, P. and Williams, T. (1980) *The Inheritance of Inequality*, London: Routledge and Kegan Paul.
Brown, R. T., Reynolds, C. R. and Whitaker, J. S. (1999) 'Bias in Mental Test Since *Bias in Mental Testing*', *School Psychology Quarterly*, 14(3), 208–38.

Brown, S., McIntosh, S. and Taylor, K. (2011) 'Following in Your Parents' Footsteps? Empirical Analysis of Matched Parent–Offspring Test Scores', *Oxford Bulletin of Economics and Statistics*, 73(1), 40–58.

Brunello, G. and Checchi, D. (2007) 'Does School Tracking Affect Equality Of Opportunity? New International Evidence', *Economic Policy*, 22(52), 781–861.

Brunner, M. (2008) 'No *g* in Education?', *Learning and Individual Differences*, 18(2), 152–65.

Buchmann, C. (2002) 'Measuring Family Background in International Studies of Education: Conceptual Issues and Methodological Challenges' in Porter, A. C. and Gamoran, A. (eds) *Methodological Advances in Cross-National Surveys of Educational Achievement*, Washington, DC: National Academy Press, 150–97.

Buchmann, C. and DiPrete, T. A. (2006) 'The Growing Female Advantage in College Completion: The Role of Family Background and Academic Achievement', *American Sociological Review*, 71(4), 515–41.

Buchmann, C. and Park, H. (2009) 'Stratification and the Formation of Expectations in Highly Differentiated Educational Systems', *Research in Social Stratification and Mobility*, 27(4), 245–67.

Buchmann, M., Charles, M. and Sacchi, S. (1993) 'The Lifelong Shadow: Social Origins and Educational Opportunity in Switzerland' in Shavit, Y. and Blossfeld, H.-P. (eds) *Persistent Inequality: Changing Educational Attainment in Thirteen Countries*, Boulder, CO: Westview, 177–92.

Burawoy, M. (1979) *Manufacturing Consent: Changes in the Labor Process Under Monopoly Capitalism*, Chicago: University of Chicago Press.

Burawoy, M. (2005) 'For Public Sociology (2004 ASA Presidential Address)', *British Journal of Sociology*, 56(2), 259–94.

Burbidge, J. B., Magee, L. and Robb, A. L. (2002) 'The Education Premium in Canada and the United States', *Canadian Public Policy/Analyse de Politiques*, 28(2), 203–17.

Bynner, J. and Joshi, H. (2002) 'Equality and Opportunity in Education: Evidence from the 1958 and 1970 Birth Cohort Studies', *Oxford Review of Education*, 28(4), 405–25.

Cameron, S. V. and Heckman, J. J. (1998) 'Life Cycle Schooling and Dynamic Selection Bias: Models and Evidence for Five Cohorts of American Males', *Journal of Political Economy*, 106(2), 262–333.

Cameron, S. V. and Heckman, J. J. (2001) 'The Dynamics of Educational Attainments for Black, Hispanic, and White Males', *Journal of Political Economy*, 109(3), 455–99.

Cappell, C. L. (1995) 'An Empirical Comment on the State of Sociology', *American Sociologist*, 26(2), 78–123.

Card, D. (1999) 'The Causal Effect of Education on Earnings' in Card, D. and Orley, C. A. (eds) *Handbook of Labor Economics*, Amsterdam: Elsevier, 1801–63.

Cardak, B. A. and Ryan, C. (2009) 'Participation in Higher Education in Australia: Equity and Access', *Economic Record*, 85(271), 433–48.

Carlson, M. J. and Corcoran, M. E. (2001) 'Family Structure and Children's Behavioral and Cognitive Outcomes', *Journal of Marriage and Family*, 63(3), 779–92.

Carneiro, P. and Heckman, J. J. (2002) 'The Evidence on Credit Constraints in Post-Secondary Schooling', *Economic Journal*, 112(482), 705–34.

Carroll, J. B. (1993) *Human Cognitive Abilities: A Survey of Factor-Analytic Studies*,

New York: Cambridge University Press.
Carroll, J. B. (1995) 'Reflections on Stephen Jay Gould's *The Mismeasure of Man* (1981): A Retrospective Review', *Intelligence*, 21(2), 121–34.
Carroll, J. B. (2003) 'The Higher-Stratum Structure of Cognitive Abilities: Current Evidence Supports *g* and About Ten Broad Factors' in Nyborg, H. (ed.) *The Scientific Study of General Intelligence: Tribute to Arthur R. Jensen*, New York: Pergamon, 5–22.
Caspi, A., Moffitt, T. E., Entner Wright, B. R. and Suva, P. A. (1998) 'Early Failure in the Labor Market: Childhood and Adolescent Predictors of Unemployment in the Transition to Adulthood', *American Sociological Review*, 63(3), 424–51.
Cataldi, E. F., Laird, J. and Kewal Ramani, A. (2009) *High School Dropout and Completion Rates in the United States: 2007*, Washington, DC: National Center for Education Statistics, Institute of Education Sciences, US Department of Education.
Ceci, S. J. (1991) 'How Much Does Schooling Influence General Intelligence and Its Cognitive Components? A Reassessment of the Evidence', *Developmental Psychology*, 27(5), 703–22.
Cesarini, D. (2013) *Family Influences on Productive Skills, Human Capital and Lifecycle Income*, Department of Economics, Massachusetts Institute of Technology, Cambridge, MA: unpublished thesis.
CESifo (2011) Tuition Fees in Europe 2010/2011, *CESifo DICE Report*, 9(1), 53–5.
Charles, K. K. and Hurst, E. (2003) 'The Correlation of Wealth Across Generations', *Journal of Political Economy*, 111(6), 1155–82.
Cheung, S. Y. and Egerton, M. (2007) 'Great Britain: Higher Education Expansion and Reform – Changing Educational Inequalities' in Shavit, Y., Arum, R. and Gamoran, A. (eds) *Stratification in Higher Education: A Comparative Study*, Stanford, CA: Stanford University Press, 195–219.
Chevalier, A. and Lanot, G. (2002) 'The Relative Effect of Family Characteristics and Financial Situation on Educational Achievement', *Education Economics*, 10(2), 165–81.
Christofides, L. N., Cirello, J. and Hoy, M. (2001) 'Family Income and Postsecondary Education in Canada', *Canadian Journal of Higher Education*, 31(1), 177–208.
Cobalti, A. and Schizzerotto, A. (1993) 'Inequality of Educational Opportunity in Italy' in Shavit, Y. and Blossfeld, H.-P. (eds) *Persistent Inequality: Changing Educational Attainment in Thirteen Countries*, Boulder, CO: Westview, 155–76.
Coelli, M. and Wilkins, R. (2009) 'Credential Changes and Education Earnings Premia in Australia', *Economic Record*, 85(270), 239–59.
Cole, S. (1994a) 'Introduction: What's Wrong with Sociology?', *Sociological Forum*, 9(2), 129–31.
Cole, S. (1994b) 'Why Sociology Doesn't Make Progress Like the Natural Sciences', *Sociological Forum*, 9(2), 133–54.
Coleman, J. S. (1987) 'Families and Schools', *Educational Researcher*, 16(6), 32–8.
Coleman, J. S. (1988) 'Social Capital in the Generation of Human Capital', *American Journal of Sociology*, 94, S95–S120.
Coleman, J. S. and Hoffer, T. (1987) *Public and Private Schools. The Impact of Communities*, New York: Basic Books.

Coleman, J. S., Campbell, E. S., Hobson, C. J., McPartland, J., Mood, A. M., Weinfeld, F. D. and York, R. L. (1966) *Equality of Educational Opportunity*, Washington, DC: US Government Printing Office.

Coleman, J. S., Hoffer, T. and Kilgore, S. (1982) *High School Achievement: Public, Catholic, and Private Schools Compared*, New York: Basic Books.

Collins, R. (1971) 'Functional and Conflict Theories of Educational Stratification', *American Sociological Review*, 36(6), 1002–19.

Colom, R. and Flores-Mendoza, C. E. (2007) 'Intelligence Predicts Scholastic Achievement Irrespective of SES Factors: Evidence from Brazil', *Intelligence*, 35(3), 243–51.

Comber, L. C. and Keeves, J. P. (1973) *Science Education in Nineteen Countries.* International Studies in Evaluation I, New York: John Wiley and Sons.

Conley, D. (2001) 'Capital for College: Parental Assets and Postsecondary Schooling', *Sociology of Education*, 74(1), 59–72.

Conley, D. and Glauber, R. (2008) 'All in the Family? Family Composition, Resources, and Sibling Similarity in Socioeconomic Status', *Research in Social Stratification and Mobility*, 26(4), 297–306.

Connelly, R. (2012). 'Social Stratification and Cognitive Ability: An Assessment of the Influence of Childhood Ability Test Scores and Family Background on Occupational Position Across the Lifespan', in Lambert, P., Connelly, R., Blackburn, R. M. and Gayle, V. (eds) *Social Stratification: Trends and Processes*, London: Ashgate, 101–14.

Corak, M. (ed.) (2005) *Generational Income Mobility in North America and Europe*, Cambridge: Cambridge University Press.

Corak, M. (2006) *Do Poor Children Become Poor Adults? Lessons from a Cross Country Comparison of Generational Earnings Mobility*, Bonn: Forschungsinstitut zur Zukunft der Arbeit (Institute for the Study of Labor).

Corak, M. and Heisz, A. (1999) 'The Intergenerational Earnings and Income Mobility of Canadian Men: Evidence from Longitudinal Income Tax Data', *Journal of Human Resources*, 34(3), 504–33.

Corak, M., Lipps, G. and Zhao, J. (2003) *Family Income and Participation in Post-Secondary Education*, Ottawa: Statistics Canada.

Corcoran, M. (1992) 'Review: Background, Earnings, and the American Dream', *Contemporary Sociology*, 21(5), 603–9.

Corcoran, M., Jencks, C. and Olneck, M. (1976) 'The Effects of Family Background on Earnings', *American Economic Review*, 66(2), 430–5.

Coser, L. A. (1975) 'Presidential Address: Two Methods in Search of a Substance', *American Sociological Review*, 40(6), 691–700.

Covay, E. and Carbonaro, W. (2010) 'After the Bell: Participation in Extracurricular Activities, Classroom Behavior, and Academic Achievement', *Sociology of Education*, 83(1), 20–45.

Crook, C. (1997) *Cultural Practices and Socioeconomic Attainment: The Australian Experience*, Westport, CT: Greenwood Press.

Currie, J. and Thomas, D. (1999) 'The Intergenerational Transmission of "Intelligence": Down the Slippery Slopes of *The Bell Curve*', *Industrial Relations*, 38(3), 297–330.

Currie, J. and Thomas, D. (2001) 'Early Test Scores, School Quality and SES: Longrun Effects on Wage and Employment Outcomes', in Polachek, S. (ed.) *Worker Wellbeing in a Changing Labor Market*, Research in Labor Economics,

Volume 20, Bingley: Emerald, 103–32.
Curry, R. L. (1962) 'The Effect of Socio-Economic Status on the Scholastic Achievement of Sixth-Grade Children', *British Journal of Educational Psychology*, 32(P1), 46–9.
Curtis, D. D. and McMillan, J. (2008) *School Non-Completers: Profiles and Initial Destinations*, Longitudinal Surveys of Australian Youth Research Report 54, Melbourne: Australian Council for Educational Research.
Daniels, M., Devlin, B. and Roeder, K. (1997) 'Of Genes and IQ' in Devlin, B., Fienberg, S. E., Resnick, D. P. and Roeder, K. (eds) *Intelligence, Genes, and Success: Scientists Respond to* The Bell Curve, New York: Springer-Verlag, 45–70.
Daouli, J., Demoussis, M. and Giannakopoulos, N. (2010) 'Mothers, Fathers and Daughters: Intergenerational Transmission of Education in Greece', *Economics of Education Review*, 29(1), 83–93.
Davies, P., Telhaj, S., Hutton, D., Adnett, N. and Coe, R. (2008) 'Socioeconomic Background, Gender and Subject Choice in Secondary Schooling', *Educational Research*, 50(3), 235–48.
Davis, J. A. (1982) 'Achievement Variables and Class Cultures: Family, Schooling, Job, and Forty-Nine Dependent Variables in the Cumulative GSS', *American Sociological Review*, 47(5), 569–86.
Davis, J. A. (1994) 'What's Wrong with Sociology?', *Sociological Forum*, 9(2), 179–97.
Davis, J. T. Jr. (1995) 'The Occupational Mobility of Black Males Revisited: Does Race Matter?', *Social Science Journal*, 32(2), 121–36.
Davis, O. S. P., Haworth, C. M. A. and Plomin, R. (2009) 'Dramatic Increase in Heritability of Cognitive Development from Early to Middle Childhood: An 8-Year Longitudinal Study of 8,700 Pairs of Twins: Research Article', *Psychological Science*, 20(10), 1301–8.
Davis, P., McLeod, K., Ransom, M., Ongley, P., Pearce, N. and Howden-Chapman, P. (1999) 'The New Zealand Socioeconomic Index: Developing and Validating an Occupationally Derived Indicator of Socio-Economic Status', *Australian and New Zealand Journal of Public Health*, 23(1), 27–33.
de Graaf, N. D., de Graaf, P. M. and Kraaykamp, G. (2000) 'Parental Cultural Capital and Educational Attainment in the Netherlands: A Refinement of the Cultural Capital Perspective', *Sociology of Education*, 73(2), 92–111.
de Graaf, P. M. (1986) 'The Impact of Financial and Cultural Resources on Educational Attainment in the Netherlands', *Sociology of Education*, 59(4), 237–46.
de Graaf, P. M. (1988) 'Parents' Financial and Cultural Resources, Grades, and Transition to Secondary School in the Federal Republic of Germany', *European Sociological Review*, 4(3), 209–21.
de Graaf, P. M. and Ganzeboom, H. B. G. (1993) 'Family Background and Educational Attainment in the Netherlands for the 1891–1960 Birth Cohorts' in Shavit, Y. and Blossfeld, H.-P. (eds) *Persistent Inequality: Changing Educational Attainment in Thirteen Countries*, Boulder, CO: Westview, 75–99.
de Graaf, P. M. and Huinink, J. J. (1992) 'Trends in Measured and Unmeasured Effects of Family Background on Educational Attainment and Occupational Attainment in the Federal Republic of Germany', *Social Science Research*, 21(1), 84–112.
de Graaf, P. M., Ganzeboom, H. B. G. and Kalmijn, M. (1989) 'Cultural and

Economic Dimensions of Occupational Status' in Jansen, W., Dronkers, J. and Verrips, K. (eds) *Similar or Different? Continuities in Research on Social Stratification*, Amsterdam: SISWO, 53–74.
de Vries, J. and de Graaf, P. M. (2006) 'The Reliability of Family Background Effects on Status Attainment: Multiple Informant Models', *Quality and Quantity*, 42(2), 203–34.
Dearden, L., Machin, S. and Reed, H. (1997) 'Intergenerational Mobility in Britain', *Economic Journal*, 107(440), 47–66.
Deary, I. J. (2012) 'Intelligence', *Annual Review of Psychology*, 63, 453–82.
Deary, I. J., Der, G. and Shenkin, S. D. (2005a) 'Does Mother's IQ Explain the Association Between Birth Weight and Cognitive Ability in Childhood?', *Intelligence*, 33(5), 445–54.
Deary, I. J., Johnson, W. and Houlihan, L. M. (2009) 'Genetic Foundations of Human Intelligence', *Human Genetics*, 126(1), 215–32.
Deary, I. J., Penke, L. and Johnson, W. (2010) 'The Neuroscience of Human Intelligence Differences', *Nature Reviews Neuroscience*, 11(3), 201–11.
Deary, I. J., Strand, S., Smith, P. and Fernandes, C. (2007) 'Intelligence and Educational Achievement', *Intelligence*, 35(1), 13–21.
Deary, I. J., Taylor, M. D., Hart, C. L., Wilson, V., Smith, G. D., Blane, D. and Starr, J. M. (2005b) 'Intergenerational Social Mobility and Mid-Life Status Attainment: Influences of Childhood Intelligence, Childhood Social Factors, and Education', *Intelligence*, 33(5), 455–72.
Deary, I. J., Whiteman, M. C., Starr, J. M., Whalley, L. J. and Fox, H. C. (2004) 'The Impact of Childhood Intelligence on Later Life: Following Up the Scottish Mental Surveys of 1932 and 1947', *Journal of Personality and Social Psychology*, 86(1), 130–47.
Denny, K., Harmon, C. and O'Sullivan, V. (2004) *Education, Earnings and Skills: A Multicountry Comparison*, Dublin: Institute of Fiscal Studies.
Devlin, B., Fienberg, S., Resnick, D. and Roeder, K. (eds) (1997) *Intelligence, Genes, and Success: Scientists Respond to* The Bell Curve, New York: Springer-Verlag.
Devroye, D. and Freeman, R. (2001) *Does Inequality in Skills Explain Inequality of Earnings Across Countries?*, Cambridge, MA: National Bureau of Economic Research.
DiMaggio, P. (1982) 'Cultural Capital and School Success: The Impact of Status Culture Participation on the Grades of US High School Students', *American Sociological Review*, 47(2), 189–201.
DiMaggio, P. and Mohr, J. (1985) 'Cultural Capital, Educational Attainment, and Marital Selection', *American Journal of Sociology*, 90(6), 1231–61.
DiPrete, T. A. and Grusky, D. B. (1990) 'Structure and Trend in the Process of Stratification for American Men and Women', *American Journal of Sociology*, 96(1), 107–43.
Downey, D. B., von Hippel, P. T. and Broh, B. A. (2004) 'Are Schools the Great Equalizer? Cognitive Inequality During the Summer Months and the School Year', *American Sociological Review*, 69(5), 613–35.
Dronkers, J. (1993) 'Is the Importance of the Family Decreasing? Evidence Regarding Dutch Sibling Data and Educational Attainment' in Meeus, W., de Goede, M., Kox, W. and Hurrelmann, K. (eds) *Adolescence, Careers and Cultures*, Berlin: Walter de Gruyter, 267–78.

Dronkers, J. and Robert, P. (2008) 'Differences in Scholastic Achievement of Public, Private Government-Dependent, and Private Independent Schools: A Cross-National Analysis', *Educational Policy*, 22(4), 541–77.
Dumais, S. A. (2002) 'Cultural Capital, Gender, and School Success: The Role of Habitus', *Sociology of Education*, 75(1), 44–68.
Dumais, S. A. and Ward, A. (2010) 'Cultural Capital and First-Generation College Success', *Poetics*, 38(3), 245–65.
Dumay, X. and Dupriez, V. (2008) 'Does the School Composition Effect Matter? Evidence from Belgian Data', *British Journal of Educational Studies*, 56(4), 440–77.
Duncan, G., Kalil, A., Mayer, S. S., Tepper, R. and Payne, M. R. (2005) 'The Apple Does Not Fall Far from the Tree' in Bowles, S., Gintis, H. and Osborne Groves, M. (eds) *Unequal Chances: Family Background and Economic Success*, Princeton, NJ: Russell Sage Foundation, Princeton University Press, 23–79.
Duncan, O. D. (1961) 'A Socioeconomic Index for all Occupations' in Reiss, A. J. J. (ed.) *Occupations and Social Status*, Glencoe, IL: Free Press, 109–38.
Duncan, O. D. (1966) 'Path Analysis: Sociological Examples', *American Journal of Sociology*, 72(1), 1–16.
Duncan, O. D., Featherman, D. L. and Duncan, B. (1972) *Socioeconomic Background and Achievement*, New York: Seminar Press.
Dunlop, J. T., Harbison, F. H., Kerr, C. and Myers, C. A. (1975) *Industrialism and Industrial Man Reconsidered*, Princeton: The Inter-University Study of Human Resources in National Development.
Duru-Bellat, M. (2008) 'Recent trends in Social Reproduction in France: Should the Political Promises of Education be Revisited?', *Journal of Education Policy*, 23(1), 81–95.
Duru-Bellat, M. and Kieffer, A. (2000) 'Inequalities in Educational Opportunities in France: Educational Expansion, Democratization or Shifting Barriers?', *Journal of Education Policy*, 15(3), 333–52.
Eaves, L., Heath, A. C., Martin, N. G., Maes, H., Neale, M., Kendler, K., Kirk, K. and Corey, L. (1999) 'Comparing the Biological and Cultural Inheritance of Personality and Social Attitudes in the Virginia 30,000 Study of Twins and Their Relatives', *Twin Research*, 2(2), 62–80.
Eckland, B. K. (1965) 'Ability, Education, and Occupational Mobility', *American Sociological Review*, 30(5), 735–46.
Eckland, B. K. (1967) 'Genetics and Sociology: A Reconsideration', *American Sociological Review*, 32(3), 173–94.
Eide, E. R. and Showalter, M. H. (1999) 'Factors Affecting the Transmission of Earnings Across Generations: A Quantile Regression Approach', *Journal of Human Resources*, 34(2), 253–67.
Epstein, D. and Winship, C. (2005) 'Mental Ability – Uni or Multidimensional? An Analysis of Effects' in Morgan, S. L., Grusky, D. B. and Fields, G. S. (eds) *Mobility and Inequality: Frontiers of Research from Sociology and Economics*, Stanford, CA: Stanford University Press, 259–89.
Erikson, R. and Goldthorpe, J. H. (1992) *The Constant Flux: A Study in Class Mobility in Industrial Nations*, Oxford: Clarendon Press.
Erikson, R. and Goldthorpe, J. H. (2010) 'Has Social Mobility in Britain Decreased? Reconciling Divergent Findings on Income and Class Mobility', *British Journal of Sociology*, 61(2), 211–30.

Erikson, R. and Jonsson, J. O. (1996) 'Explaining Class Inequalities in Education: The Swedish Test Case' in Erikson, R. and Jonsson, J. O. (eds) *Can Education Be Equalized? The Swedish Case in Comparative Perspective*, Boulder, CO: Westview, 1–63.

Erikson, R. and Rudolphi, F. (2010) 'Change in Social Selection to Upper Secondary School – Primary and Secondary Effects in Sweden', *European Sociological Review*, 26(3), 291–305.

Erikson, R., Goldthorpe, J. H. and Portocarero, L. (1979) 'Intergenerational Class Mobility in Three Western Societies: England, France and Sweden', *British Journal of Sociology*, 30(4), 415–41.

Erikson, R., Goldthorpe, J. H., Jackson, M., Yaish, M. and Cox, D. R. (2005) 'On Class Differentials in Educational Attainment', *Proceedings of the National Academy of Sciences of the United States of America*, 102(27), 9730–3.

Ermisch, J. and Francesconi, M. (2004) 'Intergenerational Mobility in Britain: New Evidence from the British Household Panel Survey' in Corak, M. (ed.) *Income Mobility in North America and Europe*, Cambridge: Cambridge University Press, 147-89.

Evans, M. D. R., Kelley, J. and Kolosi, T. (1992) 'Images of Class: Public Perceptions in Hungary and Australia', *American Sociological Review*, 57(4), 461–82.

Evans, M. D. R., Kelley, J., Sikora, J. and Treiman, D. J. (2010) 'Family Scholarly Culture and Educational Success: Books and Schooling in 27 Nations', *Research in Social Stratification and Mobility*, 28(2), 171–97.

Eysenck, H. J. (1979) *The Structure and Measurement of Intelligence: With Contributions from David W. Fulker*, Berlin: Springer-Verlag.

Faasse, J. H., Bakker, B., Dronkers, J. and Schiff, H. (1987) 'The Impact of Educational Reform: Empirical Evidence from Two Dutch Generations', *Comparative Education*, 23(3), 261–77.

Fagerlind, I. (1975) *Formal Education and Adult Earnings: A Longitudinal Study on the Economic Benefits of Education*, Stockholm: Almquist and Wiksell.

Farber, H. S. and Gibbons, R. (1996) 'Learning and Wage Dynamics', *Quarterly Journal of Economics*, 111(4), 1006–47.

Farkas, G. (2003) 'Cognitive Skills and Non-Cognitive Traits and Behaviours in Stratification Processes', *Annual Review of Sociology*, 29, 241–62.

Farkas, G., Grobe, R. P., Sheehan, D. and Shuan, Y. (1990) 'Cultural Resources and School Success: Gender, Ethnicity, and Poverty Groups Within an Urban School District', *American Sociological Review*, 55(1), 127–42.

Featherman, D. L. and Hauser, R. M. (1976) 'Prestige or Socioeconomic Scales in the Study of Occupational Achievement?', *Sociological Methods and Research*, 4(4), 403–22.

Featherman, D. L. and Hauser, R. M. (1978) *Opportunity and Change*, New York: Academic Press.

Featherman, D. L., Jones, F. L. and Hauser, R. M. (1975) 'Assumptions of Social Mobility Research in the US: The Case of Occupational Status', *Social Science Research*, 4(4), 329–60.

Fejgin, N. (1995) 'Factors Contributing to the Academic Excellence of American Jewish and Asian Students', *Sociology of Education*, 68(1), 18–30.

Fergusson, D. M., Horwood, L. J. and Ridder, E. M. (2005) 'Show Me the Child at Seven II: Childhood Intelligence and Later Outcomes in Adolescence and Young

Adulthood', *Journal of Child Psychology and Psychiatry and Allied Disciplines*, 46(8), 850–8.
Fergusson, D. M., Horwood, L. J. and Boden, J. M. (2008) 'The Transmission of Social Inequality: Examination of the Linkages Between Family Socioeconomic Status in Childhood and Educational Achievement in Young Adulthood', *Research in Social Stratification and Mobility*, 26(3), 277–95.
Fertig, A. R. (2003) 'Trends in Intergenerational Earnings Mobility in the United States', *Journal of Income Distribution*, 12(3–4), 108–30.
Fienberg, S. E. and Resnick, D. P. (1997) 'Reexamining *The Bell Curve*' in Devlin, B., Fienberg, S. E., Resnick, D. P. and Roeder, K. (eds) *Intelligence, Genes, and Success: Scientists Respond to* The Bell Curve, New York: Springer-Verlag, 3–19.
Fisher, C. S., Hout, M., Jankowski, M. S., Lucas, S. R., Swidler, A. and Voss, K. (eds) (1996) *Inequality by Design: Cracking* The Bell Curve *Myth*, Princeton, NJ: Princeton University Press.
Flerea, S., Krajnca, M. T., Klanjšeka, R., Musila, B. and Kirbiša, A. (2010) 'Cultural Capital and Intellectual Ability as Predictors of Scholastic Achievement: A Study of Slovenian Secondary School Students', *British Journal of Sociology of Education*, 31(1), 47–58.
Fletcher, J. M. (2009) 'Beauty vs. Brains: Early Labor Market Outcomes of High School Graduates', *Economics Letters*, 105(3), 321–5.
Flynn, J. R. (1984) 'The Mean IQ of Americans: Massive Gains 1932 to 1978', *Psychological Bulletin*, 95(1), 29–51.
Flynn, J. R. (1987) 'Massive IQ Gains in 14 Nations: What IQ Tests Really Measure', *Psychological Bulletin*, 101(2), 171–91.
Flynn, J. R. (1999) 'Searching for Justice: The Discovery of IQ Gains Over Time', *American Psychologist*, 54(1), 5–20.
Foley, K., Gallipoli, G. and Green, D. A. (2009) *Ability, Parental Valuation of Education and the High School Dropout Decision*, London: Institute for Fiscal Studies.
Foshay, A. W., Thorndike, R. L., Hotyat, F., Pidgeon, D. A. and Walker, D. A. (1962) *Educational Achievement of Thirteen-Year-Olds in Twelve Countries*, Hamburg: UNESCO Institute for Education.
Frey, M. C. and Detterman, D. K. (2004) 'Scholastic Assessment or *g*? The Relationship Between the Scholastic Assessment Test and General Cognitive Ability', *Psychological Science*, 15(6), 373–8.
Fukuyama, F. (2006) *The End of History and the Last Man*, New York: Free Press.
Fullarton, S., Walker, M., Ainley, J. and Hillman, K. J. (2003) *Patterns of Participation in Year 12*, Longitudinal Surveys of Australian Youth Research Report 33, Melbourne: Australian Council of Research.
Gabay-Egozi, L., Shavit, Y. and Yaish, M. (2010) 'Curricular Choice: A Test of a Rational Choice Model of Education', *European Sociological Review*, 26(4), 447–63.
Galindo-Rueda, F. and Vignoles, A. (2005) 'The Declining Relative Importance of Ability in Predicting Educational Attainment', *Journal of Human Resources*, 40(2), 335–53.
Gamoran, A. (1996) 'Curriculum Standardization and Equality of Opportunity in Scottish Secondary Education: 1984–90', *Sociology of Education*, 69(1), 1–21.
Gamoran, A. (2001) 'American Schooling and Educational Inequality: A Forecast for the 21st Century', *Sociology of Education*, (Special Issue), 135–53.

Gamoran, A. and Mare, R. D. (1989) 'Secondary School Tracking and Educational Inequality: Compensation, Reinforcement, or Neutrality?', *American Journal of Sociology*, 94(5), 1146–83.

Ganzach, Y. (2000) 'Parent's Education, Cognitive Ability, Educational Expectations and Educational Attainment', *British Journal of Educational Psychology*, 70(3), 419–41.

Ganzeboom, H. B. G. and Treiman, D. J. (1993) 'Preliminary Results on Educational Expansion and Educational Opportunity in Comparative Perspective' in Becker, H. A. and Hermkens, P. L. J. (eds) *Solidarity of Generations*, Amsterdam: Thesis Publishers, 467–506.

Ganzeboom, H. B. G. and Treiman, D. J. (1996) 'Internationally Comparable Measures of Occupational Status for the 1988 International Standard Classifications of Occupations', *Social Science Research*, 25(3), 201–39.

Ganzeboom, H. B. G. and Treiman, D. J. (2007) 'Ascription and Achievement in Occupational Attainment in Comparative Perspective', presented at *Sixth Meeting of the Russell Sage Foundation/Carnegie Corporation University Working Groups on the Social Dimensions of Inequality*, Los Angeles, CA: UCLA.

Ganzeboom, H. B. G., de Graaf, P. M. and Treiman, D. J. (1992) 'A Standard International Socio-Economic Index of Occupational Status', *Social Science Research*, 21(1), 1–56.

Ganzeboom, H. B. G., Treiman, D. J. and Ultee, W. C. (1991) 'Comparative Intergenerational Stratification Research: Three Generations and Beyond', *Annual Review of Sociology*, 17, 277–302.

Gesthuizen, M., de Graaf, P. M. and Kraaykamp, G. (2005) 'The Changing Family Background of the Low-Educated in the Netherlands: Socio-Economic, Cultural, and Socio-Demographic Resources', *European Sociological Review*, 21(5), 441–52.

Giddens, A. (1978) *Capitalism and Modern Social Theory: An Analysis of the Writings of Marx, Durkheim and Max Weber*, Cambridge: Cambridge University Press.

Giddens, A. (1980) *The Class Structure of Advanced Societies,* 2nd edn., London: Hutchinson and Co.

Giddens, A. (1990) *Consequences of Modernity*, Cambridge: Polity Press.

Giddens, A. and MacKenzie, G. (eds) (1982) *Social Class and the Division of Labour: Essays in Honour of Ilya Neustadt*, Cambridge: Cambridge University Press.

Gilbert, D. L. and Kahl, J. A. (1992) *The American Class Structure: A New Synthesis*, 4th edn., Belmont, CA: Wadsworth Publishing Company.

Glaeser, E. L. and Maré, D. C. (2001) 'Cities and Skills', *Journal of Labor Economics*, 19(2), 316–42.

Goldberger, A. S. (1978) 'The Nonresolution of IQ Inheritance by Path Analysis', *American Journal of Human Genetics*, 30(4), 442–8.

Goldthorpe, J. H. (1982) 'On the Service Class: Its Formation and Future' in Giddens, A. and Mackenzie, G. (eds) *Social Class and the Division of Labour*, Cambridge: Cambridge University Press, 162–85.

Goldthorpe, J. H. (1990) 'A Response' in Clark, J., Mogdil, C. and Mogdil, S. (eds) *John H. Goldthorpe: Consensus and Controversy*, London: Falmer, 399–440.

Goldthorpe, J. H. (1996a) 'Class Analysis and the Reorientation of Class Theory: The Case of Persisting Differentials in Educational Attainment', *British Journal of Sociology*, 47(3), 481–505.

Goldthorpe, J. H. (1996b) 'Problems of "Meritocracy"' in Erikson, R. and Jonsson, J. O. (eds) *Can Education Be Equalized? The Swedish Case in Comparative Perspective*, Boulder, CO: Westview, 255–83.

Goldthorpe, J. H. (1997) 'Problems of Meritocracy' in Halsey, A. H., Lauder, H., Brown, P. and Wells, A. S. (eds) *Education: Culture, Economy, and Society*, Oxford: Oxford University Press, 663–82.

Goldthorpe, J. H. (2000) *On Sociology: Numbers, Narrative and the Integration of Research and Theory*, Oxford: Oxford University Press.

Goldthorpe, J. H. (2007) 'Cultural Capital: Some Critical Observations', *Sociologica*, 2007(2), 1–22.

Goldthorpe, J. H. and Hope, K. (1972) 'Occupational Grading and Occupational prestige' in Hope, K. (ed.) *The Analysis of Social Mobility: Methods and Approaches*, Oxford: Clarendon Press, 17–79.

Goldthorpe, J. H. and Llewellyn, C. (1977) 'Class Mobility in Modern Britain: Three Theses Examined', *Sociology*, 11(2), 257–87.

Goldthorpe, J. H., Llewellyn, C. and Payne, C. (1987) *Social Mobility and Class Structure in Modern Britain*, 2nd edn., Oxford: Clarendon Press.

Gorard, S. (2006) 'Is There a School Mix Effect?', *Educational Review*, 58(1), 87–94.

Gorard, S. (2008) 'A Re-consideration of Rates of 'Social Mobility' in Britain: or Why Research Impact Is Not Always a Good Thing', *British Journal of Sociology of Education*, 29(3), 317–24.

Gordon, R. A. and Rudert, E. E. (1979) 'Bad News Concerning IQ Tests', *Sociology of Education*, 52(3), 174–90.

Gottfredson, L. S. (1997a) 'Mainstream Science on Intelligence: An Editorial with 52 Signatories, History, and Bibliography', *Intelligence*, 24(1), 13–23.

Gottfredson, L. S. (1997b) 'Why *g* Matters: The Complexity of Everyday Life', *Intelligence*, 24(1), 79–132.

Gottfredson, L. S. (2008) 'Of What Value Is Intelligence?' in Prifitera, P., Saklofeske, D. H. and Weiss, L. G. (eds) *WISC–IV Clinical Assessment and Intervention*, 2nd edn., Amsterdam: Elsevier, 545–63.

Gottschalk, P. and Joyce, M. (1998) 'Cross-National Differences in the Rise in Earnings Inequality: Market and Institutional Factors', *Review of Economics and Statistics*, 80(4), 489–501.

Gould, S. J. (1996) *The Mismeasure of Man*, Revised edn., New York: W. W. Norton and Company.

Gouldner, A. W. (1970) *The Coming Crisis of Western Sociology*, New York: Basic Books.

Gouldner, A. W. (1979) *The Future of Intellectuals and the Rise of the New Class*, New York: Seabury Press.

Goyder, J. and Curtis, J. E. (1977) 'Occupational Mobility in Canada Over Four Generations', *Canadian Review of Sociology and Anthropology*, 14(3), 303–19.

Graetz, B. (1988) 'The Reproduction of Privilege in Australian Education', *British Journal of Sociology*, 39(3), 58–75.

Grawe, N. D. (2006) 'Lifecycle Bias in Estimates of Intergenerational Earnings Persistence', *Labour Economics*, 13(5), 551–70.

Grogger, J. and Eide, E. (1995) 'Changes in College Skills and the Rise in the College Wage Premium', *Journal of Human Resources*, 30(2), 280–310.

Grönqvistb, E., Öcker, B. and Vlachos, J. (2010) *The Intergenerational Transmission of Cognitive and Non-Cognitive Abilities*, Stockholm, Swedish Institute for Labour Market Policy Evaluation.
Grusky, D. B. and DiPrete, T. A. (1990) 'Recent Trends in the Process of Stratification', *Demography*, 27(4), 617–37.
Gustafsson, J. E. (2001) 'Schooling and Intelligence: Effects of Track of Study on Level and Profile of Cognitive Abilities', *International Education Journal*, 2(4), 166–86.
Guterman, S. S. (1979) 'IQ Tests in Research on Social Stratification: The Cross-Class Validity of the Tests as Measures of Scholastic Aptitude', *Sociology of Education*, 52(3), 163–73.
Güveli, A., Need, A. and de Graaf, N. D. (2007) 'Socio-Political, Cultural and Economic Preferences and Behaviour of the Social and Cultural Specialists and the Technocrats: Social Class or Education?', *Social Indicators Research*, 81(3), 597–631.
Habermas, J. (1975) *Legitimation Crisis*, Boston, MA: Beacon Press.
Habermas, J. (1984) *The Theory of Communicative Action, Volume 1: Reason and the Rationalization of Society*, London: Heinemann Educational.
Habermas, J. (1987) *The Theory of Communicative Action, Volume 2: Lifeworld and System: A Critique of Functionalist Reason*, London: Heinemann Educational.
Haegeland, T., Klette, T. J. and Salvanes, K. G. (1999) 'Declining Returns to Education in Norway? Comparing Estimates Across Cohorts, Sectors and Over Time', *Scandinavian Journal of Economics*, 101(4), 555–76.
Halsey, A. H. (1977) 'Towards Meritocracy. The Case of Britain' in Karabel, J. and Halsey, A. H. (eds) *Power and Ideology in Education*, New York: Oxford University Press, 173–85.
Halsey, A. H., Heath, A. F. and Ridge, J. M. (1980) *Origins and Destinations: Family, Class, and Education in Modern Britain*, Oxford: Clarendon Press.
Hamermesh, D. S. and Biddle, J. E. (1994) 'Beauty and the Labor Market', *American Economic Review*, 84(5), 1174–94.
Hansen, K. T., Heckman, J. J. and Mullen, K. J. (2004) 'The Effect of Schooling and Ability on Achievement Test Scores', *Journal of Econometrics*, 121(1–2), 39–98.
Hansen, M. (2010) 'Change in Intergenerational Economic Mobility in Norway: Conventional Versus Joint Classifications of Economic Origin', *Journal of Economic Inequality*, 8(2), 133–51.
Hansen, M. N. and Mastekaasa, A. (2006) 'Social Origins and Academic Performance at University', *European Sociological Review*, 22(3), 277–91.
Hanushek, E. A. (2006) 'School Resources' in Hanushek, E. A., Welch, F. (eds) *Handbook of the Economics of Education, Volume 2*, Amsterdam: North-Holland, 865–908.
Harden, K. P., Turkheimer, E. and Loehlin, J. C. (2007) 'Genotype by Environment Interaction in Adolescents' Cognitive Aptitude', *Behavior Genetics*, 37(2), 273–83.
Harding, D. J., Jencks, C., Lopoo, L. M. and Mayer, S. E. (2005) 'The Changing Effect of Family Background on the Incomes of American Adults' in Bowles, S., Gintis, H. and Groves, M. O. (eds) *Unequal Chances: Family Background and Economic Success*, Princeton, NJ: Russell Sage. Foundation Press, Princeton University Press, 100–44.

Harker, R. and Tymms, P. (2004) 'The Effects of Student Composition on School Outcomes', *School Effectiveness and School Improvement*, 15(2), 177–99.

Harper, B. (2000) 'Beauty, Stature and the Labour Market: A British Cohort Study', *Oxford Bulletin of Economics and Statistics*, 62(Suppl.), 771–800.

Hattie, J. A. C. (2009) *Visible Learning: A Synthesis of Over 800 Meta-Analyses Relating to Achievement*, London: Routledge.

Hauser, R. M. (1969) 'Schools and the Stratification Process', *American Journal of Sociology*, 74(6), 587–611.

Hauser, R. M. (1970) 'Context and Consex: A Cautionary Tale', *American Journal of Sociology*, 75(4), 645–64.

Hauser, R. M. (1974) 'Contextual Analysis Revisited', *Sociological Methods and Research*, 2(3), 365–73.

Hauser, R. M. (2000) *Meritocracy, Cognitive Ability, and the Sources of Occupational Success*, Department of Sociology, Center for Demography and Ecology, University of Wisconsin-Madison.

Hauser, R. M. (2010) *Intergenerational Economic Mobility in the United States: Measures, Differentials, and Trends*, CDE Working Paper, Madison: Department of Sociology, Center for Demography and Ecology, University of Wisconsin-Madison, unpublished.

Hauser, R. M. and Huang, M. H. (1997) 'Verbal Ability and Socioeconomic Success: A Trend Analysis', *Social Science Research*, 26(3), 331.

Hauser, R. M. and Mossel, P. A. (1988) 'Fraternal Resemblance in Educational Attainment and Occupational Status', *American Journal of Sociology*, 91(3), 650–73.

Hauser, R. M. and Sewell, W. H. (1986) 'Family Effects in Simple Models of Education, Occupational Status and Earnings: Findings from the Wisconsin and Kalamazoo Studies', *Journal of Labor Economics*, 4(3), S83–S115.

Hauser, R. M. and Warren, J. R. (1997) 'Socioeconomic Indexes for Occupations: A Review, Update, and Critique', *Sociological Methodology*, 27(1), 177–298.

Hauser, R. M. and Wong, R. S.-K. (1989) 'Sibling Resemblance and Intersibling Effects in Educational Attainment', *Sociology of Education*, 62(3), 149–71.

Hauser, R. M., Tsai, S.-L. and Sewell, W. H. (1983) 'A Model of Stratification with Response Error in Social and Psychological Variables', *Sociology of Education*, 56(1), 20–46.

Hauser, R. M., Warren, J. R., Huang, M.-H. and Carter, W. Y. (2000) 'Occupational Status, Education, and Social Mobility in the Meritocracy' in Arrow, K., Bowles, S. and Durlauf, S. (eds) *Meritocracy and Economic Inequality*, Princeton, NJ: Princeton University Press, 179–229.

Haveman, R. and Wolfe, B. (1995) 'The Determinants of Children's Attainments: A Review of Methods and Findings', *Journal of Economic Literature*, 33(4), 1829–78.

Hearn, J. C. (1984) 'The Relative Roles of Academic, Ascribed, and Socioeconomic Characteristics in College Destinations', *Sociology of Education*, 57(1), 22–30.

Hearn, J. C. (1988) 'Attendance at Higher Cost Colleges: Ascribed, Socioeconomic, and Academic Influences on Student Enrollment', *Economics of Education*, 7(1), 65–76.

Hearn, J. C. (1991) 'Academic and Nonacademic Influences on the College Destinations of 1980 High School Graduates', *Sociology of Education*, 64(3), 158–71.

Heath, A. C., Berg, K. J. E., Lindon, J., Solaas, M. H., Corey, L. A., Sundet, J. M., Magnus, P. M. and Nance, W. E. (1985) 'Education Policy and the Heritability of Educational Attainment', *Nature*, 314(6013), 734–6.

Heath, A. F. (1981) *Social Mobility*, Glasgow: Fontana.

Heath, A. F. (2000) 'The Political Arithmetic Tradition in the Sociology of Education', *Oxford Review of Education*, 26(3), 313–31.

Heath, A. F. and Clifford, P. (1990) 'Class Inequalities in Education in the Twentieth Century', *Journal of the Royal Statistical Society, Series A*, 153(1), 1–16.

Heath, A. F., Mills, C. and Roberts, J. (1992) 'Towards Meritocracy? Recent Evidence on an Old Problem' in Crouch, C. and Heath, A. (eds) *Social Research and Social Reform*, Oxford: Clarendon Press, 217–43.

Heckman, J., Stixrud, J. and Urzua, S. (2006) 'The Effects of Cognitive and Noncognitive Abilities on Labor Market Outcomes and Social Behavior', *Journal of Labor Economics*, 24(3), 411–82.

Heckman, J. J. and Rubinstein, Y. (2001) 'The Importance of Noncognitive Skills: Lessons from the GED Testing Program', *American Economic Review*, 91(2), 145–9.

Hedström, P. and Swedberg, R. (1996) 'Rational Choice, Empirical Research, and the Sociological Tradition', *European Sociological Review*, 12(2), 127–46.

Heineck, G. and Anger, S. (2010) 'The Returns to Cognitive Abilities and Personality Traits in Germany', *Labour Economics*, 17(3), 535–46.

Heise, D. R. (1972) 'Employing Nominal Variables, Induced Variables, and Block Variables in Path Analysis', *Sociological Methods and Research*, 1(2), 147–73.

Hellevik, O. (2013) 'Measuring Social Inequality in Educational Attainment' in Birkelund, G. E. (ed.) *Class and Stratification Analysis*, Comparative Social Research Vol. 30, Bingley: Emerald, 319–39.

Hemmings, B. and Kay, R. (2010) 'Prior Achievement, Effort, and Mathematics Attitude as Predictors of Current Achievement', *Australian Educational Researcher*, 37(2), 41–58.

Herrnstein, R. J. and Murray, C. (1994) *The Bell Curve: Intelligence and Class Structure in American Life*, New York: Free Press.

Hertz, T. (2005) 'Rags, Riches and Race: Intergenerational Economic Mobility of Black and White Families in the United States' in Bowles, S., Gintis, H. and Osborne Groves, M. (eds) *Unequal Chances: Family Background and Economic Success*, Princeton, NJ: Russell Sage Foundation, Princeton University Press, 165–91.

Hertz, T. (2006) *Understanding Mobility in America*, Washington, DC: Center for American Progress.

Hertz, T., Jayasundera, T., Piraino, P., Selcuk, S., Smithy, N. and Verashchagina, A. (2007) 'The Inheritance of Educational Inequality: International Comparisons and Fifty-Year Trends', *B. E. Journal of Economic Analysis and Policy*, 7(2), Article 10.

Hill, M. and Duncan, G. J. (1987) 'Parental Family Income and the Socioeconomic Attainment of Children', *Social Science Research*, 16(1), 39–73.

Hirvonen, L. H. (2008) 'Intergenerational Earnings Mobility Among Daughters and Sons: Evidence from Sweden and a Comparison with the United States', *American Journal of Economics and Sociology*, 67(5), 777–826.

Hobcraft, J. (2001) 'Intergenerational Transmission of Inequality in a British Birth

Cohort', Paper Presented at Population Association of America Annual Meeting, Washington, DC, 29–31 March.

Hodge, R. W., Treiman, D. J. and Rossi, P. H. (1966) 'A Comparison Study of Occupational Prestige' in Bendix, R. and Lipset, S. M. (eds) *Class, Status and Power: Social Stratification in Comparative Perspective*, 2nd edn., New York: Free Press, 309–21.

Holm, A. and Jæger, M. M. (2009) *Selection Bias in Educational Transition Models: Theory and Empirical Evidence*, Copenhagen: Centre for Applied Microeconometrics, Department of Economics, University of Copenhagen.

Holm, A. and Jæger, M. M. (2011) 'Dealing with Selection Bias in Educational Transition Models: The Bivariate Probit Selection Model', *Research in Social Stratification and Mobility*, 29(3), 311–22.

Horn, D. (2009) 'Age of Selection Counts: A Cross-Country Analysis of Educational Institutions', *Educational Research and Evaluation*, 15 (4), 343–66.

Horowitz, I. L. (1994) *The Decomposition of Sociology*, New York: Oxford University Press.

Hout, M. (2007) 'Maximally Maintained Inequality Revisited: Irish Educational Mobility in Comparative Perspective' in Hilliard, E. and Phádraig, M. N. (eds) *Changing Ireland in International Comparison*, Dublin: Liffey Press, 23–39.

Hout, M. and Dohan, D. P. (1996) 'Two Paths to Educational Opportunity: Class and Educational Selection in Sweden and the United States' in Erikson, R. and Jonsson, J. O. (eds) *Can Education Be Equalized? The Swedish Case in Comparative Perspective*, Boulder, CO: Westview, 183–206.

Hout, M. and Garnier, M. A. (1979) 'Curriculum Placement and Educational Stratification in France', *Sociology of Education*, 52(3), 146–56.

Hout, M., Raftery, A. E. and Bell, E. O. (1993) 'Making the Grade: Educational Stratification in the United States, 1925–1989' in Shavit, Y. and Blossfeld, H.-P. (eds) *Persistent Inequality: Changing Educational Attainment in Thirteen Countries*, Boulder, CO: Westview, 25–49.

Huang, L. (2009) 'Social Capital and Student Achievement in Norwegian Secondary Schools', *Learning and Individual Differences*, 19(2), 320–5.

Huber, J. (1995) 'Institutional Perspectives on Sociology', *American Journal of Sociology*, 101(1), 194–216.

Hunter, J. E. and Hamilton, M. A. (2002) 'The Advantages of Using Standardized Scores in Causal Analysis', *Human Communication Research*, 28(4), 552–61.

Husen, T. (1967) *International Study of Achievement in Mathematics. A Comparison of Twelve Countries*, Oxford: Pergamon Press.

Hyman, H. H. (1966) 'The Value Systems of Different Classes: A Social Psychological Contribution to the Analysis of Stratification' in Bendix, R. and Lipset, S. M. (eds) *Class, Status and Power: Social Stratification in Comparative Perspective*, 2nd edn., New York: Free Press, 488–99.

Iannelli, C. (2008) 'Expansion and Social Selection in Education in England and Scotland', *Oxford Review of Education*, 34(2), 179–202.

Ichou, M. and Vallet, L. A. (2011) 'Do All Roads Lead to Inequality? Trends in French Upper Secondary School Analysed with Four Longitudinal Surveys', *Oxford Review of Education*, 37(2), 167–94.

Inglehart, R. (1997) *Modernization and Postmodernization: Cultural, Economic, and Political Change in 43 Societies*, Princeton, NJ: Princeton University Press.

Irwing, P. and Lynn, R. (2006) 'The Relation Between Childhood IQ and Income in Middle Age', *Journal of Social, Political, and Economic Studies*, 31(2), 191–6.

Ishida, H. (1993) *Social Mobility in Contemporary Japan*, Hong Kong: Stanford University Press.

Jackman, M. R. and Jackman, R. W. (1983) *Class Awareness in the United States*, Berkeley, CA: University of California Press.

Jackson, M. (2006) 'Personality Traits and Occupational Attainment', *European Sociological Review*, 22(2), 187–99.

Jackson, M. (ed.) (2013) *Determined to Succeed?: Performance Versus Choice in Educational Attainment*, Stanford, CA: Stanford University Press.

Jackson, M., Erikson, R., Goldthorpe, J. H. and Yaish, M. (2007) 'Primary and Secondary Effects in Class Differentials in Educational Attainment', *Acta Sociologica*, 50(3), 211–29.

Jæger, M. M. (2007) 'Educational Mobility Across Three Generations: The Changing Impact of Parental Social Class, Economic, Cultural and Social Capital', *European Societies*, 9(4), 527–50.

Jæger, M. M. (2009) 'Equal Access But Unequal Outcomes: Cultural Capital and Educational Choice in a Meritocratic Society', *Social Forces*, 87(4), 1943–72.

Jæger, M. M. (2011) 'Does Cultural Capital Really Affect Academic Achievement? New Evidence from Combined Sibling and Panel Data', *Sociology of Education*, 84(4), 281–98.

Jæger, M. M. and Holm, A. (2007) 'Does Parents' Economic, Cultural, and Social Capital Explain the Social Class Effect on Educational Attainment in the Scandinavian Mobility Regime?', *Social Science Research*, 36(2), 719–44.

Jansen, G. (2011) *Social Cleavages and Political Choices: Large Scale Comparisons of Social Class, Religion and Voting Behaviour in Western Democracies*, Nijmegen, Interuniversity Center for Social Science Theory and Methodology.

Jencks, C. and Tach, L. (2006) 'Would Equal Opportunity Mean More Mobility?' in Morgan, S. L., Grusky, D. B. and Fields, G. S. (eds) *Mobility and Inequality*, Stanford, CA: Stanford University Press, 23–58.

Jencks, C., Bartlett, S., Corcorcan, M., Crouse, J., Eaglesfield, D., Jackson, G., McClelland, K., Mueser, P., Olneck, M., Schwartz, J., Ward, S. and Williams, J. (1979) *Who Gets Ahead? The Determinants of Economic Success in America*, New York: Basic Books.

Jencks, C., Crouse, J. and Mueser, P. (1983) 'The Wisconsin Model of Status Attainment: A National Replication with Improved Measures of Ability and Aspiration', *Sociology of Education*, 56(1), 3–19.

Jencks, C., Smith, M., Acland, H., Bane, M. J., Cohen, D., Gintis, H., Heyns, B. and Michelson, S. (1972) *Inequality: A Reassessment of the Effect of Family and Schooling in America*, New York: Basic Books.

Jensen, A. R. (1969) 'How Much Can We Boost IQ and Scholastic Achievement?', *Harvard Educational Review*, 39(1), 1–123.

Jensen, A. R. (1980) *Bias in Mental Testing*, New York: Free Press.

Jensen, A. R. (1998) *The* g *Factor: The Science of Mental Ability*, Westport, CT: Praeger.

Jensen, A. R. and McGurk, F. C. J. (1987) 'Black–White Bias in "Cultural" and "Noncultural" Test Items', *Personality and Individual Differences*, 8(3), 295–301.

Jerrim, J. and Micklewright, J. (2012) *Socioeconomic Gradients in Children's Cognitive Skills: Are Cross-Country Comparisons Robust to Who Reports Family Background?* DoQSS Working Paper: Department of Quantitative Social Science, Institute of Education, University of London.

Johnson, R. C. and Nagoshi, C. T. (1985) 'Parental Ability, Education and Occupation as Influences on Offspring Cognition in Hawaii and Korea', *Personality and Individual Differences*, 6(4), 413–23.

Johnson, W., Brett, C. E. and Deary, I. J. (2010a) 'Intergenerational Class Mobility in Britain: A Comparative Look Across Three Generations in the Lothian Birth Cohort 1936', *Intelligence*, 38(2), 268–81.

Johnson, W., Brett, C. E. and Deary, I. J. (2010b) 'The Pivotal Role of Education in the Association Between Ability and Social Class Attainment: A Look Across Three Generations', *Intelligence*, 38(1), 55–65.

Johnstone, B. D. (2004) 'The Economics and Politics of Cost Sharing in Higher Education: Comparative Perspectives', *Economics of Education Review*, 23(4), 403–10.

Jones, F. L. (1979) 'Inequality Across Generations: One Hypothesis – Half an Answer' in Martin, J. I. (ed.) *Counter-Predictive Research Outcomes*, Departmental Monograph No. 2, Canberra: Department of Sociology, Research School of the Social Sciences, Australian National University, 67–86.

Jones, F. L. (1989) 'Occupational Prestige in Australia: A New Scale', *Australian and New Zealand Journal of Sociology*, 25(2), 187–99.

Jones, F. L. and McMillan, J. (2001) 'Scoring Occupational Categories for Social Research: A Review of Current Practice with Australian Examples', *Work, Employment and Society*, 15(3), 539–63.

Jones, J. D., Vanfossen, B. E. and Ensminger, M. E. (1995) 'Individual and Organizational Predictors of High School Track Placement', *Sociology of Education*, 68(4), 287–300.

Jonsson, J. O. (1987) 'Class Origin, Cultural Origin, and Educational Attainment: The Case of Sweden', *European Sociological Review*, 3(3), 229–41.

Jonsson, J. O. (1993) 'Persisting Inequalities in Sweden' in Shavit, Y. and Blossfeld, H.-P. (eds) *Persistent Inequality: Changing Educational Attainment in Thirteen Countries*, Boulder, CO: Westview, 101–32.

Jonsson, J. O., Grusky, D. B., Carlo, M. D., Pollak, R. and Brinton, M. C. (2009) 'Microclass Mobility: Social Reproduction in Four Countries', *American Journal of Sociology*, 114(4): 977–1036.

Jonsson, J. O., Mills, C. and Müller, W. (1996) 'Half a Century of Increasing Openness? Social Class, Gender and Educational Attainment in Sweden, Germany and Britain' in Erikson, R. and Jonsson, J. O. (eds) *Can Education Be Equalized? The Swedish Case in Comparative Perspective*, Boulder, CO: Westview, 183–204.

Judge, T. A. and Cable, D. M. (2004) 'The Effect of Physical Height on Workplace Success and Income: Preliminary Test of a Theoretical Model', *Journal of Applied Psychology*, 89(3), 428–41.

Judge, T. A., Higgins, C. A., Thoresen, C. J. and Barrick, M. R. (1999) 'The Big Five Personality Traits, General Mental Ability, and Career Success Across the Lifespan', *Personnel Psychology*, 52(3), 621–52.

Judge, T. A., Klinger, R. L. and Simon, L. S. (2010) 'Time Is on My Side: Time,

General Mental Ability, Human Capital, and Extrinsic Career Success', *Journal of Applied Psychology*, 95(1), 92–107.

Jungbauer-Gans, M. (2004) 'The Influence of Social and Cultural Capital on Reading Achievement: A Comparison of Germany, France, and Switzerland Using PISA 2000 Data', *Zeitschrift für Soziologie*, 33(5), 375–97.

Kahl, J. A. (1953) 'Educational and Occupational Aspirations of "Common Man" Boys', *Harvard Educational Review*, 23(Summer), 186–203.

Kalmijn, M. and Kraaykamp, G. (1996) 'Race, Cultural Capital, and Schooling: An Analysis of Trends in the United States', *Sociology of Education*, 69(1), 22–34.

Karen, D. (2002) 'Changes in Access to Higher Education in the United States: 1980–1992', *Sociology of Education*, 75(3), 191–210.

Kariya, T. and Rosenbaum, J. E. (1999) 'Bright Flight: Unintended Consequences of Detracking Policy in Japan', *American Journal of Education*, 107(3), 210–30.

Katsillis, J. and Rubinson, R. (1990) 'Cultural Capital, Student Achievement, and Educational Reproduction: The Case of Greece', *American Sociological Review*, 55(2), 270–9.

Kaufman, A. S. (2010) '"In What Way Are Apples and Oranges Alike?" A Critique of Flynn's Interpretation of the Flynn Effect', *Journal of Psychoeducational Assessment*, 28(5), 382–98.

Kaymak, B. (2009) 'Ability Bias and the Rising Education Premium in the United States: A Cohort-Based Analysis', *Journal of Human Capital*, 3(3), 224–67.

Keeves, J. P., Morgenstern, C. and Saha, L. J. (1991) 'Educational Opportunity and Equality of Opportunity: Evidence from Studies Conducted by IEA in Ten Countries in 1970–71 and 1983–84', *International Journal of Educational Research. Special Edition, Comparing Opportunity. Further Research on Educational Opportunity*, 15(1), 61–80.

Keister, L. A. (2005) *Getting Rich: America's New Rich and How They Got That Way*, Cambrige: Cambridge University Press.

Kelley, J. (1990) 'The Failure of a Paradigm: Log-Linear Models of Social Mobility' in Clark, J., Modgil, C. and Modgil, S. (eds) *John H. Goldthorpe: Consensus and Controversy*, London: Falmer Press, 319–46.

Kerckhoff, A. C. and Trott, J. M. (1993) 'Educational Attainment in a Changing Educational System: The Case of England and Wales' in Shavit, Y. and Blossfeld, H.-P. (eds) *Persistent Inequality: Changing Educational Attainment in Thirteen Countries*, Boulder, CO: Westview, 133–53.

Kerckhoff, A. C., Campbell, R. T. and Trott, J. M. (1982) 'Dimensions of Educational and Occupational Attainment in Great Britain', *American Sociological Review*, 47(3), 347–64.

Kerckhoff, A. C., Mason, W. M. and Poss, S. S. (1973) 'On the Accuracy of Children's Reports of Family Social Status', *Sociology of Education*, 46(2), 219–47.

Kerckhoff, A. C., Raudenbush, S. W. and Glennie, E. (2001) 'Education, Cognitive Skill, and Labour Force Outcomes', *Sociology of Education*, 74(1), 1–24.

Kerr, C. (1983) *The Future of Industrial Societies: Convergence or Continuing Diversity?*, Cambridge, MA: Harvard University Press.

Kerr, C., Dunlop, J. T., Harbinson, F. H. and Myers, C. A. (1964) *Industralism and Industrial Man: The Problems of Labor and Management in Economic Growth*, London: Heinemann.

Khoo, S. T. and Ainley, J. (2005) *Attitudes, Intentions and Participation*,

Longitudinal Surveys of Australian Youth Research Report 41, Melbourne: Australian Council for Educational Research.

Kifer, E. and Robitalle, D. F. (1989) 'Attitudes, Preferences and Opinions' in Robitaille, D. F. and Garden, R. A. (eds) *The IEA Study of Mathematics II: Contexts and Outcomes of School Mathematics*, Oxford: Pergamon Press, 178–208.

Kiker, B. F. and Condon, C. M. (1981) 'The Influence of Socioeconomic Background on the Earnings of Young Men', *Journal of Human Resources*, 16(1), 94–105.

Kim, J.-O. and Ferree, G. D. (1981) 'Standardization in Causal Analysis', *Sociological Methods and Research*, 10(2), 187–210.

King, G. (1986) 'How Not to Lie with Statistics: Avoiding Common Mistakes in Quantitative Political Science', *American Journal of Political Science*, 30(3), 666–87.

Kingston, P. W. (2000) *The Classless Society*, Studies in Social Inequality, Stanford, CA: Stanford University Press.

Kingston, P. W. (2001) 'The Unfulfilled Promise of Cultural Capital Theory', *Sociology of Education*, 2001(Extra Issue), 88–99.

Kingston, P. W. (2006) 'How Meritocratic Is the United States?', *Research in Social Stratification and Mobility*, 24(2), 111–30.

Kirsh, I. S., Jungeblut, A., Jenkins, L. and Kolstad, A. (1993) *Adult Literacy in America: A First Look at the Results of the National Adult Literacy Survey*, Washington: National Center for Education Statistics.

Klein, D. B. and Stern, C. (2006) 'Sociology and Classical Liberalism', *Independent Review*, XI(1), 37–52.

Knighton, T. and Bussière, P. (2006) *Educational Outcomes at Age 19 Associated with Reading Ability at Age 15*, Ottawa: Culture, Tourism and the Centre for Education Statistics Division, Statistics Canada.

Koenig, K. A., Frey, M. C. and Detterman, D. K. (2008) 'ACT and General Cognitive Ability', *Intelligence*, 36(2), 153–60.

Korenman, S. and Winship, C. (2000) 'A Reanalysis of *The Bell Curve*: Intelligence, Family, Background and Schools' in Arrow, K., Bowles, S. and Durlauf, S. (eds) *Meritocracy and Economic Inequality*, Princeton, NJ: Princeton University Press, 137–78.

Korupp, S. E., Ganzeboom, H. B. G. and van der Lippe, T. (2002) 'Do Mothers Matter? A Comparison of Models of the Influence of Mothers' and Fathers' Educational and Occupational Status on Children's Educational Attainment', *Quality and Quantity*, 36(1), 17–42.

Koucký, J., Bartušek, A. and Kovařovic, J. (2010) *Who Gets a Degree? Access to Tertiary Education in Europe 1950–2009*, Prague, Czech Republic: Education Policy Center, Charles University.

Kraus, V., Schild, E. O. and Hodge, R. W. (1978) 'Occupational Prestige in the Collective Conscience', *Social Forces*, 56(3), 900–18.

Kristensen, P., Gravseth, H. M. and Bjerkedal, T. (2009) 'Educational Attainment of Norwegian Men: Influence of Parental and Early Individual Characteristics', *Journal of Biosocial Science*, 41(6), 799–814.

Kristol, I. (1972) 'About Inequality', *Commentary*, 54, 41–7.

Kumar, K. (1995) *From Post-Industrial to Post-Modern Society: New Theories of the Contemporary World*, Oxford: Blackwell.

Kuo, H.-H. D. and Hauser, R. M. (1995) 'Trends in Family Effects on the Education of Black-and-White Brothers', *Sociology of Education*, 68(2), 136–60.

Lambert, P., Prandy, K. and Bottero, W. (2007) 'By Slow Degrees: Two Centuries of Social Reproduction and Mobility in Britain', *Sociological Research Online*, 12(1).
Lamont, M. and Lareau, A. (1988) 'Cultural Capital: Illusions, Gaps, and Glissandos in Recent Theoretical Developments', *Sociological Theory*, 6(2), 153–68.
Lampard, R. (2012) 'Parental Characteristics, Family Structure and Occupational Attainment in Britain', *Sociology*, 46(6), 1020–38.
Lareau, A. and Weininger, E. B. (2003) 'Cultural Capital in Educational Research: A Critical Assessment', *Theory and Society*, 32(5/6), 567–606.
Le, A. T., Miller, P. W., Slutske, W. S. and Martin, N. G. (2011) 'Opportunity and Educational Outcomes in Australia', *Economic Record*, 87(Suppl. 1), 125–35.
Lee, V. E. and Bryk, A. S. (1989) 'A Multilevel Model of the Social Distribution of High School Achievement', *Sociology of Education*, 62(3), 172–92.
Lee, Y. L. and Miller, P. W. (2000) *Literacy, Numeracy and Labour Market Success*, Canberra: Department of Education, Training and Youth Affairs.
Leigh, A. (2007) 'Intergenerational Mobility in Australia', *B. E. Journal of Economic Analysis and Policy*, 7(2), Article 6.
Lenski, G. (1988) 'Rethinking Macrosociological Theory', *American Sociological Review*, 53(2), 163–71.
Levine, D. I. and Mazumder, B. (2007) 'The Growing Importance of Family: Evidence from Brothers' Earnings', *Industrial Relations*, 46(1), 7–31.
Levy, M. (1966) *Modernisation and the Social Structure of Modern Societies*, Princeton, NJ: Princeton University Press.
Lichtenstein, P., Pedersen, N. L. and McClearn, G. E. (1992) 'The Origins of Individual Differences in Occupational Status and Educational Level', *Acta Sociologica*, 35(1), 13–31.
Lien, N., Friestad, C. and Klepp, K. I. (2001) 'Adolescents' Proxy Reports of Parents' Socioeconomic Status: How Valid Are They?', *Journal of Epidemiology and Community Health*, 55(10), 731–7.
Lipset, S. M. (1994) 'The State of American Sociology', *Sociological Forum*, 9(2), 199–220.
Lipset, S. M. and Bendix, R. (eds) (1959) *Social Mobility in Industrial Society*, Berkeley, CA: University of California Press.
Lipset, S. M. and Zetterberg, H. L. (1959) 'Social Mobility in Industrial Societies' in Lipset, S. M. and Bendix, R. (eds) *Social Mobility in Industrial Society*, Berkeley, CA: University of California Press, 11–75.
Liu, H. and Zeng, J. (2009) 'Genetic Ability and Intergenerational Earnings Mobility', *Journal of Population Economics*, 22(1), 75–95.
Lockwood, D. (1958) *The Black-Coated Worker*, Fairlawn, NJ: Essential Books.
Loehlin, J. C. (2005) 'Resemblence in Personality and Attitudes between Parents and Their Children: Genetic and Environmental Contributions' in Bowles, S., Gintis, H. and Osborne Groves, M. (eds) *Unequal Chances: Family Background and Economic Success*, Princeton, NJ: Russell Sage Foundation, Princeton University Press, 192–207.
Looker, E. D. (1989) 'Accuracy of Proxy Reports of Parental Status Characteristics', *Sociology of Education*, 62(4), 257–76.
Lucas, S. R. (1996) 'Selective Attrition in a Newly Hostile Regime: The Case of 1980 Sophomores', *Social Forces*, 75(2), 511–33.
Lucas, S. R. (2001) 'Effectively Maintained Inequality: Education Transitions, Track

Mobility, and Social Background Effects', *American Journal of Sociology*, 106(6), 1642–90.

Lucas, S. R. (2009) 'Stratification Theory, Socioeconomic Background, and Educational Attainment', *Rationality and Society*, 21(4), 459–511.

Lucas, S. R., Fucella, P. N. and Berends, M. (2011) 'A Neo-Classical Education Transitions Approach: A Corrected Tale for Three Cohorts', *Research in Social Stratification and Mobility*, 29(3), 263–85.

Luo, D., Thompson, L. A. and Detterman, D. K. (2003) 'The Causal Factor Underlying the Correlation Between Psychometric *g* and Scholastic Performance', *Intelligence*, 31(1), 67–83.

Lynn, R. (1996) 'Racial and Ethnic Differences in Intelligence in the United States on the Differential Ability Scale', *Personality and Individual Differences*, 20(2), 271–3.

Lynn, R. (2009a) 'Fluid Intelligence But Not Vocabulary Has Increased in Britain, 1979–2008', *Intelligence*, 37(3), 249–255.

Lynn, R. (2009b) 'What Has Caused the Flynn Effect? Secular Increases in the Development Quotients of Infants', *Intelligence*, 37(1), 16–24.

Lynn, R. and Kanazawa, S. (2008) 'How to Explain High Jewish Achievement: The Role of Intelligence and Values', *Personality and Individual Differences*, 44(4), 801–8.

Lynn, R. and Mikk, J. (2009) 'National IQs Predict Educational Attainment in Math, Reading and Science Across 56 Nations', *Intelligence*, 37(3), 305–10.

Lynn, R., Hampson, S. L. and Magee, M. (1983) 'Determinants of Educational Achievement at 16+: Intelligence, Personality, Home Background and School', *Personality and Individual Differences*, 4(5), 473–81.

Lynn, R., Meisenberg, G., Mikk, J. and Williams, A. (2007) 'National IQs Predict Differences in Scholastic Achievement in 67 Countries', *Journal of Biosocial Science*, 39(6), 861–74.

Maani, S. A. and Kalb, G. (2007) 'Academic Performance, Childhood Economic Resources, and the Choice to Leave School at Age 16', *Economics of Education Review*, 26(3), 361–74.

Magnusson, P. E. K., Rasmussen, F. and Gyllensten, U. B. (2006) 'Height at Age 18 Years Is a Strong Predictor of Attained Education Later in Life: Cohort Study of Over 950,000 Swedish Men', *International Journal of Epidemiology*, 35(3), 658.

Manski, C. E. (1993) 'Adolescent Econometricians: How Do Youth Infer the Returns to Schooling?' in Clotfelter, C. T. and Rothschild, M. (eds) *Studies of Supply and Demand in Higher Education*, Chicago: University of Chicago Press, 43–60.

Marcenaro-Gutierrez, O., Galindo-Rueda, F. and Vignoles, A. (2007) 'Who Actually Goes to University?', *Empirical Economics*, 32(2–3), 333–57.

Marcuse, H. (1964) *One-Dimensional Man: Studies in the Ideology of Advanced Industrial Society*, Boston, MA: Beacon Press.

Mare, R. D. (1980) 'Social Background and School Continuation Decisions', *Journal of the American Statistical Association*, 75(370), 295–305.

Mare, R. D. (1981) 'Change and Stability in Educational Stratification', *American Sociological Review*, 46(1), 72–87.

Mare, R. D. (1993) 'Educational Stratification on Observed and Unobserved Components of Family Background' in Shavit, Y. and Blossfeld, H.-P. (eds) *Persistent Inequality: Changing Educational Attainment in Thirteen Countries*, Boulder, CO: Westview Press, 351–76.

Marks, G. N. (2005) 'Cross-National Differences and Accounting for Social Class Inequalities in Education', *International Sociology*, 20(4), 483–505.

Marks, G. N. (2006) 'Are Between- and Within-School Differences in Student Performance Largely Due to Socio-Economic Background? Evidence from 30 Countries', *Educational Research*, 48(1), 21–40.

Marks, G. N. (2007) 'Do Schools Matter for Early School Leaving? Individual and School Influences in Australia', *School Effectiveness and School Improvement*, 18(4), 429–50.

Marks, G. N. (2008) 'Are Father's or Mother's Socioeconomic Characteristics More Important Influences on Student Performance? Recent International Evidence', *Social Indicators Research*, 85(2), 293–309.

Marks, G. N. (2009a) 'Accounting for School-Sector Differences in University Entrance Performance', *Australian Journal of Education*, 53(1), 19–38.

Marks, G. N. (2009b) 'Modernization Theory and Changes Over Time in the Reproduction of Socioeconomic Inequalities in Australia', *Social Forces*, 88(2), 917–44.

Marks, G. N. (2010a) 'Meritocracy, Modernization and Students' Occupational Expectations: Cross-National Evidence', *Research in Social Stratification and Mobility*, 28(3), 275–89.

Marks, G. N. (2010b) 'School Sector and Socioeconomic Inequalities in University Entrance in Australia: The Role of the Stratified Curriculum', *Educational Research and Evaluation*, 16(1), 23–37.

Marks, G. N. (2010c) 'What Aspects of Schooling Are Important? School Effects on Tertiary Entrance Performance in Australia', *School Effectiveness and School Improvement*, 21(3), 267–87.

Marks, G. N. (2011) 'Issues in the Conceptualisation and Measurement of Socio-Economic Background: Do Different Measures Generate Different Conclusions?', *Social Indicators Research*, 104(2), 225–51.

Marks, G. N. (2012) 'Are School-SES Effects Theoretical and Methodological Artifacts? ', *Teachers College Record*, 114(ID Number: 16872).

Marks, G. N. (2013) 'Reproduction of Economic Inequalities: Are the Figures for the United States and United Kingdom Too High?' in Birkelund, G. E. (ed.) *Class and Stratification Analysis*, Comparative Social Research, Volume 30, Bingley: Emerald, 341–63.

Marks, G. N. and Fleming, N. (1998) *Factors Influencing Youth Unemployment in Australia, 1980–1994*, Longitudinal Surveys of Australian Youth Research Report 7, Melbourne: Australian Council for Educational Research.

Marks, G. N. and McMillan, J. (2003) 'Declining Inequality? The Changing Impact of Socioeconomic Background and Ability on Education in Australia', *British Journal of Sociology*, 54(4), 453–71.

Marks, G. N. and McMillan, J. (2007) 'Changes in Socioeconomic Inequalities in University Participation in Australia' in Shavit, Y., Arum, R. and Gamoran, A. (eds) *Stratification in Higher Education: A Comparative Study*, Stanford, CA: Stanford University Press, 351–73.

Marks, G. N., Fleming, N., Long, M. and McMillan, J. (2000) *Patterns of Participation in Year 12 and Higher Education in Australia: Trends and Issues*, Longitudinal Surveys of Australian Youth Research Report 17, Melbourne: Australian Council for Educational Research.

Marks, G. N., Cresswell, J. and Ainley, J. (2006) 'Explaining Socioeconomic Inequalities in Student Achievement: The Role of Home and School Factors', *Educational Research and Evaluation*, 12(2), 105–28.

Marsh, C. (1982) *The Survey Method: The Contribution of Surveys to Sociological Explanation*, Contemporary Social Research Series No. 6, London: Allan and Unwin.

Marshall, G. and Swift, A. (1993) 'Social Class and Social Justice', *British Journal of Sociology*, 44(2), 187–211.

Marshall, G. and Swift, A. (1996) 'Merit and Mobility: A Reply to Peter Saunders', *Sociology*, 30(2), 375–86.

Massagli, M. P. and Hauser, R. M. (1983) 'Response Variability in Self- and Proxy Reports of Paternal and Filial Socioeconomic Characteristics', *American Journal of Sociology*, 89(2), 420–31.

Mayer, K. U., Muller, W. and Pollack, R. (2007) 'Germany: Institutional Change and Inequalities of Access in Higher Education' in Shavit, Y., Arum, R. and Gamoran, A. (eds) *Stratification in Higher Education: A Comparative Study*, Stanford, CA: Stanford University Press, 240–65.

Mayer, S. E. (1997) *What Money Can't Buy: Family Income and Children's Life Chances*, Cambridge, MA: Harvard University Press.

Mayer, S. E. and Lopoo, L. M. (2005) 'Has the Intergenerational Transmission of Economic Status Changed?', *Journal of Human Resources*, 40(1), 169–85.

Mazumder, B. (2001) *Earnings Mobility in the US: A New Look at Intergenerational Mobility*, Chicago: Federal Reserve Bank of Chicago.

Mazumder, B. (2005) 'Fortunate Sons: New Estimates of Intergenerational Mobility in the United States Using Social Security Earnings Data', *Review of Economics and Statistics*, 87(2), 235–55.

Mazumder, B. (2008) 'Sibling Similarities and Economic Inequality in the US', *Journal of Population Economics*, 21(3), 685–701.

McCall, R. B. (1977) 'Childhood IQ's as Predictors of Adult Educational and Occupational Status', *Science*, 197(4302), 482–3.

McIntosh, J. (2010) 'Educational Mobility in Canada: Results from the 2001 General Social Survey', *Empirical Economics*, 38(2), 457–70.

McMillan, J., Beavis, A. and Jones, F. L. (2009) 'The AUSEI06: A New Socio-economic Index for Australia', *Journal of Sociology*, 45(2), 123–49.

McNiece, R., Bidgood, P. and Soan, P. (2004) 'An Investigation into Using National Longitudinal Studies to Examine Trends in Educational Attainment and Development', *Educational Research*, 46(2), 119–36.

Mead, L. M. (2005/06) 'Why Anglos Lead', *National Interest*, 2005/06(Winter), 1–8.

Menard, S. (2011) 'Standards for Standardized Logistic Regression Coefficients', *Social Forces*, 89(4), 1409–28.

Meyer, J. W., Ramirez, F. O. and Soysal, Y. N. (1992) 'World Expansion of Mass Education, 1870–1980', *Sociology of Education*, 65(2), 128–49.

Micklewright, J. and Schnepf, S. V. (2006) *Response Bias in England in PISA 2000 and 2003*, Southampton: Southampton Statistical Sciences Research Institute (S3RI) University of Southampton.

Miller, P. and Chiswick, B. R. (1997) 'Literacy, Numeracy and the Labour Market' in McLennan, W. (ed.) *Aspects of Literacy: Assessed Skill Levels, Australia 1996,*

Canberra: Australian Bureau of Statistics, 73–9.
Miller, P., Mulvey, C. and Martin, N. (1995) 'What do Twins Studies Reveal about the Economic Returns to Education? A Comparison of Australian and US findings', *The American Economic Review*, 85(3), 586–99.
Miller, P., Mulvey, C. and Martin, N. (1996) 'Multiple Regression Analysis of the Occupational Status of Twins: A Comparison of Economic and Behavioural Genetics Models', *Oxford Bulletin of Economics and Statistics*, 58(1), 227–38.
Miller, P., Mulvey, C. and Martin, N. G. (2001) 'Genetic and Environmental Contributions to Educational Attainment in Australia', *Economics of Education Review*, 20(2), 211–24.
Mood, C. (2010) 'Logistic Regression: Why We Cannot Do What We Think We Can Do, and What We Can Do About It', *European Sociological Review*, 26(1), 67–82.
Morgan, S. L. and Kim, Y.-M. (2005) 'Inequality of Conditions and Intergenerational Mobility: Changing Patterns of Educational Attainment in the United States' in Morgan, S. L., Grusky, D. B. and Fields, G. S. (eds) *Mobility and Inequality: Frontiers of Research from Sociology and Economics*, Stanford, CA: Stanford University Press, 165–94.
Mueller, C. W. and Parcel, T. L. (1981) 'Measures of Socioeconomic Status: Alternatives and Recommendations', *Child Development*, 52(1), 13–30.
Mullen, A. I., Goyette, K. A. and Soares, J. A. (2003) 'Who Goes to Graduate School? Social and Academic Correlates of Educational Continuation After College', *Sociology of Education*, 76(2), 143–69.
Muller, S. M. (2010) 'Another Problem in the Estimation of Intergenerational Income Mobility', *Economics Letters*, 108(3), 291–5.
Müller, W. and Karle, W. (1993) 'Social Selection in Education Systems in Europe', *European Sociological Review*, 9(1), 1–23.
Müller, W., Lüttinger, P., König, W. and Karle, W. (1989) 'Class and Education in Industrial Nations', *International Journal of Sociology*, 19(3), 3–39.
Mulligan, C. B. (1999) 'Galton Versus the Human Capital Approach to Inheritance', *Journal of Political Economy*, 107(S6), S184–S224.
Mullis, I. V. S., Dossey, J. A., Foertsch, M. A., Jones, L. R. and Gentile, C. A. (1991) *Trends in Academic Progress: Achievement of US Students in Science, 1969–70 to 1990, Mathematics, 1973 to 1990, Writing, 1984 to 1990.*, Washington, DC: Office of Educational Research and Improvement, US Department of Education.
Murnane, R. J., Willett, J. B. and Levy, F. (1995) 'The Growing Importance of Cognitive Skills in Wage Determination', *Review of Economics and Statistics*, 77(2), 251–66.
Murnane, R. J., Willett, J. B. and Tyler, Y. D. J. H. (2000) 'How Important Are the Cognitive Skills of Teenagers in Predicting Subsequent Earnings?', *Journal of Policy Analysis and Management*, 19(4), 547–68.
Nagel, I. and Ganzeboom, H. B. G. (2002) 'Participation in Legitimate Culture: Family and School Effects from Adolescence to Adulthood', *Netherlands Journal of the Social Sciences*, 38(2), 102–20.
Nagoshi, C. T. and Johnson, R. C. (2005) 'Socioeconomic Status Does Not Moderate the Familiality of Cognitive Abilities in the Hawaii Family Study of Cognition', *Journal of Biosocial Science*, 37(6), 773–81.
Nakhaie, M. R. and Curtis, J. (1998) 'Effects of Class Positions of Parents on

Educational Attainment of Daughters and Sons', *Canadian Review of Sociology and Anthropology*, 35(4), 483–515.

Nash, R. (2001) 'Class, "Ability" and Attainment: A Problem for the Sociology of Education', *British Journal of Sociology of Education*, 22(2), 189–202.

Nash, R. (2003a) 'Inequality/Difference in Education: Is a Real Explanation of Primary and Secondary Effects Possible?', *British Journal of Sociology*, 54(4), 433–51.

Nash, R. (2003b) 'Is the School Composition Effect Real? A Discussion with Evidence from the UK PISA Data', *School Effectiveness and School Improvement*, 14(4), 441–57.

NCES (1996) *NAEP 1996 Trends in Academic Progress: The Nations Report Card*, Washington, DC: National Center for Educational Statistics, Institute of Education Sciences, US Department of Education.

NCES (2008) *NAEP 2008 Trends in Academic Progress: The Nations Report Card*, Washington, DC: National Center for Educational Statistics, Institute of Education Sciences, US Department of Education.

Neiss, M. and Rowe, D. C. (2000) 'Parental Education and Child's Verbal IQ in Adoptive and Biological Families in the National Longitudinal Study of Adolescent Health', *Behavior Genetics*, 30(6), 487–95.

Neisser, U., Boodoo, G., Bouchard, J. (Jr.), Boykin, A. W., Brody, N., Ceci, S. J., Halpern, D. F., Loehlin, J. C., Perloff, R., Sternberg, R. J. and Urbina, S. (1996) 'Intelligence: Knowns and Unknowns', *American Psychologist*, 51(2), 77–101.

Nettle, D. (2003) 'Intelligence and Class Mobility in the British Population', *British Journal of Psychology*, 94(4), 551–61.

Ng, I. Y. H., Shen, X. and Ho, K. W. (2009) 'Intergenerational Earnings Mobility in Singapore and the United States', *Journal of Asian Economics*, 20(2), 110–19.

Ng, T. W. H., Eby, L. T., Sorensen, K. L. and Feldman, D. C. (2005) 'Predictors of Objective and Subjective Career Success: A Meta-Analysis', *Personnel Psychology*, 58(2), 367–408.

Nicolaou, N., Shane, S., Cherkas, L., Hunkin, J. and Spector, T. D. (2008) 'Is the Tendency to Engage in Entrepreneurship Genetic?', *Management Science*, 54(1), 167–79.

Nielsen, F. (1995a) 'Happy Days Are Here Again!' Review Article: *Inequality by Design: Cracking the Bell Curve Myth*, by Claude S. Fischer; Michael Hout; Martin Sanchez Jankowski; Samuel R. Lucas; Ann Swidler; Kim Voss', *Social Forces*, 76(2), 701–4.

Nielsen, F. (1995b) 'Review Article: *The Bell Curve: Intelligence and Class Structure in American Life*, by Richard J. Hernstein; Charles Murray', *Social Forces*, 74(1), 337–42.

Nielsen, F. (2004) 'The Vacant "We": Remarks on Public Sociology', *Social Forces*, 82(4), 1619–27.

Nielsen, F. (2006) 'Achievement and Ascription in Educational Attainment: Genetic and Environmental Influences on Adolescent Schooling', *Social Forces*, 85(1), 193–216.

Nyborg, H. and Jensen, A. R. (2001) 'Occupation and Income Related to Psychometric *g*', *Intelligence*, 29(1), 45–55.

Nyhus, E. K. and Pons, E. (2005) 'The Effects of Personality on Earnings', *Journal of Economic Psychology*, 26(3), 363–84.

Oakes, J. (1985) *Keeping Track: How Schools Structure Inequality*, New Haven, CT: Yale University Press.

OECD (1999) *Classifying Educational Programmes: Manual for ISCED-97 Implementation in OECD Countries*, Paris: Organisation for Economic Co-operation and Development.

OECD (2001) *Knowledge and Skills for Life: First Results from the OECD Programme for International Student Assessment*, Paris: Organisation for Economic Co-operation and Development.

OECD (2004) *Learning for Tomorrow's World: First Results from PISA 2003*, Paris: Organisation for Economic Co-operation and Development.

OECD (2005) *Learning a Living: First Results of the Adult Literacy and Life Skills Survey*, Paris and Ottawa: Organisation for Economic Co-operation and Development and Statistics Canada.

OECD (2007a) *Science Competencies for Tomorrow's World: Programme for International Student Assessment*, Paris: Organisation for Economic Co-operation and Development.

OECD (2007b) *Science Competencies for Tomorrow's World. Volume 1, Programme for International Student Assessment*, Paris: Organisation for Economic Co-operation and Development.

OECD (2009a) *Education at a Glance: OECD Indicators 2009*, Paris: Centre for Education Research and Innovation, Indicators of Educational Systems, Organisation for Economic Co-operation and Development.

OECD (2009b) *Growing Unequal? Income Distribution and Poverty in OECD Countries*, Paris: Organisation for Economic Co-operation and Development.

OECD (2010a) *Changes in Student Performance Since 2000, Programme for International Student Assessment*, Paris: Organisation for Economic Co-operation and Development.

OECD (2010b) *Pathways to Success: How Knowledge and Skills at Age 15 Shape Future Lives in Canada*, Paris: Organisation for Economic Co-operation and Development.

OECD (2010c) *PISA 2009 Results: Overcoming Social Background. Equity in Learning Opportunitiers and Outcomes*, Paris: Organisation for Economic Co-operation and Development.

OECD and Statistics Canada (2000) *Literacy in the Information Age: Final Report of the International Adult Literacy Survey*, Paris: Organisation for Economic Co-operation and Development.

OECD and Human Resources Development Canada (1997) *Literacy Skills for the Knowledge Society: Further Results from the International Adult Literacy Survey*, Paris: Organisation for Economic Co-operation and Development.

Oesch, D. (2008) 'The Changing Shape of Class Voting: An Individual-Level Analysis of Party Support in Britain, Germany and Switzerland', *European Societies*, 10(3), 329–55.

Olneck, M. R. (1977) 'On the Use of Sibling Data to Estimate the Effects of Family Background, Cognitive Skills and Schooling: Results from Kalamazoo Brothers Study', in Taubman, P. (ed.) *Kinometrics: Determinants of Socioeconomic Success Within and Between Families*, Amsterdam: Elsevier North-Holland, 125–50.

Olneck, M. R. and Bills, D. B. (1980) 'What Makes Sammy Run? An Empirical Assessment of the Bowles–Gintis Correspondence Theory', *American Journal of Education*, 89(1), 27–61.

Opdenakker, M.-C. and van Damme, J. (2001) 'Relationship Between School Composition and Characteristics of School Process and Their Effect on Mathematics Achievement', *British Educational Research Journal*, 27(4), 407–32.
Orr, A. J. (2003) 'Black–White Differences in Achievement: The Importance of Wealth', *Sociology of Education*, 76(4), 281–304.
Osborne Groves, M. (2005a) 'How Important Is Your Personality? Labor Market Returns to Personality for Women in the US and UK', *Journal of Economic Psychology*, 26(6), 827–41.
Osborne Groves, M. (2005b) 'Personality and the Intergenerational Transmission of Economic Status' in Bowles, S., Gintis, H. and Osborne Groves, M.(eds) *Unequal Chances: Family Background and Economic Success*, Princeton, NJ: Russell Sage Foundation, Princeton University Press, 208–31.
Pakulski, J. and Waters, M. (1996) *The Death of Class*, London: Sage.
Parcel, T. L. and Dufur, M. J. (2001) 'Capital at Home and at School: Effects on Student Achievement', *Social Forces*, 79(3), 881–912.
Parkin, F. (1979) *Marxism and Class Theory: A Bourgeois Critique*, Cambridge: University Press.
Paterson, L. and Iannelli, C. (2007) 'Social Class and Educational Attainment: A Comparative Study of England, Wales, and Scotland', *Sociology of Education*, 80(4), 330–58.
Paul, S. M. (1980) 'Sibling Resemblance in Mental Ability: A Review', *Behavior Genetics*, 10(3), 277–90.
Pekkarinen, T., Uusitalo, R. and Kerr, S. (2009) 'School Tracking and Intergenerational Income Mobility: Evidence from the Finnish Comprehensive School Reform', *Journal of Public Economics*, 93(7–8), 965–73.
Perry, L. B. and McConney, A. (2010) 'Does the SES of the School Matter? An Examination of Socioeconomic Status and Student Achievement Using PISA 2003', *Teachers College Record*, 112(4), 1137–62.
Peters, H. E. (1992) 'Patterns of Intergenerational Mobility in Income and Earnings', *The Review of Economics and Statistics*, 74(3), 456–66.
Pfeffer, F. T. (2008) 'Persistent Inequality in Educational Attainment and its Institutional Context', *European Sociological Review*, 24(5), 543–65.
Pfeffer, F. T. (2011) 'Status Attainment and Wealth in the United States and Germany' in Smeeding, T. M., Erikson, R. and Jännti, M. (eds) *Persistence, Privilege, and Parenting: The Comparative Study of Intergenerational Mobility*, New York: Russell Sage Foundation, 109–37.
Pistolesi, N. (2009) 'Inequality of Opportunity in the Land of Opportunities, 1968–2001', *Journal of Economic Inequality*, 7(4), 411–33.
Plomin, R., Fulker, D. W., Corley, R. and DeFries, J. C. (1997) 'Nature, Nurture, and Cognitive Development from 1 to 16 Years: A Parent–Offspring Adoption Study', *Psychological Science*, 8(6), 442–7.
Plug, E. and Vijverberg, W. (2003) 'Schooling, Family Background, and Adoption: Is It Nature or Is It Nurture?', *Journal of Political Economy*, 111(3), 611–41.
Popper, K. (1976a) 'The Logic of the Social Sciences' in Adey, G. and Frisby, D. (trans.), *The Positivist Dispute in German Sociology*, London: Heinemann, 87–104.
Popper, K. (1976b) 'Reason or Revolution' in Adey, G. and Frisby, D. (trans.), *The Positivist Dispute in German Sociology*, London: Heinemann, 288–300.
Raftery, A. E. and Hout, M. (1993) 'Maximally Maintained Inequality: Expansion,

Reform, and Opportunity in Irish Education, 1921–1975', *Sociology of Education*, 66(1), 41–62.

Rawls, J. (1971) *A Theory of Justice*, Cambridge, MA: Harvard University Press.

Reisel, L. (2011) 'Two Paths to Inequality in Educational Outcomes: Family Background and Educational Selection in the United States and Norway', *Sociology of Education*, 84(4), 261–80.

Resh, N. (1998) 'Track Placement: How the "Sorting Machine" Works in Israel', *American Journal of Education*, 106(3), 416–39.

Reynolds, A. J. and Walberg, H. J. (1992) 'A Process Model of Mathematics Achievement and Attitude', *Journal for Research in Mathematics Education*, 23(4), 306–28.

Richards, M. and Sacker, A. (2003) 'Lifetime Antecedents of Cognitive Reserve', *Journal of Clinical and Experimental Neuropsychology*, 25(5), 614–24.

Richardson, K. (2002) 'What IQ Tests Test', *Theory and Psychology*, 12(3), 283–314.

Rijken, S. (1999) *Educational Expansion and Status Attainment. A Cross-National and Over-Time Comparison*, Netherlands: Inter–University Center for Social Science Theory and Methodology.

Rijken, S., Maas, I. and Ganzeboom, H. B. G. (2007) 'The Netherlands: Access to Higher Education – Institutional Arrangements and Inequality of Opportunity' in Shavit, Y., Arum, R. and Gamoran, A. (eds) *Stratification in Higher Education: A Comparative Study*, Stanford, CA: Stanford University Press, 266–93.

Rindermann, H. (2006) 'What Do International Student Assessment Studies Measure? School Performance, Student Abilities, Cognitive Abilities, Knowledge or General Intelligence?', *Psychologische Rundschau*, 57(2), 69–86.

Rindermann, H. (2007) 'The *g*-factor of International Cognitive Ability Comparisons: The Homogeneity of Results in PISA, TIMSS, PIRLS and IQ-Tests Across Nations', *European Journal of Personality*, 21(5), 667–706.

Rindermann, H. (2008) 'Relevance of Education and Intelligence at the National Level for the Economic Welfare of People', *Intelligence*, 36(2), 127–42.

Rindermann, H. and Thompson, J. (2011) 'Cognitive Capitalism: The Effect of Cognitive Ability on Wealth, as Mediated Through Scientific Achievement and Economic Freedom', *Psychological Science*, 22(6), 754–63.

Ringdal, K. and Birkelund, G. E. (2001) *Social Background and Educational Attainment, Norway 1973–1995*. Paper presented at the RC28 Social Mobility and Stratification Research Committee, Mannheim, Germany, April 25–28.

Ringen, S. (2006) 'The Truth about Class Inequality', *Sociologicky Casopis [Czech Sociological Review]*, 42(3), 475–91.

Rivera-Batiz, F. L. (1992) 'Quantitative Literacy and the Likelihood of Employment Among Young Adults in the United States', *Journal of Human Resources*, 27(2), 313–28.

Roberts, B. W., Kuncel, N. R., Shiner, R., Caspi, A. and Goldberg, L. R. (2007) 'The Power of Personality: The Comparative Validity of Personality Traits, Socio-economic Status, and Cognitive Ability for Predicting Important Life Outcomes', *Perspectives on Psychological Science*, 2(4), 313–45.

Robinson, W. S. (1950) 'Ecological Correlations and the Behavior of Individuals', *American Sociological Review*, 15(3), 351–7.

Rodgers, J. L. and Wänström, L. (2007) 'Identification of a Flynn Effect in the NLSY: Moving from the Center to the Boundaries', *Intelligence*, 35(2), 187–96.

Roksa, J., Grodsky, E., Arum, R. and Gamoran, A. (2007) 'United States: Changes in Higher Education and Social Stratification' in Shavit, Y., Arum, R. and Gamoran, A. (eds) *Stratification in Higher Education: A Comparative Study*, Stanford, CA: Stanford University Press, 165–91.

Rönnlund, M. and Nilsson, L. G. (2008) 'The Magnitude, Generality, and Determinants of Flynn Effects on Forms of Declarative Memory and Visuospatial Ability: Time-Sequential Analyses of Data from a Swedish Cohort Study', *Intelligence*, 36(3), 192–209.

Rothman, S. (2003) 'The Changing Influence of Socioeconomic Status on Student Achievement: Recent Evidence from Australia', Paper Presented at the Annual Meeting of the American Educational Research Association, Chicago, April 21–25.

Rowe, D. C. (1997) 'A Place at the Policy Table? Behavior Genetics and Estimates of Family Environmental Effects on IQ', *Intelligence*, 24(1), 133–58.

Rowe, D. C., Jacobson, K. C. and van den Oord, E. J. C. G. (1999a) 'Genetic and Environmental Influences on Vocabulary IQ: Parental Education Level as Moderator', *Child Development*, 70(5), 1151–62.

Rowe, D. C., Vesterdal, W. J. and Rodgers, J. L. (1999b) 'Herrnstein's Syllogism: Genetic and Shared Environmental Influences on IQ, Education, and Income', *Intelligence*, 26(4), 405–23.

Rumberger, R. W. (1983) 'The Influence of Family Background on Education, Earnings, and Wealth', *Social Forces*, 61(3), 755–73.

Rumberger, R. W. (2010) 'Education and the Reproduction of Economic Inequality in the United States: An Empirical Investigation', *Economics of Education Review*, 29(2), 246–54.

Rumberger, R. W. and Palardy, G. J. (2005) 'Does Segregation Still Matter? The Effect of Student Composition on Academic Achievement in High Schools', *Teachers College Record*, 107(9), 1999–2045.

Sackett, P. R., Kuncel, N. R., Arneson, J. J., Cooper, S. R. and Waters, S. D. (2009) 'Does Socioeconomic Status Explain the Relationship Between Admissions Tests and Post-Secondary Academic Performance?', *Psychological Bulletin*, 135(1), 1–22.

Sandefur, G. D., Meier, A. M. and Campbell, M. E. (2006) 'Family Resources, Social Capital, and College Attendance', *Social Science Research*, 35(2), 525–53.

Saunders, P. (1995) 'Might Britain Be a Meritocracy?', *Sociology*, 29(1), 23–41.

Saunders, P. (1996) *Unequal But Fair? A Study of Class Barriers in Britain*, Choice in Welfare Issue 28, London: Institute of Economic Affairs, Health and Welfare Unit.

Saunders, P. (1997) 'Social Mobility in Britain: An Empirical Evaluation of Two Competing Explanations', *Sociology*, 31(2), 261–88.

Saunders, P. (2002) 'Reflections on the Meritocracy Debate in Britain: A Response to Richard Breen and John Goldthorpe', *British Journal of Sociology*, 53(4), 559–74.

Saunders, P. (2010) *Social Mobility Myths*, Institute for the Study of Civil Society, London: Cromwell Press Group.

Scarr, S. and Weinberg, R. A. (1978) 'The Influence of "Family Background" on Intellectual Attainment', *American Sociological Review*, 43(5), 674–92.

Scheerens, J. and Bosker, R. J. (1997) *The Foundations of Educational Effectiveness*, Oxford: Pergamon.

Scheerens, J. C. J., Bosker, R. J. and Creemers, B. P. M. (2000) 'Time for Self-Criticism: On the Viability of School Effectiveness Research', *School Effectiveness and School Improvement*, 12(1), 131–57.

Schmidt, F. L. and Hunter, J. (2004) 'General Mental Ability in the World of Work: Occupational Attainment and Job Performance', *Journal of Personality and Social Psychology*, 86(1), 162–73.

Schmidt, W. H. and Kifer, E. (1989) 'Exploring Relationships Across Systems Population A Systems' in Robitaille, D. F. and Garden, R. A. (eds) *The IEA Study of Mathematics II: Contexts and Outcomes of School Mathematics*, Oxford: Pergamon Press, 209–31.

Schneider, T. (2004) 'The Influence of Parental Income on School Choice', *Zeitschrift für Soziologie*, 33(6), 471–92.

Schofer, E. and Meyer, J. W. (2005) 'The Worldwide Expansion of Higher Education in the Twentieth Century', *American Sociological Review*, 70(6), 898–920.

Schoon, I. (2008) 'A Transgenerational Model of Status Attainment: The Potential Mediating Role of School Motivation and Education', *National Institute Economic Review*, 205(1), 72–82.

Schultz, T. W. (1977) 'Investment in Human Capital' in Karabel, J. and Halsey, A. H. (eds) *Power and Ideology in Education*, New York: Oxford University Press, 313–24.

Sen, A. and Clemente, A. (2010) 'Intergenerational Correlations in Educational Attainment: Birth Order and Family Size Effects Using Canadian Data', *Economics of Education Review*, 29(1), 147–55.

Sewell, W. H. and Hauser, R. M. (1975) *Education, Occupation and Earnings: Achievement in the Early Career*, New York: Academic Press.

Sewell, W. H. and Shah, V. P. (1968) 'Social Class, Parental Encouragement, and Educational Aspirations', *American Journal of Sociology*, 73(5), 559–72.

Sewell, W. H. and Shah, V. P. (1977) 'Socioeconomic Status, Intelligence and the Attainment of Higher Education' in Karabel, J. and Halsey, A. H. (eds) *Power and Ideology in Education*, New York: Oxford University Press, 197–215.

Sewell, W. H., Haller, A. O. and Ohlendorf, G. (1970) 'The Educational and Early Occupational Status Attainment Process: Replication and Revision', *American Sociological Review*, 35(5), 1014–27.

Sewell, W. H., Haller, A. O. and Portes, A. (1969) 'The Educational and Early Occupational Attainment Process', *American Sociological Review*, 34(1), 82–92.

Sewell, W. H., Hauser, R. M., Springer, K. W. and Hauser, T. S. (2004) 'As We Age: A Review of the Wisconsin Longitudinal Study, 1957–2001' in Leicht, K. T. (ed.) *Research in Social Stratification and Mobility, Volume 20*, London: Elsevier, 3–111.

Sewell, W. H., Hauser, R. M. and Wolf, W. C. (1980) 'Sex, Schooling, and Occupational Status', *American Journal of Sociology*, 86(3), 551–83.

Shavit, Y., Arum, R. and Gamoran, A. (eds) (2007a) *Stratification in Higher Education: A Comparative Study*, Stanford, CA: Stanford University Press.

Shavit, Y. and Blossfeld, H.-P. (eds) (1993) *Persistent Inequality. Changing Educational Attainment in Thirteen Countries*, Boulder, CO: Westview.

Shavit, Y. and Featherman, D. L. (1988) 'Schooling, Tracking, and Teenage Intelligence', *Sociology of Education*, 61(1), 42–51.

Shavit, Y. and Westerbeek, K. (1998) 'Educational Stratification in Italy: Reforms,

Expansion, and Equality of Opportunity', *European Sociological Review*, 14(1), 33–47.
Shavit, Y., Yaish, M. and Bar Haim, E. (2007b) 'The Persistence of Persistent Inequality' in Scherer, S., Pollak, R., Otte, G. and Gangl, M. (eds) *From Origin to Destination: Trends and Mechanisms in Social Stratification Research*, Frankfurt: Campus Verlag, 37–57.
Shayer, M. and Ginsburg, D. (2009) 'Thirty Years On – A Large Anti-Flynn Effect? (II): 13- and 14-Year-Olds: Piagetian Tests of Formal Operations Norms 1976–2006/7', *British Journal of Educational Psychology*, 79(3), 409–18.
Sieben, I. and de Graaf, P. M. (2001) 'Testing the Modernization Hypothesis and the Socialist Ideology Hypothesis: A Comparative Sibling Analysis of Educational Attainment and Occupational Status', *British Journal of Sociology*, 52(3), 441–67.
Sieben, I. and de Graaf, P. M. (2003) 'The Total Impact of the Family on Educational Attainment – A Comparative Sibling Analysis', *European Societies*, 5(1), 33–68.
Sikora, J. and Saha, L. J. (2007) 'Corrosive Inequality? Structural Determinants of Educational and Occupational Expectations in Comparative Perspective', *International Education Journal*, 8(3), 57–78.
Silles, M. A. (2007) 'The Returns to Education for the United Kingdom', *Journal of Applied Economics*, 10(2), 391–413.
Silles, M. A. (2009) 'Personality, Education and Earnings', *Education Economics*, 18(2), 131–51.
Silventoinen, K., Kaprio, J. and Lahelma, E. (2000) 'Genetic and Environmental Contributions to the Association Between Body Height and Educational Attainment: A Study of Adult Finnish Twins', *Behavior Genetics*, 30(6), 477–85.
Sirin, S. R. (2005) 'Socioeconomic Status and Academic Achievement: A Meta-Analytical Review of Research', *Review of Educational Research*, 75(3), 417–53.
Smith, J. (1995) 'Emancipating Sociology: Postmodernism and Mainstream Sociological Practice', *Social Forces*, 74(1), 53–79.
Snijders, T. A. B. and Bosker, R. J. (2012) *Multilevel Analysis: An Introduction to Basic and Advanced Multilevel Modelling*, 2nd edn., Los Angeles, CA: Sage.
Sokal, A. (1996) 'Transgressing the Boundaries: Towards a Transformative Hermeneutics of Quantum Gravity', *Social Text*, 46/47(Spring/Summer), 217–52
Solon, G. (1992) 'Intergenerational Income Mobility in the United States', *American Economic Review*, 82(3), 393–408.
Solon, G. (1999) 'Intergenerational Mobility in the Labor Market' in Ashenfelter, O. and Card, D. (eds) *Handbook of Labor Economics*, Amsterdam: North-Holland, 1761–800.
Solon, G. (2002) 'Cross-Country Differences in Intergenerational Earnings Mobility', *Journal of Economic Perspectives*, 16(3), 59–66.
Sørensen, A. B. (2000) 'Toward a Sounder Basis for Class Analysis', *American Journal of Sociology*, 105(6), 1523–58.
Sorjonen, K., Hemmingsson, T., Lundin, A. and Melin, B. (2011) 'How Social Position of Origin Relates to Intelligence and Level of Education When Adjusting for Attained Social Position', *Scandinavian Journal of Psychology*, 52(3), 277–81.
Spearman, C. (1904) 'General Intelligence Objectively Determined and Measured', *American Journal of Psychology*, 15(2), 201–92.
Sternberg, R. J. (1996) 'Myths, Countermyths, and Truths About Intelligence', *Educational Researcher*, 25(2), 11–16.

Sternberg, R. J., Grigorenko, E. L. and Bundy, D. A. (2001) 'The Predictive Value of IQ', *Merrill–Palmer Quarterly*, 47(1), 1–41.

Stolzenberg, R. M. (1992) 'Educational Continuation by College Graduates', *American Journal of Sociology*, 99(4), 1042–77.

Stolzenberg, R. M. (2008) 'Methodological Shamanism and the Review Process', *Sociological Methodologist*, 2008(Winter), 1–3.

Strenze, T. (2007) 'Intelligence and Socioeconomic Success: A Meta-Analytic Review of Longitudinal Research', *Intelligence*, 35(5), 401–26.

Sullivan, A. (2001) 'Cultural Capital and Educational Attainment', *Sociology*, 35(4), 893–912.

Sullivan, A. (2007) 'Cultural Capital, Cultural Knowledge and Ability', *Sociological Research Online*, 12(6), 1.

Sundet, J. M., Barlaug, D. G. and Torjussen, T. M. (2004) 'The End of the Flynn Effect? A Study of Secular Trends in Mean Intelligence Test Scores of Norwegian Conscripts During Half a Century', *Intelligence*, 32(4), 349–62.

Swift, A. (2004) 'Would Perfect Mobility Be Perfect?', *European Sociological Review*, 20(1), 1–11.

Tach, L. M. and Farkas, G. (2006) 'Learning-Related Behaviors, Cognitive Skills, and Ability Grouping When Schooling Begins', *Social Science Research*, 35(4), 1048–79.

Tambs, K., Sundet, J. M., Magnus, P. and Berg, K. (1989) 'Genetic and Environmental Contributions to the Covariance Between Occupational Status, Educational Attainment, and IQ: A Study of Twins', *Behavior Genetics*, 19(2), 209–22.

Tate, W. F. (1997) 'Race–Ethnicity, SES, Gender, and Language Proficiency Trends in Mathematics Achievement: An Update', *Journal for Research in Mathematics Education*, 28(6), 652–79.

Taubman, P. (1976a) 'The Determinants of Earnings: Genetics, Family, and Other Environments: A Study of White Male Twins', *American Economic Review*, 66(5), 858–70.

Taubman, P. (1976b) 'Earnings, Education, Genetics, and Environment', *Journal of Human Resources*, 11(4), 447–61.

Taubman, P. and Wales, T. (1972) *Mental Ability and Higher Educational Attainment in the 20th Century*, New York: McGraw–Hill.

Teachman, J. D. and Paasch, K. (1998) 'The Family and Educational Aspirations', *Journal of Marriage and the Family*, 60(3), 704–14.

Teachman, J. D., Paasch, K. and Carver, K. (1997) 'Social Capital and the Generation of Human Capital', *Social Forces*, 75(4), 1343–59.

Teachman, J. D. (1996) 'Intellectual Skill and Academic Performance: Do Families Bias the Relationship?', *Sociology of Education*, 69(1), 35–48.

Teasdale, T. W. and Owen, D. R. (1984) 'Heredity in Intelligence and Educational Level: A Sibling Study and Familial Environment', *Nature*, 309(5969), 620–2.

Teasdale, T. W. and Owen, D. R. (1989) 'Continuing Secular Increases in Intellgence and a Stable Prevalence of High Intelligence Levels', *Intelligence*, 13(3), 255–62.

Teasdale, T. W. and Owen, D. R. (2008) 'Secular Declines in Cognitive Test Scores: A Reversal of the Flynn Effect', *Intelligence*, 36(2), 121–6.

Tellegen, A., Lykken, D. T., Bouchard, T. J. J., Wilcox, K. J., Segal, N. L. and Rich,

S. (1988) 'Personality Similarity in Twins Reared Apart and Together', *Journal of Personality and Social Psychology*, 54(6), 1031–9.
Thienpont, K. and Verleye, G. (2004) 'Cognitive Ability and Occupational Status in a British Cohort', *Journal of Biosocial Science*, 36(3), 333–49.
Thomas, G. E., Alexander, K. L. and Eckland, B. K. (1979) 'Access to Higher Education: The Importance of Race, Sex, Social Class, and Academic Credentials', *School Review*, 87(2), 133–56.
Thomson, S., De Bortoli, L., Nicholas, M., Hillman, K. and Buckley, S. (2010) *Challenges for Australian Education: Results from PISA 2009*, Melbourne: Australian Council for Educational Research.
Thorlindsson, T. (1987) 'Bernstein's Sociolinguistics: An Empirical Test in Iceland', *Social Forces*, 65(3), 695–718.
Thorn, W. (2009) *International Adult Literacy and Basic Skills Surveys in the OECD Region*, Paris: Organisation for Economic Co-operation and Development.
Thorndike, R. L. (1962) 'International Comparison of the Achievement of 13-Year-Olds' in Foshay, A. W., Thorndike, R. L., Hotyat, F., Pidgeon, D. A. and Walker, D. A. (eds) *Educational Achievement of Thirteen-Year-Olds in Twelve Countries*, Hamburg: UNESCO Institute for Education, 21–55.
Thorndike, R. L. (1973) *Reading Comprehension Education in Fifteen Countries. An Empirical Study*, International Studies in Education, International Association for the Evaluation of Educational Achievement, New York: John Wiley and Sons.
Thrupp, M., Lauder, H. and Robinson, T. (2002) 'School Composition and Peer Effects', *International Journal of Educational Research*, 37(5), 483–504.
Tieben, N., de Graaf, P. M. and de Graaf, N. D. (2010) 'Changing Effects of Family Background on Transitions to Secondary Education in the Netherlands: Consequences of Educational Expansion and Reform', *Research in Social Stratification and Mobility*, 28(1), 77–90.
Torche, F. (2011) 'Is a College Degree Still the Great Equalizer? Intergenerational Mobility Across Levels of Schooling in the United States', *American Journal of Sociology*, 117(3), 763–807.
Treas, J. and Tyree, A. (1979) 'Prestige Versus Socioecomic Status in the Attainment Processes of American Men and Women', *Social Science Research*, 8(3), 201–21.
Treiman, D. J. (1970) 'Industrialization and Social Stratification', *Sociological Inquiry*, 40(Special Issue: Stratification Theory and Research), 207–34.
Treiman, D. J. (1977) *Occupational Prestige in Comparative Perspective*, New York: Academic Press.
Treiman, D. J. and Ganzeboom, H. B. G. (2000) 'The Fourth Generation of Comparative Mobility Stratification Research' in Quah, S. R. and Sales, A. (eds) *The International Handbook of Sociology*, London: Sage, 123–50.
Treiman, D. J. and Terrell, K. (1975) 'The Process of Status Attainment in the United States and Great Britain', *American Journal of Sociology*, 81(3), 563–83.
Treiman, D. J. and Yamaguchi, K. (1993) 'Trends in Educational Attainment in Japan' in Shavit, Y. and Hans-Peter, B. (eds) *Persistent Inequality: Changing Educational Attainment in Thirteen Countries*, Boulder, CO: Westview, 229–49.
Treiman, D. J. and Yip, K.-B. (1989) 'Education and Occupational Attainment in 21 Countries' in Kohn, M. L. (ed.) *Cross National Research in Sociology*, Newbury Park: Sage, 373–94.
Treiman, D. J., Ganzeboom, H. B. G. and Rijken, S. (2003) *Educational Expansion*

and Educational Achievement in Comparative Perspective, Los Angeles, CA: Callifornia Centre for Population Research, University of California.
Trow, M. (2006) 'Reflections on the Transition from Elite to Mass to Universal Access: Forms and Phases of Higher Education in Modern Societies since WWII', in Forest, J. J. F. and Altbach, P. G. (eds), *International Handbook of Higher Education*, Dordrecht, The Netherlands: Springer, 243–80.
Turkheimer, E., Haley, A., Waldron, M., D'Onofrio, B. and Gottesman, I. I. (2003) 'Socioeconomic Status Modifies Heritability of IQ in Young Children', *Psychological Science*, 14(6), 623–8.
Turner, J. (1992) 'If Not Positivism, Then Why Is Sociology Important?', *Canadian Journal of Sociology*, 17(1), 54–61.
Vallet, L.-A. (2002) *The Dynamics of Inequality of Educational Opportunity in France: Change in the Association Between Social Background and Education in Thirteen Five-Year Cohorts (1908–1972)*, Paper presented at the XV ISA World Congress of Sociology, Brisbane, Australia, July 7–13.
van de Werfhorst, H. G. (2010) 'Cultural Capital: Strengths, Weaknesses and Two Advancements', *British Journal of Sociology of Education*, 31(2), 157–69.
van de Werfhorst, H. G. (2011) 'Skill and Education Effects on Earnings in 18 Countries: The Role of National Educational Institutions', *Social Science Research*, 40(4), 1078–90.
van de Werfhorst, H. G. and Mijs, J. J. B. (2010) 'Achievement Inequality and the Institutional Structure of Educational Systems: A Comparative Perspective', *Annual Review of Sociology*, 36(1), 407–28.
van de Werfhorst, H. G., Sullivan, A. and Cheung, S. Y. (2003) 'Social Class, Ability and Choice of Subject in Secondary and Tertiary Education in Britain', *British Educational Research Journal*, 29(1), 41–62.
van Doorn, M., Pop, I. and Wolbers, M. H. J. (2011) 'Intergenerational Transmission of Education Across European Countries and Cohorts', *European Societies*, 13(1), 93–117.
van Leeuwen, M., van den Berg, S. M. and Boomsma, D. I. (2008) 'A Twin-Family Study of General IQ', *Learning and Individual Differences*, 18(1), 76–88.
Veroff, J., McClelland, L. and Marquis, K. (1971) *Measuring Intelligence and Achievement Motivation in Surveys*, Ann Arbor, MI: Survey Research Center, Institute for Social Research, University of Michigan.
Voitchovsky, S., Maitre, B. and Nolan, B. (2012) 'Wage Inequality in Ireland's "Celtic Tiger" Boom', *Economic and Social Review*, 43(1), 99–133.
Vollebergh, W. A. M., Iedema, J. and Raaijmakers, Q. A. W. (2001) 'Intergenerational Transmission and the Formation of Cultural Orientations in Adolescence and Young Adulthood', *Journal of Marriage and Family*, 63(4), 1185–98.
von Stumm, S., Gale, C. R., Batty, G. D. and Deary, I. J. (2009) 'Childhood Intelligence, Locus of Control and Behaviour Disturbance as Determinants of Intergenerational Social Mobility: British Cohort Study 1970', *Intelligence*, 37(4), 329–40.
von Stumm, S., Macintyre, S., Batty, D. G., Clarke, H. and Deary, I. J. (2010) 'Intelligence, Social Class of Origin, Childhood Behavior Disturbance and Education as Predictors of Status Attainment in Midlife in Men: The Aberdeen Children of the 1950s Study', *Intelligence*, 38(1), 202–11.

Vrooman, J. C. and Dronkers, J. (1986) 'Changing Educational Attainment Processes: Some Evidence from the Netherlands', *Sociology of Education*, 59(2), 69–78.

Walker, I. and Zhu, Y. (2008) 'The College Wage Premium and the Expansion of Higher Education in the UK', *Scandinavian Journal of Economics*, 110(4), 695–709.

Wanner, R. A. (1999) 'Expansion and Ascription: Trends in Occupational Opportunity in Canada, 1920–1994', *Canadian Review of Sociology and Anthropology*, 36(3), 409–42.

Wanner, R. A. (2005) 'Twentieth-Century Trends in Occupational Attainment in Canada', *Canadian Journal of Sociology/Cahiers Canadiens de Sociologie*, 30(4), 441–67.

Warren, J. R., Sheridan, J. T. and Hauser, R. M. (2002) 'Occupational Stratification Across the Life Course: Evidence from the Wisconsin Longitudinal Study', *American Sociological Review*, 67(3), 432–55.

Watkins, M. P. and Meredith, W. (1981) 'Spouse Similarity in Newlyweds with Respect to Specific Cognitive Abilities, Socioeconomic Status, and Education', *Behavior Genetics*, 11(1), 1–21.

Weakliem, D. L., McQuillan, J. and Schauer, T. (1995) 'Toward Meritocracy? Changing Social-Class Differences in Intellectual Ability', *Sociology of Education*, 68(4), 271–86.

Weiss, L. G. (2010) 'Considerations on the Flynn Effect', *Journal of Psychoeducational Assessment*, 28(5), 482–93.

West, P., Sweeting, H. and Speed, E. (2001) 'We Really Do Know What You Do: A Comparison of Reports from 11 Year Olds and Their Parents in Respect of Parental Economic Activity and Occupation', *Sociology*, 35(2), 539–60.

Whelan, C. T. and Hannan, D. F. (1999) 'Class Inequalities in Educational Attainment Among the Adult Population in the Republic of Ireland', *Economic and Social Review*, 30(3), 285–307.

White, K. R. (1982) 'The Relationship Between Socio-Economic Status and Academic Achievement', *Psychological Bulletin*, 91(3), 461–81.

White, S. B., Reynolds, P. D., Thomas, M. M. and Gitzlaff, N. J. (1993) 'Socio-economic Status and Achievement Revisited', *Urban Education*, 28(3), 328–43.

Whitt, H. P. (1986) 'The Sheaf Coefficient: A Simplified and Expanded Approach', *Social Science Research*, 15(2), 174–89.

Willis, P. E. (1977) *Learning to Labour: How Working Class Kids Get Working Class Jobs*, Westmead: Saxon House.

Willms, J. D. (2010) 'School Composition and Contextual Effects on Student Outcomes', *Teachers College Record*, 112(4), 1008–37.

Winship, C. and Korenman, S. (1997) 'Does Staying in School Make You Smarter? The Effect of Education on IQ in *The Bell Curve*' in Devlin, B., Fienberg, S. E., Resnick, D. P. and Roeder, K. (eds) *Intelligence, Genes, and Success: Scientists Respond to* The Bell Curve, New York: Springer-Verlag, 215–34.

Winship, C. and Korenman, S. (1999) 'Economic Success and the Evolution of Schooling with Mental Ability' in Mayer, S. and Peterson, P. (eds) *How Schools Matter*, Washington, DC: Brookings Institute, 49–78.

Wolf, F. M. (1986) *Meta-Analysis: Quantitative Methods for Research Synthesis*, Quantitative Applications in the Social Sciences, Volume 59, Beverly Hills, CA: Sage.

Wolfe, J. R. (1982) 'The Impact of Family Resources on Childhood IQ', *The Journal of Human Resources*, 17(2), 213–35.

Wright, E. O. (1980) 'Varieties of Marxist Conceptions of Class Structure', *Politics and Society*, 9(3), 323–70.

Xie, Y. (2011) 'Values and Limitations of Statistical Models', *Research in Social Stratification and Mobility*, 29(3), 343–9.

Yaish, M. and Andersen, R. (2012) 'Social Mobility in 20 Modern Societies: The Role of Economic and Political Context', *Social Science Research*, 41(3), 527–38.

Young, M. (1994) *The Rise of the Meritocracy 1870–2033: The New Elite of Our Social Revolution,* Reprint edn., New Brunswick: Transaction Publishers.

Zagorsky, J. L. (2007) 'Do You Have to Be Smart to Be Rich? The Impact of IQ on Wealth, Income and Financial Distress', *Intelligence*, 35(5), 489–501.

Zax, J. S. and Rees, D. I. (2002) 'IQ, Academic Performance, Environment, and Earnings', *Review of Economics and Statistics*, 84(4), 600–16.

Zhang, L. (2005) 'Advance to Graduate Education: The Effect of College Quality and Undergraduate Majors', *Review of Higher Education*, 28(3), 313–33.

Zimdars, A., Sullivan, A. and Heath, A. F. (2009) 'Elite Higher Education Admissions in the Arts and Sciences: Is Cultural Capital the Key?', *Sociology*, 43(4), 648–66.

Zimmer, R. W. and Toma, E. F. (2000) 'Peer Effects in Private and Public Schools Across Countries', *Journal of Policy Analysis and Management*, 19(1), 75–92.

Zimmerman, D. J. (1992) 'Regression Toward Mediocrity in Economic Stature', *American Economic Review*, 82(3), 409–29.

Index